Asian Indigenous Law

In Interaction with Received Law

Edited by
Professor Masaji Chiba

Routledge
Taylor & Francis Group
NEW YORK AND LONDON

First published in. 1986 by Kegan Paul International

This edition first published in 2009 by
Routledge
2 Park Square, Milton Park, Abingdon, Oxon, OX14 4RN

Simultaneously published in the USA and Canada
by Routledge

711 Third Avenue, New York, NY 10017
Routledge is an imprint of the Taylor & Francis Group, an informa business

First issued in paperback 2013
Transferred to Digital Printing 2009

British Library Cataloguing in Publication Data
A catalogue record for this book is available from the British Library

ISBN 13: 978-0-710-30113-0 (hbk)
ISBN 13: 978-0-415-86169-4 (pbk)

Publisher's Note
The publisher has gone to great lengths to ensure the quality of this reprint but points out that some imperfections in the original copies may be apparent. The publisher has made every effort to contact original copyright holders and would welcome correspondence from those they have been unable to trace.

Preface

Western law is normally regarded as universal when considered from the fact that it has been received and utilized by non-Western countries as the basis of their own state legal systems. It is accordingly natural that jurisprudence, among both Western and most non-Western scholars as well, tends to observe the development of a non-Western legal system as a history of received Western law. In fact, because of their different underlying cultural histories, there have been countless incongruities and conflicts between received Western law and indigenous non-Western law. However, these points have rarely been taken seriously by orthodox jurisprudence – a situation which may seem reasonable from the Western point of view, but is certainly not from the non-Western.

Non-Western peoples have each cherished their indigenous law as an integral part of their cultural heritage. During their long histories their law has on occasions encountered foreign law, whether voluntarily or not, and these encounters have led sometimes to peaceful assimilation and sometimes to destructive struggle between indigenous and received law. The indigenous law may sometimes have failed to maintain itself, while at others it may have succeeded either by rejecting the encountered law or by adapting itself to conserve its cultural identity. Contemporary non-Western law is thus seen as one in a current state in an ongoing process of self-developing indigenous law whether successfully or not. Truly, the reception of Western law by non-Western countries in modern times is the most influential encounter of non-Western law with foreign law. However, it is still only one of many encounters in the long history of each non-Western law. The major portion of this book is a collection of descriptions of typical non-Western countries from this viewpoint by native scholars.

The scope of this collection is limited to only six Asian communities among many for two reasons: first, theoretically, because Asian cultures have maintained many established legal ideas in comparison with the Western in their great religious or philosophical traditions; and second, practically, because in the organizational stage of the work it was in these communities that I was able to reach collaborators who were in a position to carry through this joint project. Also, "Asia" here means not so much a geographical area as it does a collection of nations who maintain cultures which originated in Asia. In this respect, I regret that I was unable at that time to reach others such as the Chinese and Indonesian. This limitation in the scope of the project both necessitated and facilitated the construction of theoretical hypotheses for the accurate observation and analysis of working Asian law. The Introduction and Conclusion of this book were written for that purpose, and also in the hope that the scheme set forth herein may be enlarged to apply to non-Western situations in general.

This book could not have been completed without the continuing encouragement of many friends both foreign and Japanese, including Professor Adam Podgoreki of Carlton University, Ottawa, Professor Peter G. Sack of the Australian National University, Canberra, Professor Marc Galanter of the University of Wisconsin, Madison; and the timely assistance of several agencies. Among the agencies, the International House of Japan, Tokyo, chaired by Mr Shigeharu Matsumoto, extended invaluable moral efforts and assistance which helped me to gain financial support from other sources; the Mitsubishi Foundation, Tokyo, and the Ford Foundation, New York, both of whom were generous in bearing the research expenses of the collaborators; and the East-West Seminar, Tokyo, chaired by Mr Masahide Shibusawa, provided grants which covered the major part of the expense of completing the manuscript. To them, and to many others too numerous to list, I tender my heartfelt thanks.

In addition I record my deep respect for the enduring friendly co-operation of the collaborators during the ten-year duration of this project. Each of them was assailed by difficulties which might easily have discouraged him from cooperating. To cite just a few, Dr Yassin suffered the tragic loss of his wife after a protracted illness, Professor Nezami had to leave his beloved country because of the political upheaval, Dr Tiruchelvam was called upon several times to participate in official business to tackle so-called ethnic affairs, and Professors Baxi and Preedee were for some years occupied with important duties connected with the presidencies of their universities. The factor which enabled them to overcome these difficulties was, I believe, their enthusiasm for our common purpose, backed by the encouragement of their wives. Finally I would like to mention my own wife, Mieko, who has been a source of constant encouragement and support to me.

Masaji Chiba

Contents

1 Introduction[1]

Masaji Chiba

I. Problem

There has been a long-established belief among both specialists and laymen that law is a special mechanism for social control isolated from other social mechanisms and, for this reason, that the scientific study of law should be confined to the special capacity of traditional, model jurisprudence. But since the beginning of the twentieth century this common belief has been challenged by new ideas concerning both the objectives and methods of the study of law. As a result it has become evident that law is so inseparably rooted in society as to be approachable by sociological methods. Furthermore, it has also become accepted that law must be recognized as an aspect of the total culture of a people, characterized by the psychological and ideational features as well as the structural and functional features of each fostering people, and may therefore be approached by anthropological methods.

The popular negligence of the cultural factor of law may have been partly caused by the alleged universal nature of traditional jurisprudence, prevailing as in *the* model science of law in the world. Contemporary model jurisprudence is indeed established on a universal basis. Its overwhelming prevalence in the world seems to leave little room either for serious consideration of its cultural specificity or for doubt as to its applicability to the different cultural specificities of other countries. But the Western conception of law, created and supported by model jurisprudence, has been bereft of its cultural specificity when comparatively analysed with the conceptions of law in other cultures (cf. David, 1975; Sawer, 1975). Truly, contemporary model jurisprudence is a product of long Western history and is coloured by a Western culture based on the Hellenistic and Christian view of man and society. While we acknowledge the universalistic achievements of Western jurisprudence as the most advanced science of law ever accomplished by man, we cannot disregard its cultural specificity. That specificity may have been in some cases diffused by or assimilated into different specificities of different cultures, but in other cases it has conflicted with or been rejected by them. In all cases, model jurisprudence, convinced of its universality, will not pay due attention to the cultural problems which accompany such diffusion or conflict between Western specificity and non-Western specificities (Chiba, 1984).

At the same time it is true that the peoples and scholars of non-Western countries who have cherished their own jurisprudence with specificities quite different from the Western, have not succeeded nor even attempted to present the achievements of their jurisprudence before the world circle of legal science forcibly enough to cause the proponents of Western jurisprudence to doubt their conviction of its universality. Without presenting the achievements of their own jurisprudence before world bodies specifically aimed at self-reflection of model jurisprudence, they would be disqualified from criticizing the ethnocentricity of the latter, as recently pointed out by some Western scholars (Chiba, 1980: 37), and insisting upon the *raison d'être* of their own jurisprudence. Such a negative or passive attitude may be another reason why model jurisprudence has in general disregarded the jurisprudence of different cultures – jurisprudence with due respect to indigenous law in non-Western countries. Vital to the proper understanding of law in non-Western culture is, firstly, for native scholars to present their own data and views positively in order not to negate the significance of model jurisprudence, but to maintain a sound understanding of its nature when utilized in different cultures.

We, the authors, from six countries with traditional cultures of Asian origin, want here to present the results of our joint project initiated by the above aspiration. Our purpose is, after all, accurately to identify the structural position and function of the indigenous laws of the countries concerned in terms of the state laws which are, by and large, based on received Western law.

Asian cultures have yielded a variety of philosophies and religions comparable to Western ones. Some of them have survived to our time with far-reaching influences upon the culture and society of various peoples. When they were confronted with the different systems of law received from Western countries, they must have struggled with that received law at the risk of their cultural identities. The general state of law found today in Asian countries is nothing but the result of those struggles. In some cases, the struggles may have ended earlier with happy or unhappy results; in others, the struggle may still be continuing. We wish to take a step forward in establishing how such struggles developed, or are developing, whether harmoniously or with conflict, and also to determine whether the results should be judged as successful or unsuccessful. We know that the answers to such questions cannot be given in an instant. We want to try, however, to begin our approach to the problem encouraged by the above aspiration, overcoming some admitted difficulties arising from our own different cultural and personal backgrounds. The countries here included are India, the Hindu society; Thailand, a Buddhist society; Egypt, a Sunni-Islamic society; Iran, an Islamic society; Sri Lanka, multi-religious society; and Japan, the peculiar Shinto society.[2]

II. Method

How then is it possible to observe and analyse the whole structure of law of a people as a phase of their culture and as a result of the struggles between received law and indigenous culture, particularly of the six countries here included? In other words, what frame of reference is effectively available for our purpose? We are disappointed to note that there is no ready-made scheme or framework on which we can rely. That one has never been presented is a reasonable result of the attitude of model jurisprudence on the one hand, which ignores the cultural nature of law by limiting its scope to the instrumental and technical nature, and of both sociology and anthropology on the other, which have thus far excluded investigation of the special mechanism of law. Accordingly, we first have to try to devise an appropriate frame of reference for ourselves.

Happily, we have some forerunners who have left us invaluable suggestions as to the cultural nature of law. In the nineteenth century, we find such scholars as Wundt, Savigny, Hegel, Maine, Post, and Kohler. Early in the twentieth century, Ehrlich (1936: 486–506) established the concept of "living law" in every human group to include in law a certain type of conventional social norm; and Weber (1967: 233) typified ideally "the particular principles underlying the religious ethics" which limit the structure and function of secular law. Malinowski (1926: 46–49) found the social mechanism of "publicity" and "reciprocity" to be the essence of law in a society without government and formal law. Hoebel (1954: 97–126) collected data concerning the function of "jural postulates" of primitive peoples. Pospisil (1971: 71–126) emphasized "the multiplicity of legal systems within a society". Some comparative scholars, derivating from model jurisprudence, noted differences in cultural factors among different peoples in discussing classification of different systems of law into the "families of law" (cf. David & Brierley, 1968: 9–17). And recently "legal pluralism" has come to be taken for granted not only in non-Western but also in Western countries (cf. Hooker, 1975).

The above suggestions are invaluable. The point is that the whole structure of law of a people is not limited to the monistic system of state law as maintained by model jurisprudence in accordance with its methodological postulates. The whole structure of law as an aspect of culture should include all regulations, however apparently different from state law, which the people concerned observe as law in their cultural tradition, including value systems; the very cultural identity of a people demands that we include all of them in a whole structure. Thus, the whole structure of law is plural, consisting of different systems of law interacting with one another harmoniously or conflictingly. Our first methodological requirement then is to frame a new conceptual scheme sufficient to allow us to observe the relevant facts accurately and to analyse them into theoretical formulations. Thus we arrive at our first working hypothesis: The three-level structure of law.

Cultural problems in the three-level structure of law of non-Western countries may be found in great variety. But the most conspicuous among them are those related to the cultural origin of law and which are inevitably related to the problem of reception of law. Reception of law is one of the topics frequently discussed by the proponents and students of model jurisprudence. But their point of view is, generally speaking, limited to confirming how Western law has been adopted or permeated into the official legal systems of non-Western countries, with only occasional recognition of its conflict with or rejection by indigenous systems. In this view, main concern is given to the destiny of the received Western law rather than to the receiving indigenous systems. For the receiving peoples, in contrast, main concern must be given to the whole structure of their indigenous systems, with focus upon assimilation of the received law while firmly maintaining their cultural identities. Unfortunately, the point of view clearly centring on that concern has been neither established nor systematically attempted. This, then, would be second methodological requirement necessary for our purpose: Interaction between received law and indigenous law.[3]

III. Working hypotheses

1. THE THREE-LEVEL STRUCTURE OF LAW

The whole structure of law is seen from a formal aspect to be composed of three levels of law: official law, unofficial law, and legal postulate.

Official law is the legal system sanctioned by the legitimate authority of a country. *State law* is ordinarily understood as a typical official law or even the only official law. Truly, it is directly sanctioned by the legitimate authority of the government of a state to have overall jurisdiction over the country. But as a matter of nature it is only one among many official laws of a country, however dominant it may appear over the others. For instance, as in most contemporary countries with established religions, religious law may be partially included in or accommodated by state law, but partially functioning out of the jurisdiction of the latter, thus forming its own system different from state law. Canon law, Islamic law, Hindu law, Buddhist law, and Judaic law are among typical examples. Other examples may be found in the laws of marriage and family, land and farming, local organizations, professional guilds, castes and stratifications, ethnic minorities, and so on, insofar as officially sanctioned by state law in one form or another. Each of these official laws of a country is sanctioned first by an authority of its own. But all of them are required to keep consonance with one another. To fulfil this requirement, each of them must, finally, be sanctioned by the state authority. However, as far as each of them forms an independent system of law, it may in actuality work in indifference to the other official laws and, accordingly, be in conflict with them.

Unofficial law is the legal system not officially sanctioned by any legitimate authority, but sanctioned in practice by the general consensus of a certain circle of people, whether within or beyond the bounds of a country. That general consensus may be either consciously recognized and expressed in formal rules, or unconsciously observed in particular patterns of behaviour. However, not all such unofficial practices supported by general consensus are to be included in unofficial law. Unofficial law is here limited to those unofficial practices which have a distinct influence upon the effectiveness of official law; in other words those which distinctively supplement, oppose, modify, or undermine any of the official laws, including state law. The effectiveness of the total system of official law is thus dependent upon the *status quo* of the unofficial law of the country concerned. One of the most important problems of unofficial law is therefore its positive or negative influence upon official law as well as its cultural background. While model jurisprudence has tended to disregard it, unofficial law has been treated in various rubrics in sociological and anthropological trends. For example, such rubrics are frequently found as customary law, living law, law in action, primitive law, tribal law, native law, and folk law[4], although their specific connotations should be carefully distinguished from one another.

A *legal postulate*[5] is a value principle or value system specifically connected with a particular official or unofficial law, which acts to found, justify and orient the latter. It may consist of established legal ideas such as natural law, justice, equity, and so on in model jurisprudence; sacred truths and precepts emanating from various gods in religious law; social and cultural postulates affording the structural and functional basis for a society as embodied in clan unity, exogamy, bilineal descent, seniority, individual freedom, national philosophy, and so on; political ideologies, often closely connected with economic policies, as in capitalism or socialism; and so on. The legal postulates of a country, whether official or unofficial, are as a whole required to keep a certain degree of consonance with one another. But complete consonance cannot be expected. First, because as each legal postulate is in support of a particular system of official or unofficial law, the potential of conflict with other systems, as pointed out above, is high. Second, because the legal postulate may tend to upset the *status quo* of its supported official or unofficial law in order to improve or even replace the latter. Formally speaking, a minimum integration among the legal postulates of a country should be preserved if the people are to maintain their national identity. But the nature of integration, and accordingly its modes and degrees, may differ from culture to culture.

2. INTERACTION BETWEEN RECEIVED LAW AND INDIGENOUS LAW

The whole structure of law of a non-Western country is, seen from a cultural point of view, formed in the interaction between received law and indigenous law.

Received law is, in a broad sense, that law which is received by a country from one or more foreign countries. Reception may take place in a variety of forms or processes; for instance, partially or wholly, systematically or unsystematically, formally or substantially, rapidly or gradually, voluntarily or involuntarily, in one or more of the three levels, exclusively between Western or non-Western countries, or, finally, between Western *and* non-Western countries. Most crucial for our purposes, however, is the reception of Western state law by non-Western countries in modern times, which we might consider as the narrower sense of "reception of law". It is crucial because it is the one in which the cultural conflict between received law and indigenous law is most conspicuous, and because the reception process, in the truest meaning, has not yet been completed. The modern reception has taken place rather formally and systematically in the level of official state law, whether imposed by Western countries or voluntarily accepted by non-Western countries, and some might see the reception as completed by the formal enforcement of received law. But in the actual process of the history of the receiving countries, it is only the beginning of their struggles to assimilate the foreign systems of law of different cultures with their own indigenous law. Notable is the fact that in this struggle process the foreign law originally received can be more or less assimilated with existing indigenous law so that it may assume a character of indigenous law, while it may still be discriminated as a different system of law.

Indigenous law[6] is, in a broad sense, law originated in the native culture of a people. But in consideration of the general trend of cultural diffusion in human society, it would be next to impossible to find purely indigenous law in contemporary society. The available concept of indigenous law should be limited by relative features useful for our purpose, that is, meaningful in dichotomy against received law, especially in its narrower sense. It may thus be defined as law existing indigenously in the native culture of a people prior to the reception of Western state law in modern times, although it may include some assimilated law which was originally received in earlier times. Whether and how indigenous law has developed in the struggles with received law in this process of reception is the most urgent problem to be here explored, as evidenced by the insistence of some scholars upon adopting the concept of "imposition" in place of "reception" (Burman & Harrell-Bond, 1979).

The actual interaction between received law and indigenous law differs widely from country to country. Generally speaking of the reception in a narrower sense, state law is framed after Western models in its formal structure, adopting into its substantial contents various rights, duties, and legal institutions and procedures originated in Western law. However, it has also adopted various indigenous laws such as those relating to marriage, family, status, land, etc. into its formal structure, and furthermore, some indigenous institutions and procedures by reformulating their essence in accordance with that formal structure. But interaction is not limited to such a static structure. It takes place rather in a dynamic process of mutual influences between both types of law, whether through institutional revisions at a long range, or through individual authoritative judgements and peoples' behaviour at a short range. It is a process of accommodation or conflict, with legal postulates for both types of law playing an important role as they ideationally encourage the peoples concerned to protect or reformulate the law they support against rivalling law. Official law other than state law may originate in indigenous law or in received law as in the case of established religious law, though generally assimilated as if indigenous. Unofficial law is mostly occupied with indigenous law, except in cases where new reformative ideas of rights, such as environmental or consumers' rights, or legal institutions such as socialist ones in capitalistic countries, come to have certain effective influence as unofficial law. And finally, legal postulates constantly accompany all forms and cases of official and unofficial law, both received and indigenous.

Such are our initial working hypotheses: a frame of reference, against which the data in the following chapters should be considered and, where possible, verified.

Notes

1 For points of Introduction, cf. Chiba, 1979.

2 If the Asian cultures were to be adequately represented, some other countries should have been added, particularly China and Indonesia. But, frankly speaking, it was not possible when this project was drawn up to include all representatives at once. In spite of this lack of a few representative countries, we are convinced of the unprecedented significance of the study of the six countries included herein for the benefit of future advancement of this direction of study.

3 As may be clearly understood by the above argument, "law" is used here in a broader meaning not limited to rigid law advocated by model jurisprudence, but including the most systematized, prevalently applicable means of social control valid in a certain society, legitimated by the authority or general consensus of the society, as is referred to in the sociology and anthropology of law. Law, in this meaning, consists of various factors such as rights and duties, positive and negative sanctions, guiding ideas and principles, rules and legislations, and specific institutions as far as identified by formal expressions and certain patterns of behaviour.

4 "Folk law" is the term adopted as the main objective of study by the Commission on Folk Law and Legal Pluralism, International Union of Anthropological and Ethnological Sciences. It is a label to be used to isolate related social phenomena in three levels: first, "the substantive law of social groups of various sorts (other than the modern state)"; second, "involv[ing] social processes, namely procedures and legally-relevant behavior governed by folk law in the first sense"; third, "involved in a variety of kinds of interaction, on the levels of substance and of process, with other folk law and with state law" (from *Terms of Reference* prepared by the IUAES Commission on Folk Law and Legal Pluralism).

5 "Legal postulate" was first labelled as "basic law" (Chiba, 1979) and then as "jural postulate" (Chiba, 1982). But the essence of the terms are the same.

6 "Indigenous law" has been used by Marc Galanter for another specific meaning: "social ordering which is indigenous . . . to be found in a variety of institutional settings – in universities, sports leagues, housing developments, hospitals, etc." (1981: 17–18).

References

Burman, Sandra B., & Harrel-Bond, Barbara E., eds.
1979. *The Imposition of Law*. London: Academic Press.

Chiba, Masaji.
1979. Three-Level Structure of Law in a World of Many Cultures. *Law and Future of Society*, Archiv für Rechts- und Sozialphilosophie, Beiheft Neue Folge, Nr. 11: 293–302.
1980. Doubts on the Utility of "Traditional vs. Modern:" From an Asian Point of View. *Law and Development*, University of Philippines Law Center, 1978/1979 Issue: 34–45.
1982. The Unofficial Jural Postulates Underlying Attitudes toward Law. *Zeitschrift für Rechtssoziologie* 3(1): 59–73.
1984. Cultural Universality and Particularity of Jurisprudence. In *Essays on Third World Perspectives in Jurisprudence*, M. L. Marasinghe and W. E. Conklin, eds., Singapore: Malayan Law Journal.

David, René,
1975. Introduction to Ch.1: The Different Conceptions of Law. In *International Encyclopedia of Comparative Law*, René David, ed., 2: 3–13.

David, René, & Brierley, John E. C.
1968. *Major Legal Systems in the World Today: An Introduction to the Comparative Study of Law*. New York: The Free Press.

Ehrlich, Eugen.
1936. *Fundamental Principles of the Sociology of Law*. Walter L. Moll, transl. Cambridge, Mass.: Harvard University Press.

Galanter, Marc.
1981. Justice in Many Rooms: Courts, Private Ordering, and Indigenous Law. *Journal of Legal Pluralism*, 19: 1–47.

Hoebel, E. Adamson.
1954. *The Law of Primitive Man*. Cambridge, Mass.: Harvard University Press.

Hooker, M. B.
1975. *Legal Pluralism: An Introduction to Colonial and Neo-Colonial Laws*. Oxford: Clarendon Press.
1978. *A Concise History of South-Eastern Asian Law*. Oxford: Clarendon Press.

Malinowski, Bronislaw K.
1926. *Crime and Custom in Savage Society*. London: Routledge & Kegan Paul.

Pospisil, Leopold.
1971. *Anthropology of Law: A Comparative Theory*. New York: Harper & Row.
Sawer, Geoffrey.
1975. The Western Conception of Law. In *International Encyclopedia of Comparative Law*, René David, ed., 2: 14–48.
Weber, Max.
1967. *On Law in Economy and Society*. E. D. Shils & Max Rheinstein, transls. New York: Simon & Schuster.

2 Development of Plural Structure of Law in Egypt, A Sunni-Islamic Society

El Sayed Yassin

The movement of Islamic conquest which took place under various substantive and historic conditions followed the advent of Islam in the Arab Peninsula.

In AD641, 20 *Hijra* (Islamic year), the Islamic armies marched towards Egypt and inflicted defeat on the Roman forces of occupation. From that date onwards Egypt became an integral part of the Islamic provinces which, in their entirety, constituted the Abode of Islam. As a result, a process of substitution of new legal systems drawn from Islamic law "Shari'a" gradually set in at both the structural and functional levels.

This fundamental legal change was the outcome of a number of socio-political and doctrinal transformations in Egypt, with Islam steadily growing until it became the dominant feature of the Egyptian society.

The following is a review of the changes which occurred in the Egyptian society.

I. Brief Introduction to the History of the Egyptian Legal System

The student of the history of Egyptian law in the Islamic era is faced with two problems:

First, the dearth of historic documents which illustrate how law applied to social relations and hence the correlation between the Islamic (Koranic Sunni) text and the social structure, and eventually the relationship between tradition and innovation.

Second, the scarcity of historic studies specializing in Egyptian Islamic law and establishing the link between this system and the socio-political edifice in its various dimensions.

As a matter of fact, these difficulties are bound to have a negative impact on our endeavour to get acquainted with the distinctive features of the Egyptian identity in its interaction with Islamic law, Shari'a, which prevailed over this society until the emergence of the movement of modernization or "revival" in modern times.

This study will focus on the most fundamental historical changes, rather than on the historical, political and economic realities. Moreover, this study is meant to highlight the structure of the national legal system and its components within the framework of the theory of the source of law during the Islamic era. It is common knowledge that when Egypt became one of the administrative provinces (*wilaya*) in the Abode of Islam this resulted in the application of Shari'a on a regional level.

As for personal status, the phenomenon of legal duality continued to govern this vital area of legislation up to modern times. This was the result of the Islamic theory which governed the relationship between the Islamic state and the People of the Covenant (non-Moslems) and the legal model which was established to delineate the limits of the relationship between the majority and the minority. This development had its repercussions on the enforcement of both the Christian and Jewish laws within the framework of the law on personal status, these laws being considered as one of the sources of the comprehensive legal structure of the Egyptian society.

In view of the preceding facts we shall examine the Egyptian legal system during the Islamic era in the light of the theory of the sources of law prevailing in Egypt at the time. We shall also discuss customs, non-Moslem laws, Jewish laws and the legislations promulgated by the authorities, as well as Islamic law, Shari'a.

1. THE EGYPTIAN LEGAL SYSTEM IN THE ISLAMIC ERA

A. Customs

Customs remained one of the major components of the Egyptian legal system, thus reflecting the impact of the social and class movement on the process of formulating the legal control of the movement of society. However, insofar as the Egyptian legal system is concerned, this source of law played a preponderant role in expressing the identity of the Egyptian law during the period of foreign occupation, when authentic Egyptian features prevailed through the continued implementation of Egyptian legal principles.

This situation led to the emergence of the phenomenon of dual structure as one of the fundamental features of Egyptian law prior to the Islamic conquest, a phenomenon which eventually brought about the supremacy of Egyptian law with its deeply rooted Pharaonic principles. This is apart from the legal system brought into the country by occupation, a feature confirmed by the detailed examination of the legal principles which governed the process of legal development before the Islamic era.

The Islamic conquest of Egypt led to the total collapse of the Egyptian legal system which had prevailed during the Roman rule, but this ostensible collapse failed to have any radical impact on the substance of the legal principles. For the fact that these principles were stripped of their official legislative character, led to their transformation into customary legal principles which it was not easy to keep away from the legal organization of relations and other societal systems. They consequently remained the major source of the Egyptian legal system at the beginning of the Islamic era.

Thus, Egyptians continued to implement these rules within the context of relations governing their private lives, apart from the fact that the first two conquerors did not apply the Shari'a at the outset of their conquest. This was so because Islamic legal principles had not yet been fully delineated, nor was there a sufficient number of religious scholars in a position to cope with the new situation or apply legislative models to the newly developing reality which had been governed by one of the most advanced legal systems in ancient civilizations.

One of the most outstanding factors in this connection lies in the fact that the initial principles underlying Islamic law in the area of business relations had not yet been fully outlined.

An evidence of the central place occupied by customs in this connection is the fact that they constitute one of the auxiliary sources in the legal structure of the Shari'a, a situation which made possible the continued application of the Egyptian legal principles which prevailed under the Romans. The preponderance of these principles continued but only to the extent that it did not conflict with the Shari'a as exemplified in Koran and Sunna.

This special role of the Egyptian customary laws continued as one of the basic components of the comprehensive legal edifice of the society, together with a quantitative as well as qualitative growth of the Shari'a and its legal models, taking as a point of departure the dynamism and development of the Abode of Islam. This situation led to the emergence of a broad sector of a ruling Islamic elite, namely the class of Islamic scholars.

Generally speaking, customs as one of the auxiliary sources of the legal structure of the Shari'a played an effective role in the development of Islamic jurisprudence.

With respect to Egypt in particular, customary legal rules contributed to the enrichment of activities in the field of jurisprudence and legislation. In fact, the Egyptian legal system made it possible for many of the followers of the schools of Islamic jurisprudence to get acquainted with their fundamental features, the habits and customs of the Egyptian people, together with their legal implications. It was thus natural that these rules should have had an impact on Islamic scholars in their application of Islamic legal norms and concepts to these customary rules. Thus we can find out to what extent the rules which were in line with the norms of the Shari'a continued to prevail, and whether other contrary norms were applied.

B. Non-Islamic laws

Most of the historic and legal studies of Islamic Egypt, whose aim is to determine the components of the structure of the Egyptian legal system in this period, tend to be selective when examining non-Islamic legislations. In fact, they select Coptic laws, to the exclusion of all other religious laws.

This method constitutes a gross historic oversight of some of the other sources of law, which can be called non-Islamic laws and which prevailed in Egypt prior to the Islamic conquest. The non-Islamic sector of the legal system is made up of two parts: Coptic laws and Jewish laws, which form part of the laws on personal status which are characterized by a plurality of systems, and the implementation of which differs according to the religious status of the individual in the Egyptian society.

Nevertheless, we can by no means elucidate the various aspects of the application of these two legislations as two distinctive systems in the legal structure, without delving deep into the Islamic concept *vis-à-vis* non-Moslems in the Abode of Islam and the legal model governing personal relations under family law. This law comprises the matrimonial model divorce and the legal implications involved in the dissolution of the marriage bonds. We will then deal with the Coptic canon law and the various sources which made up its fundamental features, both in theory and application.

We will then deal with the Jewish laws and their internal sources.

(1) Islam's theoretical attitude vis-à-vis *non-Moslems: model and practice*

In Islamic jurisprudence the term "People of the Covenant" applies to non-Moslems, such as Christians, Jews, Zoroastrians, which are aligned to the Islamic state by a covenant, by virtue of which the Islamic state is committed to defend them in return for their payment of the head tax (*geziah*). It may be said with some-scientific reservation that the head tax under the Islamic taxation concept is equivalent to the defence tax under modern taxation systems.

This Islamic outlook *vis-à-vis* non-Moslems is determined by the Koran and the Sunna which constitute the source of Islamic theory *vis-à-vis* the problem of plurality in the Abode of Islam. Thus, Koranic verses and the sayings of the Prophet (*Hadith*) determined the general framework of Islamic tolerance when they established the principle of freedom of belief for non-Moslems in return for the payment of the head tax.

However non-Moslems were not committed to the payment of any other taxes, with the exception of the head-tax. In fact, funds involved in domestic trade were exempted from taxation, whereas those involved in foreign trade were subject to a tax amounting to half the tithe. Cultivated lands on the other hand were subject to land tax (*khurag*) for Moslems and non-Moslems alike.

It is worth noting that the internal affairs of non-Moslems were to be left to themselves so long as no dispute arose, but in case a litigation was referred to the Moslem *Wali* (Governor) they were passed in accordance with the general rules of Shari'a.

These are the broad lines of the history of Egyptian law in the period under review. We will now get acquainted with the method of application of these general rules as seen from the historical perspective.

(2) Coptic law

Christianity saw the light in Alexandria prior to the Islamic conquest, where it spread among the Greek community, then to the Egyptians of Lower Egypt and Upper Egypt. It was only three centuries later that the Egyptian Coptic diocese was founded, headed by an Egyptian archbishop.

Due to interaction with Hellenistic culture and the prevailing historic and substantive conditions, there emerged generation after generation of clergymen who set out to formulate the principles of Coptic law. Foremost among these were Archbishops Cantinos, Clemendes, Origanos, Athenasios and Shenouda. In the words of Assiouti, Egyptian historian, "the head of the Church of Alexandria was the head of the entire world."

Meanwhile, the Christian religion centred its attention and teachings on bringing about a change in man by relying on the Christian doctrines, ethics and religious rites without proceeding to the legal organization of social relations among its followers. According to researchers, this may be due to the fact that the communities in the midst of which Christianity emerged were legally organized, and thus were in no need of regulatory laws, but only of doctrinal and ethical guidelines.

A Coptic law gradually emerged in Egypt. At the outset this law governed the family, then proceeded to include other social relationship. The basic outlines of Coptic law derived from the principles of natural law and those related to positive law which were in harmony with the principles of Christianity.

Conflict with the Roman occupier ended when the Roman state embraced Christianity, which became the official state religion. At this juncture the Egyptian Church was vested with powers to consider cases of a religious nature or personal status such as marriage and divorce. Clerical laws including biblical rules and principles applied, in addition to the decisions passed by the Christian clerical synod and those emanating from both local and public religious institutions.

These rules, as previously stated, were influenced by the positive rules derived from Pharaonic laws, which in turn had been influenced by both Greek and Roman laws following their adaptation to Christian fundamental principles.

Such were the Coptic legal principles which prevailed prior to the arrival of Amr Ibn El Aas to Egypt.

But following his conquest of Egypt, Amr Ibn El Aas carried

out the administrative reorganization of the country, which became one of the Islamic provinces (*wilaya*) which he in turn subdivided into small administrative units. He then appointed in each of these units a Coptic judge who was vested with legal powers, to pass judgements in any dispute that arose between non-Moslems in the field of personal status in accordance with their laws.

As for the disputes which arose between Moslems and non-Moslems, jurisdiction for their settlement fell to a legal council comprising judges from both parties. Thus in the Moswiya province a Moslem (Arab) judge joined his non-Moslem counterpart with the result that the Coptic judge no longer enjoyed full jurisdiction except in those disputes which involved personal status and which were governed by Christian canon laws.

Meanwhile, Islamic legal rules began gradually to take shape by grappling with new problems, whereas the administration took on an Arab colouring. With the spread of Islam, the various strata of the Egyptian society eventually began to be governed by Islamic law. As a result, Copts no longer enjoyed any legal or legislative jurisdiction outside the scope of personal status.

(3) Jewish law

In the early Islamic era, a great deal of ambiguity surrounded Islam's attitude *vis-à-vis* the Jews and their history in the Egyptian society. It may however be said with a sufficient measure of historic reliability that Jews received equal treatment with the other people of the Covenant in conformity with the principles of freedom of belief and religious tolerance. This view is substantiated by the neutral stand of the Jews *vis-à-vis* the Arab conquest. In fact, they did not show any opposition to the conquerors, an attitude which may be attributed to their poor economic status, their long-standing conflict with the Greeks and the hatred the Romans felt for them.

When Amr signed the so-called "Alexandria reconciliation" pact, the document stipulated that the Jews should remain in Alexandria. Furthermore the Jewish canon law was drawn from the *Turah* (Old Testament) which was its primary source. Unlike the Bible, it comprised secular regulatory principles side by side with doctrinal rules. Another source of law is the Talmud which is made up of the *Meshnah*, called in Jewish canon law the verbal or second *Turah*, and the *Jamrah* or explanations and comments added to the *Meshnah*.

It is believed that the attitude of Islam towards the Jewish canon law was the same as its attitude towards Coptic canon law, particularly in the field of personal status which was regulated by Jewish canon law.

All other areas were governed by the rules of the Shari'a.

(4) Legislations emanating from the authorities

This source of law played a major role in developing the process of legislation and in harnessing it to regulate the new socioeconomic relationship of the Egyptian society.

It was agreed among the scholars of Islamic jurisprudence that authorities were to be allowed to pass legislations in those areas which were not governed by either Koranic or Sunni provisions, i.e. this was to be done in accordance with the principle of legitimate policy.

This was to constitute a supplementary source of law.

(5) The legal system of the Shari'a

As stated earlier, a consensus was reached among historians on the application of the legal provisions of the Shari'a to socioeconomic as well as legal relationships. Generally speaking, it appears that the history of such an application is nothing but the repercussion of the development and growth of the Islamic edifice as a whole.

Whereas this trend, which prevails in historic and legal studies, is valid in most cases, nevertheless Egypt's legal reality, which constituted an ever-developing civilizational and legal process, played a special role prior to the Arab conquest. This understanding was the result of the ambiguity which prevailed in the works of Egyptian historians concerning the legal system which existed in Egypt during the Islamic era, a situation which called for thorough study in order to dissipate the obscurity of that period, and to know how Islamic law was applied.

2. SHARI'A

In our attempt to get acquainted with Islamic law, which constitutes one of the components of Egypt's legal system, and how it was applied in Islamic Egypt, it is necessary to examine the internal structure of the Shari'a. It is common knowledge that the sources of Islamic law are subdivided into a number of branches. However, the prevalent division is that which breaks it up into fundamental and rational sources.

Under the former division we have the Koran and the Sunna, that is the rules and the integrated legal provision. It is a self-evident fact that legal provisions are few in the Koran, and that these are governed by the following two systems:

First, the system of *hudud*[1] (sing. *had*) or standardized penalties which constitutes the Islamic penal code. According to religious scholars, it aims at safeguarding the fundamental interests of the Islamic society and upgrading them to the level of the moral interests of the community. This system involves crimes of defamation, theft, adultery, highway robbery, corruption, all of which are governed by *hudud*.

Second, the system of business relations which is made up of the family laws (matrimonial bonds, dissolution of marriage and the legal implications involved) in addition to certain regulations governing contracts, administration of justice and profession of faith.

As for the rational sources, they are being determined by opinions and personal reasoning. Under this general division we find diverse forms such as *ijmah* (consensus), *qiyas* (analogy) and *istihsan* (preponderance of opinion). Fundamentalists have called them borrowed or rational evidence, while in actual fact they are nothing but technical methods meant to develop Islamic jurisprudence to suit the movement of change which involved the Islamic societies.

As for the legal application of the Shari'a in Egypt, in accordance with the principle of regionality of laws in the Abode of Islam, Islamic law was preponderant; but following its evolution and its interaction with Egyptian law and following the advent of Amr and up to the hanging of Touman Bay, it became the general law which was to apply in cases of crime and business relations with the exception of personal status for non-Moslem Egyptians.

3. EGYPTIAN LEGAL STRUCTURE: INDICATIONS OF CHANGE

There was a second indication of change in the context of the Egyptian legal structure, an indication which may be called changes from the outside. It coincided with the increase in the number of Circassian Mamelukes.

At this time a number of Tartar laws which had been laid down by Genghis Khan replaced earlier laws. These new laws were to apply to civil matters side by side with the previously outlined Egyptian body of law. With the new and borrowed sources of law, the Shari'a could no longer cope with the new situations, with the result that the supremacy of the Shari'a became jeopardized and the scope of its application narrower and narrower becoming eventually confined to family and *wakf* (public endowments) laws. This duality of law was perpetuated until Ottoman colonialists set foot in Egypt. This situation calls for thorough examination in view of the systematic cultural and legal infiltration that occurred despite the presence of the Shari'a. This was apart from the backwardness which afflicted the Egyptian society, bringing to a halt many of its legal and civilizational functions.

Following the victory of the Ottomans over the Mamelukes at Merg Dabek and Raydaneyah in AD1517, a change occurred in Egypt's status, converting it from an Abbassid province into an Ottoman province, with the result that Egypt was engulfed in the darkness of civilizational decline.

Occupation brought about a number of changes in both the political and legal systems.

One of these changes took place within the religious elite, involving religious scholars (*ulemas*) and the administration in the judicial system, their relationship with the central and local governments, the administration of justice, religious denominations and "dervish" as well as the nature of the relationship binding these two professional groups of religious men with the military and civil elites.

According to researchers, another change occurred in the structural make-up of the law and the Shari'a in the dissociation between the rules of the Shari'a on the one hand, and religious and judicial organizations on the other.

Conflict began between customs as a source of law and Islamic law as another source which had so far enjoyed hegemony and supremacy. This change appears more evident, however, when examining the relation between the application of the Islamic penal code (the *hudud* of Islam) and the restrictions imposed by the political system on its application, ever since the military and the bureaucrats (people working in the administration) imposed restrictions on the application of Islamic penalties. As a result, they had the authority of initiating legal proceedings against criminals, and of passing life-sentences on them without intervention from the judiciary, and far from the procedural restrictions of the courts.

Ottoman rule gave rise to a growing number of legislations emanating from authorities, a situation which brought about a revolution in the administrative, fiscal and legal systems in Egypt.

At the same time, closing the door of *ijtihad* (personal reasoning) played a role in bringing about the growth of these legislations and the emergence of a class working in the legal field, *ulemas*. These had to grapple with the changing situations, and hence came to enjoy vast powers in this field.

Furthermore, the deterioration of the legal system in Egypt was a dominant feature in the decline which the country suffered under Ottoman rule.

At the same time, international political conditions led to the emergence of one of the most serious legal, political and social phenomena in Egyptian history – that of foreign concessions, which constituted a substantive factor behind a number of legal and political changes, as will be explained later.

Foreign concessions assumed a preponderant place in the Egyptian legal system. The application of this system widened the scope of these concessions, with the result that foreigners came to enjoy a number of freedoms: freedom of belief, residence, movement, employment, trade in banned goods, tax exemption unless approved by their country of origin. Moreover, foreigners were not subject to either the legislative or judicial systems of the country, with jurisdiction in these fields falling upon the consulates.

These concessions led to a state of total anarchy and the continued duality of the prevailing legal edifice, e.g. a national system and a foreign system. This situation alarmed the government and the elite, so much so that their abolition became one of the pressing demands of the national movement until the signing of the Montreux agreement.

4. THE EGYPTIAN LEGAL EDIFICE AND THE IMPACT OF THE FRENCH EXPEDITION

During Ottoman rule, the Egyptian civilization witnessed a sharp decline, followed by an upsurge which had an effective impact on Egyptian history. It was the Napoleonic expedition to Egypt which initiated a process of true knowledge of modern Egyptian civilization by the Egyptians in general and the elite in particular. This interaction between Egyptian and French cultures gave rise to a number of significant political and social phenomena, particularly *vis-à-vis* Egyptian women and their quest for freedom. Another outstanding landmark was the summoning of the first Egyptian Parliament in modern times.

An important event occurred when, during the first meeting of the administration (*Diwan 'aam*) on 15 October 1798, Napoleon proposed to apply the Napoleonic code, both civil and penal, in Egypt. He had raised the matter earlier before the members of the Scientific Association at its first meeting on 23 August 1798, when he proposed the examination of reforms that could be introduced in both the legislative and judicial systems, particularly in the civil and criminal aspects. This would involve reconsideration of criminal and civil procedures, and laws governing property, inheritance and taxation. It was, however, decided in the administration *Diwan 'aam* that the provisions of the Shari'a and the existing judicial system would continue to apply. But the process of practical application led to a number of changes which faced the traditional Egyptian society, such as the French commitment to the French criminal code, a step which reached its climax following Kleber's assassination. In fact the trial was carried out according to French norms which constituted the Latin aspect of modern legal civilization, and which underscored the defective application of the Shari'a by the Ottomans and the Mamelukes.

Meanwhile, the French introduced numerous changes in the judiciary by establishing a commercial court, made up of twelve merchants, half of them Copts and the others Moslems, headed by a Copt. It devolved upon this court to settle disputes in the fields of commerce and inheritance. This experience however failed to produce the results expected of it. Jurisdiction once again fell to the Islamic judge in these matters.

Meanwhile steps were undertaken by Menou to set up a new legal system in Egypt, but international political developments and internal conflicts between the leaders of the expedition, its soldiers and national resistance hampered the implementation of the project and led to the departure of the expedition from Egypt.

It may be said that the reason behind the refusal by the elite, which had established the first Egyptian Council under French occupation, to apply French laws lies in the status, class composition and intellectual make-up of this elite, which owed its allegiance to the *ulemas* with their various religious trends. Their strength was bound to have an impact on the existing political system and to play a role in conferring legitimacy to it. To accept foreign positive laws constituted a blow to the system and to the pivotal role played by this elite in the Egyptian society of the time.

5. EGYPTIAN LAW FROM MOHAMMED ALI TO THE PROMULGATION OF MODERN LEGISLATION

With the advent of Mohammed Ali on the Egyptian political scene, his assumption of power, and the approval of the Sublime Porte of the Egyptian popular administration, a crucial stage set in with the completion of the process of change as well as the social and cultural development which had taken root at the time of the French expedition. This process had aimed at modernizing the Egyptian society within limits which would permit the realization of the military and economic ambitions of the new ruler.

However, the focus of the modernization efforts indirectly led to the establishment of the foundations of a modern Egyptian state. Under those new conditions, Egypt set out to establish contacts with the modern legal civilization, most particularly in the area of Latin legal culture in its French sector. But this was achieved only intermittently.

Mohammed Ali thus embarked on a process of change by introducing reforms in the traditional, cultural and political structure of Egyptian society; aware as he was of the failure of Ottoman experience, Mohammed Ali, a man of the religion, set out to liquidate the semi-feudal class of the Mamelukes which were the actual rulers of the country. He thus carried out the physical liquidation of his opponents, and went as far as to get rid of the source of traditional legitimacy in the Egyptian society. The actual starting point was a change in production, relationships in agriculture, industry and trade, which brought about a number of structural changes in the closed economic edifice which had regulated all socioeconomic relations in Egypt before the Napoleonic expedition.

From the theoretical point of view supremacy was given to the Shari'a, but the process of building a modern state ready for external expansion necessitated funds, administrative cadres and an institutional system, steps which had a decisive impact on building up the legal base of the country.

The major trait of the Egyptian legal structure in its legislative aspect was the lack of general positive legislation in civil dealings, according to the historian Omar Mamdouh. Thus from the theoretical point of view it was the Shari'a which was supreme.

These rules, with the exception of the traditional penal code of the Shari'a, lacked the required competence to wipe out the elements of the closed economic edifices and build up state monopolies and the new administrative and legal systems they required in order to achieve the new objectives of the society, and to ensure political domination of the ruler over the country.

Certain Egyptian researchers are of the view that when modern penal legislation was introduced in Egypt only a few propositions of Islamic law relating to retribution and blood money (for injuries) were applied. As for the *hudud*, Egypt had followed in the footsteps of the Ottoman empire and had totally discarded them for hundreds of years. New positive legislations were promulgated to govern the socioeconomic relations of the Egyptian society in the new era.

First, the Peasant Law was promulgated in January 1830. It constituted the beginning of infiltration of positive law into the structure of the Egyptian society at this stage. This law aimed at organizing Egyptian agriculture in the light of the new changes. But a technical and social analysis of its rules would lead us to say that these rules were mostly pre-emptive and penal. In July 1837 Mohammed Ali promulgated the law on Royal policy, which was meant to regulate the internal government and administrative edifice while organizing work relations between public civil servants and the state, indicating the duties to be performed and the penalties to be imposed in case of breach of duty. This law was made up of a preamble, three chapters and sixty-one articles. In 1842 a law governing bridge construction, irrigation and the recruitment of seasonal workers, as well as relations between directors and irrigation engineers was promulgated. In 1844 a law called *Siyasat El La'eha* was promulgated regulating public offices.

This plethora of legislative rules and regulations, together with the anarchy it created and the difficulty of obtaining precise knowledge about their provisions, led the government to compile and organize them in bodies of law without introducing any new rules.

However the most serious change that took place in modern Egyptian thought was the recession of the supremacy of Islamic law and the borrowing of western positive laws, with the result that the application of the Shari'a to social relations was subject to the will of the ruler. Thus, in cases falling outside the scope of relations between the ruler and the masses, supremacy was to the Shari'a. This recourse to Islamic law, however, fell short of coping with other crimes related to the government's aim at ensuring change and at mobilizing the society to go beyond the national boundaries and look to the outside world.

It may be said that the stage of legal amalgamation with modern Latin civilization was launched during Mohammed Ali's rule. As a result, a thorough examination of the history of Egyptian law reveals a new phenomenon, that of the duality of existing legal cultures. Thus, there were legal rules and regulations which found their origin in Islamic law, while others had their roots in borrowed western culture and civilization, particularly Latin.

The decline of the socio-economic edifice in the country and its systematic deterioration after Mohammed Ali's death led to the growth of foreign concessions, particularly after the collapse of the state commercial and industrial monopolies, together with a growing foreign penetration into the country. This situation led to the perpetuation of this phenomenon in both its legal and judicial aspects.

It therefore appears that foreign concessions in Egypt assumed serious proportions, unlike the case in other Ottoman provinces. This gave rise to the promulgation of a legislation whereby foreigners were to be governed by the laws of their own countries, and the application of these laws fell to the jurisdiction of consular courts.

Meanwhile the spread of this phenomenon, with the submission of most foreigners to non-Egyptian laws, caused a state of anarchy which had a profound impact on socioeconomic relations. Inequality between Egyptian and foreigners led to the introduction of legislative and judicial reforms which initiated a new stage in the development of Egyptian law.

6. MODERNIZATION OF THE EGYPTIAN LEGAL STRUCTURE FROM THE JUDICIAL REFORM TO THE MONTREUX AGREEMENT

The anarchy that prevailed in the legislative and judicial systems as a result of widespread foreign concessions and the attitude of European countries *vis-à-vis* this phenomenon, together with the elite's desire to lay down a well-balanced legal system which would be governed by the same principles as modern European laws, particularly French, gave rise to the need for judicial reform.

Thus, Nubar Pasha in his report to Khedive Ismail called for a reform of the judiciary and the creation of mixed courts side by side with the promulgation of new laws. Thus, the judicial system which governed foreigners served to introduce European legislations into Egypt. Before giving their consent for judicial reforms, the European countries set as a condition that these new courts draw their legislations from European laws. In January and February 1873 an international committee met in Istanbul to lay down a final draft for judicial reforms providing for the creation of Mixed Egyptian Courts, which obtained the approval of the countries concerned and of the Egyptian government between 1874 and 1875. On 18 June 1875 Khedive Ismail officially inaugurated the Mixed Courts, and in February 1876 they met in their first sitting.

The Egyptian government eventually entrusted Manoury, a French lawyer from Alexandria, with the task of drafting a body of law on the European model. He set out to borrow from French legislations while introducing partial modifications based on Islamic law and on certain provisions of the Egyptian law. As a result, there emerged a body of mixed rules, such as laws governing commerce, maritime trade, civil, commercial and criminal proceedings, as well as penal codes.

On 14 June 1883 a decree was passed providing for the creation of national courts. A technical committee was set up to draft new national laws which were an exact reformulation of previous laws, with only slight modifications which by no means altered the substance of the legal rules they contained. On 18 October and 13 November 1883, the new national laws were promulgated in French, but were later translated into Arabic.

The process of borrowing from French models constituted an innovation in the Egyptian legal system. In the light of the changes which occurred in Egyptian society, the Criminal and Penal Codes were amended in 1904 so as to fall in line with modern criminal systems. Consequently, Egypt became imbued with modern French legal culture, with the scope of application of Islamic law becoming confined to personal status. This situation caused drastic changes in the structure of Egyptian law.

Thus, positive legislations drawn from French laws stood at the top of the general legal edifice, while those drawn from the Shari'a concerning personal status and those governing non-Moslems assumed narrower proportions in this structure. Furthermore, customary law dwindled by reason of repeated state intervention in the field of legislation.

7. THE MONTREUX AGREEMENT: ABOLITION OF FOREIGN CONCESSIONS AND PROMULGATION OF MODERN EGYPTIAN LEGISLATIONS

Abolition of foreign concessions and the establishment of national liberation and independence were at the core of national aspirations. Thus, the most important achievement of the glorious national movement was the agreement reached with the concession countries on their elimination. In fact Egypt succeeded in concluding the Montreux Agreement in 1937, by virtue of which consular courts were to be abolished and their jurisdiction was to devolve on the mixed courts. These were to remain in existence for another twelve years, after introducing modifications into their system, thus bringing them closer to national courts.

After the expiry of the period determined by the Agreement, mixed courts were to be replaced by national courts in all the areas of their jurisdiction. Paragraph One of Article Two of the Agreement reads as follows:

> "Subject to the principles of international law, foreigners are to be governed by Egyptian legislation in the criminal, civil, commercial, administrative and financial fields, etc. . . ."

This meant the elimination of one of the abnormal features of Egyptian law. The judicial system and Egyptian law were unified, initiating a new stage in the history of modern Egyptian law. The most salient change in this connection was the drafting of modern bodies of law which were to apply to social relations following the unification of the legal and judicial systems.

II. Constants and Variables in Modern Egyptian Legal Structure

Studies of positive jurisprudence within the context of French legal culture follow an abstract methodology in their examination of the prevailing legal systems and their components in a given society at a given historical period.

As a result, legal and social structures are dissociated from one another. The first is dealt with as a purely legal edifice, or more precisely, an edifice devoid of its social class and historical content.

This phenomenon gives a false impression about the neutrality of the legal edifice *vis-à-vis* social problems, and the relationship between political powers in the political society under consideration, although in actual fact legal problems cannot be tackled in any given society by drawing a demarcation line between the legal edifice on the one hand and the socio-economic structure on the other. This is because the legal edifice is one of the components of the superstructure of the society and is characterized by a specific peculiarity and effectiveness in its dialectical relationship with the infrastructure.

In fact this law, being determined through social relations which in the final analysis are relations of production, is not, however, a mechanical reflection of a negative nature. For it has the ability to enjoy relative independence which enables it to have an impact on such relations by organizing and consolidating some of them and by reorganizing others.

We therefore can by no means grasp the developments associated with the borrowing of French positive laws and Egypt's shift to French legal culture, together with the presence of certain Islamic as well as non-Islamic laws in its modern legal system, and the inevitable outcome of the regression of Islamic law application to socio-economic relations in Egypt; we cannot fully grasp the social and legal structures.

As a matter of fact, we cannot unravel the far-reaching changes which involved the socio-economic and cultural structures in Egypt in this historic period, nor can we reveal the dialectical relations or deep-rooted interaction that occurred in the process.

Taking this as a point of departure it would be possible to study the determining factors which brought about the transfer of an advanced western legal culture to a backward society, while examining the factors which determined national acceptance and assimilation of an alien culture.

1. DECISIVE FACTORS IN NATIONAL ACCEPTANCE OF AN ALIEN LEGAL CULTURE

Needless to say, this attempt to pinpoint the determining factors that led to the borrowing of western legal culture, whether in its structural form as modern and comprehensive codifications which organized a changing social reality, or as an expression of philosophical and legal concepts which as a whole constituted an integrated abstract edifice, does not stop at the details of every determining factor separately, but would aim at rising above the details but without overlooking them when determining their major components. This in the final analysis constituted the core of the process of national acceptance and assimilation of this modern civilization in the era under review.

In other words, we shall focus on the general in every single factor without overlooking the particular, so that we may ultimately determine the general traits of the Egyptian society's assimilation of this borrowed culture.

(1) Socio-political factors

It may be said that the changes which occurred in the economic edifice during Mohammed Ali's rule constitute the actual beginning of a new socio-economic and cultural reality which made it possible for the ruling class to borrow French positive laws and apply them to Egyptians in their various forms of relations.

Moreover the period of Mohammed Ali's rule, 1805–1849, which constitutes a stage in modern Egyptian history with all its achievements and failures, represents one of the most significant experiences in the fields of modernization and development. In fact the focal point of all the changes brought about by the Egyptian ruler in this connection was "to create a military power by consolidating his own personal position to the detriment of big landowners on the one hand, and the traditional powers which dominated social relationships in Egypt at the time as well as foreign interests" (Herrschlag, 1973: 108) on the other, while strengthening his own relationship with the Ottoman Empire.

As a matter of fact a major portion of the changes which came over the Egyptian structure took place to some degree within the framework of modernization of the Egyptian military institution. This was so because, in the words of Herrschlag, the methods adopted by Mohammed Ali in achieving his objectives in this field reflected the efforts of a central government in a backward agricultural country to achieve rapid industrialization with scarce capital and little competitive power when compared with the ever-growing economic development in Europe. Thus, in order to realize his aspiration of curbing the influence of foreigners, and in order to counterbalance British domination in an area which constituted the road to India, Mohammed Ali preferred to rely on French assistance particularly in organizing and training his army. This was so despite the fact that he had concluded successful deals with the British in 1811 and 1812.[2]

The change effected by Mohammed Ali by force of law in the

agricultural sector, may be summed up in the following. He drew up a new agricultural policy within the framework of an economic policy which aimed at achieving his imperial aims in the then prevailing international balance of power, and within the context of his relationship with the Ottoman Empire.

In the course of his policy of creating state monopolies[3] Mohammed Ali effected radical changes in the Egyptian agricultural structure particularly in the following fields:

1 System of real estate property in agricultural lands
2 irrigation and drainage system
3 marketing system of agricultural crops
4 system of agricultural production
5 extension services in agriculture
6 system of taxation in agriculture (Hassanein, 1974: 35).

As a matter of fact, the most radical of these changes in the agricultural structure, with all their social impact, is the change which occurred in the system of real estate property in agricultural lands.[4] In this connection, changes did not occur all at once[5] but gradually, with the abolition of the system of *iltizam* whereby a person was appointed as tax-collector in a certain district and the system of *wakf* whereby the ownership of agricultural lands was transferred to it. Egypt became in the eyes of some people a monopoly assumed by Mohammed Ali himself (ibid.: 36).

As for Ismail's rule (1862–71), it was said to have been aimed at increasing production and wealth with a view to realizing the dream of an African empire. He therefore gave great attention to irrigation and the increase of the area of cultivated land in addition to the changes that he introduced in the property system (see ibid.; Herrschlag, 1973: 146).

Thus, the tendency to realize the dream of a model of western civilization, with its far-reaching effects on the nature of the Egyptian system and its various structures, paved the way for the ruling class to accept the west as a model to be followed. The most salient feature of such an acceptance was the attempt by both Ismail and Nubar Pasha to carry out a process of reform of the judiciary system within the framework of relations between nationals and foreigners through the creation of mixed courts, in addition to the borrowing of mixed laws, followed by a comprehensive legal reform of both the legal and judiciary systems of the country.

(2) Social factors

The various developments which involved the Egyptian economic system had a wide range of social and cultural repercussions. The social system was most affected by these changes, particularly by the changes which occurred during the reign of Mohammed Ali's successors, specially Ismail. It has thus been proved that changes occurred in the social and class structure with certain western patterns and models entering into the Egyptian society. These changes also included architectural patterns with their relevant mechanisms and social repercussions.

Furthermore, the emergence of new social classes influenced by western models had its repercussions on the borrowing of positive laws.

(3) Cultural factors

A thorough analysis of the changes which occurred in the national cultural structure in its legal context, indicates a starting point which coincides with the Napoleonic expedition which to most researchers constitutes the origin of relations with the west – what may be called the trend towards "Westernization" or western polarization.

This is a consensus on the basis of scientific evidence that the French expedition which put forward a liberal French model to the Egyptian intelligentsia, particularly the *ulemas*, interacted with certain hesitant and relatively rational elements within the framework of the religious institutions. It thus sowed the seeds of unrest within the ranks of the Sunnis. As a matter of fact, the beginning of the transfer of positive legal culture, with its Latin origin, had begun to infiltrate both in Ottoman laws and in the laws promulgated by Mohammed Ali, which carried within them a trend towards incrimination as a means of controlling social relations with the state and its various activities.

The process of transfer of modern codes represents in actual fact a shift in the history of Egyptian culture, as it constitutes a rift in certain aspects of national legal culture in its traditional Islamic Sunni context, and ushers in secular thought in Egypt. This process in its legal aspect confirms the link that exists between the legislative process and the state, and the break between the legal base and any other non-positive source of law. The researcher is of the view that the beginning of secular thought coincides with the borrowing of legal culture from the French model, together with the ideas which the period of European Enlightenment embodied.

Hence the effective historical beginning for the unravelling of the dialectical process in the cultural edifice coincides with the rule of Mohammed Ali. At the outset, there emerged a methodological difficulty in explaining the process of cultural change in its legal context, more so in that the pattern of transfer from an advanced and developing culture to a traditional one carried within it the seeds of instability and unrest

How can the process of borrowing or transfer be explained? In his small but persuasive article, Gustave E. von Grunebaum (1953) first reviewed the four theses which Arnold Toynbee presented in interpreting the phenomenon of cultural borrowing (Toynbee, 1953: esp. 67–71). The Toynbee theses were (a) the peculiarities of the foreign culture, from which the process of borrowing emanates, are in general more acceptable than the recipient culture, (b) the power of penetration of any cultural radiation is in inverse proportion to the cultural value of such a radiation, (c) as most important, the process of acceptance of an element from a foreign culture is bound to drag the rest in its train, and (d) this single element may be more unsettling to the recipient culture than if the foreign culture were adopted in its entirety.

However, von Grunebaum expressed a certain reservation in his critical approach to the theory of borrowing as adopted by Toynbee, to the effect that there is another more important consideration in the process of borrowing. According to him, when a certain civilization or culture seeks to borrow from another, it is when it is incapable with its own resources of grappling with a certain problem.

He considers that a difference exists between the process of borrowing which occurred during the first Abbassid era and the borrowing which took place in modern times. He thinks "foreign goods are the only means to hamper infiltration or political and economic domination and that Islam at the time was not in a defensive position but adopted these foreign models for its own good. It did so with a great deal of caution because the pressure under which it fell did not come from the outside, but was rather spurred by the period of development through which it was passing." Von Grunebaum concludes his analysis of Toynbee's theory and its application to these two historic stages of the Islamic world by saying that the political circumstances which guide cultural borrowing in our modern age are those which make such a borrowing difficult from the psychological and social points of view and cause the disruption of the groups which receive this culture. (Grunebaum, 1953: 188)

Von Grunebaum goes on to say that the first borrowing of a substantial element from a foreign civilization will inevitably lead in time to the borrowing of all the other fundamental elements. Furthermore, technological transfer will of necessity cause changes in social and intellectual attitudes. These changes will in turn bring about other forms of scientific and philosophical borrowings and may ultimately involve religious elements.

As a matter of fact, this critical approach to the various elements which constitute Toynbee's theory of cultural borrowing is predominantly an external one from outside the borrowing culture – that is an approach which does not delve deeply into the determining factors of the process of cultural borrowing from an advanced society to a backward one. This is particularly so in the societies which enjoy historical continuity and in which past heritage weighs heavily on them and hampers their present movement, as in the case of the Egyptian society under consideration.

Toynbee's and Grunebaum's viewpoints coincide with certain prevalent trends in western sociology with respect to the explanation of the process of cultural change. However, such explanations can by no means cope with all the details of the Egyptian case, for a study of the structural changes in Egypt at the time of Mohammed Ali, insofar as the fundamental system and class composition are concerned, underscore the determining factors in the process of borrowing from western positive laws.

It has been proved that one of the two most important changes effected by Mohammed Ali in the social edifice was the liquidation of the upper strata of *multazimin* (tax collectors) appointed in fixed districts, either physically or socially, by abolishing the system of *iltizam* (a system of tax collection), as a result of which these people were stripped of their wealth (Barakat, 1970). In the words of Helen Revlin, "the class of former land-owners was annihilated or stripped of their land and this paved the way for the emergence of a new class of landowners" (cf. ibid.).

Another important change in this connection was the fact that the vanguard of the Egyptian bourgoisie, made up of merchants and craftsmen, which emerged at this time, played a social role in the struggle against the French expedition and culminated in Mohammed Ali's investment. This class received a deadly blow when the Egyptian ruler established state monopolies with all their adverse effects on trade opportunities and operations (ibid.).

These measures also met with strong resistance on the part of men of religion and the *ulemas* which represented the middle-class intelligentsia, with the result that the *sheikhas* (men of religion) and *ulemas* of El Azhar joined the *multazimin* in their opposition to the abolition of the *iltizam* system. These measures, which put an end to the social status of the *ulemas*, eventually weakened their political role.[6]

These crucial changes were carried out simultaneously with other measures such as the creation of state monopolies, and the establishment of an up-to-date military institution, with modern technology, discipline and an advanced adminstrative system, all of which were aimed at achieving his ambitions. It is at this juncture that ideas of modernization coincided with the process of updating the military institution. In other words, these socio-economic and political changes constituted the root causes of indirect cultural change which was made possible by the dwindling influence of religious groups and their institutions.

2. APPLICATION OF THE THEORY OF THE THREE LEVELS OF LAW TO THE EGYPTIAN LEGAL SYSTEM

To what extent has traditional national culture as exemplified in Islamic law, Shari'a, faced continuity and interruption – the Shari'a which shifted from a traditional legal edifice governing social relations and identified with them to a modern legal structure governing such relations in a changing society? How far did it merge with international economic relations, eventually becoming subservient to the international market and the relations established within its framework? How far have these national legal rules affected the internal arrangement of all the principles which make up the whole structure and its subsidiary systems?

This analysis constitutes an attempt by scientific and methodological approach based on confrontation between the legal rules drawn from the Shari'a and those derived from western positive sources; in other words, an investigation into the areas of crisis in the whole legal edifice. This signifies an attempt at determining where perturbations and other non-technical factors, whether political or social, occur, as these factors make up the crux of the problem of application of the Shari'a to the Egyptian political system.

Thus, an analytical review of the elements of this crisis at the structural level will open the door to a more thorough outlook, while ascertaining the validity of the opinion that it is necessary to replace the existing legal edifice as a whole and create an integrated body of law, the rules and provisions of which would derive from the traditional Shari'a which has proved suitable for application to the ever-changing and complex society.

Thus the modern Egyptian legal edifice is analysed from this angle in the light of the technical and descriptive study of its composition insofar as its component sources are concerned, particularly following modern legislation, i.e. following the Montreux Agreement and the abolition of foreign concessions with all their legal problems, effects and crises. This is so because the historic era which preceded modern codifications was largely marked, as stated earlier, by the gradual recession of Islamic laws in favour of a systematic growth of borrowed French positive laws. This analysis therefore centres on the civil legal system and personal status.

As for the other legal systems such as pleadings for the defence and criminal procedures, penal code, commercial law and all other laws governing employment, social insurance etc., these emerged totally divorced from the source of Islamic law. In fact, these laws are European positive laws which are in total contrast, from the historical point of view, to the Shari'a, which had enjoyed supremacy over the Egyptian society, at least from the theoretical point of view, since the Islamic conquest and until the onset of the movement of modernization towards the end of the last century.

Following are the national legal rules and principles in the Egyptian legal structure as represented in the personal status and civil law.

(1) Personal status in change and continuity

Personal status together with the family laws that involve it, constitutes a legal subdivision which regulates the propositions and fundamental legal principles derived from the national rules which had prevailed prior to borrowing from western positive law. In fact, the area of personal status had remained subject to positive religious legislations (certain non-Islamic rules derived from clerical power and customs).

But the social relations which came under the umbrella of the legal rules of the family and other personal status, were governed by rules and principles derived from the Shari'a and other non-Islamic codes (Jewish and Christian) which were applied by Islamic courts.

It was proven that the civil codification which was promulgated together with the judicial reform did not incorporate any provisions regulating the family. Thus Islamic courts applied to Moslem Egyptians the most preponderant opinions of the Hanafite doctrine (Shehata, 1961: 116).

However, complaint about commitment to the most preponderant opinion of the Hanafite doctrine in passing judgements in lawsuits, together with the development of social conditions, led to the promulgation of a number of legislations pertaining to the family system. These regulations derived their rules from various doctrines and from the views of religious scholars (ibid.: 116; Madkour, 1969: 111).

This occurred in the light of the changes which took place in the society. A committee of senior *ulemas* from the four schools of Islamic law was set up in 1915 headed by the Minister of Justice, and it set out in 1916 to promulgate a law governing marriage and divorce. In carrying out its activity the committee was not bound by the Hanafite school as being the official doctrine of the state, but went beyond it to other schools of Islamic jurisprudence and no further. However, this draft was never enforced because of the opposition of certain *ulemas* of the official legal institution, El Azhar.

Thus, the matter was confined to strict avoidance of certain rules and matters to which the rules of the Hanafite school failed to apply in favour of the people. In the light of the new outlook whereby certain rules and provisions of the Hanafite school were not applicable, a decree providing for law No. 25 for the year 1920 was promulgated governing certain issues of personal status and incorporating matters related to alimony of the divorcee and divorce proceedings and *udah* (period of retirement before remarriage) as well as missing persons. The provisions of this law were derived from the Shafi'ite and Malikite schools.

However, changes were not merely confined to only a branch of personal status. For in 1923 law No. 25 for the year 1920 was promulgated providing for a minimum age for marriage, 16 years for females and 18 for males, as a means of safeguarding social interests and avoiding the mishaps of early marriage.[7]

Shafik Shehata considers that this reform was not provided for by a positive legislation, but was promulgated in the form of an amendment to the statute regulating Islamic courts, an amendment which was passed in 1910, by virtue of which the case would not be heard if the age of the husband at the time of the signature of the contract was below 18 and that of the wife below 16 (cf. Note 7).

Certain religious scholars consider that the new rule incorporated in this legislative amendment did not have any backing in either of the four doctrines or any other well-known doctrine, and that the authors of this amendment had sought legal backing from a legal opinion by Ibn Sherma, one of the exponents of an obsolete doctrine, by Osman El Betti and Abu El Asam, with the result that this law was merged with the statute governing Islamic courts which was promulgated in 1931 (cf. references in Note 7).

This development in the outlook of the elite whereby they were no longer bound by the official doctrines of the State, the Hanafite school, together with the borrowing of certain Islamic rules to remedy shortcomings in certain Hanafite principles which had caused some kind of maladjustment in the changing Egyptian reality of that time, led to the borrowing of certain rules from other doctrines.

In keeping with this new methodology, the Council of Ministers approved on 9 December 1936 a proposal presented by the Minister of Justice for the establishment of a committee to be entrusted with drafting a new law governing personal status in all its ramifications: bridal money, alimony, divorce proceedings, inheritance for the divorcee, parenthood and age of custody, as well as laws governing cases of missing persons, *wakfs* and bequest.

However, it was decided that the committee would not be bound by any single orthodox rite to the exclusion of the others, but it would draw its decisions from opinions of Islamic scholars, whichever was more favourable to people's interests and to social development. Steps in this connection would start with those cases which gave rise to a great deal of complaint and criticism (Madkour, 1969: 113).

With these guidelines the committee proceeded with its work by considering the draft law on inheritance by reason of its limited scope of change. This was due to the fact that most of its rules were characterized by rigidity, since its basic source was the Koran, the fundamental source of the principles of Islamic law. In consequence of this fact, law No. 77 for the year 1943 was promulgated, incorporating all rules governing inheritance, and those derived from definitive legal rulings such as those dealing with the owners of lawful shares and paternal relations.[8]

Some consider that the most important rules introduced by this new law, and which came in contrast to previous practices, was the right of inheritance granted to brothers and sisters despite the existence of the grandfather, while earlier his existence would have excluded them. At the same time, what remained after the distribution of lawful shares was to revert back to the living partner in case the deceased did not have any inheritor. Furthermore, by virtue of the law, a person responsible for homicide was banned from the inheritance, whereas accidental homicide was no reason for such a ban (Madkour, 1969).

Another law, No. 48 for the year 1946, was promulgated introducing amendments to the *wakf* system. This new law derived its rules from the various religious doctrines with the provisions regulating the *wakf* becoming closer to those governing inheritance. Law No. 71 governing bequests was likewise promulgated in 1946.[9]

These partial innovations in the traditional jurisprudence came within the framework of *ijtihad.* But following the promulgation of the law providing for the unification of the judiciary (law No. 462 for the year 1955), the need was felt to draft comprehensive law for personal status incorporating matters related to marriage, divorce and separation, and relevant issues, in addition to the rights of children, next-of-kin, inheritance, bequest and *wakfs*.

But the Ministry of Justice ignored this draft, by reason of the controversy and opposition to which each of the new drafts gave rise. In fact, any attempt at partial innovation, even within the framework of traditional Islamic principles as exemplified in the legal opinions of the four religious doctrines, met with opposition, and accusation of departing from the Shari'a was levelled by the *ulemas*. This attitude constitutes a contradiction, at least in appearance, in view of the history of the traditional official religious institution and its relationship with the political system and the ruling class.

This contradiction may find its explanation in the fact that the Shari'a in its codified aspect, i.e. in the field of personal status, was the only area where the *ulemas*' dwindling role would mean a diminution of their social role and their religious influence on the ruling class and the political system. For any attempt at innovation outside their purview would constitute a deviation which could not be tolerated. In fact large-scale religious mobilization with political overtones was conducted by the religious institution whenever there was any attempt at introducing amendments, even if partial, from the outside.

There was, furthermore, another attempt at drawing up a comprehensive code for personal status at the beginning of 1967. It was put for consideration by the Parliament and the one single political party (the Socialist Union)[10] as well as by the press. But the defeat of June 1967 and the collapse of the entire social system caused this law to fall into oblivion. However, the issue was raised once again during the 70s and constituted one of the factors of conflict in the Egyptian political scene, becoming the focus of sharp division between the various political tendencies.[11] In fact there was constant complaint about the application of certain aspects of the law on personal status.

However, the political regime which was used as a tool to strike at secular and radical trends within the political movement tried, in an apparently contradictory move, to introduce partial amendments in the structure of personal status, particularly in the laws relating to the family such as divorce and alimony. What may explain this apparent contradiction was the relationship existing between the regime and issues of Islamic law principally. It was a pragmatic relationship, i.e. by virtue of its balanced outlook and ideology, the regime made use of this issue to strike a balance between the two major currents of the Egyptian political society, the secular and radical trend on the one hand and the right-wing religious trend on the other.

This explanation may help elucidate the contradiction at the level of legislative practice through the use of the legal system known as Presidential decrees. An example of the excessive use of such a system was when a Presidential decree, passed in 1979 and providing for law No. 44 which amended certain provisions of the law on personal status, gave rise to heated discussions in the Parliament and the press as well as among the *ulemas* themselves, as to the degree of conformity between its provisions and the principles of Islamic law. This issue will be the object of socio-political analysis from the point of view of the attitude of the fundamentalist group and the ruling class.

This law contained a number of amendments with respect to personal status. It would, however, be difficult to pinpoint the exact place of change, as it was brought about by the new legislative principles which covered the entire structure of personal status. But how far these principles could cope with the new changes in the society in terms of practical application, in the light of the change of attitude towards women and the development that occurred in the family as a social institution, would be difficult to assess unless we examine the bases on which this legislative modification was founded. Examination would also have to involve issues related to personal reasoning and innovation in Islamic thought. This may be understood from the explanatory note issued by the drafters of the law – a note which comprises the set of ideas underlying these changes.

The authors of this draft postulate that the first consideration on which the new amendments were based was the following: "Islamic law towers over all other laws because it emanates from God". And if the rules and principles underlying these changes have been relinquished in matters where they should have remained fixed, in other matters general rules have been drawn up involving provisions which would suit the changing times and the new happenings. Islamic authorities were furthermore entrusted with the task of drafting laws in accordance with the principles of the Shari'a as a means of improving the lot of Moslems and raising their standard of living.

The authors of this draft considered that "the doctrines of Islamic law had enriched Islamic jurisprudence by drawing from the Holy Koran and the Sunna and that the divergence of view between religious scholars did not involve radical or clearly defined decisions, but were matters in which personal reasoning played a major role."

Proceeding from this traditional understanding, which constituted a perpetuation of the Islamic Sunni heritage as represented in El Azhar, this amendment aimed at coping with the changes which had occurred in the society since the promulgation of law No. 78 for the year 1931, law No. 25 for 1920 and law No. 25 for 1929, which had been in application for over 50 years – changes both material and moral – which had their repercussions on special relations. But as application revealed shortcomings in certain provisions of the existing laws, the need was therefore felt to look into the Shari'a for provisions to govern the new society, without impeaching any established right for any of the members of the family.

The basic purpose behind such changes was to regulate the enjoyment of some of these rights.[12] In other words, the legislative amendment which was based on the idea of partial change, aimed not at departing from the traditional norms, but only at regulating the use of certain rights without going to the length of formulating a new law for a new pattern of life. These changes were meant more precisely to regulate relations within the marriage institution and family system in keeping with the changes which had occurred in modern Egyptian society. Another purpose behind such partial amendment may also have been the fear of direct confrontation with the *ulemas*.

The most important amendments which occurred in the obsolete laws on personal status and the attitudes of the various forces *vis-à-vis* these changes may be summed up in the following:

(2) Personal status for Moslems

i. Divorce The authors of the draft considered that an investigation into cases of divorce indicated that certain husbands divorced their wives in their absence and hid the news from them, thus causing them a great deal of harm in addition to leaving them in unsettled conditions. In some cases husbands registered the divorce in the registry office and kept the divorce document in their own possession, acting as if the marriage were running its normal course. At the first sign of conflict they produced the divorce document in an attempt to rob the wife of her rights. The authors of the draft considered that there was nothing new in this law, since the scholars of the Hanafite doctrine had earlier faced cases in which the divorce was hidden from the wife by postponing the *udah* until the time when the husband admitted that the divorce had taken place.[13]

Proceeding from this analysis of the problem the authors of the draft considered that the solution lay mainly in regulating the way by which the wife would know of her divorce, so that no conflict would arise between the partners if the husband hid the news of the divorce. Thus Article 5 bis stipulated that when the husband wished to bring about the divorce, he should go to the registry office for official registration. This article, Paragraph 2, regulated the implication of the divorce on the wife from the date of notification.[14]

ii. Divorce of other than the first wife[15] This is a principle already established as part of the provisions of law No. 25 for the year 1929, and the new amendments considered that having more than one wife was a social problem, and that it constituted a harm which entitled the wife to ask for a divorce. The legislator deemed fit to consider a second marriage as constituting a harm to the first wife, thereby giving her the right to divorce in case the second marriage was unacceptable to her, or if the husband concealed that he was already married at the time of the second marriage.[16]

According to the legislators, this amendment formed an integral part of the Shari'a and did not constitute a departure from its principle. At the same time, polygamy would be allowed only with the wife's acceptance. This amendment gave rise to conflict of opinion between the *ulemas* as some considered it a departure from the principles and rules of Islamic law, constituting a restriction of the husband's right to divorce his wife, as this right was the privilege of the husband alone. According to them the restriction constituted an impingement on this right.

iii. Right of ta'a Article 6 bis, Paragraph 2 regulated the husband's right of *ta'a* (asking the wife to come to the husband's house in case of unlawful desertion) to ensure his wife's return to his home, when it stipulated that the wife's failure to obey her husband unjustifiably implies an end to the payment of the alimony from the date of refusal. She would be considered disobedient if she failed to return to the husband's home after having been asked to do so through a letter delivered by a court usher. In this case, the husband was to specify the address of the house.[17]

The legislator allowed the wife the right to object by filling a form wherein she would indicate the legitimate grounds for her objection. A penalty was imposed in case the grounds for objection were not clearly indicated, namely, the court may rule that it rejects the objection.

Moreover, the alimony is stopped from the day the husband notifies his wife to return, and if objection is not made at the prescribed time, the alimony is halted at the fixed deadline. But when the wife's objection has sufficient legal backing, the court should interfere of its own accord, or in response to a request by one of the partners, to put an end to the conflict and reconcile them. This article has also provided for a number of legal and technical points,[18] which have been either derived from the Malikite doctrine textually or inferred from its provisions.

iv Muta *(compensation to the divorcee)* When the marriage is contracted for the purpose of sexual pleasure, Article 18 bis has established a new provision whereby the wife whose marriage has been consummated would, in case of divorce without her approval or for no fault of hers, be entitled over and above the compensation due to her *udah* to a two-year alimony at least, depending on the financial status of the husband, the circumstances of the divorcee and the length of the marriage. The court may allow the husband to pay this alimony in instalments. This amendment remedies a shortcoming in the law whereby such a compensation was not due to the wife so long as she had received the *mahr* (bridal money) in full and since she was entitled to the *udah* compensation. As for this compensation, *muta*, it was recommended but not compulsory. But the initiators of this law, considering that generosity and manliness had dwindled in modern times, ruled that the divorcee was in need of assistance beyond the *udah*, which would help her face up to the consequences of divorce.

At the same time, this new compensation would curb hasty divorces. This provision was derived from the new doctrine of Imam El Chafei.[19]

v. Child alimony Article 8 bis, Paragraph 2 has introduced a new provision for a child whereby if it has no income of its own it would be supported by the father. This would go on until a girl's marriage or until she is able to support herself, and until a boy reaches fifteen years of age or is able to provide for himself adequately. But in case of physical or mental disability or for reasons of education or in case of inability to support himself, a boy would be continuously supported by the father.

Thus the father would be committed to support his children and provide adequate housing for them so as to ensure for them a living comparable to that of people of the same social standing.

The legislator considers that it is only proper and fair that education requirements should make alimony compulsory, in case education is provided by the state and does not conflict with religion, and provided the student is progressing in his education. The girl's alimony is made compulsory until marriage or until she is able to support herself adequately, because her sex in itself constitutes some kind of handicap.

vi. Castigation of the husband if he fails in the duties demanded by the law This new ruling was derived from the scholars of the Hanafite doctrine who consider that castigation is a penalty which should be left to the discretion of the judge, and varying according to the crimes. Imprisonment may be the only penalty, or it may be associated with another such as a fine. This penalty was approved by Imam Abu Youssef and certain scholars of the Shaf'ite doctrine and in some points from the doctrine of Imam Ahmed Ibn Hanbal. Proceeding from this legal analysis, Article 23 bis incriminates the husband if he fails in his legal duties as provided for in Article 5 bis of the law and its explanatory note, as well as the duties devolved on him by virtue of the same Article and those prescribed in Article 6 bis of the law. The notary public is also to be penalized if he fails in his obligations under Article 23 bis, Paragraph 2 of the Penal Code.[20]

vii. Wife's alimony Article 2[21] of the amendment provides that Article 1 of law No. 25 for the year 1920 governing alimony and certain matters related to personal status be replaced by new provisions, the most important of which being Paragraph 2 which stipulates that the wife's illness does not preclude her from being entitled to an alimony, which includes food, clothing, housing, medical expenses and any other expenses required by customs.

The legislators have derived this provision from the Zaidieh doctrine, which falls in line with the doctrine of Imam Malik, whereby medical expenses form part of the wife's alimony. However the Egyptian legislator has in this context deviated from the provisions of the Hanifite doctrine. In Paragraph 4, the legislator has indicated cases in which the alimony is forfeited such as the wife's apostasy, unjustified refusal to surrender to the husband, etc., as well as cases in which the wife's departure from home is without her husband's consent. Paragraph 6 stipulates that the wife's alimony constitutes a debt to be borne by him from the day he refrains from supporting his wife. Such an alimony is dropped through payment, a provision derived from the Shaféite doctrine and which had been in application in the existing law.

viii. Frozen alimony The legislator has provided that no legal proceedings would be conducted in cases of alimony covering a period of over one year ending on the day legal action is brought against the husband. In this it differs from the provisions of Article 99 of the Presidential Decree providing for law No. 78 for the year 1931 governing Islamic courts, which fixed this period at three years ending on the day legal action is taken against the husband; the legislator deemed that this period was too long.

Furthermore, Article 16 has established rules for estimating the wife's alimony.

ix. Custody Article 20 of this law introduces new provisions governing custody and its time-limit, in the light of the analysis of conflicts arising in judicial application. The legislator has fixed a mother's custody of a boy to the age of ten and a girl to the age of twelve.

However it was left to the discretion of the judge to decide to keep a boy in his mother's custody until fifteen and the girl until she marries, as derived from the Malikite doctrine. He then devised certain well-balanced rules to govern relationship in this connection, such as not granting custody to the father. He further regulated the parents' right to see the child, and provided for negotiated solutions in case it is difficult to organize visits, etc.

But in view of the housing crisis which prevails in Egypt, the law has introduced provisions governing the custodian's home which are derived from the Hanafite doctrine. Independent accommodation for a divorcee and her child should be provided in the home rented by her former husband unless he makes other adequate accommodation available.

This presentation indicates the reformatory trend which guided the legislator, and reflects the response to the religious opposition which had earlier stood against a draft law proposed by the Minister of Social Affairs.[22]

However, certain religious groups rejected the Presidential Decree system which provided for the law governing the opposition, the most prominent among these being the *ulemas* of El Azhar, the Moslem Brotherhood and other Islamic groups.

As a matter of fact, the recourse by the legal system to show its ability to initiate certain reforms ran counter to the views of Islamic groups whose political role gained momentum towards the end of the 70s, under the impact of the wave of Islamic fundamentalism.

(3) Personal status for non-Moslems

The foregoing analysis of the law on personal status for Moslems and its component parts, together with a review of its historical development, is evidence of the fact that it constitutes one of the areas of traditional and national legal culture, and that the law on personal status for non-Moslems remains subject to the control of the Coptic Church, a role which was further consolidated under foreign concession.

In actual fact, non-Moslem laws remained confined to the limits of family laws, particularly under the Islamic concept of the legal status for non-Moslems in the Abode of Islam. However, such an attitude was not restricted to the Christian religion with its various denominations but extended to the Jews with their two sects, the Rabanites and the Karaites. A historical analysis of the evolution of this branch of the legal system indicates that non-Moslems had not for a very long time been governed by official legislations.

As far as Coptic canon law is concerned,[23] it had roots in a body of canon rules promulgated by Kyrollos (Patriarch of Alexandria) in the thirteenth century, and another passed by the scholar Abu El Fada'el Ben El Asaal. There was still another body of law governing personal status which was elucidated by Archbishop Philothaos Awad in 1896 (cf. references in Note 24). In fact, these sources remained for many years the legal reference for *millah* courts and had the force of law on the ground that they constituted decisions taken by a local institution (cf. ibid.).

Eventually a committee stemming from the *millah* courts for Coptic Orthodox laid down another body of law on 9 May 1938, in which all laws governing personal status were rewritten in a modern version and ratified by the general *millah* court. Another body of law on personal status for Copts was also ratified by the general Assembly of the *millah* courts and put for consideration to the synod in 1955. The purpose behind its promulgation was that it should serve as a legal base for civil courts in cases of litigation between Coptic Orthodox (Sharkawy, 1966: 68). The Patriarch of the Coptic Orthodox Church furthermore passed a Papal decree No. 7 on 18 November 1971 allowing for divorce in one case only – that of adultery – whereas the Papal decree No. 8 which was passed on 18 December 1971 barred divorced women from remarrying.[24]

As far as the Greek Orthodox denomination is concerned, a body of law made up of 30 articles regulating the institution of marriage, its impediments, reasons for divorce and its implications was passed on 15 March 1927, and eventually amended in February 1950 (Assiouty, 1974: 193).

As for the Armenian Orthodox a number of legal provisions were laid down by Mokhtar Gosh during the twelfth century, and eventually in 1940 a code was promulgated governing personal status, with jurisdiction devolving upon the *millah* courts, prior to their abolition. A book entitled *El Huda* (The Right Path) was published in the thirteenth century by Abu El Farah, better known as Ibn El 'Ebri, and another by El Ghazali, where the influence of Islamic jurisprudence is widely felt. These books regulated the life of the members of the Syrian Church. Another legislation governing personal status was passed in Jerusalem in 1929, and its provisions, from the point of view of Islamic jurisprudence, do not differ much from those of the Coptic canon law (Yehia, 1970/71: 9).

With respect to the Eastern Catholics, their sources of law are the same as those governing Coptic Orthodox.[25] And the Catholic canon law was codified in an integrated manner in 1917. But this was not the case with the Eastern denominations, whose canon laws were not codified in the same way as western canon laws. Thus, the laws governing marriage in the Eastern Catholic denomination were passed incorporating provisions applicable to the Eastern Church, and were eventually ratified by a decree from the Pope of Rome in 1949 (Sharkawy, 1966).

As for the Protestants living in Egypt they were considered by the Egyptian legislator as belonging to one and the same denomination as the National Anglicans. In fact, a law governing their personal status was passed in March 1906, and remained in force until the abolition of the *millah* courts in 1955 (cf. Yehia, 1970/71: 52 and references).

As for the Jews, they were divided into two sects, the Rabanites and the Karaites. This split may be due to a divergence which emerged after the time when the Talmud was considered in Jewish canon law as being as binding as the Old Testament. This split became all the more pronounced when Anan Ibn Daoud became the leader of the Karaites, who are few in number but who do not believe in the Talmud as constituting a source of law (Sharkawy, 1966: 79 onwards). They therefore rely on the Old Testament rather than on the Talmud as a source of legislation, while introducing *qiyas* in cases where no provisions are established, in addition to the *ijmah* and established norms or customs (ibid.: 80).

This historical survey of the sets of legal rules which make up the system of personal status for non-Moslems in Egypt indicates the rift that existed between the various religious groups in the country. This situation constituted an abnormality and inequality in the legal edifice, the like of which is not to be found in any modern society. However, this situation can not be oversimplified because it is due to the very nature of Egypt's historical development and the religious composition of its society, together with the role of religion and the political system in this context. Furthermore, the issue has far deeper causes by reason of the fact that it is linked to the legal national edifice in general and the focal problems which constitute its historic crisis in particular. This lack of equilibrium or rift in the legal edifice motivated Egyptian legal experts to call for a remedy to this shortcoming and for the need to substitute this plural system by another which would apply to all Egyptians regardless of creed.[26]

In this connection, a partial change took place as part of the process of evolution, represented in a plurality of judicial systems in Egypt, this being for political, economic and socio-religious reasons. Under these circumstances Egyptian Moslems were governed by the rules of the Shari'a courts, whereas Egyptian non-Moslems (Christians and Jews) were to fall under the jurisdiction of the *millah* courts. This situation runs counter to the concept of State supremacy and the principles of public law whereby, according to the explanatory note of law No. 462 for the year 1955, the State was to have absolute sovereignty, in addition to the fact that the population, regardless of their nationality, were to be subject to national laws and courts and one legal jurisdiction irrespective of the types of litigation involved or the law that applied to them.[27]

In the meantime, the plurality of systems and jurisdiction continued until the promulgation of law No. 462 for 1955, by virtue of which conflict of jurisdiction was eliminated through the abolition of the Shari'a and *millah* courts.

As a result, cases which had earlier been referred to the latter were referred to national courts, in accordance with the provisions of the law on pleadings. However, unification of the judiciary in matters of personal status for Egyptians did not bring about a structural change in the substantive rules which governed such relations, as they remained in force. Thus Article 6 of the previous law stipulates that rulings in cases of litigation related to personal status and *wakfs*, which had originally fallen within the competence of Shari'a courts, were to be passed in accordance with Article 280 of the statute regulating such courts. In other words, Egyptian Moslems were to be subject to the provisions enshrined in the statutes regulating Shari'a courts and to the most preponderant opinions in the Hanafite doctrine.

As for non-Moslem nationals, Article 6, Paragraph 2 stipulates that "concerning litigation related to personal status for non-Moslem Egyptians who had well-established judicial systems at the time this law was promulgated" relevant rulings were to be passed within the framework of the general system in accordance with their canon law.[28]

The previously depicted Egyptian model represents a unique example from the historical and social points of view, inasmuch as it reflects the existence of multiple and conflicting systems in the traditional legal edifice which governs personal status in the less advanced countries.

This phenomenon we will attempt to highlight in our next research when examining the relationships between the traditional legal principles and western substantive laws. However, this vital area of personal status remained subject to national legal rules (Shari'a and non-Moslem canon law) despite the socio-economic changes which motivated the borrowing of the western laws. This new structural change in the Egyptian legal edifice was required to complete the process of involvement of the Egyptian economy in the international capitalist economic market as an affiliate unit. However, the field of personal status, which was viewed as being of lesser importance, reflected the crisis prevailing in the legal edifice and in the Egyptian culture and dissent that existed in the intelligentsia and divided them into a secular and religious groups.

In other words, the perpetuation of this area of personal status in this way was a genuine expression of this split and conflict, while religious groups continued to exercise their domination.

(4) Civil law

Public civil law, together with other public laws, came as an expression of a new socioeconomic and political reality on the Egyptian scene, and of the attitude of the ruling class *vis-à-vis* the national heritage and the western legal model.[29] Thus, public civil law together with the theory of obligations was an almost exact replica of the Napoleonic Civil Code passed in 1802, was based on the same principles, and consequently was divorced from the general trend of rules of business relations as provided for in the Shari'a, which had prevailed prior to the reform of the judiciary.[30]

Some consider that certain provisions of the Egyptian civil code have been influenced by the Shari'a (see Note 30). The clearest evidence of this fact, in our view, is the prohibition by virtue of the mixed civil code to sell future crops (Article 33) in view of the peril it involves. This code determines the loss which falls on the seller as one-fifth, a proportion fixed by fundamentalist legal experts (Article 336/419). Apart from this influence of the Shari'a, both the former and latter codes stated that the buyer should have seen the produce as a precondition for a sound transaction. The

Egyptian code furthermore considered that any transaction agreed upon would, in case of fatal disease of the buyer, constitute some kind of testament in accordance with the provisions of the Shari'a. However, the Egyptian code differs from the French in that damage caused to the produce prior to delivery should be borne by the buyer in accordance with the provisions of the Shari'a.

Among the principles influenced by Islamic law was the provision for insurance against hidden or undetected blemish or defect in the produce. This influence extended to the so-called non-defined contracts called "shared burdens" in Islamic jurisprudence. In this connection, Shehata says: "The obligation arising from the lease contract was construed by the Egyptian legislator as being a negative obligation which does not compel the buyer to assume responsibility for repairing the leased unit."[31]

Under the chapter on bail, the legislator has instituted what is called caution money, which is one of the forms of contract under Islamic law. A special provision is found in the public civil code concerning *farouka*, a type of contract known in Egyptian customs since the dawn of history (Article 553).

Although it has been established, following socioeconomic and cultural analysis, that the movement of codification called movement of reform constituted a shift in Egyptian legal history and gave expressions to substantive laws in the sociopolitical system; this net result also applied to the second wave of codification which followed the abolition of foreign concessions. According to the historian Sarwat Anis El Assiouti, the movement of codification which accompanied the elimination of mixed courts in 1949 was the first sign of the advent of national capitalism as a substitute for foreign capitalism.

Consequently the new civil code came as a true reflection of the needs of the semi-feudal, semi-capitalist ruling class, while preserving the general traits of western capitalism with a few slight amendments, apart from the fact that it genuinely reflected individualistic approach and its fundamental principles.[32]

At the same time the legal and political discussions which took place in the Parliament (with both Houses) constituted a historic document which truly reflected the status of the ruling class and its social composition, as well as its attitude *vis-à-vis* the law as a tool of class domination. In fact, heated discussions arose in the House of Representatives at the time between the majority as represented in semi-feudal forces adhering to the right of pre-emption and a minority whose aim was to reject this principle (a principle derived from Islamic jurisprudence) and hence to limit big landholdings which were provided for by the law.[33]

The best evidence put forward by El Assiouti in this connection is confiscation as one of the means of acquiring property (Article 874, Paragraph 3), and legal speculations whereby state lands are seized under the pretext of reclamation. These lands were eventually mortgaged at the Real Estate Credit Bank with view to forming large landholdings. The new civil code therefore resorted to nationalization as a means of banning foreigners from competing with the Egyptian ruling class.

The most eloquent example that may be cited concerning the position of the dominant social class *vis-à-vis* the civil code as an important tool for domination was the provision enshrined in the law whereby the right of property had a social function. But this provision was rejected by the feudal class in the Senate on the ground that it was a reflection of a philosophical creed, and because it conflicted with legal interpretations. (see Note 33)

This elementary socio-political and economic analysis of the new civil code is a true reflection of the attitude of the ruling class and its concept of the role of rule of law in the society, as well as the nature of the legal base and the civilizational model from which the civil code drew its theories, provisions and principles, all of which will constitute the object of a survey in the next chapter. We should however highlight the shift in the attitude of the new civil code *vis-à-vis* Islamic law and its historic and legal heritage. In fact the Shari'a was one of the sources from which the rules of the new code were derived, although only partly, for it was used as a last resort after legislation and customs (Article 2). Thus this "referral to Islamic law was meant to remedy the shortcomings and loopholes of the legal system. However, such a referral did not mean a total adherence to the detailed provisions of any particular doctrine, but was to be resorted to provided it did not conflict with the fundamental principles of the Egyptian legal system" (Assiouti, 1974: 193).

As a matter of fact this outlook towards the provisions and principles of the Shari'a in business relations which are derived from the principles and heritage of Islamic jurisprudence, reflects the viewpoint of the legislators, El Sanhouri and Lambert, on the possibility of drawing from the Shari'a and of reformulating some of the many aspects of jurisprudence. Thus, El Sanhouri, an authority in Egyptian jurisprudence considered, even prior to the drafting of the new code, that the Shari'a should "receive a greater share of attention on the part of the Egyptian legislator when revising the code. For the Shari'a was the source of law of the country prior to the adoption of current laws, and still is in a major part of the civil code, namely the area of personal status, as well as certain fields of business relations. Thus having recourse as much as possible to Islamic law as a source of legislation is in conformity with the Egyptian legal traditions, and is in keeping with the view whereby the law cannot be created all at once but grows and develops gradually with its past continuing into its present" (Sanhouri, 1938: 119).

This outlook was nevertheless linked, in the opinion of the great jurist, "to the need for the revival of a powerful scientific movement which would recover its seriousness and shake off the dust of intellectual stagnation which had prevailed in the East for long years, in addition to breaking the shackles of imitation to which the backward had been bound" (ibid.: 120–121).

However, despite this fact and under these circumstances, thinking stopped at the revision of the civil code which was considered a rich source from which the Egyptian law-giver could borrow many of the legal principles of the new draft (ibid.). This was all the more true, in that the Egyptian law-giver had drawn certain provisions from the Shari'a, such as those governing the *wakf* and pre-emption.

The great jurist, in the meantime, drew up a plan which reflected his concept concerning the possibility of borrowing from the Islamic heritage when redrafting laws governing business relations. His concept boils down to the opinion that borrowing, to use his own words, "is beneficial in updating the principles of Egyptian law, and in redressing its shortcomings". For updating the principles of legislation should be done through the general theories which fall in line with the various aspects of the law. Thus, there exist certain theories in Islamic law which are in harmony with the most up-to-date concepts underlying modern legislations, as well as with legal traditions, and hence should be adopted as a basis. The Shari'a will therefore serve as a criterion when adopting stands towards the not-so-well-established theories, but in case these theories had some origin in the Shari'a, then they were likely to be endorsed (ibid.: 127–128).

As a matter of fact the Egyptian law-giver drew certain

provisions from the Shari'a, the most important being, in so far as the general spirit is concerned, those in which the materialistic or substantive trend was predominant; this is a trend which falls in line with the provisions of the legal heritage. Furthermore, the most significant theory adopted by the legislator was the one related to the abuse of rights, which in the Shari'a had a broader scope than in European substantive legislations. In the meantime, the lawgiver kept "most of the provisions which public law had drawn from Islamic legislations, while adding to them certain deep-seated Islamic principles such as the idea of the contract council (Article 94) side by side with the theory of contract. Another theory which was included was the *i'zar* under the chapter on lease (Article 608), in addition to considering release from commitment as a unilateral legal procedure which would not require approval of the contractor. This constituted one of the concepts incorporated in Islamic jurisprudence (Shehata, 1961: 144–145).

The new code, moreover, introduced the principle of unforeseen accidents which had been adopted by the French administrative justice, rather than the civil, and which the Egyptian legislator eventually adopted on the strength of the theory of necessity in Islamic law. In addition to these general theories, the lawgiver drew from the Shari'a numerous detailed provisions, such as those governing the *wakf* lease and monopolies, the lease of agricultural land, the destruction of crops in the leased area, the termination of the lease contract with the death of the lessee or through a breach of faith, and unilateral remission of debt, in addition to many other matters which the code borrowed from the Shari'a – the planting of trees in the leased area as well as provisions pertaining to common walls and the period of time limitation, eligibility grants, and pre-emption. This was apart from the principle, whereby there could be no inheritance except after the payment of debts, all of which were issues taken from the Shari'a.

As a matter of fact the process of borrowing from the Islamic legal tradition which constituted an attempt on the part of the intelligentsia to introduce certain traditional legal components into the civil code, reflected an attitude based on compromise on the part of the legislators and the ruling class on the one hand and of the other trends on the other. In fact, according to Borham Atallah there were three major trends which attempted to influence the provision of the civil code *vis-à-vis* the Shari'a. The first was the secular trend which considered that no reference should be made to Islamic law, in view of the fact that the evolution of modern life no longer recognized that the Shari'a should be of any assistance to the judge in the settlement of litigations. The second view expressed an Islamic trend (the Moslem Brotherhood, the *ulemas* and certain judges) which deemed it necessary to lay down a civil code which would derive all its provisions from Islamic law. In this connection, they formulated a draft law on obligations, the provisions of which were drawn from the Shari'a. The third and intermediate view was that advocated by El Sanhouri, one of the drafters of the law, and one which finally prevailed. According to this view, Islamic law was to constitute a reserve source of law, next to legislations and customs, keeping in mind that the objective trend of the civil code should fall in line with the spirit of the general provisions of the Shari'a in addition to keeping abreast with modern times (Atallah, 1968: 75–76).

It therefore proves that the success of the Egyptian experiences, insofar as borrowing from western laws is concerned, was due to a number of decisive factors which governed the shift from a positive legal culture to a traditional one, and emphasizes the gradual emergence of secular roots in the very core of traditional culture. Thus, despite the presence of certain conflicts of a sociopolitical nature, this by no means detracted from the success of the experience, a success unprecedented in this field. This experience nevertheless had negative repercussions on controversial issues such as the relationship between the incoming legal culture and the recipient traditional legal edifice, and the effect of such a borrowing on the national identity. In short, the Egyptian problems involved in the experience also differed from those which arose in the developing countries of Africa, problems pertaining to the relationship between the traditional legal heritage and the process of integrated development of these societies. For such a legal heritage was considered as an impediment to its legal, cultural and social development.[34]

III. Relationship between National Legal Culture and Western Positive Laws

The relationship between the elements of traditional culture and those borrowed from western positive culture is one of the fundamental issues which confront the legal system in developing societies. This relationship likewise faces a crisis when it comes to application, a crisis linked to the issues of integrated development as a means of breaking the shackles of the traditional society with its negative repercussions.

With all the historic crisis that it involved, this issue, despite its being one of the central ones faced by the Egyptian society, yet had world-wide dimensions, in view of the fact that it had socioeconomic as well as political connotations in Third World countries, particularly the African.

This situation led UNESCO to entrust the International Society for Legal Sciences to draw up a detailed plan for the study of the legal systems of the newly-independent countries, while pin-pointing the changes which had occurred in these systems during the colonial era. This study was aimed at examining changes and modifications that could be introduced into the systems so that they would effectively respond to the dictates of development in these countries. The study was to deal in its first stage with the African countries alone (Tunc, 1968: 3).

This underscores the significance of the relationships that exist between the rules of traditional law and those borrowed from western positive law, and how far this affects the cause of progress and development in its various aspects.

However, while acknowledging in principle the importance of these problematic issues in Africa, conflict arose between researchers in this field, some advocating reform, such as Kibambaye and B. Anwabizi[35], and others of a more conservative view, such as Max Gluckman, who tended to highlight the human values entrenched in African life and the richness of African traditions in the field of law and the administration of justice. The latter therefore encouraged respect for traditional legal systems, emphasizing the danger inherent in adopting amendments and applying them to a majority of Africans. On this point, an author endorsed the conservative view of the eminent anthropologists Max Gluckman and René Gendarme, to the effect that a far-too-advanced legal system, ill-adjusted to existing socioeconomic and intellectual structures, was no less dangerous than an outdated one (*see* Tunc, 1968).

This controversy became more acute, hence truly reflecting the depth of the crisis that confronted the African societies, and gave an example of the various dimensions of the problems when examined in the light of the Egyptian reality. In fact, these problems would have to be viewed in an integrated manner which would involve the entire social, legal and cultural edifice and all related issues, and in the final analysis would be interlinked with the political movement of the Egyptian society. Hence, a study of the relationships between the various elements of the national legal heritage and those borrowed from the modern Latin legal civilization in its French aspects, would set the stage for a thorough examination of the demand for the application of Islamic law and jurisprudence with a view to adjusting them to the realities of a changing society. Some go as far as to ask for its substitution for the existing legal edifice.

A reservation should however be entered with respect to the Egyptian case, which differs from its African counterpart, to which reference was made with a view to highlighting the gravity of these central issues. This is so because the modernization of the Egyptian legal system differs historically and qualitatively from that of the African, insofar as its relationship with the issues of progress and development are concerned and because Egypt's borrowing of western substantive law occurred at a relatively earlier date that was the case in Africa. Egypt's shift to the west ushered in a process of modernization with the introduction of the western liberal model which the society easily assimilated. However, the conflict that arose in this connection was of a socio-political nature, being linked to the roots of the political movement, and in some other aspects to the historic crisis of the edifice of national culture, as well as to the composition of the intelligentsia since the time it established channels of communication with modern European civilization towards the end of the nineteenth century.

There is one final observation. The previous study of the components of the Egyptian legal edifice has underlined the phenomenon of dual legal culture which dominated Egyptian legal structure, and its cultural roots which are partly traditional and partly borrowed from western positive laws. This duality is the outcome of numerous socio-political and economic changes, as a result of which the traditional rules of the Shari'a lagged behind and consequently could no longer play their functional role, nor could they adjust to the new conditions. On the strength of these reservations and the previous limitations it would be possible to examine the relationships existing between the indigenous legal principles and the positive principles and components of the Egyptian legal edifice at three levels:

1. DIMENSION OF INTEGRATION BETWEEN POSITIVE LAW AND TRADITIONAL NATIONAL CULTURE

The Egyptian code on personal status in its Islamic aspect which represents the laws governing non-Moslems is the ideal area of integration between the traditional legal culture and the legal edifice as a whole, because this subsidiary system has a functional role in governing personal relations.

But despite the recurrent call for changing this system to suit the societal changes and the relations prevailing in the family as a social institution, the relationship between husband and wife, rights and obligations of both parents and their effects on children, the fruit of marriage, issues such as divorce, custody and alimony, as well as the reforms introduced through the most recent law which amended certain of its fundamental provisions – despite all the issues, yet this area has withstood radical or structural change. In fact this area represents the core of the Shari'a system next to the system of *hudud*, which is an area of great importance to the *ulemas* and to the fundamentalist institution.

We have earlier dealt with the system of personal status, its historic development and the amendments which were introduced to it.

2. DIMENSION OF CONFLICT BETWEEN WESTERN POSITIVE LAW AND NATIONAL LEGAL PRINCIPLES

It may be said that there are numerous areas of conflict between borrowed positive laws and traditional national principles. The following are the areas of conflict, in order of importance:

(1) Conflict between the positive penal code and the Islamic system of *hudud*

But the penal and procedural laws, as subsidiary systems of the legal edifice, have constituted models which withstood integration. This conflict coincided with the process of modernization which pits the national legal principles derived from Islamic jurisprudence and heritage against the principles drawn from western positive law. Furthermore, the penal code in its substantive and procedural aspects was borrowed almost literally from the French code. In other words, an integrated penal code modelled on the western system was laid down side by side with a system of criminal justice. As a matter of fact this penal code, on both the substantive and procedural levels, does not represent an alternative to or a substitute for the Islamic penal model, which includes retribution, consolidation, and *hudud*, and it therefore constitutes the core of conflict between two contrasting models with respect to sources, framework and guidelines.

A critical review of the Islamic criminal code confirms a view advocated even by those who favour Islamic law and its penal code for modern society. According to this view, the phenomenon of incrimination, which was rendered necessary by modern systems as a result of social evolution and its increasing demands, is catered for by the system of *ta'zir* (consolidation, crimes for which penalties are not specified) which constitutes the legal basis for the secular side of Islamic criminal law. Such a system is capable not only of keeping abreast of modern civilizational systems, but also of taking care of all the criminal procedures devised to control criminal manifestation and their diverse causes, in societies where corruption and dissolution have infiltrated, with crime becoming a serious social illness (Rashed, 1975: 8–9).

The *ta'zir* can therefore assimilate many of the changes which occurred in the edifice of criminal culture, and the modifications inherent in the application of modern criminal procedures. What remains therefore is the area of the *hudud* and the right of the "avenger of blood" in crimes of retribution and blood-money,[36] which constitute the core of conflict between positive law and the Shari'a. This is a fundamental area where, according to some people, Islamic law should apply. This demand aims for the most part at implementing the Islamic code of *hudud* in crimes of retribution and blood indemnities.

Conflict arose at the academic legal level, pitting the *ulemas* and Islamic groups against legal men of western culture, as to whether Islamic law could apply *in toto* or in part to modern social relations. Conflict also arose at the political level between the political authorities and certain Islamic currents and trends within the official *ulema* group. In the eyes of many, this represents the key to the issue of application of Islamic law to the modern Egyptian legal system; also it is an issue which constitutes the core of a long socio-political conflict in the Egyptian society.

(2) Conflict between certain rules of business relations in civil law

and the principles of the Shari'a

Most of the legal rules which made up both the old and the new Egyptian legal edifices constitute a model area of western legal rules, in their theories and general ideas, and therefore do not conflict with the legal principles derived from the Egyptian national heritage. Also there exists an area of integration and interaction where state law as derived from the western heritage is adopted side by side with certain Islamic rules in the field of business relations. But despite this fact, the Egyptian civil code incorporates a set of rules which run counter to certain important religious principles of the traditional legal edifice which had been prevailing in the Egyptian society.

The set of rules which conflicted with traditional Islamic principles focused on the issue of interest rates and usury which were banned by the Shari'a. Thus, mixed civil codes determined the maximum rate of interest at 12% in civil matters and 12% in all commercial matters, and in cases of common consent this rate should not exceed 12% of the original debt. However, an amendment was introduced through a decree passed on 6 April 1882 reducing the former to 7% and the latter to 9%, while the maximum rate even in cases of common consent should not exceed 12%.

In 1883, the Egyptian legislator adopted a set of civil codes related to maximum official and unofficial rates of interest. Another amendment was introduced on 10 July 1892 modifying rates of interest to 5%, 7% and 9%. With the promulgation of a decree, these rates were lowered to 5%, 6% and 8%. However, the national legislator intervened to put an end to usury, which constituted a manifestation contrary to the principles of the Shari'a, by promulgating law No. 49 for the year 1923.

Shafik Shehata considers that this reform constituted a step towards the elimination of this type of dealing which was known in the early Islamic days. This was in fact some kind of credit practice which was rendered unnecessary through two kinds of mortgage: estate mortgage through non-acquisition, a system adopted in the Egyptian civil code and which had been unknown to Islamic jurisprudence, and the estate mortgage through acquisition which was current in Islam and adopted by the Egyptian civil code on a larger scale than in the French civil code.[37]

It may therefore be said that the new civil code carried within it a somewhat stringent trend *vis-à-vis* usury, this being evident in the reduction of rates of interest to 4% in civil matters, 5% in commercial matters, and 7% in cases of common consent. It eventually banned, in the most explicit terms, compound rates of interest, as well as any increase in rates of interest on capital.

However, such a conflict was not restricted to the legal rules governing various rates of interest which were based on principles of the French positive civil code and those emanating from Islamic law, but extended also to the rules of time limitation, *takadum*: 15 or 5 years depending on the circumstances, and three years in cases of claims of invalidation (Shehata, 1961: 73). This had to be achieved because the rules concerning business relations in Islam did not adopt the principle of time limitation for the abrogation of rights. However, under the 1971 Constitution, Islam was considered as the primary source of legislation, and by virtue of this fact time limitation, whatever its length, was rejected on the grounds that it constituted a western concept contrary to the rules of the Shari'a and thereby was not enshrined in its provisions.

As a matter of fact, trends prevailing in the Egyptian legal profession and among certain religious groups favoured the opinion that the civil code should not be tampered with but that there should preferably be amendment on a partial basis. This was to be achieved by the elimination of any principle running counter to Islam, such as the system of interest rates, which was construed by many religious groups as being tantamount to usury, and that of time limitation. However, some of the people sitting on the committee working on the application of the Shari'a were of the view that it was necessary to draw all the rules which make up the civil code from Islamic law, to the exclusion of any derived from western models.

This opinion constitutes an unrealistic and unscientific approach, in view of the absence of theories which could be used in laying down such Islamic civil codes, in addition to the impact which such a view could have on issues of legal application and social stability, apart from the existence of a longstanding heritage of judicial application in Egypt.

3. DIMENSION OF INTERACTION BETWEEN NATIONAL AND WESTERN POSITIVE PRINCIPLES: HARMONY AND CONFLICT BETWEEN OFFICIAL LAW AND UNOFFICIAL LAW

We have earlier indicated that the Egyptian civil code had adopted a number of concepts and principles derived from Islamic jurisprudence which were reformulated and incorporated in the system of business relations, and that these Islamic legal principles represented an area of traditional national culture in the State legal edifice. These rules and principles therefore reflected an interaction between the rules of traditional national law and borrowed western positive law. For in the process of judicial application and jurisprudential elucidation, a theoretical interaction also takes place, since the elucidation of these Shari'a rules proceeds from western positive parameters, thus driving this interaction between these patterns of legal rules to unprecedented richness. As a result, there appears on the levels of elucidation and judicial application some kind of interaction and harmony between these two patterns of rules.

The present era has witnessed a dwindling of the historic role played by customs and customary rules in governing relations and social interactions, more particularly in the advanced societies. This was the result of the developments and deep changes which involved human society, as well as the growing role of the state and its functions, in addition to the shift of its pattern from one of non-intervention to one of intervention, together with an evolution of the legislative role of the State. In fact, custom was relegated to the background and was to be resorted to only in cases when legislative treatment was absent. Thus, its place in the legal hierarchy as a source of law in the Latin as well as Egyptian systems comes second in the legal base and serves only as a supplement to positive legislations.

In this manner, customs do not come into conflict with the borrowed positive legal rules, because the positive legislator recognizes that customs should have a role in cases of absence of explicit provisions to deal with any social problem. As a result, customs have come to play a marginal role in modern life, particularly following the growing impact of state functions. However, such a role supplements the positive legal edifice, and may serve as a source of legislative rules which the legislator reformulates in the light of the attitude of the dominant forces and their socio-political interests, in addition to integrating them in the auxiliary system to which they belong.

However, custom, or unofficial law as it is commonly called, plays another role different from the previously mentioned supplementary one. This role is a conflicting one, though limited in scope, dimensions and impact, and is mainly confined to tribal areas, such as the New Valley, and the cases of the western Desert most particularly in the Awlad Ali tribal society. In fact, the customary rules which govern social relations in the Awlad Ali society play the same role as the broad positive official laws in the Egyptian society.[38] We shall detail the general traits of these rules.

It is worth pointing out that certain studies attempted to put Malinowski's and Radcliffe-Brown's theories on tribal laws and the role of customs in the traditional society of the Awlad Ali community (Mohsen, 1975; Mahgoub 1976) to the test. The same objective was sought in an article by Safia Mohsen entitled *Conflict and Law among Awlad Ali of the Western Desert* (1975) and a study by Ahmed Abu Zeid (1962) on *Blood-Vengeance* in an Upper Egyptian village.

One of the most salient traits which characterize the Awlad Ali community is the absence of a representative body or legislative council to legislate legal rules and principles which would govern the behaviour of the political group. There are also no courts which would determine the extent to which citizens should abide by these abstract rules which are devoid of any legislations. Neither is this community acquainted with the post of Public Prosecutor. Mahgoub further maintains that they are not aware of the existence of such professions as that of a lawyer, who assumes their defence, or the police force, or the coercive implementation of penalties provided for in the penal code and supplementary laws.[39] The code which governs relations in the Awlad Ali community is not divided into two systems, one for business relations, the other for penalties, as is found in official legislations.

There is furthermore the system of *muradi* (conciliator) who is chosen by the litigants (the defendant and the prosecutor, to use the official terminology of the pleading system) in order to rule in the *mi'ad* (customary council) which meets to deliberate on the accusation or prosecution and determine penalties (material or moral) in accordance with the rules of the *derbah* (legislations). There is also the system of *awakel* (wise men), or chiefs who enjoy traditional authority and who attend the deliberation council to represent the litigants who delegate them. Another system is that of *nuzzar* (blood-money) which determines the harm caused to the victim, so that the conciliator may apply the law and fix the adequate compensation. (Information in Mahgoub, 1976: 245 onwards)

As a matter of fact, customary law in the Awlad Ali tribal community is based on substituting official laws by the rules of the traditional local system. Some maintain that the elderly in the Awlad Ali community still recall the *Hagfa* meeting in which they set out to pass customary laws or *derbah* which comprises 67 articles governing relations between members of the same family unit, or *aman* (peaceful relationships) between distinctive political units. These laws provide for the breach of the general principles of good conduct, and the types of penalties that befall the criminals, as well as methods of settling tribal disputes.[40] There is a traditional system of penalties provided for in the *derbah* governing *nuzzar* etc., as well as oaths of allegiance.

An examination of the provisions of the customary law of the Awlad Ali community confirms the nature of the conflict existing between this law and the official national law, in particular the conflict prevailing in the official penal code and the tribal code.

In fact Article 1 of their tribal customary law stipulates that in the case of premeditated murder, blood-money amounting to 400 Egyptian pounds is to be paid, with 300 pounds in the case of an accidental killing. Article 4 of the same law stipulates that in cases of aggression resulting in injury, the conciliator determines the value of the blood-money to be paid in accordance with the gravity of the injury. The blood-money is to be estimated in relation to the material harm, incapacitation or damage caused to the victim or the group to which he belongs. (Mahgoub, 1976: 248)

It is therefore evident that these provisions are in contrast to the official criminal and penal rules which do not include such systems, because the Egyptian criminal code (penal code and code of procedures) has relinquished the system of retribution and blood-money which had prevailed prior to the modernization of the Egyptian legal system in the nineteenth century. Furthermore, blood-money, *diyah* (a certain amount of money paid as compensation to the family of the victims) and *kebara* (which is estimated at a certain amount of money and certain animals) comprise, at the level of legal principles, a conflict with one of the general principles of the modernized official legal edifice, which provides for the equality of all citizens before the law. But the *kebara* differs according to the legal status of the individual who has been the victim of aggression, or according to the structural distance which separates the two political groups, that of the aggressor and that of the victim of aggression, and the type of aggression committed.[41]

Although the official penal code acknowledges a modern criminal principle, namely the personalization of the penalty, the penal system of the Awlad Ali provides that the distinctive political unit in their community involves joint responsibility in the payment or acceptance of blood-money. There are for instance cases in which the thief has to pay four times the value of the goods stolen from the victim, a system called *el tarbah* (quadruple) (Article 23), if the stolen goods are found in his house, store, or hands, or if he is caught red-handed. The *tarbah* is to be paid from the thief's own money without any assistance from his family. This constitutes a special type of penalty in the Awlad Ali community. (Information in Mahgoub, 1976: 253–255.)

This disparity between the traditional rules and the official law constitutes one of the areas of conflict between traditional legal rules and borrowed modern laws or positive laws. It may be said that the conflicting role of the customary tribal (traditional) law of the Awlad Ali community has relatively but slowly dwindled under the impact of the socio-cultural achievements of the state on their traditional culture. In fact these achievements have contributed to the structural and political change of this community, a change which was brought about by the modern equipment of land reclamation and cultivation as well as by new settlements. Those were aimed at promoting and developing this traditional society in addition to introducing new political activities such as the Arab Socialist Union, the political parties with all their impact on the traditional tribal system, and new key posts in the traditional community (ibid.: 333–335).

Conflict, therefore, is a socio-political as well as a cultural and structural feature which governs the relationship between the principles of tribal traditional law and the state official legislations. This unofficial law which stands in contrast to state laws contains a pattern of legal principles and ideas of a tribal nature which contradict those on which modern state legislations are based, namely, integrated historical considerations.

The area of traditional customary law in the Awlad Ali community, although standing in conflict with State laws, yet identifies with it in unofficial traditional rules which govern certain social aspects like those prevailing in Upper Egypt, such as the phenomenon of blood-vengeance.

In a study by Ahmed Abu Zeid on blood-vengeance in Beni-Sami, one of the villages of Upper Egypt, and through the use of the anthropological method, he formulated the law on vengeance on the basis of a descriptive and analytical study of this social phenomenon, with all its implications and repercussions. This law may be summed up in the following axiom (Zeid, 1962: 48 onwards): "The battle occurs in the extended family, but blood falls on the nucleus family"; it is a well-known proverb which sums up the view of Awlad Ali concerning killing and vengeance. In other words, the murder of a family member represents the humiliation of a closely-knit and co-operative group, with the result that the scope of responsibility widens the area of conflict. Another axiom is that the person who is killed should be avenged by the murder of one member from the family of the aggressor, or whatever families are related to it, regardless of the status of both families (ibid.: 51). Again, the extended family should avenge the blood of its victims at the hands of its sons or any of the extended families, on the grounds that the one single extended family constitutes an integrated unit. Moreover, very often a blood-enmity arises between two or more *bedna* (extended families). Finally, changes have occurred in the laws on blood-vengeance, represented in certain departures from the old traditions concerning the accosting and harming of women and children (ibid.: 62 onwards).

Blood-vengeance laws which have been derived from an anthropological study of the Beni Sami village reflect the situation in many Upper Egyptian villages where customary laws, as unofficial legislations in a local area, are unapproved by the state and stand in contradiction in both their structure and component parts to the rule incorporated in the state penal code.

One word remains on the social developments which occurred in the traditional society during the last few years: it is that they relegated the rules of traditional law into the background, and eventually subdued the conflict between these traditional, tribal rules and state official legislations.

4. CONCLUSION: RELATIONSHIP BETWEEN THE GENERAL PRINCIPLES OF THE EGYPTIAN CIVIL CODE AND THE PRINCIPLES OF THE SHARI'A

The theory governing the sources of law in the Egyptian civil code has endorsed the principles of natural law and rules of justice as a supplementary or reserve source of law (Article 1, Paragraph 1, Egyptian Civil Code); they are second in rank to the principles of

Islamic law, Shari'a.[42] The judge may have recourse to them in case the legislations, customs or the Shari'a do not provide a principle to govern relations between the litigant parties. The principles of natural law and the rules of justice constitute a major source of the components of the western legal edifice with both its general and subsidiary systems. These principles[43] play a pivotal and functional role in the overall legal structure and endow it with legitimacy, while ensuring a minimum of integration between its component parts.

In the context of the Egyptian civil code there exists a predominant view whereby when adopting the provisions of Islamic jurisprudence, consideration should be given to co-ordinating these provisions with the general rules and principles underlying civil legislations in general. It is in fact inadmissible to adopt a provision of Islamic jurisprudence which would run counter to one of these principles, as this would jeopardize its cohesiveness and harmony (Badrawy, 1969/70: 225).

The idea behind such a trend is that both in theory and application there is no conflict between the principles of the Shari'a and those of natural law or the rules of justice. This is so because the latter principles constitute one of the fundamentals of modern legislation in western legal patterns, and their basic theories would be preponderant in cases of recourse to the principles of Islamic jurisprudence and in cases of conflict between them and the general overall principles of the civil code. However, practical experience indicates the presence of a certain conflict between the Shari'a and the general principles of law and justice as we have earlier indicated in our analysis.

Notes

AUTHOR'S NOTE: The author wishes to thank his assistant Mr. Nabil Abdel Fattah who has played a major role in the documentation of this research as well as in the preliminary drafting of some of its points.

1 *Had* in arabic is originally a distinction or demarcation between two things so that one does not encroach on the other.

2 See Herrschlag, 1973: 108 and Dodwell, 1931, reference to which is made in Herrschlag, 1973.

3 The process of adjustment of Mohammed Ali's global economic policies or sectoral policies still constitutes an object of controversy in Egyptian Islamic jurisprudence. Thus some consider that this policy relied mainly on the principle of national economic independence on the one hand, and the principles of state socialism on the other. Among these is Said, 1954: 50. The same trend is adopted by Hassanein, 1974. Others maintain that Mohammed Ali adopted an economic system which may be called a "Collective system" (O'Brien, 1966: 39). Reference is made to this fact in a book by Metwalli in which he considers this system as being state capitalism (1974: 40).

4 An issue arises in this connection: that of the various effects caused by the changes introduced by Mohammed Ali in the field of real estate property. Helen Ann Revlin maintains that these policies were not affected by the movement of Turkish reform alone, but also by the agricultural reforms carried out by the French during their occupation of Egypt. She finds that French reforms did not in most cases go beyond the stage of planning, basing her information on Egyptian sources such as El Gabarty, El Azhar Sheikhs, and Copts which were in close contact with the new developments during the French occupation. In her view, these people together with the French who remained behind after the withdrawal of the French expedition and those who came during Mohammed Ali's rule may have encouraged reforms similar to those advocated by Napoleon and Menou. She is however uncertain about the actual sources of her information. See Revlin, 1963: 66.

5 Review in Revlin, 1963: 79–90, covering the various changes which occurred in this connection and the ensuing social interaction between the religious institution and the state together with the fundamentalists' opposition to some of the changes involving their social standing.

6 In his aforementioned letter, Ali Barakat considers that the collapse of the *iltizam* system was due to the seizure of the charitable *wakfs*. Some of these were *multazimin* and the others were *wakf* superintendents, and their political role dwindled following the clash which occurred between Mohammed Ali and Omar Makram. It was therefore natural that their role in social life should recede due to the new secular trends, the mission despatched to Europe by Mohammed Ali and the borrowing from western sciences. Cf. Barakat, 1970: 151–152.

7 For details, see Shehata, 1961: 116–117; Madkour, 1969; 112–113.

8 Madkour, 1969: 113–114. This fundamentalist jurist considers that all the committee had to do with the rules drawn from definitive judgements was to reformulate them.

9 Madkour, 1969: 114. The entire *wakf* system was abolished by virtue of law No. 180 for the year 1952. This same scholar considers that the rules of bequest did not follow one specific doctrine of the four religious doctrines. Its most fundamental principles were those of compulsory bequest, whereby grandchildren excluded from inheritance from their grandfather or grandmother would enjoy the right of inheritance provided their grandparents did not bequeath anything to them. This decision was derived from legal followers. The law furthermore permitted bequest to the heir within the limits of one-third of the legacy without the approval of the rest of the heirs.

10 Review these changes in Madkour, 1969: 115.

11 When Aicha Rateb, Minister of Social Affairs, submitted the new draft law on personal status, a confrontation between the *ulemas* and the Minister took place, and El Azhar students staged a demonstration in opposition to this law, with the result that political rulers had to go back on it, temporarily, under the impact of confrontation with the religious groups.

12 Explanatory note of the Presidential decree providing for law No. 44 for 1979, concerning the amendment of some provisions of the law on personal status.

13 In Abdin, n.d. (Pt. 2, the chapter on the *udah*), it is said that if the husband divorces his wife and keeps the news hidden from her, then acknowledges it at a later date, the *udah* starts only from the time of his acknowledgement. If an earlier date is given for the divorce, it will not be acknowledged. See the explanatory note in Note 12.

14 Article 5 bis, Paragraph 3 provides for ways to inform the wife of the divorce, including attendance of registration. If she does not attend, the husband notifies her through a court usher at her place of residence or through a next-of-kin. All this is to be carried out in accordance with procedures incorporated in a decision by the Minister of Justice. The authors of the draft see that the need to register the divorce and to regulate the method of notification must

not impinge on the right of divorce which was granted by God to the husband.

15 The principle of divorce for wives other than the first was established in Article 6 of law No. 25 for the year 1925, which reads as follows: If the wife claims that the husband has done her wrong to the extent that marriage can no longer be tolerated she can ask the judge for divorce. Irrevocable divorce is pronounced if the wrong done to her is proved and if reconciliation becomes impossible between them. This provision is taken from the Malikite doctrine and that of Imam Ahmed ibn Hanbal, and is in contrast to the doctrines of both Imam Abu Hanifa and Chafei.

16 Article 6 bis, Paragraph 2 stipulates that "a husband's second marriage without his wife's prior consent is considered harmful to her, in case she had specified as a precondition in the marriage contract that he does not take a second wife, or in case the husband conceals from his new wife an earlier marriage." In its last paragraph, this article restricts this right of the wife by not giving her all latitude to use it whenever or wherever she wants, but estimates the period when she can use this right to one year, provided she has good grounds for it and in case she had not explicitly or implicitly accepted to remain under his *esmah* (matrimonial authority). (See Note 12.) In order to ensure the wife's knowledge the article provides in its first paragraph that at the signing of the marriage contract the husband has to specify the name of the wife or wives under his *esmah* and their places of residence. The notary is then bound to notify wives of the new marriage by registered mail (see Article 6 bis).

17 Article 6 bis, Paragraph 2 of the Presidential decree providing for law No. 44 for the year 1979 concerning amendments of certain provisions of the law on personal status and the relevant explanatory note.

18 See Article 6 bis of the previous law for 1979. The legislators consider that the motives behind the third provision does not conflict with the principles of the Shari'a, since it was not banned by the Koran. This has become imperative nowadays as it has become a means of revealing right from wrong and abolishing harm.

19 The legislators consider that the principle behind the law on compensation for the divorce aimed at providing a source of comfort for the woman and that it was one of the principles of charity and generosity called for in the Shari'a. This compensation was made compulsory for the divorce when the marriage was consummated and when separation was not due to a fault on her part.

20 Article 23 bis of the previously mentioned law provides for the following: The husband is to be punished with imprisonment for a period not exceeding six months, and a fine of not more than 200 Egyptian pounds, or either of the two penalties in case of breach of

any of the provisions of Article 5 bis of this law, or when he gives false information on his social status, residence of his wife, wives or divorce. The notary is also to be punished with imprisonment for a period not exceeding one month and a fine not exceeding 50 pounds, in case of breach of any of the duties imposed by law. He may be suspended or dismissed from his work for a period not exceeding one year.

21 This article stipulates that the alimony is due to the wife by the husband from the date of consummation of the marriage, whether both partners embrace the same religion or not. The wife's illness does not preclude her from enjoying this right.

The alimony is dropped in a case of the wife's apostasy or if she wilfully refuses to surrender to her husband for no fault of his. On the other hand, leaving the matrimonial home without her husband's consent in cases permitted by the Shari'a or by customs, or in times of need, does not constitute sufficient ground for forfeiting the wife's right to the alimony. Nor does leaving the house to carry out legitimate work forfeit such a right unless she misuses this right in a way that runs counter to the family interest and unless she fails to comply with her husband's wish for her to stay at home. This alimony constitutes a debt on the husband from the day he refrains from supporting his wife. Legal proceedings cannot be carried out in cases of alimony covering up to a one-year period ending on the day the complaint is lodged.

22 Aicha Rateb, Minister of Social Affairs, in the Cabinet of Prime Minister Mamdouh Salem.

23 The Orthodox creed includes four denominations: Copts Orthodox, Greek Orthodox, Armenian Orthodox and Syrian Orthodox. It is considered that each of these denominations has its own private as well as common sources of law, while the dissolved *millah* courts (village courts) exercised jurisdiction over them. See Yehia, 1970/71: 149 and also Awad, 1896 and, for the common sources of canon law for Christians, see Sharkawy, 1966: 59 onwards.

24 Sharkawy, 1966: 68–69. Sharkawy considers that the two previous bills cannot be considered legislations by reason of the absence of binding rules. According to him this may be due to the fact that the body of law of 1938 was not submitted to the *millah* court, which in any case was not competent in the field of legislation. Such a competence fell to the clerical synod to which this body of law was not submitted. As for the 1955 body of law, the synod failed to adopt it, in accordance with the rules governing its meeting. This ruling was incorporated in a resolution which was passed on 12 August 1920 and which was approved by only a few. It therefore failed to acquire any legitimacy. In this connection, see Ismail, 1950.

25 The denominations of the Catholic creed are:

1. The Copts Catholics who are of Egyptian origin,
2. the Greek Orthodox who are of non-Egyptian origin (Greek),
3. the Armenian Catholics who are of Armenian origin,
4. the Syrian Catholics who are of Syrian origin,
5. the Maronite Catholics who are of Lebanese origin,
6. the Chaldean Catholics who are of Iraqui origin,
7. the Latin Catholics who are of European origin.

All these denominations are subject to the authority of the Pope of Rome, and are considered separate entities. From the historic regional and racial points of view, see Yehia, 1970/71.

26 See in this connection Yehia, 1970/71: 11; Farag, 1969: 22 onwards; Badrawy, 1968: 13; Kira, n.d.: 394.

27 See the explanatory note of law No. 462 for 1955 concerning the unification of the laws on personal status for all nationals.

28 See Yehia & Salama, 1962. Yehia points out that this provision incorporates the rule of "ascription" (*isnad*) of an Islamic tradition because it determines the applicable law in cases of personal status without indicating the substantive ruling for these cases (ibid.: 9). See various legal discussions concerning the application of this article in the previous references in Note 26.

29 The eminent legal expert Sarwat Anis El Assiouti considers that Egypt borrowed French laws towards the end of the 19th century when foreign capitalists had the upper hand in Egypt's economic life, hence transferring capitalist laws to Egypt to strengthen their economic stronghold. See his important book (1974: 116).

30 Explanation of the technical aspects and principles underlying the theory of obligations in public law is seen in Shehata, 1961: 135 onwards.

31 Shehata considers that the lease contract in Islamic law entitles the lessee to enjoy the right of use, and hence does not compel the landlord to repair the house after he has conceded to the lessee one of the elements of ownership (1961: 139).

32 This is a thorough analysis of the composition of the semi-feudal, semi-capitalist ruling class, particularly those sitting in Parliament. In fact an analysis of the Egyptian Parliament and its social structure in this historic stage, together with the discussion of these laws, confirm the truth of this opinion. Review Assiouti, 1974: 118. One of the most salient features of this new code is the principle whereby a contract constitutes a law governing the contracting parties (Article 147, Paragraph 1) and that the implementation of Islam should be compulsory on the debtor (Article 234, Paragraph 1). Consequently this code, as rightly pointed out by El Assiouti, centres mainly on tying the hands of the debtor and submitting him as a slave to the creditor, as the Romans did in the past, in addition to its great emphasis on everything pertaining to the individual will. Within the

framework of liability, the general principle whereby no liability would be entailed without fault still prevailed (Article 163) etc. It failed, however, to give due attention to public interest, and dealt with it only in part. On the other hand, this code underscored the influence of the Sunni-feudal class in the Egyptian Parliament, and encouraged the formation of large landholdings by all possible means, etc. See Assiouti, ibid.: 119 onwards.

33 This important survey can be reviewed in the book written by the great expert Sarwat Anis El Assiouti (1974: 120). Also review the set of preparatory works of the Civil Code, Chap. 1, p. 373 onwards and Chap. 6, p. 13 onwards.

34 There exists an Arabic translation of this report (Tunc, 1968).

35 Kibambaye, first President of the Supreme Court in Senegal during the preparation of this report. B. Anwabizi, Professor at the Faculty of Law, Lagos University, at the time of the preparation of this report.

36 Ali Rashed maintains that Islamic criminal legislations distinguish three areas in the field of crimes and penalties, from the point of view of the rights engendered by man's actions and behaviour. This distinction involves the rights of God, and the rights of his servant or the individual on the one hand, and these rights and those of the community on the other. Thus, there are crimes which entail punishment for God's sake, such as the crimes of *hudud* and others, as a result of which direct harm is incurred by individuals when crimes affect their own persons, lives or physical bodies; consequently the penalty involves the right of individuals either in an absolute or preponderant manner, as in crimes of retribution or blood money. There are other crimes which are by no means related to the rights of individuals or the society; these are crimes for which penalties are non-specified. (Rashed, 1975: 15–16)

37 Shehata, 1961: 139–140. Information concerning the rules and provisions introduced by the mixed and national codes, as well as by the Ottoman decrees governing the rates of interest and their limits, are taken from Shehata, ibid.

38 Some maintain that the anthropologists, in examining the various aspects of the problems of social control in the traditional (primitive) societies, should take into consideration all the systems which have the same functions as those achieved by law in modern society, regardless of whether these social systems have the same elements as those found in modern legal systems. This is because these conditions and elements are of a formal nature and do not lead to any change in the nature of these systems or their social functions. (See Mahgoub, 1976: 241) Malinowski tends in his study "*Crime and Custom in Savage Society*" (1926) to widen the scope of the concept of traditional law so as to include all the components of the existing

culture. This contributes in one way or another to the establishment of security and social control. He and his followers do not therefore consider customs in traditional societies, as being equivalent to law in modern societies. (See Mahgoub, 1976: 56, 241)

39 See Mahgoub, 1976: 245. There exists a Court of Summary Proceedings in the New Valley, which falls within the administrative jurisdiction of the Guizeh Court of the First Instance (information obtained from some authors and Safeya Mohsen).

40 Mahgoub, 1976: 246. One of the things which proves the conflict existing between official law and the bodies in charge of its application on the one hand, and customary traditional law on the other, is the administrator's attendance at reconciliation councils in order to give them an official character, without their having any effective role either in passing judgements or in their implementation. This is due to the fact that they deliberate issues and settle litigations involving infringement of public rules far from the authorities and without any interference on their part (ibid.: 247–248).

41 See Article 53 of the *derbah* to which reference is made in Mahgoub, 1976: 249, which comprises descriptive information.

42 Article 1 of the preliminary draft does not specifically state that the Shari'a constitutes a third source of the Egyptian civil code. Thus, Article 1, Paragraph 2 states the following: In case of absence of applicable legislation, the judge may rule according to customs, if not, then in accordance with the principles of natural law and the rules of justice. However, the review committee decided to add the Shari'a in its second paragraph, and amended the paragraph to read as follows: In case of absence of applicable legislation, the judge may rule according to customs, if not, then in accordance with the principles of the Shari'a which are most consonant with the provisions of this law without abiding by any specific doctrine. Some people eventually proposed the deletion of the last sentence of the second paragraph, so that referral to the principles of the Shari'a may be unrestricted, a proposal which was approved by the committee. See Badrawy, 1969/70: 224; also see the set of preparatory works of the Egyptian Civil Code, pp. 191–192.

43 Atallah maintains that the term "natural law" points to a body of rules elicited by the human mind from the nature of social relations and serving as a whole to achieve the notion of justice (1968: 76). He considers that natural law has played an undeniable role in the evolution of modern law, a role which it would be difficult to assess. As a result, speaking about natural law would take the form of irrational mediations which would be inconceivable in modern times. See in this connection the definition of Abdel Hay Hegazi (1966: 322–323); Badrawy, 1969/70: 226.

References

Abdin, Ibn
n.d. *El Dar El Mokhtar*. Cairo.
Assiouti, Sarwat Anis El.
1974. *Principles of Law*. Cairo: Dar El Nahda El Arabia.
Atallah, Borham Mohammed.
1968. *Fundamentals of the Civil Code*. Cairo: Dar El Ma'arif.
Awad, Archbishop Philothaos.
1896. *Legal Gist of Personal Status for Copts Orthodox*. 2nd rev. ed. Guirguis Philothaos Awad, ed., 1913. Cairo: El Maktaba'a El Misriya El Ahliyah.
Badrawy, Abdel Moneim El.
1968. *Introduction to Private Law*. Cairo: Waba.
1969/70. *Principles of Law*. Cairo: Waba.
Barakat, Ali.
1970. *Development of Land Ownership in Egypt between 1813–1914 and its Impact on the Political Movement*. Cairo: Dar El Thakafa El Jadida.
Dodwell, Henry.
1931. *The Founder of Modern Egypt*. Cambridge: Cambridge University Press.
Farag, Tewfik Hassan.
1969. *Provisions on Personal Status for Non-Moslem Egyptians*. Alexandria: U. Publishing House.
Grunebaum, Gustave E. von.
1953. Westernization in Islam and Theory of Cultural Borrowing. In: *Islam: Essays in the Nature and Growth of a Cultural Tradition*. ed. Grunebaum, G. E. von. London: Routledge & Kegan Paul.
Hassanein, Ahmed Said.
1974. *Egyptian Agricultural Policy: Theory and Application*. Cairo: U. Publishing House.
Herrschlag, Z. Y.
1973. *Introduction to the Modern Economic History of the Middle East*, transl. Mostafa El Husseiny. Beyrouth: Dar El Hakita.
Hegazi, Abdel Hay.
1966. *Introduction to the Study of Legal Sciences*. Cairo: U. Publishing House.
Ismail, Ihab.
1950. *Dissolution of Marriage in Coptic Canon Law*. Ph.D. thesis at Cairo University.

Kira, Hassan.
n.d. *Origins of the Law*. 2nd ed. Alexandria; Dar El Thakafa.
Madkour, Mohammed Salama.
1969. *Introduction to Islamic Jurisprudence: History, Sources and General Principles*. Cairo: Dar El Nahda El Arabia.
Mahgoub, Mohammed Abdou.
1976. *Political Anthropology*. Alexandria: The General Book Organization.
Malinowski, Bronislaw K.
1926. *Crime and Custom in Savage Society*. London: Routledge & Kegan Paul.
Metwalli, Mahmoud.
1974. *Historic Roots of Egyptian Capitalism and its Development*. Cairo: The General Book Organization.
Mohsen, Safia.
1975. *Conflict and Law among Awlad Ali of the Western Desert*. Cairo: National Centre for Social and Criminological Research.
O'Brien, Patrick.
1966. *The Revolution in Egypt's Economic System*. London: Oxford University Press.
Rashed. Ali.
1975. Philosophy of the Criminal Code, Part Two. In: *Criminal Thought in the Arab World: Lessons to Ph.D. and Post-graduate Students in Criminal Code*. Cairo: Faculty of Law, Ein Shams University.
Revlin, Helen.
1963. *Economy and Administration in Egypt at the Beginning of the 19th Century*. Transls. Ahmad Abdel Rehim Mostafa & Mostafa El Husseiny. Cairo: Dar El Ma'aref.
Said, Gamal El Dine.
1954. *Economic Development in Egypt*. Alexandria.
Sanhouri, Abdel Razzak El.
1938. On Which Basis is the Revision of the Egyptian Civil Code to be Conducted? In: *Golden Book of National Courts*, Part Two. Cairo: El Amiriuah.
Sharkawy, Gamil El.
1966. *Personal Status for National Non-Moslems and Foreigners*, 2nd ed., orig. 1917. Transl. Mourad Farag. Cairo: Al-Nahda Publishing House.
Shehata, Shafik.
1961. *History of the Movement of Innovation in Legal System in Egypt since Mohammed Ali's Rule*. Cairo: The Egyptian Society for Historic Studies.
Toynbee, Arnold J.
1953. *The World and the West*. London: Oxford University Press.

Tunc, André.
1968. Les aspects juridiques du développement economique. In: *Selected Articles on Economic Planning and Development.* Cairo: The Egyptian Society of Political Science, Statistics and Legislations.
Yehia, Abdel Wadoud Ali.
1970/71. *Provisions of Family Law for Non-Moslem Egyptians.* Cairo: Dar El Nahda El Arabia.
Yehia, Abdel Wadoud, & Ahmed, Salama.
1962. *Personal Status for Non-Moslem Nationals and Foreigners*, 7th ed. Cairo: U. Publishing House.
Zeid, Ahmed Abu.
1962. *Blood-Vengeance: Anthropological Study in an Upper Egyptian Village.* Cairo: The National Centre for Social and Criminological Research.

Glossary

aman	peaceful relationships
awakel	wise men
bedna	extended families
derbah	customary laws, legislations
Diwan 'aam	a Council created by Napoleon
diyah	a certain amount of money paid as compensation to the family of the victim
esmah	husband's matrimonial authority
el tarbah	quadruple
farouka	a type of contract known in Egyptian customs
geziah	head tax
had (pl. *hudud*)	a punishment specified in the Koran
Hadith	Sayings of the Prophet
Hagfa	a meeting in which the Awlad Ali tribal community set out to pass customary laws
Hijra	Islamic Year
ijmah	consensus
ijtihad	the process of extracting and formulating new rules from the Koran and other authentic sources of the Shari'a
iltizam	a system of tax collection
istihsan	preponderance of opinion
isnad	ascription, or tracing of a *Hadith* to the Prophet Mohammed
i'zar	release from commitment
Jamrah	explanations and comments added to the *Meshnah*
kebara	compensation estimated at a certain amount of money and certain animals
khurag	land tax
mahr	bridal money
Meshnah	verbal or second *Turah*
mi'ad	customary council
millah	village
multazimin	tax collectors
muradi	conciliator
muta	compensation to the divorcee
nuzzar	blood-money
qiyas	analogy

Shari'a	Islamic law
sheikhas	men of religion
Sunna	the Tradition of the Prophet Mohammed
ta'a	asking the wife to come to the husband's house in case of unlawful desertion
takadum	the passing of a certain time which may lead to the loss of a right
ta'zir	crimes for which penalties are not specified
Turah	Old Testament
udah	period of retirement before remarriage
ulema	religious scholar
wakf	public endowments
wilaya	administrative provisions
Wali	Governor, Administration

3 Modern Law and Judiciary Reform in Iran – An Islamic Society

M. A. Nezami Talesh

Introduction

After repeated military defeats by Russia in the first quarter of the nineteenth century, Iran, hitherto a great power in the region, was shocked by a sudden awakening to its weakness *vis-à-vis* the West and thus began a conscious attempt to modernize, i.e. to copy the West. As contact with the West increased, a profound sense of generalized inferiority which shook the very foundations of the society set in, and modernity came to be seen as contrary to and incompatible with all aspects of the traditional ways of life.

This view was not of course shared by all involved. To some Westernization was a dream and to others a spectre. Caught up between the two conflicting currents were the masses, who were perplexed by a paralysing dissonance, to say the least.

One of the areas which most sharply reflected the contrast between Iran and the West was the system of justice, and thus "demand for law," in both the political as well as the judiciary senses of the term, came to be the most important ideological force in Iran throughout the nineteenth century.

If the strictly political aspect of this "demand for law" met the opposition of the country's age-old absolutistic political establishment and led to a bloody constitutional revolution, its judiciary side was not any easier. It meant on the one hand intrusion in the domain of, and direct threat to the vested interests of, a most powerful group, the *ulama* (Islamic clergy), and on the other hand supplementation if not supersession of a highly rigid and well-established judiciary system, the Sharia, which for centuries had been regarded sacred and immutable.

This paper is concerned with the latter aspect, the judiciary reform. The process, as we shall see, was tedious and, as the revolution of 1978 and its aftermath substantiate, the new Westernized judiciary system failed to achieve an appreciable degree of institutionalization in the society or integration with the traditional Sharia judiciary. Conceived as the antitheses of the traditional system and carried out without proper attention to the socio-political elements involved, the judiciary reform boiled down to an inarticulate explanation of an inherently alien system in a vastly different socio-cultural environment; the system thus created emerged as a shocking example of cultural discontinuity and gap.

To provide a complete picture of the reform, its outcome and background, we shall devote the first part of this chapter to a short but comprehensive description of the traditional judicial system in Iran. In the second part the process of reform from its beginning in the nineteenth century to the end of the Pahlavi period will be discussed. In the third part I shall take a static look at the modern law and judiciary in Iran, and shall examine the various codes from the point of view of their legislative technique, legal structure and underlying philosophy. And finally, in part four, an attempt will be made to draw certain conclusions from the whole project.

I. The Traditional Judiciary System of Iran: A Historical Sketch

In the year 640, eight years after the death of the Prophet Mohammed, when the Arabs finally defeated the Sassanid army, the Islamic history of Iran began. True, complete Islamization of the vast Persian Empire took centuries, and in the process Iran provided a fertile soil for the growth of the most heterodox sectarian movement in Islam, the Shiism; but throughout, Iran never entertained doubts in accepting Islam as the most important, if not the only, source of inspiration for shaping its culture and social institutions.

Nowhere has this supreme reign of Islam been so total as in the realm of law, and the observation that "law is the distilled essence of the civilization of a people" (Anderson, 1976:1) is definitely more true of the Sharia in Iran – as well as in other Islamic societies – than of any other religious law anywhere.

This does not of course mean that other types of law did not exist in the country. To be sure, *orf* (customary law), laws imposed by the conquerors, and above all decree legislation by the rulers were all at times important parts of the country's judiciary system. But leaving aside the exceptional cases, these non-Sharia laws were always used as a supplement to, and at least in theory, in accordance with, the general rules of the Sharia. As has been observed, the Sharia all down the centuries was ". . . the most effective agent in moulding the social order and community life of Muslim peoples and in holding the social fabric of Islam compact and secure through all the fluctuations of political fortunes" (Hamilton Gibb, quoted in Anderson, ibid.).

But given the dogmatic nature of the Sharia, which prevented any change after its formative years in the eighth century, this domination by the Sharia meant a stagnation in the country's judicial system which lasted more than a millenium. In the nineteenth century when Iran like other Islamic societies came into close contact with the West, this age-old stagnation appeared as a shocking gap and led to a struggle for "reception"[1] of the Western judicial system which itself created more gaps and cultural lags.

In this part we will briefly review the development and basic features of the Sharia and other elements of the traditional judicial system in Iran, and with this as a background will follow the story of the judiciary reform in the country which began in the nineteenth century.

1. THE DEVELOPMENT OF THE SHARIA

Like all religions, Islam consists of two basic divisions: the *Eateqadat* (beliefs) and the *Ahkam* (rules and laws), called Sharia or *Fiqh*. The former constitute the "foundation", and reign over the realm of human mind and cognition; but being abstract, they can be judged only in terms of their concrete, i.e., behavioural manifestations; hence the *Ahkam*, which constitute the operational definitions of the *Eateqadat*, and govern the realm of human conduct.

In the *Ahkam*, human conduct, and thus the Sharia itself, is classified on two bases. The first, an ordinal classification, has as its basis the "degree of desirability" of conduct, and hence the well-known quintuple: *commanded, recommended, indifferent, reprobated* and *forbidden* behaviour. The second typology, a nominal one, is based on the nature or the immediate objective of the conduct, and hence the dichotomy: the *Ibadat* (acts of worship) or "services to God", on the one hand,[2] and the *Moamalat* (social actions) which relate to the rights of God's servants and cover a wide area from family to international relations, on the other.

As the direct and primary indicators of the beliefs, the *Ibadat* and their related rituals occupy a major part of a Moslem's life and thus a major part of the Sharia[3]; on these the rules were set and fully developed during the lifetime of the Prophet, and are applied uniformly – leaving aside some minor variations of later development between different schools of the Sharia – throughout the Islamic community.

The situation with the other part, the *Moamalat*, however, was very different. With the phenomenal expansion of Islam after the death of the Prophet it became increasingly obvious that the simple social rules which had developed in the tribal community of the Madinah under the Prophet (622–632) and his Four Caliphs (632–661) were far from sufficient to meet the exigencies of the vastly complex new territories. Under the Umayyads (661–757), limited areas of public law, such as fiscal matters and the treatment of the non-Moslem subjects, were uniformly ruled by the directives of the central administration; the rest, especially the sphere of private law, was almost entirely left to the discretion or *raay* (sound opinion) of the local officials, who were charged with the duty of *qada* (litigation). As much as possible, these *qadis* (judges) sought solutions to the new problems, which inevitably arose between the old and the new orders, by direct reference to or interpretation of the Quran and *Sunna* (the tradition of the Prophet) and in most cases allowed the old practices to continue.[4]

From the beginning of the eighth century however, changes started to take place. Disturbed by the increasing erosion of the Islamic ethics under the Umayyads, a group of pious scholars began systematic work on the Islamic law, and this marked the beginning of a movement which lasted for about 150 years, having a lasting impact on the future of the Islamic civilization.

The main purpose of the movement was to fill the persistent gap which separated the community of the Prophet from the rest of the Islamic Empire and to end the wide divergences which existed in the administration of justice between, and even within, the cities. Under normal conditions, this would be done through either new legislation or "reception." But given the basic premise of Islam which considered legislation an exclusively divine prerogative, the process, though inherently the same, took a different form and name – *ijtehad* which, broadly speaking, meant the process of extracting new laws from the Quran and other authentic sources.

But what constituted an "authentic source" and what was the nature and process of "extraction" were jurisprudential questions which were not easy to answer. On these there developed a number of schools,[5] each with its own doctrine of jurisprudence and independent set of laws. Leaving aside technical questions, the main point of conflict between these schools was the degree to which human reasoning was permissible in the process of *ijtehad.* While one group, called *Ahlol Hadith*, advocated a closer adherence to the traditions of the Madinah, another, *Ahl or-Raay* assigned a greater role to the systematic legal reasoning in the process.

This conflict continued throughout the Islamic history, and ultimately ended in the victory of the conservative traditionalism. In the formative years of the Sharia, however, it reached its closest resolution in the work of the most renowned architect of the Islamic law, Mohammad ibn Idris ash-Shafei (767–820) whose work has rightly been termed as "the greatest individual achievement in the Islamic jurisprudence" (Schacht 1955a: 54).

Like others, Shafei's theory was also built on the four basic sources or *osul* (roots): the Quran, the *Sunna, ijmaa* (consensus) and *qiyas* (reasoning by analogy), all of which had been elaborated before him. But Shafei redefined these concepts and welded them into a more coherent scheme which both made "the essential thesis of the Traditionalists prevail in the Islamic law" and "brought systematic legal reasoning to its zenith."[6]

After Shafei, interest in jurisprudence in general and in systematic reasoning in particular declined. In the unprecedented upsurge towards traditionalism which followed, there developed some highly conservative schools,[7] and by the end of the ninth century all groundwork for a climax was laid: there was the Quran, whose authenticity had never been questioned; there was the *Sunna*, which had been critically sifted and compiled,[8] and finally there was the Sharia which, through the efforts (*ijtehad*) of the Grand *Mojtahids* (doers of *ijtehad*) and their disciples, had been extracted in detail and to the fullest possible degree. Thus, by the beginning of the tenth century, a consensus developed among the scholars of all schools that the "doors of *ijtehad* were closed;" from that time on, all Moslems were to be the *moqallids* (followers) of the established schools, and the juristic activity of the scholars came to be confined to the explanation, application and, at the most, interpretation of the laws which had thus been formulated once and for all. In the subsequent centuries, although occasional objections to the closing of the doors of *ijtehad* were voiced and even though there developed several "personal" schools of law, the doctrine took a firm hold and the formative period of Sharia came to an end. Gradually the various minor schools which failed to attract many followers, became extinct[9] and from 1300 the schools of Hanafi, Maliki, Shafei and Hanbali became the only recognized ones of the orthodox Sunni world; they have remained so to the present day.

2. THE SHII *FIQH*

At this point a brief mention must be made of a different development, the emergence of the Shii *Fiqh*, which has a particular relevance to the case of Iran. At the time of the Prophet's death the fact that Ali was not chosen as his successor by the selecting council of the Companions displeased him and his admirers (*shias*), and Shiism was born. After Ali's assassination (661), Shiism emerged as a heterodox political movement. In the subsequent centuries it split into various subsects of which one was the *Ithnaashariyyah* (twelvers). In 1501, when the semi-theocratic Safavid dynasty was established in Iran, the *Ithnaashari* Shiism was declared as the state religion. Ever since, it has been the dominant religion of the country; presently the Shias constitute 60% of the Iranian Moslems, and together with the Shias of the other countries, almost 10% of the world Moslem population.

Originally the conflict between the Shia minority and the Sunni majority centred on the constitutional question of the nature of sovereignty and political legitimacy. In opposition to the orthodox doctrine of the caliphate, which considered public consensus as the basis of sovereignty and legitimacy, the Shias maintained a most conservative view. According to this doctrine, known as the theory of *imamate* (the office, rule or rank of an *imam*), (1) Ali and his descendants were divinely ordained and the sole legitimate successors to the Prophet; (2) it was this fact and not the community consensus which determined political legitimacy; thus (3) not only the Umayyas but also the first three caliphs of the Prophet ruled unlawfully; and finally, (4) as a representative of God on Earth, an *imam* will always be present to reveal His Will and to uphold His Command.

Although developed as a political weapon, this doctrine obviously had tremendous judicial implications. Given the central feature of this scheme – the continuing presence of an *imam* who spoke with the supreme authority of a divine law-giver – it is obvious that in Shia jurisprudence there could be no place for human reasoning. Thus, of the four basic sources of the Sharia which had been elaborated in the orthodox schools, the Shias rejected or ignored *ijmaa* and *qiyas*. As for the *Sunna*, they of course accepted it in principle but not without modification. Of the *Sunna* which had been accepted by the Sunni Traditionalists, they rejected those which did not meet their criteria and supplemented the rest by the Traditions of their *imams*, paying special attention to the seventh *imam*, Jaafar as-Sadiq (732–765) and hence "Jaafari School,"[10] a term used by the *Ithnaashariyyah* to identify their school. As for the Quran, while they could not deny the authenticity of any part in it, they interpreted it differently whenever deemed necessary.[11]

But the theory posed some problems. First, the reason for the orthodox schools' use of *ijmaa* and *qiyas* as supplementary sources of law was the fact that the problems of the new empire could not simply be solved by literal adherence to the Quran and *Sunna*. The *ijmaa* and *qiyas* were in fact "judicial devices" by which the scholars could bridge the gap between the simple community of the Madinah and the vastly complex conquered world. This problem the Shia jurists solved at least in part, by citing a vast number of *Hadiths* from their *imams* in the same way they and the orthodox Sunnis did for the Prophet.

But there was another problem: the presumed disappearance of the last (twelfth) *imam* at the end of the ninth century and hence the interruption of the Tradition. This problem was also taken care of by a final addition to the scheme: in the absence of the *imam* – here called *imam-e mostaqarr* (established *imam*) – the affairs of the faithful must be managed by the qualified theologians, the *mojtahids*, called *imam-e mostowdaa* (entrusted *imam*), who had all the prerogatives of the "Hidden *Imam*;" as the spokesmen of the *imam* and hence God, the *mojtahids* have, the theory goes, the final say on all matters of the community, including of course, *ijtehad*, whose doors could never be closed.

Given the nature of sources used and, especially, the political perspective followed, it was natural that the Jaafari scholars varied considerably in their specific conclusions from the orthodox schools. But important as these differences might have been from the point of view of reflecting the true teachings of Islam, they are of little significance from the perspective of sociology of knowledge. Considered from this point of view, the Jaafari school was the continuation of the same trend which characterized the orthodox Sunni schools. Notwithstanding the claims of the Shii writers to the contrary, the authentic legal literature of the Shiis, especially that of the Twelvers, started around the end of the ninth century.[12] By that time, as we have seen, the development of the Sharia in the orthodox Sunni world had almost been completed: the major schools had been established and the process of *ijtehad* reached its climax. Thus, following this well-paved path, the Shii *Fiqh* started, "having the same pattern, recognizing the same principal institutions . . . expressed in the same literary form as the Sunnite law . . . (and even) directly borrowed rules developed in the Sunnite schools" (Coulson. 1964: 194–195).

3. THE BASIC CHARACTERISTICS OF THE SHARIA

The Sharia, whether of Sunni or Shii, has a set of unique characteristics which must be taken into account not only to explain its phenomenal role in the Islamic societies but also to understand the great many events which took place in the Islamic World since the beginning of the nineteenth century.

The first and most significant of these characteristics is that it is not conceived of as a reflection of the collective conscience or the will of man but as the revealed and concretized Will of God. It has exteriority and constraint, to use Durkheimian terms, not only in relation to the individual but also in relation to the whole society, and thus instead of being controlled by society, it controls it and remains immutable.

Second, although in its details and final form the Sharia was worked out by a group of specialists over a period of more than a century, and although its raw materials and even its most important theoretical concepts basically came from the pre-Islamic practices in the Umayyad and Abbasid periods,[13] it is nevertheless highly idealistic. Especially in the case of Shiism, it grew not from the practical realities of the-world-as-it-is, but from a set of preordained religious dicta; the *mojtahids* who quarrelled, sometimes for years, over even minor issues of the Sharia, were concerned not with whether the point in question was applicable or practical, but whether it reflected the true Intention or Command of God, and it is revealing to notice that the technical term for the Sharia, namely *Fiqh*, means "understanding" or "comprehension."

Third, although idealistic, the Sharia in its formative period enjoyed a degree of vitality and, taken as a whole, reflected and met the social and economic conditions of the time (Schacht, 1955b: 77). But after the "closing of the doors of *ijtehad*" in the tenth century it became stagnant and grew more and more out of touch with the developments of the state and society. Occasionally new texts were published but they rarely went beyond simple reorganization and interpretation of the ideas of the founding fathers. Yet detached and rigid as it increasingly became, it never ceased to be uniformly applied throughout the Islamic world, from Mauritania to China and from Turkey to Indonesia, irrespective of the different socio-political conditions of these societies. The situation was even worse in the Shii *Fiqh*. Although the Shii *mojtahids* did not accept the idea of closing of the doors of *ijtehad*, they always used this self-proclaimed right as a means of wielding political power – a privilege of which their Sunni colleagues were deprived.[14] Their *Fiqh* unlike the Sunni Sharia found very little, if any, chance for application until the sixteenth century, and after that it followed exactly the same course which had been followed in the Sunni world.

Fourth, to all these we must add the fact that the Sharia as it has developed is the most "totalitarian" system of religious law in the sense that it covers every aspect of life. "Every human act . . . – from murder to social etiquette, from incest to the rules of religious retreat – is thus evaluated, and may be classified," according to the widely accepted five-fold classification mentioned above, "and it is only – in theory at least – in the category of things left legally indifferent by the Almighty that there is any essential place for human regulations" (Anderson, 1957: 14).

Yet exhaustive as it seems in its scope, the content of the Sharia is more encapsulating than comprehensive. Concentrating on the relation of man to God, or the *Ibadat*, the Sharia fell short on many mundane matters in the area of *Moamalat* which were of vital interest even to the Medieval world. For example, the early *mojtahids* rarely touched the issues of constitutional law and the theories of caliphate and *imamate* which developed later were retrospective abstractions dealing more with the attributes and qualifications of the rulers than the questions of the nature of political power and its distribution. Similarly, very little attention was paid to the fields of public and procedural law. "Criminal law, for example, did not exist in the technical sense of a comprehensive scheme of offences against the public order. Homicide . . . was treated as a private and not as a public offence. For the rest, the doctrine was largely confined to the exposition of six specific offences – illicit sexual relations, slanderous allegations of unchastity, theft, wine-drinking, armed robbery and apostasy – in which the notion of man's obligations toward God predominated and which, because God himself had 'defined' the punishment therefore, were known as the *hadd* . . . offences" (Coulson, 1964: 124; Schacht, 1964: 175–187). The same could be said of fiscal matters, contracts and obligations. In short, except for the family, inheritance and pious endowments (*vaqf*), on which the Sharia had the "firmest hold" (Schacht, 1955b: 77), in other areas such as criminal law, contracts and obligations, constitutional law, fiscal matters, etc., it had a very limited reign.[15]

4. THE PROCEDURE AND ORGANIZATION OF THE SHARIA JUDICIARY

While the underlying assumptions about the nature of man and society in certain areas of the Sharia may be found to be questionable by modern sociologists and psychologists,[16] the original Islamic approach to the area of litigation was surprisingly modern. Committed to the notion of justice as its most fundamental principle, Islam from the very beginning upheld two basic principles: (1) that all litigants should be treated equally irrespective of their creed, social position or ethnicity (*asl ot-tasavi*), and (2) that all suspects should be presumed innocent until they are proven otherwise (*aslol baraah*).[17]

These rules were not only accepted in theory but were strictly adhered to in practice during the life-time of the Prophet and his Four Caliphs. During the rule of Omar, the second caliph, when Islam expanded into a vast empire, he issued orders to the *walis* (governors) and *qadis* of different regions on the observance of these rules, and one of these orders addressed to Abu Musa Ashari in 636, has become a landmark in legal history.[18]

Bearing in mind the atrocious conditions of injustice in the other areas of the world in those days, this aspect of Mohammad's mission was truly remarkable,[19] and it has been observed that this more than anything else was a factor in the appeal and expansion of Islam in its early days (cf. Tabatabaei, 1967: 388–389, 548 ff.; Saleh, 1969: 212–214).

However, in the subsequent years during which the substantive part of the Sharia underwent so astonishing a development, little attention was paid to its procedural and organizational aspects obviously because, as we said before, practical considerations were of no significant concern to the jurists.[20]

Following an old ground-rule, "Upon the claimant is the (burden of) proof (*bayyina*) and upon the defendant, the oath (of denial)," which is mentioned in the letter of Omar and which is a correlate of the second principle mentioned above, the Sharia procedure from the very beginning followed a simple but rigid course: after the plaintiff presented his claim, the *qadi* questioned the defendant; if he accepted it, the case was over; if he denied it, the *qadi* asked the claimant to produce evidence; if he failed, the *qadi* would then order the defendant to take an oath if the plaintiff so demanded; if the defendant refused to take the oath, verdict was issued against him if, according to some schools, the plaintiff took an oath; but if the defendant did take the oath, the case was dismissed – reserving the right of the claimant for a new trial. There was no appeal, nor public prosecution, nor representation by a professional attorney, although the litigants could delegate others – anyone they chose – to appear on their behalf.

To this procedural rigidity we must add another feature which reduced the role of the Sharia courts still further. The term *bayyina* used in the ground-rule mentioned above is a general term which means "evidence." In practice however it was narrowed down by three qualifications. First, the word came to mean almost exclusively "witness" or, more exactly, "oral testimony;" second, like the *qadi* himself, the person whose testimony was to be accepted as evidence had to meet a number of religious and moral qualifications which could not be found in the ordinary persons; and third, in certain cases the requirements of proof were so demanding that they were practically impossible to meet. For instance, to prove an offence of fornication (*zina*), the claimant was required to present to the court the testimony of four upright male eye-witnesses to the very act of carnal conjunction.

These were then the basic features of the Islamic procedural law. Throughout history it remained unchanged and was applied with primary emphasis "not so much on arriving at the truth as on applying certain formal rules" (Schacht, 1964: 195; Tyan, 1955: 236–278; Coulson, 1964; 124–127). Corresponding to such a formalistic procedure was, of course, a similar judiciary organization which, likewise, had a promising beginning but an abortive development.

In the beginning of Islam, "the office of judge was exercised by the Prophet personally" (Ibn Khaldun, 1958, I: 452). The first significant development in the direction of the differentiation of the judiciary from the executive took place during the rule of Omar, who appointed several judges in different parts of the Empire and on that occasion issued his above mentioned order.[21]

Important as this was as a beginning, it was yet far from an independent judicial organization. Down to the beginning of the Abbasid period (757–1258) the judiciary function was delegated to second- and third-grade officials such as "army commanders, masters of treasury, market inspectors and even officials in charge of water supply" (Coulson, 1964: 120), who were attached to the office of the *wali*. As a whole, the judiciary organization in this period had two basic characteristics: parochialism in the sense of heavy reliance on local pre-Islamic laws, and complete subordination to the executive machinery of the provinces to the extent of serving as the legal secretary to the governors. This "centralized decentralization" meant a system which, regardless of the quality of justice it provided, was at least functionally and politically consistent.

Under the Abbasid caliphs, however, both of these features changed; and with that came an incoherent dualism which has marked the Islamic judiciary up to the present day.

As a part of their effort for total Islamization of the Empire, the Abbasid caliphs paid a much greater attention to the function of *qadi*, making it a rule that only specialists in the Sharia were appointed, and they were appointed not by the provincial governors but from the centre of the Empire, and as an independent functionary of the Caliphate. Following this policy there came another development. As part of the general effort to adopt features of the Sassanid administration, Harun or-Rashid (786–809) created the office of *Qadil Qodat* (chief *qadi*) which corresponded almost exactly to the Zoroastrian *Mubadan-Mubad* (priest of priests).[22] The *Qadil Qodat* not only functioned as an important counsellor to the caliph, but also had the authority to appoint and dismiss the provincial *qadis*.[23]

These developments had two interrelated implications. They meant, first, a growing independence of the judiciary from the executive and second, a greater freedom of the *qadis* to adhere strictly to the rules of the Sharia, whose faithful application they considered an expression of their exclusive allegiance to Allah. But if sound and "healthy" from the point of view of safeguarding the Faith, this had an important social dysfunction. Given the basically academic nature of the Sharia and the rigidly formalistic approach of its procedural law, it made the Sharia judiciary increasingly detached from the realities of the vastly complex Empire; and hence the dualism of the Sharia and non-Sharia court systems which continued up to the present day.

Structurally a Sharia court consisted of (1) a single *qadi*, (2) the litigants or their delegates (*vakils*), (3) witnesses and occasionally a clerk (*katib* or *mozakki*). There was no hierarchy of courts or judges as such, although as a matter of course "cases of extreme importance were taken to eminent *mojtahids* of whom there never was a large number . . ." (Curzon, 1892, I: 453); and finally, following the simple procedure discussed above, there was no public prosecutor nor professional lawyer. But whereas this simple form remained the same throughout the centuries, there developed, especially in the two rival Safavid and the Ottoman Empires, certain religio-administrative functions which were indirectly related to the judiciary system.[24]

5. THE NON-SHARIA JUDICIARY

Given the basic features of the Sharia and the formalism and rigidity of its procedural aspects, it is obvious that no matter how devoted the community and its rulers were to Islam, the increasingly diverse needs of the Islamic world could not be met solely by the Islamic judiciary. And as the time passed, fewer and fewer of "the Muslim rulers were willing to leave the maintenance of law and order and the prevention of crime exclusively to [the] courts which were by their very nature officially bound to observe [the Islamic principles]" (Anderson, 1976: 12).

The immediate consequence of this incapacity of the Sharia judiciary was that it provided an added incentive for the sovereigns' absolutistic sense of competence in having the authority and ability to right all wrongs. Thus from the early days of the Abbasid period there developed what came to be known as the court of *mazalim* (complaints, acts of injustice). As a common pre-Islamic practice – popular especially among the Sassanid Kings[25] – it was usually a periodic Royal open-house to which every one was free to come. As a means of keeping contact with the subjects, it was, at the same time, a tribunal to which complaints against administrative officials and other citizens could be brought. Gradually the type and frequency of cases brought to these tribunals increased, and thus other officials such as ministers, governors and even local administrators were empowered to exercise *mazalim* jurisdiction.

Soon the *mazalim* courts became an autonomous institution throughout the Islamic Empire. In Iran, they existed not only during the Abbasid rule, but also after the emergence of independent indigenous dynasties. In describing these early dynasties, Lambton tells us, for example, that "Under the Saljugs [1038–1194] as under earlier rulers the *mazalim* courts became, not an exceptional appeal to the sultan in person, but an everyday application to his representative to be dealt with according to a settled practice. The general tendency was for the *mazalim* jurisdiction relative to the Sharia courts to extend."[26]

Extended indeed they became. In subsequent centuries, while the "hearing of *mazalim*" continued as an essential function of the kings and their top officials, its strictly judicial duties expanded into a rather vast administrative apparatus with varying names and a host of specific judiciary functions.[27]

From the substantive point of view, there came two complementary developments. The first was the emergence of *orf* as an independent basis of litigation. True, customary law "had contributed a great deal to the formation of Islamic law" (Schacht, 1964: 62) and had especially been used as a basis for *istihsan* in the Hanafi school and *istislah* in the Maliki school, two mechanisms used in the process of *ijtehad* in the formative years of the Sharia.[28] But with all this, conscious recognition of customary law as an independent source of litigation did not come until about the fourteenth century, since which time it was increasingly used in contracts and obligations and other areas if, theoretically, it did not contradict the Sharia (Saljuqi, 1968: 32, 46–49; Schacht, 1955b: 77–78).

But contradiction, even if it existed, could be reduced to a minimum, thanks to certain legal devices which helped to narrow the gap between the fixed system of Sharia and the more complex and changing society (cf. Vesey-Fitzgerald, 1955: 107–110). One type of mechanism, developed especially in the Hanafi school and subsequently adopted by the others, was *hiyal* (literally, tricks), a variety of evasive practices or legal stratagems used for achieving, explicitly or implicitly, illegal ends without violating the letter of the Sharia.[29]

Another such mechanism used was *siyasat osh-Shariyyah* (religious policy). Developed during the Abbasid rule in the eleventh century, this theory gave to the rulers – assuming their piety and ability to ascertain and comprehend the Divine Laws – the power to make regulations for carrying out the *Sharia*. This was the basis for "decree legislation" by the caliphs, kings and rulers which gradually increased in scope and gave an air of legitimacy to tyrannic rule in the Islamic states.

Unfortunately, no attempt has ever been made to record and compile the Iranian customary laws; of the various decree laws which have been issued at different times by different rulers, only a small portion have survived in history books. Well-known among these are the various codes which were imposed by the Mongol invaders. The most famous of these codes are the *Yasa* of Genghiz Khan,[30] the *Yerlighs* of Ghazan Khan, the *Tozuks* of Tamerlane and the so-called Law of Ozun Hasan.[31]

In the large-scale administrative reform which took place during the reign of the Safavid King, Shah Abbas the Great (1587–1629), the so-called *mahakim-e orf* (courts of customary law) were officially established and as a counterpart of the Sharia system they continued up to the twentieth century (Shayegan, 1943: 23).

In sharp contrast to Sharia courts, the *mahakim-e orf* were not bound by any strict regulations or rules of procedure; the persons who presided over them were not required to have legal training. In many cases they were responsible only to hear the litigants and collect evidence without the power to make a decision, and even if they had such a power, the evidence they used and the procedures they followed were far from acceptable by the original Sharia standards; substantively, they functioned on the basis of decree legislations, government regulations, and of course the *orf*. The latter in turn was based on oral tradition, on precedent, and on custom. "But there being no written or recognized code, it varied still more in practice according to the character or caprice of the individual who administered it; and so far from any attempt being made to hunt up precedents or to ascertain what was done in parallel cases before, the decision was as a rule promptly given and promptly executed by the civil officer . . . whose sole guide . . . was a rough sense of right and wrong" (Curzon, 1892, I: 454).

II. The Judiciary Reform in Iran

Such was then the nature and condition of the judiciary in Iran before the nineteenth century. With all its substantive and procedural shortcomings and deficiencies, the traditional judiciary in Iran had one essential characteristic: it had evolved and was rooted in the society; and as long as the society was "inner-directed", to use David Riesman's term,[32] the judiciary was consistent with the rest of its institutions and its shortcomings were not much noticed. "To the bird which is raised in a cage," using the imagery of a Persian poet, "the contrast between cage and nest is meaningless."[33]

But the contrast finally did emerge. In the beginning of the nineteenth century, direct contact with the West began, and Iran, like most of the Moslem world, found itself in an awkward condition militarily, socially and economically. Almost suddenly, the tranquillity and self-confidence of an age-old inner-directedness was gone, and a mesmerized attitude of other-directedness coupled with a shattering sense of inferiority had taken its place. As the contact increased, the contrast became more and more vivid and the urge for reform and Westernization more and more compelling.

On the cultural and institutional level, one of the most conspicuous areas of contrast was the country's system of justice which in the eyes of a Western observer appeared most "abominable" and "shocking" (Curzon, 1892, I: 456). Describing this state of shock, the observer provided an account of the system in the following words: "Not even the most generous estimate of the merits or the most lenient consideration of the failings of the judicial procedure . . . can blind us to the fact that it is lamentably deficient in the two essentials of an effective legal system, viz. a compact and systematized code of law, and a competent tribunal to administer it. Although the Ecclesiastical Law has been subjected to a rough codification, this is neither scientific, exhaustive, nor suited to modern conditions. The Common Law has no written existence, and is moulded by the arbitrary idiosyncrasies of individuals. The jurisdiction of the clerical and secular courts overlap; nor is there any intelligible distinction between their prerogatives and functions. Cases are referred to one or the other according to the fancy of the appellant, and frequently pass through the two courts in succession. Even if it be thought hazardous or unwise to interfere with the law based on the Quran, no voice can possibly defend the haphazard condition of the Common Law which is in a state of disgraceful uncertainty and, as an instrument of guidance to civil magistrates, is practically useless" (ibid.: 459).

This then was how the state of the judiciary looked in Iran in the beginning of the nineteenth century. With such a background it is not surprising that in the long process of struggle for the rule of law – "the most dominant issue in the country throughout the nineteenth century" (Adamiyat, 1975: 308) – the strictly judicial aspect of the problem was even more tedious than its political side. In any event, after the political struggle was terminated by the constitutional revolution, the judiciary reform emerged as a very important, if not the most important, problem with which the newly established Majlis (the Parliament) was concerned.

In this part we shall briefly review the process of the judiciary reform as it began in the nineteenth century, and in the subsequent sections take up the substantive and other aspects of the new judiciary system thus introduced.

1. THE IMMEDIATE FACTORS OF REFORM

Judiciary reform or, put more aptly, conscious efforts to Westernize the legal system of Iran, were enhanced by at least three immediate factors. One of them was the existence of capitulary (extra-territorial) rights for foreigners. The last Russo-Iranian war, in which Iran lost the remainder of its possessions in the Caucasus, ended in the humiliating Turkomanchi Treaty of 1828. According to this treaty, the Russian subjects came to be almost totally exempted from Iranian legal jurisdiction. Soon after, other foreign governments followed suit and assumed capitulary privileges for themselves. On the excuse that the Sharia courts did not give equal treatment to Moslem and non-Moslem litigants and that the chaotic secular courts did not dare to oppose them, the European embassies in subsequent years extended their self-proclaimed privileges and established virtually independent judiciaries of their own. The so-called "legal agencies" (*kar-gozariha*) which were attached to these embassies and their consulates became sources of such a tremendous degree of abuse that they even exempted Iranian citizens they favoured from paying taxes to their own government.[34]

On occasion these developments served as grounds for the European governments to put pressure on Iran to undertake legal reforms.[35] But as a source of humiliation, the capitulary system had a strong impact on the nationalists and reform-minded politicians, and played an important role in the effort to bring about judiciary reform up until its abolition in 1928.[36]

The second motivating factor for legal reform in Iran came from the similar developments in other Islamic countries, especially the Ottoman Turkey. As early as 1789, the Ottomans started giving serious thought to their growing weakness *vis-à-vis* the West. In 1837, a committee was established to prepare legal and administrative reforms with special attention to the adoption of European laws. This marked the beginning of what is known as the era of *Tanzimat* (a reform programme) and led to the proclamation, on 3 November 1839, of the *Khatt-e Sharif-e Golkhaneh* (Holy Edict of the Rose Chamber), which officially initiated the legal reform. After ten years of debate and discussion the results finally started appearing: Between 1850 and 1863 various codes, based almost entirely on the French codes, were promulgated. These were followed by the well-known civil code called *Majallah*, of 1876, which was based on the Sharia of the Hanafi rite, and along these, purely secular and mixed courts developed in conjunction with the traditional Sharia tribunals.[37]

With these developments in Turkey the Iranians were in close touch; the Ottoman capital was a sanctuary for the dissident Iranian intellectuals and politicians; and even if the statement that ". . . virtually the whole political vocabulary of Persian [in the nineteenth century] may be said to have been derived from the Ottoman Turkish" (Algar, 1973: 27) is not completely true, there can be little doubt that the Ottoman developments had a great impact on the reform movement in Iran, especially in the second half of the nineteenth century.

Perhaps the most significant factor behind the legal reform was the campaign by the Iranian writers. One of the popular themes which from the second half of the eighteenth century received increasing attention in Persian writings was law and its role in human society. Merchants, travellers and diplomats who visited or lived in Europe gave detailed descriptions of law, the judiciary system and civil liberties in Europe and launched, with varying degrees of openness, a massive campaign for reform and rule of law.

These included such writers as Mirza Abutalib (1752–1806) who after six years of travel in Europe, published a diary devoting two chapters to the law and political system of England;[38] Mirza Fathali Akhond-Zadeh (1812–1878) who spent years in Petersburg and Tiflis, then one of the centres of progressive thinking in Russia, and wrote devastating criticisms of Iran's reactionary religious groups, despotic rules and social and judiciary conditions;[39] and the philosopher-critic, Mirza Aqa Khan-e Kirmani (1853–92) whose uncompromising attacks, from exile in Turkey, on Iran's religious and political leaders for the lawlessness which reigned supreme in the country, led to an international dispute between Iran and the Ottoman Empire, and finally resulted in his deportation and brutal execution (cf. Adamiyat, 1967). Above all these of course stood Sayyid Jamal od-Din Asadabadi (1838–1897), the well-known pan-Islamist whose strong personality and relentless campaign against the rulers of Iran and other Islamic states was a most powerful voice for reform in the second half of the nineteenth century.

These were great intellectual and political figures for whom the question of law was part of a general plan for socio-political change. The man more directly concerned with the question of law and the legal system was Mirza Malkom Khan (1833–1908). Born to an Armenian family, he was sent to France for education. Upon his return to Iran in 1850, he entered the government service in the newly established Bureau of Translation and soon found his way to Nasir od-Din Shah's court. In 1859, on the occasion of the Shah's taking a step towards administrative reform, as we shall discuss shortly, Malkom seized the opportunity and published his famous treatise, the *Kitabcheh-ye Gheybi.*[40] After a long preamble where, among other things, the author gave lip-service to the *ulama* and assured the Shah that his proposed measures were not designed to undermine his supreme authority, he proposed a set of 180 specific proposals under 24 general headings or *qanuns* (laws), which as a whole could be regarded as a constitution.[41] Especially significant among these laws were those concerned with the establishment of a legislative body. The body was supposed (1) to systematize and codify all existing laws including the Sharia and what he called "the governmental laws," (2) to write and ratify whatever law it deemed necessary for completing the existing set of laws, and finally, (3) to publish the finalized laws in five volumes as Civil Law, Procedural Law, Penal Law, Constitutional Law, and Administrative Law (1948, Law No. 11, arts. 1–4). In addition, Malkom proposed a new and relatively modern judiciary organization which included a *divan-e aala* (supreme court) to be established in the capital, a *divan adliyyeh* (court of justice) to be established in each province and a *divan islah* (court of first instance) for each district. These courts, hierarchically organized, were to be manned by a number of judges and officials appointed by the Shah and managed by the Minister of Justice (ibid. Law No. 35). Although – in spite of his initial success – Malkom's attempts, like others before, failed to produce a lasting result, he never ceased championing for law. In private correspondence with the Shah and his high officials and in booklets which he published subsequently, Malkom expanded his original ideas and, after his retirement in 1898, he established a newspaper whose very name *Qanun* (law) was a reflection of his life-long preoccupation.[42]

In addition to those mentioned above, there were many writings, including diplomatic reports, periodicals published at home and abroad, and critical social analyses, which were involved in the campaign. While disagreeing on the course of action to be taken, they all agreed (1) that the key to Europe's progress and superiority was its system of law, (2) that Iran was in a desperate need of reform and this reform had to begin with its system of law. But as to what the exact nature of this law was and where it was to come from was a matter of disagreement, and this was a conflict which has continued up to the present day.[43]

2. THE NINETEENTH CENTURY ATTEMPTS AT JUDICIARY REFORM

Under these conditions, judiciary reform in Iran began. Until the revolution of 1978, however, Westernization or, to use a better term, "Westomania" was the most powerful force in determining the course of all reform activities, and the new legal system served as one of the best examples of the process.

While the general reform movement in Iran started from the administrative reform in the early nineteenth century,[44] judiciary reform began in a later phase. It started during the premiership of Mirza Taqi Khan Amir Kabir (1848–1852), whose efficiency, dedication and fame in Iran's modern political history is rivalled only perhaps by Dr Mossaddigh who came a century after him.[45] Of the matters of utmost importance to Amir was his Socratic observance of law and justice and his dedication to the principle of separation of the judiciary from the executive – the principle on which he founded his *Nezam-e Jadid* (new military system) (Iqbal, 1962: 307–317, esp. 309). Knowing the chronic deficiencies and the basic features and potentialities of the dual court system which had existed for centuries, he took action in both directions. He reorganized the notorious secular *orf* judiciary, then called *Divan Khaneh*, he appointed a new chief administrator, established new courts (Sheil, 1856: 169), and extended their jurisdiction.[46] At the same time he paid considerable attention to the chaotic situation of the Sharia courts. He took an uncompromising attitude toward the corrupt elements amongst the *ulama*. He removed and punished the corrupt *mollas*[47] from the bench, abolished the legal force of contradictory verdicts and did everything to restore piety and order to the Sharia courts.

In one of the darkest episodes of what Lord Curzon has called "the crime-stained and bloody pages of Persian history" (Curzon, 1892, I: 456), Amir Kabir was dismissed on 15 November 1851 and was savagely assassinated on 6 January 1852.

With this tragic event, all reform activities practically stopped. In 1855, a European-inspired code of laws which was modeled after the Ottoman *Khatt-e Sharif-e Golkhaneh* was proposed to the Shah (Lambton, 1970: 259); but as far as the records show, the project proved abortive and nothing took place in the area of law till 1858. In that year the Shah ventured into a new experiment. Dismissing the prime minister,[48] he appointed for the first time a six-member *Shura-ye Dowlat* (council of ministers) and divided the duties of the government among them. In the following year (November 1859), he took another promising step, establishing a *Maslahat Khaneh* (house of consultation), hence giving an indication that he intended to separate the legislative from the executive power. The *Maslahat Khaneh* was composed of twenty-five individuals hand-picked by the Shah on the basis of their "familiarity with the outside world," their experience, dedication and respect among the public (Adamiyat & Natiq, 1977: 189, 196–197). It had a constitution and a set of rather comprehensive procedural rules.[49] Its purpose, as stated in the constitution, was to assemble "the wise and sound-minded men of the country so that they will discuss, confer and decide on the matters which would lead to the improvement of the government, to the development of the nation and to the good of the people" (ibid.: 189).

In the first year of its existence, the *Maslahat Khaneh* was very active. It took measures on many areas of public interest such as marketing and distribution of public necessities, smallpox vaccination, and care for the homeless, giving the impression that it was going to succeed in meeting the goals for which it had been set up.[50]

Among all the new efforts which the Shah had launched, the judiciary reform occupied a high priority. Of the six new cabinet posts created, one was the Ministry of Justice, or *Adliyyeh* as it then came to be known. Assigned to the post was Abbas-Qoli Khan Moatamad od-Dowleh Javanshir. Though lacking an appreciable background in modern education, the new minister was respected for his integrity and honesty, and is remembered for the important steps he took in the direction of creating a modern and viable judiciary in Iran. Soon after he took office, he issued, on 18 November 1858, an important decree. Aimed at asserting the authority of the Ministry of Justice over the provinces and the ultimate establishment of the *adliyyeh* (secular courts) in different regions of the country, the decree barred provincial governors and local officials from conducting "trials." To ensure proper implementation of these measures, a special legal official of the ministry, called *divan-begi*, was sent to each province; functioning as a legal warehouse, the office of the *divan-begi* was first to receive all complaints and then refer them either to the Sharia or *orf* court, or if judged important, to the Central Ministry in Tehran. In addition, the *divan-begi* was to act as a watchdog over the provincial administration of justice for which important new procedural guidelines were also provided in the decree.[51]

Besides these specific efforts, the judiciary reform, notwithstanding the tremendous sensitivity of the *ulama*,[52] received other attentions as well. We are informed for instance that the *Maslahat Khaneh*, apparently with the intention of compiling different codes as had been suggested by Mirza Malkom Khan, "collected, within six months of its existence, four thousand articles of law;"[53] and in a long report written on "The Improvement of the *Maslahat Khaneh*," attention was called particularly to the need for strengthening of the secular courts and for reorganization and reform of the Sharia courts (Adamiyat & Natiq, 1977: 212–213, 215).

Following these efforts, the Shah started regular *mazalim* (acts of injustice) hearings in 1860, an institution which continued in the following decades and functioned as a court both of appeal and of first instance. In 1862 he took another step in the direction of strengthening the Ministry of Justice. By that time a norm had developed which allowed each ministry to have its own tribunals and to exercise jurisdiction over cases which either involved its employees or concerned the issues which were conceived as falling within its purview. The decree which was issued on 19 December banned this practice and reaffirmed the basic points of the 1858 decree. It gave the Ministry of Justice exclusive jurisdiction over all cases and disputes and at the same time provided a procedural manual (*dasturol amal*) for the *Divan Khaneh-ye Aazam* (the grand house of secular judiciary) or *Adliyyeh*.[54]

But given the utterly corrupt and inefficient nature of the political system, none of these innovations took root, in spite of all their initial enthusiasm and relative success. By the time this last degree was issued the *Maslahat Khaneh* had been almost completely forgotten. Moatamad od-Dowleh was replaced by a cruel and corrupt man[55] who repealed the 1858 decree, dropped the idea of establishing regional courts – on the pretext that "the provincial governors consider such courts a nuisance"[56] – and brought all the efforts of Moatamad od-Dowleh to nought. Thus, as Amir Kabir's efforts in the late 40s had proved abortive, so were the reforms of the late 50s; and except for the first two years of the 1860s, the whole decade, like the 1850s, went by in stagnation.

The 1870s began with another round of renewed interest. This time the principal player was Mirza Hoseyn Khan Moshir od-Dowleh Sepahsalar who, after Amir Kabir, was the most efficient administrator and reformer of the Quajar period.[57] As a career diplomat with twenty years of foreign service in Bombay, Tiflis and Istanbul, Moshir od-Dowleh was thoroughly familiar with the theoretical and practical aspects of reform, and like his close friends Mirza Malkom Khan and Mirza Yusof Khan (later Mostashar od-Dowleh)[58], had been a strong advocate of Westernization reform. On 23 December 1870, while in the company of the Shah during the latter's pilgrimage to the Shiite shrines of Iraq – then a part of Ottoman Turkey – he was appointed Minister of Justice and Pious Endowments,[59] a post which he assumed upon their return to Tehran on 22 February 1871. On 29 September he was given the title of *Sepahsalar* (army commander) and Minister of War, and this was followed, on 13 November by the additional post of *Sadr-e Aazam* (prime minister) (Fasai, 1972: 374).

In some seven months of his service as Minister of Justice, *Sepahsalar*'s achievements were truly remarkable, and it was this very fact that paved the way for his subsequent promotions (Mostowfi, 1945, I: 153, 155). Aided by his faithful and enthusiastic friend, the above-mentioned Yusof Khan (Mostashar od-Dowleh), *Sepahsalar* started where the early 50s and 60s had left off.

In March 1871, he issued a decree[60] introducing a vast programme of reform; three months later, on 22 June he published his 119-article "Law of the Grand Ministry of Justice and the Houses of Justice in Iran" which described the plan in full detail, and on 9 July he issued a very strongly worded decree to the provincial governors and judges on his new programme. Modelled basically on the Ottoman version of the Westernized judicial system, the programme had three basic features: ideological, organizational and procedural.

Ideologically the programme aimed at guaranteeing certain basic human rights. It forbade arrest without court order, detention after being found innocent, and undue infliction of harm and punishment on persons of lower rank or lesser influence. These ideals were especially developed and elaborated in the second decree which, at the same time, and like the Shah's decree of 1858, was intended to assert the authority of Central *Adliyyeh* over the provincial courts. The decree specifically prohibited the provincial governors from the pronouncement and "execution of physical punishment and the death penalty . . . and delimited their role in the criminal process to mere arrest, preliminary investigation and the dispatch of the case to the Ministry of Justice" (Mostowfi, 1945, I: 155; Adamiyat, 1972: 175).

To ensure proper carrying out of these plans, *Sepahsalar* created a new office: that of "*nazir*" (overseer) of *Adliyyeh*, who was dispatched to the provinces and, reminding the *divan begi* of the early 60s, charged him with supervision of the observance of the new regulations (Adamiyat, ibid.: 177). But this was too limited a measure, and the experience of the 1860s had clearly demonstrated the futility of such remedies. What was needed was a radical structural departure from the past and this was exactly what the *Sepahsalar* did. By this first decree, he created six courts or "majlises" as they were called: three specialized courts dealing respectively with crime, real estate and commerce; a court of appeals, and two other "courts": an executive court to carry out the decisions of the Ministry of Justice and a legislative court to draw up laws and regulations (cf. Adamiyat, 1972: 174–177; Bakhash, 1978: 87). The decree also provided specific guidelines on such procedural matters as regular opening of the courts, hearing of the cases by turn, registration of petitions, proceedings and decisions of the courts, taking evidence and estimating injuries (Adamiyat, 1972: 174–177).

Finally, we must also mention *Sepahsalar*'s articulate tactics. Fully aware of his potential enemies, the *ulama* and the reactionary courtiers – who ultimately brought him down – he took every precaution to ensure the success of his plans. In the prologue to the first decree, he declared his purpose to be the restoration of the spirit of the Sharia and the establishment of the conditions which would permit the state "to emulate the golden times" (ibid.). Furthermore he took full advantage of the protective shield of the Shah's position and name. He issued all decrees with the Shah's name and signature, and to put an end to the common abuses by the governors, he reminded them that punishment of crime was "reserved to the Shah alone" and it was he who had the exclusive authority to dispense justice (ibid.: 88; cf. Farhad-Moatamad, 1947: 38; Mostowfi, 1945, I: 155; Sani od-Dowleh, 1876–78, III: 6–9).

Like Amir Kabir and for the same reason, *Sepahsalar*'s hopes were also short-lived. On 20 April 1873 (after seventeen months as Prime Minister) he and his advisor and friend Mirza Malkom Khan, took the Shah on an "educational" tour of Europe. While they were abroad, reactionary forces seized the opportunity and instigated a public uproar against the Prime Minister's alleged anti-religious motives. Upon their return in early September and even before the arrival of the entourage in the capital, he resigned under duress and with that began the end of his dreams (Fasai, 1972: 379).

Thus, just as it was in the early 50s and 60s the relative

improvements of the early 70s also proved to be temporary. After *Sepahsalar*, affairs naturally returned to their "normal" state. Of his innovations only the three specialized courts (of crime, real estate and commerce) survived and continued to function up to the Constitutional Revolution of 1905.

Along with these, the archaic *mazalim* tribunal which had existed since 1860 also continued and, in view of the decreasing power of the *Adliyyeh*, became increasingly active. To these tribunals, letters of complaint poured in from all over the land, but whether they had any effect on the brutal injustices inflicted upon the helpless people by landlords and local government officials is seriously in doubt.[61]

Throughout the past decades, although the idea of the European judiciary system was at the centre of attention, no conscious attempt was ever made to translate the European codes directly and openly. But frustrated with its repeated failures, especially in view of the mounting criticism and public cry for justice, it was natural that the regime would finally resort to such a measure, a step which had been taken in Ottoman Turkey more than thirty years before.

Thus, upon his return from his third visit to Europe in September 1888, the Shah assembled the ministers and the dignitaries of the court and delivered to them a short but very hearty speech: "In this journey we realized that all the order and progress of Europe was due to their having law. We are strongly determined to create a law in Iran and work on that basis. You go and write a law" (Molk-Ara, 1982: 175).

Following that order, a committee of five individuals who were familiar with the European languages and legal systems was set up. Using the *Code Napoleon* as the main source, the committee obtained copies of other codes such as the modified version of the *Code Napoleon* prepared for the French Islamic colonies of Africa, the British code prepared for the Moslem population of India, and the codes which were prepared by the Ottoman reformers. With these sources at hand, the committee commenced the work of translation. A series of pamphlets were completed and, after the approval of the government, were signed by the Shah (ibid.: 175–177; Adamiyat, 1976: 12–13; Curzon, 1892; I: 462). But from the very start, the influential courtiers "who had learned nothing but robbing others and embezzling public funds started criticizing the laws which had taken years for the European philosophers to prepare."[62] The end, of course, was not difficult to predict. "In response to recent inquiries," wrote Lord Curzon three years later in 1891, "I am informed that nothing further has been heard of the new code, hence I am led to infer that one more excellent chance has gone into the waste-paper basket and that one more stone must be added to the cairn of abortive reforms that has been so conscientiously piled by Nasir-ed-Din Shah" (Curzon, 1892, I: 462).

But if not the last from the political point of view, this indeed was the last abortive attempt of the nineteenth century from the point of view of judiciary reform. In the spring of that year, and following the *fatva* of a grand *mojtahid*, Ayatollah Shirazi, against an infamous tobacco concession which the government had granted to a British company, mass demonstrations erupted in the country for the first time in history and forced the Shah to cancel the concession. Though not the first concession, the tobacco agreement served as a precipitating factor which touched off an explosion and that finally led to the assassination of the Shah in 1896 and to the collapse of absolute monarchy in 1906. In these years judiciary reform was almost completely pushed to the background and was not resumed until after the opening of the first legislative assembly, the Majlis, in 1906.

3. JUDICIARY REFORM FOLLOWING THE CONSTITUTIONAL REVOLUTION OF 1905

The tyranny, corruption, inefficiency and a virtually total bankruptcy which had underlain the 1892 uprising, ultimately led to a full-fledged revolution in 1905 and to the declaration of 4 August 1906 by Mozaffar od-Din Shah (1896–1906) which ended, at least in theory, the age-old absolute monarchy in Iran. Within a few months of that historical event, the first national elections were held, and on 5 September the first *Majlis-e Shura-ye Melli* or Majlis convened.

Within two weeks, the Majlis got organized, adapted its *Nizam Nameh-ye Dakheli* (rules of order) and started work. The first problem, naturally, was the adoption of a constitution. Earlier, a joint committee of the Majlis and the government representatives had drafted a code of Fundamental Law and submitted it to the government for the Shah's approval. But given the animosity which existed between the new Majlis and the government, its return to the Majlis was delayed. After a period of bargaining, threats and behind-the-scenes manoeuvres, however, the document was finally returned; after three days of heated debate in the Majlis and then in another joint committee, an agreement was reached and on 8 January 1907, it was finally signed by the Shah.[63]

Fearing the death of the ailing Shah, the Majlis prepared the Fundamental Law very hastily. It dealt more with the working of the Majlis itself,[64] and left untouched important areas such as the rights of citizens, the relationship between the government and the Majlis, and more importantly, the place of the judiciary. But as a first step it was an immense psychological and tactical victory for the revolutionaries; after that, the Majlis turned to the "real" issues. In mid-February, 1907, it appointed a seven-member committee of its most prominent members to prepare a supplement to the Fundamental Law. Using – as we shall discuss – the Belgian constitution and the relatively rich source materials which a previously established group of Saad od-Dowleh had prepared as a base, the committee drafted the Supplement and after two months of hard work submitted it to the Majlis. As expected, it met a strong resistance, but this time the opposition came not from the government but mainly from the *ulama* (cf. Taqizadeh, 1959: 54; Adamiyat, 1976: 409–432). After seven months of struggle in the Majlis backed by mounting public support, the Supplement was finalized and was signed by the new Shah on 7 October 1907.

To these important documents and their content we shall of course return. But before that let us follow our historical sketch to the end.

The successful passage of the Fundamental Law and its Supplement, however, had also its negative consequences. As it reflected a measurable success for the revolutionaries, it widened the gap between the Majlis and the newly enthroned Mohammad Ali Shah (1906–1909), but at the same time brought him additional strength. This came through the conservative wing of the *ulama*, especially an influential Ayatollah, Sheyk Fazlollah Nuri who then openly broke away from his colleagues in the Majlis and joined the counter revolutionaries headed by the Shah. On 23 June 1908, the Majlis was shelled and the second and most bloody phase of the revolution, known as Short Tyranny (*Istebdad-e Saghir*) began. After nearly seventeen months of struggle the revolutionaries, who had been marching toward the capital from the provinces, triumphantly entered Tehran; on the same day, 16 July 1909, the Shah, who had taken refuge in the embassy of Russia – a strong supporter of his (Browne, 1910: 321) – was deposed. Thus, the Short Tyranny came to an end and constitutional life was resumed.

By this time the condition of the judiciary not only had not improved in comparison to the early nineteenth century, it in many respects had even worsened.

On the eve of the revolution, the atrocious "consulate tribunals" (*kar-gozariha*) which were discussed before, had mushroomed throughout the country; of all attempts at judiciary reform in the nineteenth century only the three specialized courts of crime, real estate and commerce which were established by *Sepahsalar* in 1871 had a nominal existence in the capital city; and even these, along with the entire Ministry of Justice, had become such a vivid manifestation of injustice and inefficiency that they served as the best targets of attack and criticism during the revolution, and thus on the order of the government, the forces of Ephraim Khan, the Chief of the Police, moved in, closed the Ministry and the courts completely and took many of the judges to prison (Bastani-Parizi, 1968: 512).

After the success of the revolution, the question of the judiciary was, of course, among the top priorities; to many, including some leading revolutionaries, it was even the sole objective of the struggle (cf. Kasravi, 1940: 101–103).

The cabinet of Mirza Nasrollah Khan Moshir od-Dowleh, whose establishment in 1 August 1906[65] paved the way for the Constitutional Declaration of 4 August, marked a turning point in the revolutionary struggle. In this cabinet Mirza Ahmad Khan Moshir os-Saltaneh served as Minister of Justice, and the Ministry which had been closed before was reopened with signs of a new beginning. In addition to the three courts which had existed before, two types of courts of appeal – a lower one called *istinaf* and a higher one, the *Divan-e Tamiz* – were established, and a number of new judges appointed (Bastani-Parizi, 1968: 17, 512; Matin-Daftari, 1948, I: 7-8)

With the establishment of the first Majlis, although the new deputies were faced with innumerable problems, they did not lose sight of the gravity of the problems of the judiciary. Thus, after putting itself in order by adopting its *Rules of Order*, and while waiting for the return of the Fundamental Law from the government, the Majlis set up a committee for "translation and compilation of (European) law."[66] The committee was equipped with all necessary means, including a collection of foreign codes and legal texts and fifteen translators, and was headed by a leading deputy, Mirza Javad Khan Saad od-Dowleh who had formerly served as the charge d'affaires in Brussels and was well acquainted with Europe.[67] Within two months, the committee prepared a code for the Ministry of Justice and a new law on publications and the press which was translated from the French. After that it split into two sub-committees, one continuing the translation and codification and the other made up of legal scholars and theoreticians, devoted to editing and systematization.

But the lamentable situation of the administration of justice which had further deteriorated under the chaotic revolutionary conditions was far from remedied by these actions. For their salary, for example, the judges still depended on the meagre 15% of the settled value they received in each case (10% from the winning party and 5% from the losing party); and fearing the wrath of the *ulama*, whose hypersensitivity *vis-à-vis* the Majlis was becoming more and more apparent, they even used to call their court decisions "report to the office of the minister" instead of *hokm* (legal verdict) (cf. Forughi, 1936: 729 ff.; Saleh, 1964, II: 972).

With the end of the "Short Tyranny" which had destroyed even the meagre achievements of the first Majlis, reform activities were resumed. Before following up these developments, however, a brief mention must be made of Mirza Hasan Khan Moshir od-Dowleh Pir-niya (1873–1935), who was destined to play a crucial role in the subsequent judiciary history of Iran. He started his career as a diplomatic envoy to Russia where he had been studying law since 1884. "From that beginning, [he] was aware of the deficiencies of the legal system in Iran, and everywhere, he continued his search for its improvement" (Bastani-Parizi, 1968: 511, also 25-28; Safaei, 1965: 101). In 1899 when his father, the previously mentioned Nasrollah Khan Moshir od-Dowleh, was appointed Minister of Foreign Affairs, he was summoned to Iran. With the help of his father and younger brother, Mirza Hoseyn Khan Pir-niya (Moatamanol Molk), who later played an equally important role in the parliamentary history of the country,[68] he established the first school of political science (19 December 1899). In the subsequent years, he served as the chairman and professor of law in the school[69] and played a key role in the writing of the Fundamental Law and its Supplement.

In the first cabinet which was formed after the dethronement of

Mohammad Ali Shah, Mirza Hasan Khan Pir-niya who, after the death of his father on September 13, 1907, had received the title of Moshir od-Dowleh, was named Minister of Justice.[70] He kept this job in several of the following cabinets,[71] and in this rather long period, laid the foundations of the modern judiciary of Iran which lasted up to the revolution of 1978 (Bastani-Parizi, 1968: 517).

When he took office, he dismissed a number of judges for reasons of corruption or counter-revolutionary tendencies;[72] then he turned to his most difficult task, the completion and official enactment of modern secular laws which had been in the process of preparation in various committees by himself and his like-minded colleagues. For this, knowing the general atmosphere of the second Majlis (convened on 15 November 1909) which was still dominated by the *ulama*,[73] he resorted to an astute and, at the same time, logical tactic: with considerable difficulty, he got permission from the Majlis – and the government – to prepare laws and to put them into practice after the approval of the Judiciary Committee of the Majlis and to submit them to the entire body of the Majlis for final enactment after a period of experimental trial and possible revisions (Bastani-Parizi, 1968: 513; Foroughi, 1936: 972). This not only avoided major obstacles, but also set a precedent which, as we shall see, continued throughout the following Majlises up to the revolution of 1978.

With this permission in hand, Moshir od-Dowleh charged his deputy with the daily affairs of the Ministry of Justice and retired to his library. After six months of hard work and many private meetings and consultations with the prominent *ulama* and influential deputies, he came up (mid 1910) with two sets of law: the Law of Civil Procedures (*Osule-e Mohakamat-e Hoquqi*)[74] and the Organization Code of the Ministry of Justice (*Osul-e Tashkilat-e Adliyyeh*). But as it turned out, the difficulties in the Judiciary Committee were nearly as great as was expected from the entire Majlis. For there was the Sayyed Hasan Modarris, a highly influential and respected member of the *ulama* who at the same time acted as the representative of the top *mojtahids* of the country.

The Organization Code was accepted without much difficulty, but the Code of Civil Procedures met strong opposition from Modarris. After long debates and the addition of eight articles which the *ulama* had suggested, it also was accepted by the Committee on 13 November 1911 (Shayegan, 1943: 34). After two years of experimental trial, both codes were passed by the entire Majlis, thanks to the efforts of Mohammad Ali Forughi, another important figure in legal reform who was then the Minister of Justice.[75]

By the new code, district courts (*mahakim-e solh*), lower and higher courts of appeal (*istinaf* and *tamiz*, respectively) and the office of attorney general (*moddail omum*), an independent budget for the Ministry of Justice and regular salaries for its functionaries were established, and thus the principles of appeal and hierarchy of courts which had been introduced by *Sepahsalar* in 1871 and had been foreseen in the Supplement became an official reality.

One of the interesting contributions of Moshir od-Dowleh was a long, 139-article, law concerning registration of legal documents (*sabt-e asnad*). Though limited strictly to legal and court proceedings, this law constituted an important step in the direction of bringing the *ulama* and the Sharia courts under the control of the Ministry of Justice. It was repealed by a single act of the fourth Majlis on 17 April 1923 and was revived with a much wider scope during Reza Shah's rule.[76]

Moshir od-Dowleh was well aware that in Iran, especially in those chaotic days, no innovation, no matter how well conceived, was sure to last to the next minute. Thus, to ensure at least some degree of continuity, he employed, by the approval of the Majlis, a French jurist, Adolph Perni, who helped him in preparing the codes and remained in the service of the Ministry for fifteen years until 1926.[77]

After finishing the first two major codes, Moshir od-Dowleh began work on a code of criminal procedures. Using the French Code of Criminal Procedures as a base, he prepared, with the help of M. Perni, a relatively exhaustive code (492 articles), and submitted it to the Judiciary Committee of the Majlis in late 1911. In the middle of the second round of its deliberation, however, the Majlis adjourned (8 December 1911) and the code remained unfinished. But in view of the urgency of the matter, the Ministry of Justice organized a new committee which included the honorable Sayyed Hasan Modarris, Moshir od-Dowleh himself and M. Perni.[78] After a thorough scrutiny and the addition of fourteen more articles and after the approval of the Council of the Ministers on 12 August 1912, Momtaz od-Dowleh, then the Minister of Justice, was authorized to put it into effect (cf.

Hedayati, 1953: 11–12; Foroughi, 1936: 973). In the following year a short Code of Commercial Procedures and Drafts (in 62 articles) was also prepared but since the Majlis was adjourned the same procedure was followed, and it went in effect on 8 July 1914.[79]

Thus came to an end the first phase of the establishment of the modern judiciary in Iran. Under the direct or indirect auspices of Mirza Hasan Khan Moshir od-Dowleh, and with the help of such men as Mohammed Ali Foroughi Zakaol Molk, a modern organizational chart of the Ministry of Justice and codes of civil, criminal and commercial procedures were ratified and, along with these, other steps toward establishing a modern Western-inspired judiciary were taken. But leaving aside the quality and cultural suitability of these measures, the task was far from complete. Most conspicuous was the absence of equally modern penal and civil codes. But these were substantive laws, touching the very core of the Sharia, and any attempt at even discussing them was sure to create an uproar that no one was prepared to face.

When the third Majlis convened (4 December 1914), World War I had already begun and Iran was under Russian occupation. In the turmoil of struggle with occupying forces, the leaders of the Majlis and other nationalists were scattered; on 13 November 1915, the Majlis adjourned and did not meet again for almost six years.

The fourth Majlis (22 June 1921 – 21 June 1923) began in an entirely different climate. Internationally World War I had ended, and with this had come the October Revolution, which, insofar as it had removed the age-old menace of Czarist Russia, was "a divine gift"[80] for Iran. And domestically, on 27 February 1921, a coup had taken place in which Reza Khan had emerged victorious and was fast ascending the Iranian political pyramid.[81] In the cabinet that followed the coup he served as Minister of War, and while retaining that important post by the special acclamation of the Majlis he was appointed Prime Minister on 28 October 1923. On 31 October 1925 the Majlis deposed the last Shah of Qajar and declared Reza Khan the Shah of Iran (M5: 18, 78–79).

Notwithstanding the struggle with Reza Khan's ambitions, the fourth and fifth Majlis enjoyed a relatively substantial degree of stability and calm. In both, the special authorization for experimental laws which was initiated by the second Majlis was renewed,[82] and through the Justice Committee of the Majlis, the Westernization of the judiciary continued.

In the fourth Majlis, the Civil Procedure Code of 1911 was revised (Matin-Daftari, 1948, I: 25, 46 ff.), delimiting the jurisdiction of the Sharia-based district (*solh*) courts, and the most important step, which hitherto had not been dared, was taken: on 21 June 1923, it authorized the government "to establish a twelve-member committee of well-informed men for the preparation of a penal code" and even "to put it to experimental use if it were completed before the opening of the fifth Majlis" (M1-4: 624). The Majlis also passed on 1 December 1922, and then on 20 March 1923, a law on jury trials for the primary and appeal courts. On 14 April 1923, a law was passed specifying the qualifications, recruitment, promotion, salary scale and retirement of judges and public prosecutors (M1-4: 584–586, 611–612).

Although the fifth Majlis (11 February 1924 – 11 February 1926) had a much more stormy life due to the heightened struggle with Reza Khan, it nonetheless did make important contributions – thanks to the traditional authority of its Judiciary Committee. One of the laws it ratified was a Commercial Code (in 387 articles) which was adopted from the French Code by the help of M. Perni,[83] and which was a considerable improvement over the rudimentary Law of Commercial Draft passed in the second Majlis. Perhaps more important was the first Penal Code (*Qanun-e Jaza*) whose preparation was authorized by the fourth Majlis. It was enacted by the Judiciary Committee on 13 and 27 January 1926, and as a first major substantive code it constituted the first true challenge to the Sharia (Saleh, 1964: 994–995; Ali-Abadi, 1965, I: 25). It was a process which became more open and sweeping under Reza Shah.

4. JUDICIARY REFORM IN THE PAHLAVI PERIOD

The basic features characterizing Reza Shah's policies can be summed up as follows: (1) an autocratic centralism in excess of what the Constitution had allowed, thus arousing the opposition of the liberal nationalists who had fought for a constitutional government, (2) a strong secularism coupled with hypernationalism which was manifested in his vehement anti-clerical policies, and finally (3) an extreme pro-Western policy which clashed directly with the growing leftist groups. A few months after he ascended to the throne, the sixth Majlis (6 July 1926 – 13 August 1928) convened, and like those which followed, became an instrument, increasingly powerless, for carrying out his policies.

Besides being a part of his general desire to change Iran rapidly into a modern, Westernized nation, legal reform had a very special place in the mind of Reza Shah. First, it was an important prerequisite to the abolition of the humiliating, century-old capitulation system which still continued. Second, it was central to his anti-clerical policies and echoed what was going on in Turkey under Mostafa Kamal.

Thus in the programme which he submitted to the fifth Majlis as Prime Minister (13 April 1924), he pledged himself, among other things, to the "completion of [the secular] judiciary and the extension of the judiciary organizations into the provinces" (M5: 284). Shortly after he ascended to the throne, he chose one of his most able lieutenants, Ali Akbar Davar, who had a degree in law from the University of Geneva, for that important task. On 13 February 1927, he appointed Davar as the Minister of Justice and, to give him a free hand, dissolved the ministry.[84] For the next seven years, that is until 18 September 1933, Davar remained at the centre of judiciary and played an important role in legal reform as an important part of the massive Westernization effort of the Reza Shah era.[85]

On 16 February, only three days after Davar took office, the Majlis empowered him to reorganize the ministry of justice, to recruit new judges and to prepare new procedural laws.[86] Following the tradition set by the second Majlis it authorized him on 3 March 1928 to put into practice experimental laws after their ratification by the Judiciary Committee (cf. M6: 26–27). Following these developments came another move. On 24 April Reza Shah instructed Davar to take action to abolish the century-old capitulary rights.

With these authorizations, Davar began his tedious task. On 26 April he reopened the Ministry of Justice with new personnel, many of whom had received European educations. In the inauguration ceremony Reza Shah delivered a short speech where he expressed the importance he attached to the judiciary: "The prestige of a nation depends upon the quality of its justice. I expect of you the most honorable conduct that will at once bring justice and prestige to our country" (Quoted in Matin-Daftari 1930: 179–180).

Davar's next move was with regard to the capitulation. On 13 May letters were sent through the Ministry of Foreign Affairs to the foreign legations declaring unilateral annulment of the capitulatory rights as of 10 May 1928, thus giving them one year for signing new agreements. But given the long-used argument of the foreign embassies regarding the lack of an acceptable judiciary in Iran, Davar had to move fast. The next few months he spent on the preparation of various laws. Between December 1927 and August 1928, he enacted, through the Judiciary Committee of the Majlis, a variety of bills, some new and others revisions of the previous codes. Included were bills on the graded salary scale for the judiciary,[87] on the qualifications, recruitment, promotion and retirement of the judiciary personnel,[88] on arbitration,[89] on disputes between the citizens and government officials,[90] on trials of the cabinet ministers,[91] on procedures for the military tribunals,[92] on civil procedures and on the organization of the judiciary.[93]

Important as these measures were, they were far from meeting the requirements of a modern judiciary in substantive areas. As we said before, on 13 and 27 January 1926, the first Penal Code had been passed by the fifth Majlis; but the other important area, the civil law, was still under the exclusive domain of the Sharia. On 31 December 1927 a committee of modern and traditional scholars was set up at the Ministry of Justice and was charged with the compilation of a modern civil code. Hurrying to meet the deadline for the abolition of capitulation, the committee submitted the first volume of the *Qanun-e-Madani* (Civil Code) in 955 articles, and without detailed examination the Majlis ratified it as a package on 8 May 1928 – two days before the deadline.[94] Thus after almost fifty years of repeated attempts, Iran came to have a codified civil code and thus took another important step in the direction of having a modern – if not functional – judiciary system.[95]

A few months after the passage of the first volume of the Civil Code, the sixth Majlis came to an end, and shortly after, the seventh Majlis (5 November 1928 – 5 November 1930) began. By this time, the matters of capitulation were out of the way and Reza Shah's autocratic march toward Westernization was well under way. Throughout these years, the Majlis, which increasingly became a rubber stamp, met regularly and passed into law a variety of measures which Reza Shah and the men around him deemed necessary for building what they considered a modern Iran.

Included in these measures was of course the judiciary reform; with the continued authorization of the Majlis for experimental laws, Davar and his successors continued work on the judiciary. While the move towards evermore delimitation of the Sharia continued, attention was also occasionally paid to the pitfalls of indiscriminate copying of the foreign models.

Thus on 1 January and 4 and 8 June 1929 the early Code of Civil Procedures was revised, delimiting the jurisdiction of the Sharia courts (M7: 5, 63–64; M8: 191–197); on 3 February 1929, and then on 16 March and 13 August 1932, laws were enacted which required official registration of property, marriage, divorce and all transactions, all of which had hitherto been parts of the functions of the *ulama* and important sources of revenue for them (M7: 22–25; M8: 122–152, 157–161). In the 1930s, the anti-clerical campaign reached its climax. On 13 November 1931 the Civil Procedures and on 25 December 1935 the Organization Code of the Ministry of Justice were once more revised and the Sharia courts and the *ulama* almost completely eliminated from the judiciary.[96]

If these unceasing and hasty efforts toward Westernization met the opposition of the *ulama* on ideological grounds or on the basis of "group interest," public outcry against the modern judiciary, especially the procedural side which had developed into a labyrinth, was not less significant (cf. pp. 135–136 below). Cognizant of the unsuitability of the new system for the socio-cultural setting of the country, the architects of the new order soon began remedial measures which, as we should judge today, were far from sufficient. Thus, as early as 1929 the Majlis twice rejected the revised Code of Procedures and ordered further scrutiny and revision to make it more culturally suitable. Following this, a bill was passed on 16 November 1931 on "Speeding up of the Trials" (M8: 188–191), and at the same time committees were established for revision of the existing experimental laws.

The years from 1935 to 1940 constituted the period of maturation and refinement of the modern judiciary. In the first days of 1935 the committee which had been working on the second and third volumes of Civil Code submitted its work (in 340 articles) to the Majlis; the articles were ratified, after thorough scrutiny, between 26 January and 30 October 1935.[97] On 16 October 1937 the long awaited Code of Civil Procedure (723 articles), which had been in the process of revision for years, was submitted to the newly-convened eleventh Majlis (18 September 1937 – 18 September 1939). Throughout its two years in session, the Majlis examined the long code clause by clause, and after some revisions and additions (which brought the final version to 789 articles), passed it on 16 September 1939. This was the first time "a principal code of the Ministry of Justice was enacted in accordance with all due processes foreseen in the Constitution" (Matin-Daftari, 1948, I: 12). Basic to the new code was that it effected a balance between length and speed of trials, the extremities which characterized the codes' 1911 and 1928 versions. Furthermore, the code restored the jurisdiction of lower courts which had been delimited by an early act on speeding up of litigation and which had caused unnecessary congestion in the Court of Appeals. The code also established total jurisdiction of the secular courts over all disputes; it eased the work of local courts, state attorneys and prosecutors; for the first time, it introduced specific measures for the bailment of foreign nationals; and it took special measures to prevent litigants from delaying trials by evasive tactics (ibid.: 13–15).

Throughout these years, that is from the eighth to the thirteenth Majlis, the early penal codes also went through continuous revisions (cf. e.g. M8: 35–40, 44–50, 59–78; *Q1312*/1933, I: 46–49). On 31 May 1932 the Penal Procedure Code of 1911 was revised. In this revision, elements of the German and Swiss laws concerning judicial delegation, the jurisdiction of public prosecutors and lawyers, oral indictment and bailment were added to the French inspired code (Hedayati, 1953: 13). In 1939 two committees were set up by the Ministry of Justice to further revise the Penal Code and the Code of the Penal Procedure. With a view to shortening the time between arrest and trial and to effecting a balance between the so-called accusatory and inquisitory systems of investigation, the committees adopted the latest developments in France, Switzerland and especially in Fascist Italy, and on 16 June 1940 submitted the two revised codes to the Judiciary Committee of the Majlis (ibid.: 13–14). Though the committee did review and debate the codes, their passage in the full Majlis was interrupted by the outbreak of World War II and the occupation of Iran, which ended the rule of Reza Shah on 16 September 1941.

By this time, though far from being complete, the basic groundwork of the modern judiciary system in Iran had been laid. In the chaotic years that followed no comparable developments took place. In the subsequent Majlises the special permission for experimental laws – which actually always continued beyond their expiration date – was renewed; and except for the act on the unification of the statute law which was passed in the fifteenth Majlis (28 August 1947 – 28 August 1949), no appreciable development took place until the premiership of Dr. Mohammed Mussadegh (1951–1953). Following the extraordinary legislative powers granted him by the Senate on 2 August 1952 and by the Majlis on the following day, Mussadegh introduced a vast number of new laws – on the electoral and judiciary reforms, on finance, on public administration, and in many other areas (Saleh, 1964: 986–987).

Included in this legislation was a thorough revision of the Civil Procedure Code, which was introduced in January 1953. In this revision, the measures which were incorporated in the last revision of the code in 1939 were repealed; and speed in adjudication, even at the expense of undermining the quality of justice, was once again emphasized.[98]

With the fall of Mussadegh naturally came an end to his special process of legislation and laws which were officially annulled – on the ground that they were unconstitutional – on 9 November 1954. In the nineteenth Majlis (31 May 1956 – 30 May 1960), from which the legislative period was extended from two to four years, reform was once again resumed. Following the traditional permission for experimental legislation, about 50 new acts were introduced by Dr. Hadi Hedayati, the Minister of Justice, and by others. They covered a wide range such as judiciary organization, recruitment of judges and their dispatch abroad for training, the establishment and procedures of disciplinary courts (for the judiciary), the appealability of the decisions of the Supreme Court in certain cases, the establishment of moving tribunals, the judiciary affairs of the nomadic tribes and the establishment of the infamous National Security Organization (SAVAK).[99]

Of the most interesting and famous of these new laws were those which concerned criminal rehabilitation and civil liability. By the first, passed in 1958 and revised in 1960, criminal offenders became eligible for a reduction in their prison term upon showing good conduct, and many rehabilitative institutions were established. By the second, the Civil Liability Act, which was enacted in 1960, every individual was held liable for "any loss or damage which his unlawful act, whether done intentionally or by mere carelessness, causes to the life or liberty or property or status or business reputation or to any other right of others."[100]

In the process of the Shah's so-called "white revolution" which began in the early 60s, although attention focused largely on social and economic reforms, the judiciary also received considerable attention. In an attempt to relieve the highly overloaded, labyrinthine and utterly inefficient judiciary, two simple tribunals were created. They were introduced in July 1966 and were modified subsequently; although functioning as a part of the Ministry of Justice, they were "not bound to the formalities of the procedural law" and could "litigate in whatever manner [they] deemed appropriate."[101]

The first, called *khana-ye insaf* (house of equity),[102] was a rural tribunal, charged with settling disputes among villagers. It was composed of five "trusted" members of the community elected for four years, and had jurisdiction over criminal and civil cases, including property disputes, of up to 100,000 rials ($1,300). (Kamangar n.d., arts. 1, 2, 10–14). The second tribunal was the *shura-ye davari* (judiciary council) which was intended for urban areas. It was similarly composed of five "trusted" individuals elected for four years. It had jurisdiction over misdemeanours which entailed a fine of up to 200,000 rials and over a variety of civil cases, including property disputes, valued up to 200,000 rials.[103]

Though not strictly judicial, mention must also be made here of another act, the Family Protection Law of 7 January 1967 which has drawn considerable attention from Western analysts[104] and to whose substantive aspects we will return later.

In July 1977, among the revisions which were introduced in the preceding laws, came the last judiciary reform of the Pahlavi period. Continuing the attempt at simplification of the judiciary, an act was promulgated (Kamangar, n.d.: 621–634) by which district courts were completely discontinued (art. 1), the process of appeal was shortened (arts. 4–7), certain procedural formalities were eliminated (arts. 8–10), and the Ministry of Justice was authorized to take extraordinary measures for training new judges and for improving the hopeless conditions in which it was (arts. 35–38).

But whether these measures could perform miracles or, more likely, would simply add a few more pages to the voluminous file of the similar abortive attempts, is a question which never received an answer. Soon after, the winds of revolution which are still lashing the country started to blow. Today, gone with the wind is not only the Pahlavi dynasty but also the Westernized judiciary and all which was wrought along with it in the long and tedious process of Westernization.

III. The Modern Judiciary in Iran

Up to this point of the chapter our discussion has mainly been chronological. We reviewed in Part I the development and basic features of the traditional (Islamic) judiciary system of Iran, and in Part II the long and tedious process of efforts for its reform and Westernization.

But what was the nature of the new system? How well-integrated or "adopted" was it, functionally and psycho-culturally, with the deeply rooted Sharia system? Did the new system gain any degree of ascendancy in society? These are important questions whose answers provide the ultimate criteria for judging the success of any innovation and reform, and with these questions we shall be concerned in this part. We shall begin with an examination of the nature and substance of the various components of the modern judiciary, namely, the constitutional, civil, penal, procedural and organizational laws, and at the end, will try to draw certain conclusions from the whole enterprise.

1. THE CONSTITUTION OF 1907

By "Constitution" is meant the Fundamental Law and its Supplement which were promulgated respectively on 8 January and 7 October 1907. As is well known, these documents, like many others in the region, were based on the Belgian Constitution of 1831.[105] The way and the time-sequence in which they were prepared are extremely revealing; they clearly show how the political and tactical considerations affected the technical and structural aspects of these laws. Given the primary objective of the revolutionary struggle, which was the establishment of the Majlis, it was natural that of the provisions of the Belgian Constitution, only those which concerned the Houses of Representatives and Senate were taken up first. But here too there was a time-sequence. The matters related to parliamentary elections were expanded and put into a single document;[106] after the elections were held and the Majlis inaugurated, there came the Fundamental Law which dealt almost exclusively with the composition, procedures and the functions of the Majlis in relation to the government and the Senate. Then, after the Majlis was firmly established, at least in theory, came the Supplement, which touched upon the most sensitive and fundamental issues of a constitutional democracy.

Substantively, the Constitution represented the most radical departure, in both structure and content, not only from the age-old absolute monarchy in Iran but also from the constitutional doctrine of Shiism. Unlike the doctrine of the caliphate which had found at least some practical application from the Abbasid through the Ottoman Empires, the Shii theory of *imamate* and its derivative *velayat-e faqih* (rule by the *faqih*) had rarely found any concrete expression beyond the textbooks or polemics of the theology students.[107] Thus when the century-old campaign for reform reached its climax in 1906 it was the desire for the Western model of government which set the intellectual mood, and to this model the Shii constitutional theory had very little, if anything, to contribute. Basically, the model which was borrowed provided for a constitutional monarchy and a system of separation of powers based on popular sovereignty.

But, as we said, these measures were concessions wrung gradually from the traditional sources of power, the *ulama* and the Shah's court. The most fundamental point in the 51-article Fundamental Law was that "The Majlis is the representative of all of the Iranian people and a medium of their participation in the economic and political affairs of their country." (FL, art. 2) Following this principle, the Fundamental Law considered the Majlis as the only authority on making law, on allocation of the budget, on levying taxes, on granting concessions, on establishing companies, on assuming (foreign) loans, on ratifying treaties and on the approval of government programmes (FL, arts. 15–26). The rest of the Fundamental Law dealt with such matters as parliamentary immunity of the deputies, hearing of complaints from the public, initiation of laws to be enacted, the internal and procedural matters of the Majlis, and the establishment of the Senate as a subordinate body (FL, arts. 32–47). In all, the Fundamental Law was aimed at one single target: the curtailment of the power of the Shah and his government and the transfer of national decision-making to the Majlis as a representative of the people.[108]

Although of tremendous significance, the Fundamental Law was only a first step. Under pressure from the government, provisions were made in it for the accountability of the ministers solely to the Shah (FL, art. 28), and for the creation of a senate half of whose members were to be appointed by the Shah (FL, art. 45). These were concessions which the revolutionaries had to give. Besides, the most fundamental questions concerning the structure of power, the rights of the citizens, etc., had yet to be faced.

These and many other questions were taken up on the Supplement, of whose 107 articles 102 were translated directly from the Belgian Constitution.[109] As such the Supplement best reflected the ideological conflict which characterized the whole constitutional movement and the Majlis which it created.

At the core of this conflict lay the tension between religion and Western-inspired secular nationalism. The Supplement began with a clear victory for the former, and hence its most important deviation from the Western model on which it was based. Whereas the Belgian Constitution had taken a completely liberal stand on religion and its relation to the state (BC, arts. 14–16), the Supplement took a completely opposite position: "The official religion of Iran is Islam of the rightful *Ithnaashariyyah* rite which the Shah of Iran must always uphold and promote." (S, art. 1) Furthermore the Majlis, whose very establishment was said to have been enhanced ". . . by the Attention of His Holiness, the (Hidden) *Imam* . . . should at no time legislate laws which disagree with the Sharia." But how to implement this "eternal principle"? After a heated debate and controversy, it was finally agreed that from among a group of twenty *mojtahids* to be introduced by the *ulama*, the Majlis should select a committee of five, and these would have the final say, with veto power, on all legislation of the Majlis and the Senate.[110]

Except in the first Majlis, where the presence of a great many of the *ulama*, including two renowned *mojtahids*, among the deputies constituted a *de facto* implementation of this rule (cf. pp. 111 and n. 73) this principle was never heeded in the subsequent sessions of the Majlis.[111] It was even violated in the Supplement itself by granting "equal rights to all people of Iran" (S, art. 8; cf. BC, art. 6) which meant the Moslems and non-Moslems alike and which was contrary to the Sharia; that the qualifying phrase, "on governmental laws," in the same article was only a face-saving device for the proponents of the Sharia is seen by the fact that this very issue was among the major points of conflict with the *ulama* which delayed the ratification of the Supplement for seven months and ended only after massive public support for the nationalists outside the Majlis (cf. Taqizadeh, 1959: 54).

Following this, the Supplement lists a number of rights, directly borrowed from the Belgian Constitution, which "cannot be abridged without the special permission of the law." These include the right to security; to immunity from summary arrest and punishment; to the judges assigned by law; to sanctity of domicile; to residence; to ownership of property (S, arts. 9–16; cf. BC, arts. 6–12); to learning, teaching and publication of what is not forbidden by or inimical to the religion; to peaceful assembly; and to secrecy of correspondence (S, arts. 18–23; cf. BC, arts. 17–22).

The anti-Sharia mood found an even clearer expression in the discussion of the nature and basis of political power and sovereignty. In sharp opposition to the *imamate* theory of Shiism it explicitly states that "All powers of the State stem from the people and shall be exercised in accordance with the provisions of the Constitution." (S, art. 26; cf. BC, art. 25) Following this principle, monarchy is described as a "divine trust confided by the people to the person of the Shah;"[112] the Shah is accepted as the chief executive; but he is inviolable and his ministers are responsible to the Majlis individually and collectively; he has the right to initiate laws and his signature finalizes the acts of the parliament, but he cannot legislate. Legislation and interpretation of law are among the exclusive prerogatives of the parliament (S, arts. 26, 36, 44, 60–70; cf. BC, arts. 26–30, 89–90). The Shah cannot assume the responsibility of another state without the consent and approval of the parliament, nor can his relatives of first degree – sons, brothers and uncles – be appointed as ministers (S, arts. 43, 59; cf. BC, arts. 62, 87).

Although the adoption of these principles signified a measurable advance in the struggle against the age-old absolutism of the Shah and his government, the task was far from over. As we recall, a differentiation of the legislative and executive had been known and even experimented with since the middle of the nineteenth century. Moreover, the writers of the Fundamental Law, who understandably could not afford to engage in a second front, made no mention of the third element in Montesquieu's trio, the judiciary, as it would have caused a direct confrontation with the *ulama*. In the writing of the Supplement, however, the problem was faced and, as expected, its provisions were vehemently opposed by the *ulama*; this time, however, the opposition of the *ulama* was not purely on ideological grounds, as was the case with the concept of equality; the new arrangement reflected a threat to their material interests as they had hitherto had an official monopoly over the judiciary. But here, too, the nationalists won: a secular judiciary was added to the legislative and executive with the explicit emphasis that "The three branches must all the time remain separate and independent of each other." (S, art. 28) In this judiciary, "The Grand Office of Justice (*Divan-e Adalete Ozma*) and the secular courts of *adliyyeh*" were recognized as "the official" organs of justice administration, leaving only matters of religion to the judgment of the qualified *mojtahids*.[113] Following this general statement, basic organizational features of the secular judiciary which were described in the Belgian model were specified. These included the establishment of a national Supreme Court (of appeal) in Tehran, and lower Courts of Appeal in the provincial capitals (S, arts. 75, 86; cf. BC, arts. 95, 104); the appointment of chief judges, the establishment of regular salary for the judiciary (S, arts. 80, 84; cf. BC, arts. 99, 102) and the requirement for jury trials on political and journalistic offences.[114]

Thus came to a climax the move which began in the early nineteenth century. Except for its secondary features, the whole legal structure of the Constitution and its key concepts are borrowed from the West: equality of all before the law, popular sovereignty, constitutionalism, the trichotomous model of government, and the independent secular judiciary. Although an end to the age-old political absolutism of the ruling class and the Shah was the immediate objective of the new system being created, confrontation with religious absolutism had perhaps greater long-run significance and difficulty. In a diplomatic dispatch to the British Foreign Office the scene was described rather well: "For sure, the most important problem [in Iran] today . . . is that of religion vs. the freedom movement. . . . [Here], as in Europe, democracy views religion as its enemy and the (current) unity between the two is an unnatural one which will sooner or later turn into a most severe confrontation . . . The *ulama* are well aware of what their opponents have in mind, and to the potential danger which threatens their very existence are sensitive. But they have fallen into a trap from which escape is impossible or even dangerous."[115]

In subsequent years, though political despotism made a full

come-back, especially under Reza Shah, religious absolutism increasingly lost ground and made its most vivid reappearance after the 1978 revolution.

2. THE CIVIL CODE

Unlike the constitutional law, the civil law traditionally received a greater attention from the Sharia. It constituted almost 90% of *Moamalat* – the second division of *Ahkam* – which concerned the relationship among God's servants. Thus whereas the organizational and procedural aspects of the judiciary were the first targets of modernization efforts, the citadel of the civil law was the last to fall and its fall, as we discussed, was enhanced by a political consideration: the abolition of the notorious capitulatory rights.

The present Civil Code, *Qanun-e Madani*, consists of three volumes. The first (955 articles) was promulgated in 1928 and the second and third (281 and 79 articles respectively) in 1935.[116] It was prepared by a bilingual committee and was based on the classical texts of the Shii Fiqh,[117] similar Islamic codes, especially the *Majallah*,[118] the civil codes of France (the *Code Napoleon* of 1804), Belgium and Switzerland, and the *orf* (Shayegan, 1943: 38).

As a whole, the *Qanun-e Madani* is a codified and systematized compendium which is "much more closely based on the Sharia . . . than was the legislation in the Ottoman Empire or in British India" (Anderson, 1971: 18). Yet the code also reflects a considerable amount of non-Sharia influence. In an apparent attempt to make the new code suitable for modern conditions, the authors have drawn heavily from the European codes especially the *Code Napoleon*, as well as from the *orf*. As such, the content of the *Qanun-e Madani* can be divided into three categories: pure *Fiqh*, pure secular laws, and mixed laws. The first can be exemplified by laws of inheritance and pious endowments, the second by laws concerning legal capacity, civil rights and civil registrations and the third by laws of property, contracts and obligations.

If not the most systematic, the *Qanun-e Madani* is regarded as the most successful of the modern codes prepared in Iran. In the following pages we will briefly examine it from the points of view of its legislative technique, legal structure and underlying philosophy.

From the point of view of legislative technique, the *Qanun-e Madani*, on the whole, is a replica of the *Code Napoleon*,[119] with a minor topical rearrangement due, obviously, to the political circumstances under which it was prepared. After a short preamble "On the Publication, Effect and Application of Laws in General" which is taken verbatim from the French code, the *Qanun-e Madani* begins with "Property" followed by "Different Modes of Acquiring Property." These two topics which make the whole of Volume One (Book I and II respectively) of the *Quanun-e Madani* were treated in Book II and III of the French code; the reason for beginning from the middle of the French code seems to have been the fact that the two topics of the Volume One constituted the areas with which the capitulatory practices had basically been concerned. Hurrying to meet the deadline for the abolition of capitulation, the authors of the first volume even left out an entire chapter of the French code on "the Proofs of Obligations . . .," and, with a more general heading, "On the Proofs of Claim," treated it later as Volume Three.[120] This left only one topic, "Persons," which had been dealt with in Book I of the French code. It was treated as Volume Two of the Iranian code which along with the third volume was promulgated in 1935.

Following these general headings, there are many adoptions of the same nature from the French code; but the more we move to the inner divisions and minor headings of the *Qanun-e Madani*, the more we see the influence of the well-established typological scheme of the *Fiqh*; and this is probably one of the reasons for many inconsistencies and organizational incoherencies which characterize the code (Shayegan, 1943: 38–42.)

This mixture is even more apparent in the legal structure of the *Qanun-e Madani*. In an apparent attempt to make the code exhaustive and suitable for modern conditions, the authors have incorporated in it a great many "received" elements and concepts. For example, in the Preamble to Volume One the differential time schedule for when new laws go into effect in localities of varying distance is a direct translation from the French (QM, art. 2 = CN, art. 1). The same is true of the retroactive inapplicability of law (QM, art. 4 = CN, art. 2), of the jurisdiction of domestic laws over foreign nationals in Iran (QM, art. 8 = CN, art. 3), and of the invalidity of the illegal private contracts (QM, art. 10 = CN, art. 6). Similarly, the division of property into moveable and immoveable, the modes of acquiring property (QM, arts. 11–28; cf. CN, arts. 516–538), and the rules of usufruction (QM, arts. 40–54; cf. CN, arts., 578–624), easement and servitude (QM, arts.

93–139; cf. CN, arts. 625–730), and considerable parts of agreements and contracts, all are of French origin.[121]

Perhaps the most interesting of the European influences on the legal structure of the *Qanun-e Madani* is to be found in its Volume Two, on persons. The volume begins with a general introduction to the various aspects of "legal capacity" which it says "begins with birth and ends with death." (QM. art. 956) This conception of persons, employing both rights and obligations, strikes a delicate contrast with the Sharia which conceives of person primarily in terms of obligation (*taklif*) and thus treating rights as a residual category in the sense that A's obligation toward B implies the latter's right. With this conception has come many other borrowings: on capacity and citizenship, on civil rights of citizens and foreigners (QM, arts. 958–991; cf. CN, arts. 7–33); on divorce before civil authorities (QM, arts. 992–1001; cf. CN, arts. 34–101); on domicile (QM, arts. 1002–1010; cf. CN, arts. 102–111); on absent persons (QM, arts. 1011–1029; cf. CN, arts. 112–143); and on the mutual obligations of husbands and wives (QM, arts. 1102–1119; cf. CN, arts. 203–226).

Important as these Western concepts are in setting the conceptual framework for the legal structure of the *Qanun-e Madani* they are of course not the only non-Sharia elements in the code. Throughout the *Qanun-e Madani* we see references to the *orf* which have helped the code to achieve a greater degree of articulation, flexibility and refinement in comparison to the traditional *Fiqh* (cf. Salujuqi, 1968: 140–164). For example "ownership" or possession over unclaimed land may be established if a person "settles" the land, but what constitutes "settlement" is a matter which should be determined by *orf* (QM, art. 141). Similar references to the *orf* are made in determining the "accessories" which would automatically be considered as part of a solid object (QM, arts. 356–358) or a contract (QM, art. 1312), in determining the shares of different parties in a sharecropping (QM, art. 519), and the right of accession relative to moveable and immoveable properties (QM, art. 54; cf., arts. 107, 225, 286, 521, 542, 549, 664 and 678), and in determining the exact nature of certain legal obligations (QM, arts. 369, 1107).

In the years which followed its first promulgation, a number of articles in the *Qanun-e Madani* were revised and many new laws which would normally fall under its categories were separately enacted. But while from the point of view of the legal structure, these additions reflected no change, they constituted a significant evolution in the underlying assumptions or philosophy of the code in certain cases and this leads to the third and final area of our discussion.

From this point of view, while the conception of the individual in terms of legal capacity and its variant civil rights in the *Qanun-e Madani* could be regarded "modern" and Western, the conception of society in the code was definitely traditional and *Fiqh*-inspired. True, many elements of European laws and of the *orf* were added, but on the whole the provisions of the Sharia on such areas as inheritance, property rights and ownership, obligations, land use, and on many other areas, were retained intact and they remained so up to the revolution of 1978.

The only exception to the latter, however, was the Family Protection Law of 1967 which has been acclaimed as "a milestone in the advance of women's rights." (Bagley, 1971: 47). Leaving aside the struggle for equal rights for women which began in the late nineteenth century, the immediate history of the act could be traced to 26 January 1963 when women were allowed, for the first time, to vote "unofficially" in the referendum held on the Shah's six-point reform programme. Included in the programme was an electoral reform which granted equal voting rights to women and paved the way for subsequent developments.

The Family Protection Law of 1967, as revised in February 1975, constituted a considerable deviation from the Sharia as well as the original *Qanun-e Madani.* Banning husbands from divorcing their wives "whenever they choose" (QM, art. 1113), the Family Protection Law[122] required that "all civil disputes which are related to marriage . . . should be settled in courts . . ." (art. 1). Without being bound to "observe formal legal procedures" (ibid.), the family courts were authorized to issue certificates of incompatibility after all attempts at reconciliation and only when certain conditions were met (arts. 3–8). Furthermore, according to the act, petitions for divorce could be initiated by either husband or wife and the court were to treat them on equal footing (art. 8); no husband could remarry without the written consent of his wife, and a similar permission of the court (art. 16).

3. THE PENAL CODE

Compared to its civil law the Islamic penal law, both in the Sunni and Jaafari schools, was far more formal and inexhaustive.

Basically, it recognized two types of offence: crimes against individuals, *jenayat*, and offences against religion.[123] The first were punishable by private vengeance and the second either by *hadd*, a fixed punishment set by God, or by *taazir*, a discretionary chastisement by the *qadi*.[124] For this reason, as we said before, from the very early days, the administration of criminal justice in the Islamic societies was taken over by the state and was carried out mainly through the non-Sharia courts. But throughout these centuries, no attempt was ever made to supplement, let alone revise, the Sharia penal law for the obvious reason that it would have meant an admission of deficiency in the Sharia and an interference with the *hodud* (limits) of God.

Thus, to the architects of the new judiciary system in Iran, preparation of a penal code presented a very difficult problem. It required not only massive new legislation, but also a reconceptualization of crime to bring social order into the focus and, desirably, to replace the punitive approach of the Sharia with a more Western-inspired "restitutive" one.

For this, given the nature of the political climate and pace of change which was taking place in the country, it is obvious that the gap could be filled only with a massive borrowing. That this is exactly what took place can clearly be seen from the 289 clause, *Qanun-e Jaza*[125] (Penal Code) which was promulgated in 1926.

The Penal Code, as we said before, was prepared under the direct supervision of M. Perni, the French advisor to the Ministry of Justice; and as the *Code Napoleon* served as an important source for the *Qanun-e Madani*, the Napoleonic *Code Penal* of 1810, "the most widely followed penal code in the world"[126], seems to have been the primary if not the exclusive basis for the *Qanun-e Jaza*; and for this reason, it could be said that in the area of substantive law, the *Qanun-e Jaza* represents the most radical departure from and supplantation of the Sharia. This is seen not only in the legislative technique and legal structure of the code but also in its underlying assumptions and penal philosophy.

From the point of view of legislative technique, the *Qanun-e Jaza* is an almost exact copy of the *Code Penal*. It is organized in *Babs* (Parts). Part One, corresponding to Book I and II of the *Code Penal*, is devoted to the General Part of criminal law. Without going into any theoretical discussion, this part begins, like its French model but in a much less systematic way, with a basic conceptual framework. The framework provides a typological scheme for crime and punishment and discusses such issues as criminal liability, accessoryship, mitigating factors and merger and concurrence of offences.[127] The rest of the compendium, the Special Part, contains the actual body of criminal law arranged by types of crime. Part Two, which corresponds exactly to Title I of Book III of the *Code Penal* is devoted to "Felonies and Misdemeanours against the Public Good,"[128] and Part Three, with a similar correspondence to Title II, deals with "Felonies and Misdemeanours against Private Persons."[129] Finally, "Violations" (petty offences) which constitute Book VI of the *Code Penal* are treated in Part Four of the *Qanun-e Jaza*, as will be discussed shortly.

The treatment of felonies and misdemeanours in Part Two and Part Three is relatively exhaustive. The offences dealt with range from such problems as vagrancy (QJ, art. 273; cf. FPC, arts. 269–279), defacement of and damage to property (QJ. arts. 250–263; cf. FPC, arts. 283–290), bankruptcy, swindling (QJ, arts. 236–238; cf. FPC, arts. 402–405), betrayal of trust (QJ, arts. 239–241; cf. FPC, arts. 406–409), counterfeiting (QJ, arts. 93–112; cf. FPC, arts. 132–144), and usurpation of position (QJ, arts. 125–126; cf. FPC, arts. 258–261), to high treason and armed uprising against the state (QJ, arts. 69–79; cf. FPC, arts. 91–101). Except when, under mitigating circumstances, some of these offences are reduced to "violations," no detailed treatment has been given to the petty offence. Part Four, which is devoted to this subject, consists of only one article (276), making these offences subject to administrative regulations within limits set by the law (QJ, art. 11).

As a whole and notwithstanding its being basically "received", i.e. copied from a Western source, the *Qanun-e Jaza* does indeed reflect a relatively exhaustive picture of the penal and criminal problems of the semi-feudal Iran of the day, and in this sense, it is, needless to say, far more realistic than the Sharia penal law.

Departure from the Sharia is even more apparent in the legal structure of the code. Conscious of the sensitivity of the *ulama*, the authors of the *Qanun-e Jaza* begin the code with a careful statement: "The penalties which are specified in this code are set for the protection of social order and shall be enforced through the *Adliyyeh*. The offences which are uncovered and prosecuted in accordance with the Islamic rules shall be subject to the *hodud* and *taazirat* which are set by the Sharia" (QJ, art. 1). That the last part of the article was intended as a "legal fiction" is seen not only from the very conditional wording of the sentence (Ali-Abadi, 1965: 52), but also from the second article of the code itself, which is a verbatim translation from the *Code Penal*: "No action could be regarded criminal unless stated so by the law," i.e., the provision of the Penal Code (QJ, art. 2).

Following these preliminary remarks, the Code sets the theoretical scheme of its legal structure which is also taken directly from the French code. The scheme consists of two components. The first, a utilitarian component, is a three-fold division of offences into (1) felonies (*jenayat*), (2) misdemeanours (*jonheh*) and (3) violations or petty offences (*khalaf*) (QJ, art. 7; cf. FPC, art. 1); this is followed by the second, a legalistic component, in which a range of punishments is set for each of the three types of offence. In all, the punishments consist of (1) the death penalty, (2) imprisonment (of varying degrees), (3) banishment (from the country or residence), (4) loss of civil rights (all or some), (5) loss of freedom of movement, and finally (6) fines (of varying amount) (QJ, arts. 8–12; cf. FPC, arts. 6–9). This principle of legalism, of which the above-mentioned article 2 is the clearest expression, is then followed by the corollary principle of non-retroactivity of penal law, which, it is explicitly said, is applicable only to the imposition of and not exemption from the punishment – a point not mentioned in the *Code Penal* (QJ, art. 6; cf. FPC, art. 4).

The legal structure thus described constitutes an important departure from the Sharia, not only in form but also in content. Focusing on "social order," the new Penal Code omits such issues as apostasy, the highest religious offence which in the Sharia Penal Law incurred the death penalty. Similarly, wine-drinking and false accusation of sexual relations, which in the Sharia had been treated as independent offences, are dealt with under more general headings, "On Vagrancy and Public Use of Alcohol and Narcotics" (QJ, art. 275; cf. QJ, arts. 273–275 and FPC, arts. 269–282) and "On Moral Offences" (QJ, art. 214 *mokarrar* [i.e. the second issue]: Part B; cf. FPC, arts. 368–378) respectively. More important is the complete abandonment of the harsh and rigid *hadd* punishment on these and other offences. Instead, a more "humane" and flexible range of punishments is provided and the judge is allowed the discretion of choosing between a maximum and minimum, hence making room for the play of mitigating factors.

On these issues, although the code is basically Western, and, as we have said, in many cases a literal translation, its authors have exercised a notable degree of independence. For instance, in both the French and Iranian penal codes, adultery is regarded as a private offence, prosecuted only upon the charge of the spouse (FPC arts. 336; QJ, art. 212, last paragraph). From that point, the two codes diverge. According to the Iranian law there is no difference between a man and a woman in their right to charge adultery (as a spouse) or in incurring punishment (as a partner in adultery).[130] In the French law, however, while the male partner in adultery is sanctioned with a heavier punishment,[131] the right of a wife to charge her husband for adultery is also limited only to cases where the husband "keeps a mistress at the matrimonial home."[132]

This independence or divergence from the Western model has not of course always been in the direction of liberalism as implied by this example. In some cases punishments even harsher than and contrary to that of the Sharia are stipulated: "If a husband sees his wife in bed or in a similar situation with another man whom she could otherwise marry, and kills or injures her or him or both, he is exempt from punishment" (QJ, art. 179).

Obviously, this is the influence of the traditional mode of thinking which has occasionally led the authors of the *Qanun-e Jaza* even to forget their own theoretical framework: "If minors (of above 12) who had not reached the age of fifteen commit a felony or a misdemeanour, they shall be sentenced to flogging from ten to fifteen lashes . . ." (QJ, art. 35); as we know, flogging as a *hadd* was very common in traditional Iran but is excluded from the list of punishments set in the beginning of the Code.

The examples cited provide good clues to our third area of interest, the penal philosophy of the new code. On this, as we have indicated before, although the new code is far more restitutive than the Sharia, it nevertheless retains the basic premises of the classical school, namely legality, *mens rea* and retributive punishment, which characterize its main source of inspiration, the *Code Penal.* Minors under twelve years of age (QJ, art. 34; cf. FPC, art. 69), the insane (QJ, art. 40; cf. FPC, art. 64), and those who commit a crime in self-defence or in defence of their marital chastity (QJ, arts. 41, 179) are excluded from criminal responsibility. In a similar vein an attempted felony is regarded punishable as in the case of a completed felony (QJ, art. 20; cf.

FPC, art. 2); the accessory is subject to the same punishment as the principal, and any mitigating factors affecting one partner will not necessarily affect the other (QJ, arts. 27–29, 30, cf. FPC, arts. 59–60). The death penalty is retained; and taking the concept "innate criminal" for granted,[133] the Code, like the *Code Penal*, has no place for individualization of the penal process. Resocialization is profoundly alien to the Code; the only place where it comes close to the idea of rehabilitation of the offender is when it mentions assigning of the non-political prisoners to work in industrial or agricultural institutions. (ibid.)

Throughout the years following its first promulgation in 1926 very little change took place in this conception of crime. In the late 1950s the appearance of many rehabilitative institutions seemed to signify a new outlook; but being introduced under an increasingly repressive political climate these measures, like many others, rarely brought any meaningful change beyond the facade of an inherently degenerate system.

4. ORGANIZATION AND PROCEDURE

The organizational aspects of the modern judiciary in Iran differed widely from the other elements of the system. As they were primarily non-substantive, their modification was least offensive to the Sharia; by being among the least developed parts of the traditional judiciary system, they were amenable to a total and comprehensive reconstruction; and finally, by being the most concrete and ultimate expression of the country's system of justice, they always had top priority in the list of reform targets.

Thus, throughout the nineteenth century, as we recall, all efforts for judiciary reform centred almost exclusively on judicial organization, and after the Constitutional Revolution Moshir od-Dowleh's first and second reform acts dealt respectively with the organization and procedure of the judiciary.

As founded by Moshir od-Dowleh in 1911 and revised and expanded in subsequent years, the modern judiciary organization of Iran developed into a colossal labyrinth which not only bore no resemblance to the country's traditional system, but, as an example of "total reception", became a perfect example of cultural discontinuity, "social misfit", and what I have called Westomania.

In essence, the system consisted of the following elements: (1) a two-stage litigation, of first instance and appeal;[134] (2) a dual arrangement of the courts on the basis of (a) the nature of their jurisdiction[135] and (b) their relative jurisdiction;[136] and (3) a host of procedural features. The latter included a detailed treatment of "The Proofs of Claim" (cf. QM, arts. 1257–1335; CN, arts. 1315–1369; Esmein, 1968: 622–630) and an articulate and highly complex procedure of investigation, trial, appeal and review.

Lack of space prevents a detailed examination of these features; and in a sense, given the "totality of reception"[137] in this area, a general characterization of the system as a whole would serve the purpose. In this regard, we could do no better than to quote two men who represent two entirely different outlooks.

The first is Ayatollah Khomeini, the present ruler of Iran. In one of his polemics against the Shah's regime while in exile in Iraq, Ayatollah Khomeini based his argument for his ideal form of government, the *velayat-e faqih*, on what he regarded as one of the cornerstones of modern Iran: "The imposition of foreign laws on [our] Islamic society has been the root of endless harms and trouble . . . A dispute which in 'those days' a *qadi* of the Sharia would settle in two or three days would not finish now even in twenty years." (Khomeini, 1972: 11–12)

While one may or may not agree with the conclusions Ayatollah Khomeini draws, his basic arguments and descriptions of the scene are correct. This is attested to by the observations of a renowned scholar and keen observer, Ahmad Kasravi, who spent ten years during the height of Reza Shah's reforms, at the service of the Ministry of Justice and occupied key positions in the judiciary. Ironically, Kasravi was an unceasing opponent and critic of Shiism and the *ulama*[138] and was assassinated by the same militant group, *Fedaiyan-e Islam* (Moslem Brotherhood) which after the 1978 revolution was headed by Sheykh Sadeq Khalkhali, the-now-famous *qadi* of the Islamic Republic of Iran.

Drawing on ten years of rich experience in the Ministry of Justice, Kasravi wrote devastating criticisms of the modern judiciary in Iran and clearly demonstrated the failures and pitfalls of the indiscriminate Westernization which had characterized the system. His first treatise on the matter begins with this introduction: "The people who for years live with troubles get used to them . . . The best example of this is the story of the *Adliyyeh* in Iran" (Kasravi, 1945: 1). Then, describing the paralysing inferiority complex which swept Iran from the beginning of the nineteenth century and with which the reform movement began, the author tells us how the French judiciary system was transplanted in Iran. Following this the author examines the modern judiciary and discusses what he calls "endless adjudications," (ibid.: 14–22) or "futile red tapes" (ibid.: 22–35); and similar features. Then he cites cases where adjudication of a simple case which in theory had to be finished in two stages of litigation had lasted for twenty years and had gone through twenty or more hearings and reviews each time with a different conclusion (see also Kasravi, 1936; 1937).

IV. Conclusion

Such then was the story of law and judiciary reform in Iran. As an important part of the country's tedious efforts at modernization, it best epitomizes the agonizing gaps, paradoxes and discontinuities which have characterized the process from its very beginning.

It began in the early 19th century. After repeated humiliating defeats from the Russian army, the country, shocked by a sudden realization of the superiority of Western technology, began looking to the West for modernization. But as contact with the West began and expanded, a profound and sweeping sense of inferiority which shook the very foundation of the society gradually set in, and modernity came to be conceived of as contrary to and incompatible with all aspects of traditional ways of life, ranging from religious values and rituals to wearing traditional clothes and even to reading and studying classical Persian literature and poetry. An influential scholar and leader of the constitutional revolution, S. H. Taqizadeh, advocated in a now-famous article that "the only cure for Iran was to become Westernized internally, externally, psychically and spiritually"[139]; this was a clear expression of the same current which was, for the builders of the new Iran, a directive of deed and action, and for the hypnotized uncommitted masses, a perplexing and paralyzing mental dissonance. In such a psycho-political climate, the reform movement began. But among the various fields of reform such as the military, technology, bureaucracy and even education and the political system, the judiciary occupied a unique position. For whereas on the cultural level it was the most shocking point of contrast with the West, its reform also presented the greatest difficulty. It meant not simply "filling a vacuum" but, rather, "supplementation" or "replacement" of a highly rigid, comprehensive and well-established system which had hitherto been regarded as "sacred," "immutable" and "infallible." Furthermore, it constituted intrusion into the exclusive domain of the *ulama*, who symbolized the society's most revered values and wielded tremendous powers.

Attempts at judiciary reform began in the first part of the nineteenth century, but no significant results were achieved until after the constitutional revolution and the establishment of the first legislative assembly, the Majlis, in 1906. From that time to the abrupt closing of its 24th session during the revolution of 1978, the Majlis – notwithstanding the many fluctuations it underwent due to the political vicissitudes of the country – produced a massive body of modern Westernized laws which constituted the backbone of the legal as well as the social and political structures of modern Iran.

From the point of view of legislative history the process of legal reform in Iran was very similar, at least in one important respect, to the promulgation of the Sharia in its formative years: both constitute attempts at "reception" or, put more precisely, at the adaptation of a psycho-politically overwhelming foreign system to native conditions of a different society. But here the similarity ends. For whereas in the case of the Sharia the pre-Islamic practices and customs were cast into the Islamic moulds with so astonishing a perfection, the adoption of the Western models in Iran, as in other Islamic societies, never achieved psychologically and functionally any comparable degree of integration. True, the nature and context of the two "receptions" were totally different. But this fact itself is sociologically problematic rather than given, and it touches the very core of the immense problems and difficulties on the way of modernization of traditional societies.[140]

But the modernizing elites of Iran were neither aware of these difficulties and of the complexity of their task, nor were they, in any event, able to meet them properly. In most cases the modernization efforts, sincere and well-meaning as they might have been, boiled down to inarticulate attempts to copy and explant, even by force, alien models and systems in a culturally hostile soil. Conceived and introduced as the *anti*-theses of the traditional system, the "received" elements, superficially imposed, generated greater gaps and conflicts and created more problems than they solved.

At the risk of sounding technical, these problems, in most cases, can be described as structural disequilibrium, or simply, anomie, in the Mertonian sense of the term (Merton 1957: 131 ff.), and the modern judiciary in Iran is a clear case in point. Put in a theoretical term, the new judiciary was a normative subsystem;[141] taken almost without modification from the West, it created great incongruities and strains which, along with other factors, led to the total collapse of the political system in the 1978 revolution.

At the highest level, the value component of society, the new judiciary was the source of deep conflicts. It was based, for instance, on the assumptions of legal capacity, individual rights, judicial rationalism, popular sovereignty, populism, and a host of similar Western inspired premises; yet as expressed in the very text of its new constitution, in the behaviour and character of almost 98% of its people and in the make-up of its social and cultural institutions, the society was deeply committed to a set of religio-traditional values which were almost totally alien to and incompatible with those assumptions.

At the normative level there was what could be termed as structural discontinuity which had two distinct aspects. The first was lack of what Harold Lasswell has called "redressing." As we recall, practically every act of the judiciary reform, from the second Majlis to the 24th, was enacted as "experimental" law, and except for one or two cases in the whole period, none was ever brought before the entire body of the Majlis for scrutiny and due processing. Carried out with such a procedure and in a climate of intense anti-clerical sentiments, especially in the Pahlavi period, the new system as a whole was, and ironically was meant to be, a break with rather than a continuation of the past. Except in the area of civil law where some degree of continuity could be said to have been achieved, in other areas, namely, the constitutional, penal and especially the procedural and organizational laws, reception meant supplantation and total supersession of the traditional (Sharia) system, and the idea of need for redressing seems not to have dawned on the architects of the new system.

Yet this structural discontinuity had a second aspect which could be called lack of institutionalization. One of the distinct features of the political system in Iran, as perhaps in most of the so-called underdeveloped world, is primary "person-centredness." In such a society, the "system" as such never gains any degree of primacy as focus of attention and loyalty, and consequently, with the change of incumbents in key positions, everything under that sphere of authority changes; no innovation takes root and the society remains in a constant process of "starting from scratch." In the modern history of Iran nothing illustrates this characteristic better than its judiciary. From the time of Amir Kabir to the fall of the Shah, as we recall, time and again the Ministry of Justice was dissolved, programmes and codes which were so painstakingly prepared by one man or group were thrown away by the next, and no step taken was sure to last to the next day.

Finally, at the lowest, the operative level of the society, the incongruities of the new judiciary were not less significant. They not only resulted directly from the nature of the system as such, but were also enhanced by the strains at the higher, normative and valuative structural levels which were discussed. As such, they epitomized, most vividly and concretely, the problems and failures of the whole system, and it was at this level that the above-mentioned polemics of Ahmad Kasravi and Ayatollah Khomeini were directed. Stated very briefly, these problems included, for example, (a) the failure of the new system to properly co-opt the members of the old system, the *ulama*, hence alienating a most important power group in society; (b) rampant growth into a bureaucratic labyrinth with increasing inability to keep up with the realities and functional necessities of an ever alienating society – a point repeatedly brought up by the critics and the public at large; and finally (c) failure to preserve a minimum degree of judiciary independence to uphold justice as well as susceptibility to such corrupting tendencies as bribery, nepotism and favouritism, which have perhaps been among the rules of the game in the Persian judiciary throughout the country's history.

Such then was the story of law and modern judiciary in Iran. Assuming, as I do, that the same story is true as well of the other elements in the package of modernization, we get a deep and clear insight into the events which have been unfolding in Iran after the 1978 revolution. For no matter how one might wish to look at it, this bloody aftermath, which is of much greater sociological significance than the revolution itself, seems to make one point clear: notwithstanding the tedious efforts of the past 150 years, however sincere and well-meaning, the things introduced into the country in the package of modernity, never penetrated, in the attitudinal and cultural sense of the term, beneath the surface of society, and the revolution of 1978 was only a gate-opening for the rejection and throwing-out of all foreign elements which had been explanted into the society without gaining any root.

Notes

Author's Note 1. Professor Duncan MacRae Jr and Andy B Dicyan both read an early draft of this chapter and made valuable corrections. To both of these dear friends the author wishes to express gratitude, and to Professor MacRae his special thanks for continuous support and encouragement.

Author's Note 2. Non-English terms and names, unless they are commonly established or determined by the rules of quotation, are transliterated as they are pronounced in Persian, thus, for example, *Malik osh-Shoara* (not *Malik al-Shoara*); *wan-Nozom* (not *wa al-Nodon*); but note *qadi* (and not according to the Persian pronunciation: *qazi*).

Author's Note 3. Some important laws and law books are abbreviated as shown in the following list:

BC: The Belgian Constitution. Cf. Note 105.

CN: *Code Napoleon* (The French Civil Code). Cf. Note 119.

CPI: Civil Procedure Code of Iran. Cf. Note 134.

FL: The Fundamental Law. Cf. Note 105.

FPC: The French Penal Code. Cf. Note 126.

M: *Majmueh-ye Mosavvabat-e Majlis-e Taqniniyyeh* (Compilation of the Laws Passed by the Majlis). Cf. Note 76.

Q: *Majmueh-ye Qavanin-ye Salyaneh* (Annual Compilation of Laws). Cf. Note 97.

QJ: *Qanun-e Jaza* (Penal Code). Cf. Note 125.

QM: *Qanun-e Madani* (Civil Code). Cf. Note 116.

S: Supplement to the Fundamental Law. Cf. Note 105.

Notes on the Text

1 For the discussion of the term in the sense used here, see Rheinstein, 1956: 31–40.

2 These consist of daily prayers, religious taxes, fasting, pilgrimage to the Makkah and the holy war.

3 For example, of the 451-page *Resalah* (Khomeini, 1963) prepared as a daily manual for his followers (*moqallids*), 70% (pp. 112–322) is devoted to *Ibadat*, 20% (pp. 323–412) to *Moamalat* in the general sense we have used here, and the remaining 10% to such miscellaneous subjects as the conditions of *taqlid* (the preferential adoption and following of the views and action of a religious authority called *mojtahid*) (pp. 1–5), hunting, edible animals, religious pledge (*nazr*), etc. (pp. 413–451).

4 Of the voluminous literature on this subject, see Schacht, 1955a: 34–38; Cahen, 1975: 307; Coulson, 1964: 21–35.

5 The oldest of these schools was the Hanafi school. It was founded in Kufah, Iraq, hitherto a domain of the Sassanid empire, by a man of Persian descent, Abu Hanifa (699–767). He is known as the leader of *Ahl or-Raay* (advocates of rational reasoning) in the Islamic jurisprudence. The counterpart of this school was the Maliki School. Founded in Madinah and by a native of the city, Malik ibn Anas (711–795), it represented an opposite, conservative approach to jurisprudence, and championed the cause of *Ahlol Hadith* (Traditionalists). For a thorough discussion of those early schools, see Schacht, 1959: 6–10, 21–35; Coulson, 1964: 36–55.

6 Schacht, 1955a: 54. Shafei's theory is best discussed in his *Risalah* (1961); for a summary of his theory, see Coulson, 1964: 53–56; Schacht, 1959: 11–20 and *passim*; Schacht, 1964: 45–48.

7 These included the Hanbali and Zaheri Schools, founded respectively by Ahmed ibn Hanbal (780–855) and Dawud ibn Khalaf (815–883). While both objected to the use of human reasoning in law, the latter went so far as "to rely exclusively on the literal (*zaheri*) meaning of the Koran and Tradition," rejecting not only "the free exercise of personal opinion which had been customary before Shafii, but even the use of analogical and systematic reasoning which Shafei had retained." (Schacht, 1964: 63).

8 As the eighth century was the Golden Age of the development of the Sharia, the ninth century was the century of the Traditions. In this century an unprecedented effort began of sifting, external criticism (*isnad*) and compilation of *Hadith* and the most famous of

the many collections, namely the *Sahih* of al-Bokhari (810–870) and the *Sahih* of Moslim (821–875) were produced.

9 These were the Syrian school of Al-Awzai (707–774), its rival Iraqi school of Sofyan ath-Thowri (715–778), the school which was founded by the Quran commentator at-Tabari (839–923) and also the Zaheri school mentioned in Note 7 above.

10 That *Imam* Jaafar as-Sadiq was a man of profound erudition and a fully qualified *mojtahid* has been attested to by practically all of the *Sunni* writers, and even such a man as Abu Hanifa is said to have studied under him. Similarly, many of the Shii *imams* are among the "chains of transmitters" of *Hadith* for the Sunni Traditionalists. What is in dispute, however, is whether these holy men, pious and reclusive as most of them were, especially in the early centuries of Islam, published any work, and if they did, whether any part of it has survived. The painstaking efforts of the Shii scholars, especially after the Safavid period, in this regard have not been taken as conclusive by the *Sunni* writers and by the Western scholars as well. Cf. e.g. Schacht, 1959: 262–268; on the development of the Shii *Fiqh*, see also Coulson, 1964: 103–119; Fyzee, 1955: 113–131; 1964: *passim*.

11 This is seen for example in the law of inheritance, in the ritual of ablution, in the meaning of the term "*olol-amr*" (rulers) to whom obedience is ordered by the Quran, and in many other verses in the Quran which concern the disputed issues, or which the *Shiis* quote to prove their views.

12 Schacht, 1959: 262; Vesey-Fitzgerald, 1955: 109–110. In these formative years, the Shii *Fiqh* owes much of its success to three most eminent divines: Mohammad ibn Yaaqub al-Koleyni (d. 941); Ibn Babaweyh, Mohammad ibn Ali known as Shikh-e Saduq (932–992); and Mohammad ibn Hasan Tusi, Shikh ot-Tariqah (995–1067). In subsequent years there appeared other prominent jurors of which the followings are the most well-known: Najm od-Din Jaafar ibn Yahya, known as Mohaqqiq-e Avval (d. 1277); Shams od-Din Mohammad ibn Jamal od-Din Makki Ameli, Shahid-e Avval (1333–1384); and Zeyn od-Din Ali ibn Ahmad Ameli, Shahid-e Thani-e (1506–1557).

13 Notwithstanding the long and controversial debate over the influence of the Roman law on the Sharia, there is increasing evidence that the Persian influence on the early Islamic development went far beyond purely administrative matters. It is a well-known fact, for instance, that by order of the second caliph, Omar, a great many Sassanian fiscal and administrative laws, were retained; and furthermore, as we see in the celebrated work of Arthur Christensen, there are interesting similarities between the Islamic and the Zoroastrian jurisprudence of the Sassanid period. Particu-

lary interesting are such common elements as the concept of consensus, the nature and type of law and crime (that which is against God and that which is against people) and others. Cf. Christensen, 1944: 299–313, esp. 303, 305. Ever since William Jones raised the question of the influence of Roman law on the Sharia in his book (1781), the issue has been debated, and today a voluminous literature exists on the matter. In general, it is reckoned that the influence on the Sharia in its formative periods has much more from the Persian than from the Roman law. Cf., e.g., Schacht, 1950: 9–17; 1956; Vesey-Fitzgerald, 1951: 81–102; Hamidullah, 1973; Mazaheri, 1961.

14 On the role of the *ulama* in Iran in recent times, see, eg., Algar, 1969; Fischer, 1980.

15 Schacht, 1955b. Even the family which has been regarded as one of the most exclusive domains of the Sharia is shown by recent researchers to be dominated by customary law in many parts of the Moslem world. Cf. Anderson, 1976; 10–13; Abu-Zohra, 1955: 132–178; Coulson, 1964: 135–138.

16 The most debated here are the Islamic penal and criminal laws which are basically, to use the famous Durkheimean classification, "repressive," implying a sort of "innate" criminality. Other areas include family law, laws of inheritance, marriage and slavery. Cf. Durkheim, 1933. For an analysis and explanation of these issues in the Sharia, see Fazlur Rahman, 1980: 451–465; the essence of Rahman's argument is that the Islamic law on these issues must be viewed on two levels: legal (formal) and moral (informal). According to him, slavery and polygamy are condoned officially but not acceptable morally!

17 "Ye who believe! *Be ye staunch in justice*, witnesses for Allah, *even though it be against yourselves or (your) parents or (your) kindred, whether (the case be of) a rich man or a poor man*, for Allah is nearer unto both (than ye are). So *follow not passion lest ye lapse (from truth)* and if ye lapse or fall away, then lo! Allah is ever informed of what ye do. (The Quran IV: 135, Italics mine; see also IV: 58, V: 8, XI: 85, XVI: 90) To the same effect, there are also great many *Hadiths* from the Prophet Mohammad. In one case, for example, he is quoted by al-Bokhari to have said: "The people before you were only lost because they used to apply the law on the weak and poor and leave the strong and the rich" (quoted in Boisard, 1980: 441).

18 In the letter, Omar writes to the governor: "Understand the depositions that are made before you and decide on the basis of proof. . . . Treat all litigants equally in your court and in your attention, so that the noble will not expect you to be partial and the humble will not despair of justice from you. . . . Beware of [showing] annoyance, impatience and vexation on account of parties

in assemblies of justice for which God rewards and beautifies what is yet to come [hereafter]." For the full text of the letter and of the voluminous literature on it, see Ibn Khaldun, 1958, I: 453–454; Hamidullah, 1971: 1–50; Margoliouth, 1910: 307–326; Tyan, 1938, I: 106–113.

19 Drawing attention to the historical significance of these developments, Marcel A. Boisard has observed (1980: 440): "Until the Crusades, legal procedure in the West consisted of 'God's judgements' by boiling water or by duel or by 'ordeal' during which people were burned with red-hot irons or boiling oil, and, if they survived, declared 'not guilty.' In contrast, we have only to quote the instructions given by Omar in the seventh century to the Moslem judges to show what a chasm separated the two conceptions: "Only decide on the basis of proof, be kind to the weak . . ."

20 For a brief analysis of this aspect of the Islamic legal system, see Nawaii, 1974: esp. 189–343; Schacht, 1964: 120–134; Coulson, 1964: 120–134.

21 As reported by Ibn Khaldun (1958, I: 453), Omar "appointed Abud-Darda to be judge with him in Madinah, he appointed Shurayh as judge in al-Basrah and Abu Musa al-Ashari as judge in al-Kufah. On appointing (Abu Musa), he wrote him the famous letter . . ." We do know, however, that even during the lifetime of the Prophet at least 130 of the Companions acted occasionally as judges and of these, seven – Omar, Ali, Abdollah ibn Masud, Ayesha, Zeyd ibn Thabit, Abdollah ibn Abbas and Abdollah ibn Omar – were the most famous. These, however, were not formally appointed to the job and were referred to, with the consent of the Prophet, simply because of their recognized command over the Islamic principles. Cf. Coulson, 1964: 23–26; Nawaii, 1974: 211–212.

22 The title of *Qadil-Qodat* (literally Judge of the Judges) has, especially in some contemporary writings, been sometimes confused by another similar concept, *aqdal-qodat* (the most judicious judge). That the former position was higher and entailed a wider responsibility can be seen in such classical writings as, eg., Nakhjavani, 1934; 329. Cf. Baghdadi, 1936: 46–59; Beyhaghi, 1945: 173, 198, 210; Schacht, 1955b: 58–59; Tyan, 1938, I: 176 ff.

23 On the appointment of local judges in Iran, see Zarrinkub, 1975, :81.

24 Very briefly, these functions, as they existed in the post-Safavid Iran, were the offices of (1) the *mojtahid*, the highest religious authority, called *ayatollah* in present day Iran; (2) the *mofti*, who, especially in the Sunni world, issued *fatva* (legal opinion) on the basis of the code of the school to which he belonged; (3) the *sadr os-sodur*, the *Pontifex Maximus* of the Safavid court, corresponding to the Abbasid chief *qadi* and to the Ottoman Grand *Mofti*; (4) the

sheykhol Islam, a top religious official appointed by the ruler sometimes equal to the grand *mofti*. Besides, there were great many other functionaries of lower rank but nonetheless very important, such as the leaders of weekend prayers (*imam jomeh*), the preachers (*voaaz*) and others. Cf. Malcolm, 1815, I: 438 ff.; Sami, 1943: 120 ff; Saleh, 1969: 214–222.

25 On the *mazalim* courts, see Amedroz, 1911: 635–674; Mawardi, 1966: 77 ff.; Abu-Yaala, 1938: 60 ff. On this practice in the Sassanid courts, see also Christensen, 1944: 299–303.

26 Lambton, 1968: 227 (reference is made by the author to Amedroz, 1911: 655).

27 These names include, for example, *divan-e aala* (supreme court), *divan khaneh* (house of judiciary), *mahkameh* (tribunal), *adalat khaneh* (house of justice), etc.; and the specific functions which developed in these courts included *vakilol-jaraim* (criminal prosecutor) later called *divan begi*, *vakil or-reaya* (public prosecutor or the attorney of the subjects), *shahneh* (chief of the police), *kalantar* (magistrate), *darugheh* (sheriff), and many others. Cf. Malcolm, 1815, I: 437; Anvari, 1976.

28 *Istihsan* and *istislah* were two very similar mechanisms used in the Hanafi and Maliki schools, respectively, in settling a rule of *Fiqh* in conformity with the requirements of every day life, equity, social conditions and general public interest even though such a rule runs counter to the implications of a *qiyas*. Cf. Schacht, 1964: 152, 155, 157.

29 For instance, to evade the Sharia ban on "interest" (*riba*), the creditor, instead of lending the capital with an interest, would buy something from the debtor for the exact amount of the capital payable in cash, and then resell it to him for a price amounting to the capital plus the interest, payable in a future date. In the colloquial Persian today, this is referred to as "*kolah-e* sharii" which means, literally, a "Sharia hat." Cf. Schacht, 1955b: 78; 1964: 78–82; Coulson, 1964: 139–141.

30 Literally, *yasa* means "decree." Here, it refers to a code which is said to have originally been compiled in 1205 when Genghiz Khan invaded China. In 1219 after Genghiz Khan's forces invaded Iran the *yasa* went into effect and subsequently replaced the Quran by the decree of Genghiz Khan. It remained in force in Iran for about three centuries. Cf. Dareste, 1926: 265; Iqbal, 1933, I: 78.

31 In 1295, Ghazan Khan, a grandson of Genghiz, came to power. He embraced Islam, declared independence from the Mongul emperor and issued a host of *yerlighs* (decrees) which dealt with a variety of issues from procedural law to the rights of peasants. In these decrees there is a notable return to the Sharia, although in several points reference is also made to the *Yasa*. The *Tozuks* of Tamerlane are

discussed in Tamerlane, 1963, although the authenticity of the book has been doubted. Cf. Browne, 1951, III: 183–184. On these and other codes, see Saleh, 1969: 173–208.

32 Riesman, 1952. Although Riesman's trichotomy – inner-directed, other-directed and traditional-directed – was coined to characterize individuals, I find it useful in characterization of societies at different stages of their development or in comparison to other societies.

33 From a stanza of Abu Talib Kalim Kashani (d. 1650) who apparently, due to religious persecution of the Safavid regime, emigrated to India and became the *Malik osh-Shoara* (Master Poet) of the Shah Jihan's court. The verse in question reads: "*Kalim az hind delgiri nadarad. Pas az olfat qafas ham ashiyan ast.*" It means: "Kalim has no grief in India. After getting used to, a cage is a nest." Cf. Kashani, 1957: 131.

34 From the speech of Matin-Daftari, as quoted in Saleh, 1969: 234–235. On the history and abuses of capitulary privileges in Iran, see Matin-Daftari 1930; on the history and effects of capitulation in the Islamic world and its bearings for legal reform, see Liebesny, 1955: 309–333.

35 Thus in April 1846, the governments of Russia and England asked the government of Iran to take strict measures to abolish what Lord Curzon (1892, I: 456) called: "savage punishments and abominable tortures." Following this, Haji Mirza Aqasi, the old and ineffective prime minister of Mohammad Shah, issued an order to the governers and other officials to that effect, but of course nothing changed. In the early days of Amir Kabir's premiership, the same two governments repeated the demand (17 January 1850) which, as we know today, was among the first priorities of Amir Kabir's reform program. Cf. Adamiyat, 1975: 312–313.

36 Thus, in a diplomatic report to Mirza Said Khan, the foreign minister, dated 18 December 1882, the Iranian ambassador to Turkey, Mirza Mohsin Khan Moinol Mamalik (later Moshir od-Dowleh), one of the leading advocates of legal reform, quotes the British ambassador as having said: "If I had a cat, I would not send it to your courts, let alone a British subject or merchant." When ten years later, in January 1892, the same Moshir od-Dowleh became the Minister of Justice, he wrote a disturbing report to the Shah and called his attention to the disgraceful fact that in the disputes between Iranian and foreign subjects the officials of the Foreign Ministry of Iran "on sheer expectation of reward or for fear of losing their positions, deliberately violate the rights of their fellow citizens in favour of the other party . . . [and in these] litigations . . . the judge, in reality, is the representative of the [foreign] embassy [and] not the head of the court." (Quoted in Adamiyat, 1976: 15n, 17)

37 On the voluminous literature on these developments in Ottoman Turkey, Egypt and other Islamic countries, see Anderson, 1950–51; 1954: 29–40; 1976; 1957: 13–40; Liebesny, 1975: 46 ff.; 1967: 16–34; Onar, 1955: 292–308.

38 He reports with utmost interest that ". . . no Englishman, unless guilty of a breach of the laws, can be seized or punished at the caprice or from the gust of passion of magistrates: he may sometimes be confined on suspicion, but his life can not be affected, except on positive proof" (1810, I: 262–263). For his detailed account of government and judiciary system in England, see ibid. Chap. 15 and II; Chaps. 17, 20, *passim*. See also 1973: 231–233, 239 ff., 263 and esp. 278–279.

39 Outraged about the country's system of justice administration he wrote deploringly: ". . . there is no single textbook of law; neither crime has a definite punishment nor righteousness a discernible reward; neither the Sharia courts have a registry nor the secular tribunals any recording. In short, there is no law, no organization, nor specific authority in this system, and, instead, it is the caprice that reigns supreme." (quoted in Adamiyat, 1970: 139). On his thought, see also Hairi 1977: 243 ff.

40 This work constitutes pp. 1–52 of Malkom's collected works (1948). On the life and work of Malkom, see Algar, 1973; Nuraei, 1973.

41 These general headings, 24 in all, are numbered from 1 to 74 with many missing in between. Apparently the author had intended the booklet to be a first draft which was to be completed later.

42 For example in 1896, he wrote a long letter to the Shah and told him that "the deficiencies and the conditions of our system of justice are the greatest source of scorn in the eyes of Europeans. . . . More than anything else, these conditions of justice must be attended to; for the development of the nation, the power of the government and independence of monarchy [all] depend on a single base: the administration of justice" (quoted in Safaei, 1970: 126).

43 A great many of these writings are collected and examined in Adamiyat and Natiq, 1977.

44 It began in the early days of the Fathali Shah (1797–1834) and was followed in 1810–20s by more serious efforts by the able crown prince, Abbas Mirza, in the areas of military, public health, etc. On these, see e.g., Mostowfi, 1945, I: 37–39; Algar, 1969: 75–79; Najmi, 1957.

45 On his life and service, see Adamiyat, 1975; Iqbal, 1962.

46 For instance, traditionally, the Sharia courts gave very favourable treatment to the new converts especially on the matter of inheritance and civil disputes, and this had been a problem for the minorities (Jews, Christians and Zoroastrians) whose opportunistic members often used this device as a means of violating the rights of

others. Amir Kabir not only took these matters out of the Sharia courts, but also, to prevent possible local influences, ordered them to be dealt with exclusively at the Tehran Grand Tribunal. He also ordered to be brought before the regular secular courts all disputes between Iranian and foreign subjects which were traditionally "settled" in the Ministry of Foreign Affairs. (Adamiyat, 1975: 309–311. See also p. 20 above.)

47 A *molla* (a low-ranking member of the *ulama*) who had accepted bribes and who had given false testimony was severely punished as he was publicly stripped of his religious attire and his head disgracefully shaved. Similarly after Amir Kabir received a message from a prominent Sharia judge, Shaykh Abd or-Rahim Brujerdi, that on a pending dispute the judge was willing to comply with the wishes of the prime minister, Amir Kabir was extremely angered and immediately replaced him with Shaykh Abdol Hoseyn Tehrani. known as Shaykhol Araqayn. (Adamiyat, 1975: 308. See also Algar, 1969: 129–136.)

48 This took place on 30 August 1858. The Shah not only dismissed the prime minister and his aides but angrily dissolved the post of premier. For the quotations from the decree, see Adamiyat, 1972; 54.

49 The constitution and the procedural rules are reprinted and discussed respectively in Adamiyat, 1972: 57–63; Adamiyat & Natiq, 1977: 189–220 (the text of the rules appears on pp. 191–195).

50 It even initiated a regular bulletin, *Ruznameh*, on its activities, and there appeared several long and independent reports on its shortcomings and improvement. Cf. Adamiyat & Natiq, 1977: 200–206.

51 For the text of the decree, see Damaghani, 1966: 56–57.

52 Nothing can illustrate this phenomenon more clearly than the argument over the use of official stationery which took place in the assembly: "In the foreign [European] countries, legal documents are automatically considered binding if they are presented on official stationeries . . . and whoever presents a claim on such official papers need no further legal action [to substantiate his case]. In this Sublime Islamic Government, however, since all disputes are settled in the presence of the *ulama* and by the means of oral testimonies and proofs . . . it is immaterial whether the claim is presented on a governmental [official] paper or not . . . [thus] if [we] require the *ulama* to write their legal decisions on official papers, it is probable that they would create problems." Cf. *Ruznameh-ye Maslahat Khaneh*, Shavval 20, 1276 (Lunar) (13 May, 1860) quoted in Adamiyat & Natiq, 1977: 201.

53 Malkom Khan, 1948: 51. For the suggestions of Malkom Khan, see pp. 99–100 above.

54 For the text of the decree, see Farhad-Moatamad, 1947: 39–43. See also Mostowfi, 1945, I: 136; Bastani–Parizi, 1968: 512.

55 He was Haj Ali Khan Maraghe-ie Eatemad os-Saltaneh, an aide to the notorious prime minister, Mirza Aqa Khan Nuri, with whom he had been angrily dismissed by the Shah in August, 1858 (cf. Note 48 above and Adamiyat, 1972: 54, 81–82).

56 From the new manual (*dasturol amal*) issued by the new minister in December, 1862. Cf. ibid.: 81, n82.

57 On the life of this remarkable man, see Farhad–Moatamad, 1947

58 Like Malkom Khan with whom we have already dealt, Mirza Yusof Khan was also a staunch advocate of judiciary reform in Iran. He had served in diplomatic posts in Russia and France and was thoroughly familiar with developments in Europe. In 1870 he wrote a commentary on the French constitution whose very title, *Yek Kalimah* ("One Word") is meant to refer to the term "law" as a one-worded prescription for the ills of Iran. On his life and ideas, cf. Hairi, 1977: 30–36; Adamiyat, 1961: 182–198.

59 Cf. Sani od-Dowleh, 1876–78, III: 133.

60 The text of the first decree appears in English translation in two diplomatic dispatches from Tehran to the British Foreign Office: No. 27, 20 March 1871 and No. 45, 18 April 1871. See (British) Foreign Office Archives (FO) 60/333–334. On the text of the second decree, see Farhad–Moatamad, 1947: 43–44; also Bakhash, 1978: 415; Adamiyat, 1972: 174–187.

61 For an analysis of the letters of complaint written to this tribunal from 1882 to 1883, see Adamiyat & Natiq, 1977: 375–413.

62 Amin od-Dowleh's letter to Malkom Khan (1882), quoted in Adamiyat, 1976: 13. See also Molk Ara's account of the failure (1982: 176).

63 On the conflict between the government and the Majlis on the Constitution, see Adamiyat, 1976: 385–409.

64 There is a visible influence on the Fundamental Law from the writings of the nineteenth century especially the proposals of Mirza Malkom Khan as discussed pp. 99–100 above.

65 On the date and immediate events leading to the establishment of this cabinet, see Kasravi 1940: 163–173; the dispatch No. 205, 1 August, 1906 of the British Embassy in Tehran to the Foreign Office as translated in Hasan Moasir, 1968: 76–77.

66 The committee was established in November 1906 and included Mirza Hoseyn Khan Moatamanol Molk Pir-niya, who is said to have written the chart of the Ministry of Justice, and whose brother Mirza Hasan Khan Moshir od-Dowleh later played a very important role in the history of Iranian legal reform. Cf. Adamiyat, 1976: 409n.

67 Though he later joined the reactionary camp, he was an active member of the first Majlis and played a key role in the writing of the

Supplement. Cf. Safaei, 1966; Kirmani, 1967, I: 146, 291, 303, II: 20–22, 92, 405, *passim*.

68 Mirza Hoseyn was sent to Paris for education and was called home at the time of his brother's recall from Russia. From the second to the sixth Majlis, he was elected from Tehran and served as the president of the Majlis with tremendous ability and effectiveness. Cf. Safaei, 1965: 715–733.

69 In 1920 the name of the school was changed to "school of law" and in 1934, when Tehran University was established, it became part of the university and constituted its Faculty of Law. Cf. Bastani-Parizi, 1968: 79–83, 505–524.

70 Though the cabinet began on 19 July 1909, that is, three days after the capture of Tehran, it was not officially instituted till 14 September 1909. It was headed by Mohammed Vali Khan Tonokaboni, *Sepahdar*, who had been the commander of the Northern revolutionary forces. Cf. Safaei, 1965; 287–313, esp. 301; Navaei, 1976: 137–146, esp. 153–155.

71 Altogether, these consisted of (1) the ill-fated cabinet of Nasirol Molk which began on 20 May 1909 and ended with the dethronement of Mohammad Ali Shah on 16 July 1909; (2) a good portion of cabinets of the above-mentioned *Sepahdar*: 1 December 1909 – 20 May 1910 and 12 March – 17 July 1911; and (3) the first cabinet of Semsam os-Saltaneh Bakhtyari: 26 July – 29 November 1911. Cf. Navaei, 1976: 131, 153, 228, 253; Bastani-Parizi, 1968: 517.

72 This act was against the terms of that newly-adopted constitution and contrary to the expectations people had of Moshir od-Dowleh. But on this and similar occasions, he, unlike his equally respected brother Mirza Hoseyn Khan Moatamanol Molk Pir-niya, resorted to a legal device saying "I want the country for the constitution and not other way around." Cf. Bastani-Parizi, 1968: 513, 520–521; Bahar, 1942: 306; Alavi, 1952: 516.

73 One of the most interesting features of the constitutional history of Iran is the decreasing role of the *ulama* in the Majlis. For instance, in the first five sessions of the Majlis (1906–1925) their number among the "freshmen" deputies, i.e. those who had entered the Majlis for the first time, ranged from 32% to 18% with an average of 23%. In the eight subsequent Majlis which constituted the Reza Shah period (1925–1941) their number, which was 25% in the first (6th Majlis), reached zero in the last (13th Majlis) and averaged less than 11% for the whole period. Fluctuating between 3% and 0%, the trend continued in the post-Reza Shah era, the only exception being the 17th Majlis, the Mossadiq period, when the number of *ulama* among the freshmen jumped to a high of 20% and thus raised their average for the eight sessions of the period (14–21) to 11%. Cf. Nezami, 1968: 216 ff.

74 In the 1939 revision, this title of the code which is Arabic and ambiguous was changed to a more precise Persian term: "Aein Dadrasi Madani" (civil procedure) which became the title of the book of Matin-Daftari who had introduced the term; cf. 1948, I: 12.

75 The Organization Code was passed on 19 July 1911, and the Civil Procedures on 20 September and 12 November. Cf. Matin-Daftari, ibid.: 9; Foroughi, 1936: 973; Bastani-Parizi, 1968: 514; Mokhtari, 1946: 419.

76 Cf. *Majmueh-ye Mosavvabat-e Majlis-e Taqniniyyeh* (Compilation of the Laws Passed by the Majlis), I (covering the first to the fourth Majlis): 305–383. The subsequent volumes of this series are devoted one to each Majlis: hereinafter they will be referred to as M1-4 for the first volume; M5, M6, etc. for the other volumes.

77 The permission for this employment was granted by the Majlis on 18 May 1911. Cf. M1-4: 494–498; Bastani-Parizi, 1968: 514, 517.

78 The other members of the committee were Sayyed Nasr ol-lah Taqavi, Mohammad Ali Forughi and Mirza Reza Naeini.

79 The first draft of this law was passed on 19 May 1910. It was modified on 25 May and in the following year. Cf. M1-4: 385; Matin-Daftari, 1948, I: 9, 56.

80 Taqizadeh, 1959: 66. For a thorough examination of the Russian and British involvement in Iran, see Kazemzadeh, 1968.

81 For a concise examination of Reza Khan's ascension to power, see Wilber 1975; Makki, 1944–46.

82 In the fourth Majlis, this permission took place on 14 January 1921 and in the fifth, on 1 December 1924. Cf. M1-4: 568–569; M5: 15–16.

83 Cf. Zanganeh, n.d.: 7. The author's assertion that this was passed by the fourth Majlis is incorrect, as he himself tells in the same passage that it was passed in 1303–04 which correspond to the time of the fifth Majlis: see also M1-4: 385n.

84 For details, see *Salnameh-ye Pars*, 1927: 1–12; 1928: 1 ff.

85 For a concise treatment of Reza Shah's reforms, see Banani, 1961; Wilber 1975.

86 M6: 19–20. This authorization was renewed on 18 June 1928.

87 M6: 34–35. This was a four-article bill and was passed on 17 December 1927. It recognized 11 grades. Each grade qualified an incumbent for 50 *tumans* plus one-fourth of the cumulative amount earned in the preceding grades. This was an obvious improvement over a 1923 law (cf. p. 114 above) which recognized only 9 salary levels and much less favourable conditions.

88 M6: 49–61. This law consisted of 50 articles and was passed on 19 March 1928. It clearly shows the tremendous influence which the *ulama* still had. For as we read in the Article 3, the applicants for the judiciary functions specified were required to have a high degree of

knowledge in such Islamic sciences as logic, *Fiqh* and jurisprudence, in addition to modern fields such as civil law, constitutional law, international law, penal law and various procedural laws. Cf. also the law concerning the transfer from the executive to the judiciary ranks, which was passed on 21 July 1928, in M7: 157–158.

89 M6: 62–68. This consisted of 17 articles and was ratified on 20 March 1928.

90 M6: 118–119. This was a single article with two supplements.

91 M6: 126–130. This consisted of 15 articles and was passed on 7 July 1928.

92 M6: 159–246. This consisted of 282 articles and was passed on 21 July 1928.

93 Both the Organization Code (118 articles) and Code of Civil Procedure (308 articles) were revisions of the earlier codes which had been prepared by Moshir od-Dowleh on 12 September 1911. They were ratified on 18 July 1928. Cf. M6: 134–157; M8: 196, art. 22; Matin-Daftari, 1948, I: 10–11, *passim.*

94 M6: 117: "The government," says the Act, "is permitted, as of Ordibehesht 20, 1307 [10 May 1928] when the capitulation system is to be annulled, to put in practice the Civil Code which it submitted to the *Majlis Shura-ye Melli* till the Judiciary Committee of the Majlis declares its definite opinion on the matter."

95 Like the second, the sixth Majlis was very important in the history of legal reform in Iran. Besides the laws mentioned in the text, the sixth Majlis also made important revisions of the existing laws such as the commercial code and a code requiring, for the first time, official registration of real estates. Cf. M6: 39–42, 126.

96 M7: 71–73; M10: 98–100. According to the new law, no one could be employed as a judge without having a degree in law from either the newly established Tehran University or from a foreign university. As for those who had been employed before and lacked such a degree, they were required to take an examination on the Iranian and European laws and, if successful, could continue their work but in any event could not rise above the rank of sixth in the eleven-grade promotional scale which was established in 1928. Cf. Note 88 above; Matin-Daftari, 1948, I: 11.

97 Shayegan, 1943: 37–38; Saleh, 1964: 993; *Majmueh-ye Qavanin-e Salyaneh* (Annual Compilation of Laws), 1934/*1313*, Section I: 102. The latter is an annual series which began appearing in 1928/*1307* and continued until early 1950s (*1330s*), containing all laws – acts of the Majlis and government regulations – of a given year in a single volume. Notwithstanding the slight variation of the titles in the Persian, these volumes will hereinafter be referred to as *Q1307*/1928, etc.

98 For instance, the consent of the litigants which in the 1929 version of

the code (arts. 127, 146–147, 165, 203, 291, 297, 311, 383) had been considered as a necessary prerequisite for the convening and repetition of the court hearing was omitted or repealed. Similarly, the rule of 1939 (art. 166) that the turn of a case would be missed with the absence of either of the parties was replaced by another one, requiring the court to pass a judgement in any event. Cf. Matin-Daftari, 1955: II; 3.

99 Cf. Saleh, 1964: 988. For a detailed list of these legislations, most of which were introduced by Hadi Hedayati, see the daily *Ettelaat* 1960.

100 It was promulgated by the joint judiciary committees of both Houses on 27 April 1960. Cf. Saleh, 1964: 996.

101 Art. 17 of the law on *Shura-ye Davari* which, with its subsequent revisions (26 articles), is printed in Kamangar, n.d.: 597–621.

102 For the text of the related law with all of its revisions, see Kamangar, n.d.: 610–612.

103 The law on *Shura-ye Davari*, Kamangar, n.d. arts. 2, 11–15.

104 For the text with latest revisions (27 articles), see Kamangar, n.d.: 287–298. For an analysis, see Bagley, 1971: 47–64; Anderson, 1971: 16–27.

105 Except for minor amendments in 1925, 1957 and 1964, the Fundamental Law, 1906, and its Supplement (hereinafter referred to as FL and S respectively) remained unchanged until the 1978 revolution. For the English translation of these documents and of the Belgian Constitution (hereinafter referred to as BC), see Peaslee, 1966, II: 449–470 and III: 72–92 respectively. In the following discussion, quotations and references of FL and S will be from the original Persian text as printed in Saleh, 1969: 734–767.

106 This document, called *Nezam-nameh-ye Intekhabat* (Election Law) was promulgated on 9 September 1906, and was the first act which followed the Constitutional Decree issued by the Shah on 4 August 1906; for the text, see M1-4: 36–44. Cf. BC, Heading III, Section II: Concerning the House of Representatives.

107 During the revolution, the progressive wing of the *ulama* attempted to reconcile the Western constitutional theory with the doctrine of *imamate*. The most famous and successful of these attempts was made by a qualified Ayatollah, Mohammad Hoseyn Naeini, who for years had lived in Ottoman Turkey. In 1909 he wrote his *Tanbihol Omma va Tanzihol Milla* which won him considerable recognition. For an analysis, see Hairi, 1977; Adamiyat, 1976: 228–275.

108 On the struggle between the constitutionalists and the government over the constitution, see, e.g., Adamiyat, 1976: 383–408.

109 The few divergences from the BC are: arts. 1 and 2 dealing with religion, art. 17 which prevents action against the feudal land lords, art. 35 on the nature of monarchy and art. 63 which forbids granting

honorary ministerial titles. For similarities, the following examples would perhaps suffice: S, art. 3 = BC, art. 23; S, arts. 4–5 = BC, arts. 125–126; S, art. 6 = BC, art. 128; S, arts. 7 = BC, art. 130; S, arts. 8–16 = BC, arts. 6–12; S, arts. 18–21 = BC, arts. 17–19; S, arts. 71–85 = BC, arts. 92–103; S, arts. 87–93 = BC, arts. 105–108; S, arts. 94–107 = BC, arts. 110–120.

110 S, art. 2; while the first article of the Supplement met the opposition of many deputies and many groups outside the Majlis, its second article was opposed by the conservative religious groups who found it gave too much. It was on this issue that the prominent Ayatollah Sheykh Fazlollah Nuri defected from the ranks of the pre-constitutionalist *ulama* headed by his influential rivals, Ayatollah Behbahani and Ayatollah Tabatabaie. Cf. Adamiyat, 1976: 416–417, 429–432.

111 This was one of the arguments used against the Shah in the 1978 revolution.

112 S. art. 35. This issue is missing in BC obviously for the reason that the idea of rule by Divine Right was still alive in the mind of the Persian King.

113 S, arts. 71–72; cf. BC, arts. 92–93. Thus in a diplomatic dispatch to the Foreign Office, No. 242, November 7, 1907, translating the full text of the Supplement, the British envoy in Tehran comments: "Article No. 71 ff., though ambiguous in wording – and this is deliberate – would, if put in operation, constitute a fatal blow to the judiciary powers of the clergy . . . It remains to be seen whether this drastic change would in fact be accepted by the *Mojtahids* or not.

"Article 86, which is also ambiguous in wording, makes all court decisions, whether based on the Sharia or on *orf*, subject to appeal and review in accordance with the provisions of the Ministry of Justice. If this interpretation is correct, it is certain that the power of the *mojtahids* who rule at will would be curtailed effectively." Retranslated from the Persian in *Moasir*, 1968: 471–72. See also Taqizadeh, 1959: 54; Adamiyat, 1976: 418 ff.

114 S, art. 79; cf. BC, art. 98. It is worth noting that in the Belgian Constitution a jury is empanelled for all criminal affairs and for political and press misdemeanour. But in the Persian document, as mentioned in the text, a jury is foreseen only for "political press offences."

115 From the report of Walter Smart quoted in Adamiyat, 1976: 420–421.

116 Of the *Qanun-e Madani* there are many editions. The one used in this study, was prepared by Anvar Hamidi (1959). Reference to this code will hereinafter be made as QM.

117 The Shii *Fiqh* texts used were *Sharh-e Lomeh* and *Sharh-e Makasib*. The other sources included Sheykh Abdol Karim Hilli's *Al-Ahkamol Jaafariyyah*. Cf. Shayegan, 1943: 38.

118 The *Majallatol Ahkamil Adliyyah*, generally known as the *Majallah*, was the Ottoman Civil Code which was promulgated in 1876. It was based on the Hanafi *Fiqh* and was in force in Syria till 1944. Cf. Anderson, 1954: 29; Liebesny 1967: 20–24. See also p. 98 above.

119 The source book: *Code Napoleon* or the *French Civil Code*, 1960, literally translated from the original and official edition published in Paris in 1804, by a Barrister of the Inner Temple. This code is hereinafter referred to as CN.

120 In CN, this is Chapter VI of Title III of Book III and consists of articles 1315 to 1369 (56 articles); in QM, it is made up of 79 articles (from 1257 to 1335).

121 For instance, QM, art. 183, on the definition of contracts and agreement, is identical to CN, art. 1101. Identical or very similar are also: QN, art. 190 and CN, art. 1108 "On Conditions of Validity of Agreement"; QM, arts. 191–209 and CN, arts. 1123–1125 on capacity of contracting parties; QM, arts. 214–216 and CN, arts. 1126–1130; QM, arts. 217–218 and CN, arts. 131–133 on the cause of contract; QM, arts. 219–231 and CN, arts. 1134–1167 on the effect of obligations. The list can go on and on.

122 The text of the law appears in Kamangar, n.d.: 277–300.

123 The first group, *jenayat*, included homicide, bodily injury and damage of property, and the second category consisted of illicit sexual intercourse, slanderous allegation of unchastity, drinking alcoholic liquor, armed robbery on roads, theft and apostasy.

124 The *hodud* consisted of the death penalty, cutting off of hand and/or foot, flogging with specified number of lashes which varied for different crimes; and the *taazirs* varied from verbal reproval to flogging.

125 Published as a part of *Majmueh-ye Qavanin-e Jazaei* (Compilation of Penal Laws), 1939: 1–100. Hereinafter referred to as QJ.

126 Mueller, 1960: xiii. The French Penal Code is hereinafter referred to as FPC.

127 These subjects are treated in two chapters in QJ and in six in FPC, the latter being much more systematic. Examples of borrowing are non-retroactivism: QJ, art. 6 and FPC, art. 4; types of crime and punishment: QJ, arts. 7–12 and FPC, arts. 6–11; commencement of crime: QJ, arts. 20–23 and FPC, arts. 2–3; recidivism: QJ, arts. 24–25 and FPC, arts. 56–58; multiplicity of offence: QJ, arts. 31–33 and FPC, art. 5; accessories to an offence: QJ, arts. 27–30 and FPC, arts. 59–60.

128 Here, the "Felonies and Misdemeanours Against the Public Good" are discussed in three chapters in FPC and in six chapters in QJ. The first three chapters have identical titles in both: "Felonies and Misdemeanours" (1) "Against the Security of the state," (2) "Against the Constitutional Order" and finally (3) "Against the

Public Order." In both, though the length of treatment of each subject varies, the subtitles are almost identical. "Breach of Duty . . . of Civil Servant . . ." "Resistance, Disobedience and other Defiances of Public Authority" and "Unlawful Associations and Assemblies," which are treated as Sections 2, 4 and 7 of Chapter 3 of FPC, are topics of Chapters 4, 5 and 6, respectively, of Part Two of QJ. Besides the differential treatment of some subjects such as offences against the constitutional order, there are some topics which do not appear in both. Revealing among these is the "Breach of Peace by the Ministers of Religion . . ." which has been treated in FPC (see Section 3 of Part III) but not in QJ.

129 Here most of the subjects are identical. They are treated in fifteen chapters in QJ and in two chapters, of different number of sections (7 and 3, respectively), in FPC.

130 Thus according to art. 212 of QJ, a woman who is married and a man who himself or his partner are married shall be jailed, upon conviction to adultery, for a period from six months to three years.

131 The punishment for each partner is imprisonment from three months to two years, plus a fine of 36,000 to 720,000 francs for the male partner (FPC, arts. 337–338). In view of art. 339, those punishments for a man will have to be based on the charge of his partner's husband.

132 In this case the punishment is only a fine of 36,000 to 720,000 francs.

133 Act of Isfand 12, 1314 (2 March 1936), art. 1: 2 which has been printed as art. 13 of QJ.

134 *Civil Procedure Code of Iran*, translated into English by Musa Sabi (1972), art. 7. Hereinafter the Code is referred to as CPI.

135 Hence the horizontal arrangement of the General vs. Special courts. Examples of the latter were the disciplinary court, the court of commercial disputes and especially the Sharia courts. Cf. Matin-Daftari, 1948, I: 3, 64 ff.; Kamangar, 1974: 240–296; Damaghani, 1973 *passim*.

136 Hence the summary courts, the courts of first instance and the courts of appeals. Cf. CPI: arts. 8 and 13–21.

137 For example, a comparison of the Iranian and the French codes of criminal procedure (cf. Kamangar, 1974: 33–130 and Kock 1964) reveals clearly that although both have gone through many revisions and changes of their original editions, they are still very similar and in many areas even identical in legislative techniques and legal structure.

138 See his devastating criticism (1944) where he traces the origin and historical development of the creed.

139 From his editorial to the second series *Dowreh-ye Jadid* of the famous Persian periodical, *Kaveh*, 1920: 2, which was published in Berlin.

140 While disagreeing on "solutions," the massive body of literature which has cumulated on the subject – from the pioneering "Communist Manifesto" of Marx and Engels to Harold Lasswell's idea of "redressing" and penetrating analysis of Edward Shils – clearly demonstrates the staggering complexity of the problem of modernization and, by implication, the unbelievable naiveté with which such leaders as Kamal Ataturk, Reza Shah and many others approached the problem.

141 I have in mind Neil Smelser's hierarchy of structural components, the valuative, normative and operative elements, which correspond, with a slight variation, to Masaji Chiba's concept of basic, official and unofficial laws. Cf. Smelser 1962; Chiba 1979.

References

Note 1. Figures in italic at the end of the entries represent AH years which, unless otherwise specified, are of the solar calendar in use in Iran.
Note 2. On the spelling and transliteration of names and titles, see Author's Note 2, p. 140.

Abutalib, Mirza.
1810. *The Travels of Mirza Abutalib Khan in Asia, Africa and Europe, during the Years of 1799, 1800, 1801, 1802 and 1803.* transl. Charles Steward, Esq. 2 vols. London. Orig. *Masir-e Talibi ya Safar Nama-ye Mirza Abutalib Khan.* ed. Hoseyn Khadiv, Tehran: Ketabha-ye Jibi, *1352* (1973).

Abu-Yaala, Mohammad ibn Hasan.
1938. *Al-Ankham os-Soltaniyyah.* Cairo. *1357* (Lunar).

Abu-Zohra, Muhammad.
1955. Family Law. In Khadduri, *et al.*, 1955.

Adamiyat, Fereydoun.
1961. *Fikr-e Azadi va Moggaddimah-ye Nahzat-e Mashrutiyyat.* Tehran: Sokhan, *1340.*
1967. *Andisheh ha-ye Mirza Aqa Khan-e Kirmani.* Tehran: Tahuri, *1346.*
1970. *Andisheh ha-ye Mirza Fathali Akhond-zadeh.* Tehran: Kharazmi, *1349.*
1972. *Andisheh-ye Taraqqi va Hokumat-e Qanun.* Tehran: Kharazmi, *1351.*
1975. *Amir Kabir va Iran.* Tehran: Kharazmi, *1354.*
1976. *Idaolozhi-ye Nahzat-e Mashrutiyyat-e Iran.* Tehran: Payam, *1355.*

----- & Natiq, Homa.
1977. *Afkar Ijtemaei va Siyasi va Iqtesadi dar Athar-e Montashir Nashoda-ye Dowran-e Qajar.* Tehran: Agah, *1356.*

Alavi, Abol-Hasan.
1952. Rejal-e Sadr-e Mashrutiyyat. *Yaghma* 5(5), *1331.*

Algar, Hamid.
1969. *Religion and State in Iran: 1785–1909.* Berkeley: University of California Press.
1973. *Mirza Malkum Khan.* Berkeley: University of California Press.

Ali-Abadi, Abdol-Hoseyn.
1965. *Hoquq-e Jenaei.* Tehran: Tehran University Press, *1344.*

Amedroz, H. Frederick.
1911. The Mazalim Jurisdiction in Ahkam Sultaniyya of Mawardi. *Journal of Royal Asiatic Society*, 1911.

Anderson, J. N. D.
1950–51. Recent Developments in the Sharia Law. *The Muslim World* 40(4), 41(1, 2, 3, 4).
1954. The Sharia and Civil Law. *The Islamic Quarterly*, 1(1).
1957. Law as a Social Force in Islamic Culture and History. *Bulletin of the School of Oriental and Asian Studies*, 20.
1971. Reforms on Islamic Law in Iran. Iqbal Review: *Journal of the Iqbal Academy, Pakistan* 12(3).
1976. *Law Reform in the Muslim World.* London: The Athlone Press.
Anvari, Hasan.
1976. *Istelahat-e Divani.* Tehran: Tahuri, *1355.*
Baghdadi, Baha od-Din Mohammad ibn Moayyad.
1936. *At-Tavassolo ilat-Tarassol.* ed. Ahmad Bahmanyar. Tehran, *1315.*
Bagley, F. R. C.
1971. The Iranian Family Protection Law of 1967: A Milestone in the Advance of Women's Rights. In *Iran and Islam*, ed. C. E. Bosworth. Edinburgh: Edinburgh University Press.
Bahar, Mohammad Taqi, Malik-osh-Shoara.
1942. *Tarikhe-e Mokhtasar-e Ahzab-e Siyasi.* Tehran, *1321.*
Bakhash, Shaul.
1978. *Iran: Monarchy, Bureaucracy and Reform under the Qajars: 1858–1896.* London: Anchor Press.
Banani, Amin.
1961. *The Modernization of Iran: 1921–1941.* Stanford: Stanford University Press.
Bastani-Parizi, Ibrahim.
1968. *Talash-e Azadi: Mohit-e Siyasi va Zendagani-ye Moshir od-Dowleh Pir-niya.* Tehran: Ilmi, *1347.*
Beyhaghi, Abul-Fazl Mohammad ibn Hoseyn.
1945. *Tarikh-e Beyhaqi.* Qasem Ghani & Fayyaz, eds. Tehran, *1324.*
Boisard, Marcel A.
1980. On the Probable Influence of Islam on Western Public and International Law. *International Journal of Middle Eastern Studies*, 2.
Browne, E. G.
1910. *The Persian Revolution of 1905–1909.* London: The Cambridge University Press.
1951. *A Literary History of Persia.* 4 vols. Cambridge, Engl.: The University Press.
Cahen, Claude.
1975. Tribes, Cities and Social Organization. In Frye, 1975.
Chiba, Masaji.
1979. Three-Level Structure of Law in a World of Many Cultures. In *Law and the Future of Society*, Archiv für Rechts and Sozialphilosophie, Beiheft Neue Folge, Nr. 11.

Christensen, Arthur.
1944. *L'Iran sus le Sassanides.* Copenhagen: Ejnar Munksgaard.
Code Napoleon or the *French Civil Code*
1960. Los Angeles, Ca.: Claitir's Book Store.
Coulson, Noel J.
1964. *A History of Islamic Law.* Edinburgh: The University Press.
Curzon, George N.
1892. *Persia and the Persian Question.* 2 vols. London: Longmans Green.
Damaghani, Mohammad Taqi.
1966. Sad Sal Pish az In: Avaalin Mogarrat-e Dadrasi: Dasturol Amal-e Omana-ye Divankhaneh-ye Adliyyeh. *Hoquq va Mardon*, 1(4), *1345.*
1973. *Majmua-ye Qavanin-e Tejari.* Tehran: Amir-Kabir, Bahman, *1351.*
Dareste, Rodolphe.
1926. *Etudes d'histoire du droit.* Paris.
Durkheim, Émil.
1933. *Division of Labor in Society.* transl. G. Simpson. New York: The Free Press.
Esmein, A.
1968. *A History of Continental Criminal Procedure.* transl. J. Simpson. New York: Augustus M. Kelley.
Ettelaat [A Persian daily newspaper]
1960. *Dey* 19 (9 January, 1960), *1338.*
Farhad-Moatamad, Mahmud.
1947. *Moshir od-Dowleh, Sepahsalar-e Aazam.* Tehran: Ilmi, *1326.*
Fasai, Hasan.
1972. *History of Persia under Qajar Rule.* transl. Haribert Busse. New York: Columbia University Press. (Original: *Farsname-ye Naseri*).
Fazlur Rahman.
1980. A Survey of Modernization of Muslims Family Law. *International Journal of Middle Eastern Studies*, 2.
Fischer, Michael.
1980. *Iran: From Religious Dispute to Revolution.* Cambridge, Mass.: Harvard University Press.
Foroughi, Mohammad Ali.
1936. Tarikhcheh-ye Hoquq. *Majalleh-ye Talaim va Tarbiyat*, 6, *1315.*
Frye, R. N., ed.
1975. *The Cambridge History of Iran*, Vol. 4: *The Period from the Arab Invasion to the Saljugs.* Cambridge, Engl.: The University Press.
Fyzee, Asaf A. A.
1955. Shii Legal Theories. In Khadduri, *et al.* 1955.
1964. *Outline of Muhammadan Law.* London: Oxford University Press.
Hairi, Abdul-Hadi.
1977. *Shiism and Constitutionalism in Iran: A Study of the Role played*

by the Persian Residents of Iraq in Iranian Politics. Leiden: E. J. Brill.
Hamidi, Anvar, ed.
1959. *Qanun-e Madani*. Tehran: Amir Kabir, *1338*.
Hamidullah, Mohammad.
1971. Administration of Justice under the Early Caliphate. *Journal of the Pakistan Historical Society*, 19 (Pt. 1).
-----, ed.
1973. *Hal lil-Qanun ir-Rumiyy-i Taathiron alal-Fiqh il-Islamiyy-i*. Beirut: Darol Bohuth el-Islamiyyah, *1393* (Lunar).
Hedayati, Mohammad Ali.
1953. *Aein-e Dadrasi-ye Keyfari*. Tehran: Tehran University Press, *1332*.
Ibn Khaldun.
1958. *The Muqaddimah*. transl. F. Rosenthal. 3 vols. New York: Pantheon Books.
Iqbal, Abbas.
1933. *Tarikh-e Mofassal-e Iran*. 2 vols. Tehran, 1312.
1962. *Mirza Taqi Khan-e Amir Kabir*. Tehran: Tehran University Press, *1341*.
Jones, William.
1781. *An Essay on the law of Bailments*. London: C. Dilly.
Kamangar, Ahmad.
n.d. *Majmuah-ye Shomare-ye*, 1: *Qavanin-e Hoquqi*. Tehran: Javidan.
1974. *Majmuah-ye Shomare-ye*, 2: *Qavanin-e Jazaie*. Tehran: Javidan, *1353*.
Kashani, Abu Talib Kalim.
1957. *Divan*. ed. H. Partow Beyzaei. Tehran: Kitabforshi-ye Khayyam, *1336*.
Kasravi, Ahmad.
1936. *Dah Sal dar Adliyyeh*. Tehran: Peymen, *1315*.
1937. *Dadqah*. Tehran: Peymen, *1316*.
1940. *Tarikh-e Mashruteh-y Iran*, Vol. 1. 2nd ed. Tehran: Chapkhaneh-ye Taban, *1319*.
1944. *Shiagari*. Tehran, *1323*.
1945. *Qanun-e Dadgari*. Tehran: Chapkhaneh-ye Peymen, 1324.
Kaveh.
1920. *Dowreh-ye Jadid*, Vol. 5, No. 1 (Serial No. 36, 22 January 1920).
Kazemzadeh, Firuz.
1968. *Russia and Britain in Persia: 1864–1914*. New Haven: Yale University Press.
Khadduri, Majid, *et al.*, eds.
1955. *Law in the Middle East*, Vol. 1: *Origin and Development of Islamic Law*. Richmond: William Byrd Press.
Khomeini, Ayatollah Ruhollah.
1963. *Resalah*. Tehran, *1342*.

1972. *Velayat-e Faqih*. Tehran: Falaq, *1392* (Lunar).
Kirmani, Nazemol-Islam.
1967. *Tarikh-e Bidari-ye Iranian*. ed. Saidi Sirjani. 2 vols. Tehran: Bonyad Farhang-e Iran, *1346*.
Kock, G. L., transl.
1964. *The French Code of Criminal Procedure*. New Jersey: Fred B. Rothman.
Lambton, A. S.
1968. The Internal Structure of the Saljug Empire. In *The Cambridge History of Iran*, Vol. 5. ed. J. A. Boyle. Cambridge: The University Press.
1970. The Persian Ulama and Constitutional Reform. In *Le Shiisme Imamite*, ed. T. Fahd, Paris.
Liebesny, Herbert.
1955. The Development of Western Judicial Privileges. In Khadduri, *et al.* 1955.
1967. Stability and Change in Islamic Law. *The Middle East Journal*, 21.
1975. *The Law of the Near and Middle East*. Albany: State University of New York Press.
Majmueh-ye Mosavvabat-e Majlis-e Taqniniyyeh (Compilation of the Laws Passed by the Majlis).
n.d. [Abbreviated in this chapter as M.] Tehran: The Majlis Press.
Majmueh-ye Qavanin-e Jazaei (Compilation of Penal Laws).
1939. [Abbreviated in this chapter as QJ.] Tehran: *Isfand, 1317*.
Majmueh-ye Qavanin-e Salyaneh (Annual Compilation of Laws).
n.d. [Abbreviated in this chapter as Q.] Tehran: Iran Publishing House.
Makki, Hoseyn.
1944–46. *Tarikh-e Bist Salah-ye Iran*. 3 vols. Tehran: Ilmi, *1323–25*.
Malcolm, Sir John.
1815. *The History of Persia from the Earliest Period to the Present Time*. 2 vols. London.
Malkom Khan, Mirza.
1948. *Majmueh-ye Athar-e Mirza Malkom Khan*. ed. and introd. Mohit Tabatabaie. Tehran: Kitabkhanah-ye Danesh, 1327.
Margoliouth, D. S.
1910. Umar's Instructions to the Kadi. *Journal of the Royal Asiatic Society of Great Britain and Ireland*.
Matin-Daftari, Ahmad.
1930. *La suppression des capitulations en Perse: L'ancien regime et le statut actuel des entrangers dans l'Empire du "lion et soleil."* Paris.
1948, 55, 58. *Aein Dadrasi Madani va Bazargani*. 3 vols. Tehran: Tehran University Press, 1327, 34, 37.
Mawardi, Abol Hasan.
1966. *Al-Ahkam os-Saltaniyya val-Velayat od-Diniyya*. Cairo: Albabi al Halabi.

Mazaheri, Aly.
1961. Le droit sassanide comparé au le droit musulman. *La Pensee Chiite*, Paris, 7 (Janvier).
Merton, R. K.
1957. *Social Theory and Social Structure*. New York: The Free Press.
Moasir, Hasan.
1968. *Tarikh-e Istegrar-e Mashrutiyyat dar Iran*: Translation of the Diplomatic Dispatches of the British Embassy in Iran during the Constitutional Revolution of 1905. Tehran: Ibn Sina, *1347*.
Mokhtari, Habibollah.
1946. *Tarikh-e Bidari-ye Iranian*. Tehran, *1325*.
Molk-Ara, Abbas Mirza.
1982. *Sharh-e Hal-e Abbas Mirza Molk-Ara*. Ed. A. Navaei. Tehran: Intesharat-e Babak, *1361*.
Mostashar od-Dowleh, Mirza Yusof Khan.
1870. *Yek Kalimah*. Paris.
Mostowfi, Abdollah.
1945. *Sharh-e Zendagani-ye Man Ya Tarikh-e Ijtemaei va Idari-ye Dowreh-ye Qajariyyeh*. 2 vols. Tehran: Mohammad Ali Ilmi, *1324*.
Mueller, Gerhard, ed.
1960. *The French Penal Code*. Jean F. Moreau, et al., transls. N.J.: Fred B. Rothman.
Naeini, Mohammad Hoseyn.
1954. *Tanbihol Omma va Tanzihol Milla*. Tehran: Firdowsi, *1373* (Lunar).
Najmi, Nasir.
1957. *Iran dar Miyan-Tufan ya Sharh-e Zendagani Abbas Mirza*. Gilan: Kanun-e Maarifat, *1336*.
Nakhjavani, Mohammad ibn Hindu-Shah.
1934. *Tajarob os-Salaf*. Ed. Abbas Iqbal. Tehran, *1313*.
Navaei, Abdol-Hoseyn.
1976. *Dowlatha-ye Iran az Aghaz-e Mashrutiyyat ta Ultimatum*. Tehran: Intenshat-e Babak, *1355*.
Nawaii, Abdol Khaliq.
1974. *Al Alaqat od-Dowliyyah wan-Nazmol Qadaiyya Fi ash-Shariatel Islamiyya*. Beirut: Darol Kotobel Arabiyya.
Nezami, Mohammad Asaad.
1968. *The Persian Political Elite*. Unpublished doctoral dissertation, The University of Chicago. Thesis No. T17286.
Nuraei, Fereshteh.
1973. *Tahqiq dar Afkar-e Mirza Malkom Khan-e Nazem od-Dowleh*. Tehran: Ketabha-ye Jibi, *1352*.
Onar, S. S.
1955. The Majalla. In Khadduri *et al.* 1955.
Peaslee, Amos J.
1966. *Constitutions of Nations*. 4 vols. The Hague: Martinus Nijhoff.

Rheinstein, Max.
1956. Type of Reception. *Annales de la Faculte de Droit de Istanbul*, No. 6.
Riesman, David.
1952. *The Lonely Crowd.* New Haven: Yale University Press.
Sabi, Musa, transl.
1972. *Civil Procedure Code of Iran.* Tehran:
Safaei, Ibrahim.
1965. *Rahbaran-e Mashruteh.* Tehran: Kitabforushi-ye Sokhan, *1344.*
1966. *Rahbaran-e Mashruteh: Dowrah-ye* 2: Biography 8. Tehran: Kitabforushi-ye Sokhan, *1345.*
1970. *Asnad-e Now-yafteh-ye Dowran-e Qajar.* Tehran: Kitabforushi-ye Sokhan, *1349.*
Saleh, Ali-Pasha.
1964. Qovveh-ye Moqannineh va Qovveh-ye Qazaiyyeh. In *Iran Shahr*, 2 vols., Tehran: Tehran University Press, *1343.*
1969. *Sargozasht-e Qanun: Mabahethi az Tarikh-e Hoquq.* Tehran: Tehran University Press, *1348.*
Salnameh-ye Pars.
1927. Vol. 2, *1306.*
1928. Vol. 3, *1307.*
Saljuqi, Mahmud.
1968. *Naqshe Orf dar Hoquq Madani.* Tehran, *1347.*
Sami, Mirza.
1943. *Tadhkirat al-Moluk.* English version, V. Minorsky, transl. London: Hefner and Sons.
Sani od-Dowleh (also Eatemad os-Saltaneh), Mohammad Hasan Ali Mogaddam Maraghe–ei.
1876–78. *Miratol Boldan.* 4 vols, *1294–96* (Lunar).
Schacht, Joseph.
1950. Foreign Elements in Ancient Islamic Law. *Journal of Comparative Legislation and International Law*, 32.
1955a. Pre-Islamic Background and Early Development of Jurisprudence. In Khadduri *et al.* 1955.
1955b. The Schools of Law and Later Developments of Jurisprudence. In Khadduri *et al.* 1955.
1956. *Droit Byzantin et droit Musulman.* Rome: Academia Nazionale del Lincei.
1959. *Origins of Muhammadan Jurisprudence.* London: Oxford University Press.
1964. *An Introduction to Islamic Law.* London: Oxford University Press.
Shafei, Mohammed Ibn Idris.
1961. *Risalah.* English version, transl. Majid Khadduri. Baltimore: Johns Hopkins University Press.

Shayegan, Sayyed Ali.
1943. *Hoquq-e Madani-ye Iran.* 3rd ed. Tehran, *1322.*
Sheil, Lady Mary Leonara.
1856. *Glimpse of Life and Manners in Persia.* London.
Smelser, Neil J.
1962. *The Theory of Collective Behavior.* Glencoe, Ill.: The Free Press.
Tabatabaei, Mohammad Mohit.
1967. Dadgostari dar Iran az Inqeraz-e Sasanid ta Ibteda-ye Mashrutiyyat. *Vahid*, 4, *1346.*
Tamerlane.
1963. *Tozukat va Malfuzat-e Teymur.* Mojtaba Minovi, ed. Tehran: Offset, *1342.*
Taqizadeh, Sayyed Hasan.
1959. *Khetabeh.* Tehran, *1338.*
Tyan, Émile.
1938. *Histoire de l'organization judiciaire en pays d'Islam.* 2 vols. Paris.
1955. Judicial Organization. In Khadduri *et al.* 1955.
Vesey-Fitzgerald, S. G.
1951. The Alleged Debt of Islamic to the Roman Law. *Law Quarterly Review*, 67.
1955. Nature and Source of the Sharia. In Khadduri *et al.* 1955.
Wilber, Donald N.
1975. *Reza Shah Pahlavi: The Resurrection and Reconstruction of Iran.* Hicksville, N. Y.: Exposition Press.
Zanganeh, Abdol-Hamid Aazami.
n.d. *Hoquq-e Bazargani.* ed. Sohrab Aminian. Tehran.
Zarrinkub, Abdol-Husain.
1975. The Arab Conquest of Iran and Its Aftermath. In Frye, 1975.

Glossary

adalat khaneh	house of justice
adliyyeh	the ministry of justice; (secular) court
aein-e dadrasi-ye madani	civil procedure
ahkam	statutes, ordinances and laws (of Islam) which concern human conduct (cf. *eateqadat*)
ahl or-raay	people of opinion; those who advocated rational reasoning in the process of *Ijtehad* (cf. *ahlol hadith*)
ahlol hadith	people of *hadith*: those who advocated strict adherence to the Traditions of the Prophet Mohammad in the process of *itjehad* (cf. *ahl or-raay*)
aqdal-qodat	the most judicious judge (cf. *qadil qodat*)
aslol baraah	the principle of presuming innocence until guilt is proven
asl ot-tasavi	the principle of equality (of all people before law)
ayatollah	sign of God: a relatively modern title of respect for leading Shii *mojtahids*
bayyinah	proof
darugheh	sheriff
dasturol amal	procedural and operational manual
divan	ministry; office of administration
divan-begi	a high legal official; public prosecutor
divan-e aala	the supreme court
divan-e adalat-e ozma	the grand office of justice
divan-e adliyyeh	(secular) court; chief magistrate court
divan-e islah	the court of first instance
divan-e tamiz	the high court of appeal
divan-khaneh	ministry (of justice); (secular) court
divan-khaneh-ye aazan	the grand house of secular judiciary
dowreh-ye jadid	the new series
eateqadat	doctrines pertaining to matters of belief (cf. *ahkham*)
fatva, pl. *fatava*	a sentence or opinion pronounced by a *mojtahid* or a *mofti*
Fedaiyan-e Islam	the devotees of Islam: a contemporary zealotic movement in Iran similar to the Moslem Brotherhood in the Arab world
fiqh	comprehension: science of the Sharia; Islamic jurisprudence

faqih	a specialist in *fiqh*
hadd, pl. *hodud*	limit: punishment specified in the Koran
Hadith	sayings of the Prophet Mohammad
hiyal	tricks: legal fictions
hokm	a legal verdict
Ibadat	the division of *ahkam* or Sharia which pertains to man's duties in relation to God; rituals and matters of worship (cf. *Moamalat*)
ijmaa	consensus (of the Islamic community or jurors)
ijtehad	endeavour: the process of extracting and formulating new rules from the Koran and other authentic sources of the Sharia (cf. *taqlid*)
imam	in general, anyone who occupies a leading position (in religious matters); in Shiism, any one of the twelve descendants of Ali, regarded as the legitimate successor of the Prophet Mohammad and hence the rightful rule of the Islamic community (equivalent to caliph in Sunnism)
imamate	the office, rule or rank of an *imam*
imam-e mostaqarr	permanent or established *imam*
imam-e mostowdaa	temporary or entrusted *imam*
imam jomeh	the leader of the congregational Friday prayers
isnad	ascription or tracing of a *hadith* to the Prophet Mohammad by an examination and assertion of the (uninterrupted) chain of authorities who have transmitted it
Istebdad-e Saghir	Short Tyranny: the period of 1909–1911 in which Mohammad Ali Shah of Qajor abolished the newly established *Majlis* (parliament) and constitution of Iran and ruled as an absolute monarch
istihsan	a method of *ijtehad* in the Hanafi Schools, in which ruling was done by consideration of public interest and equity even though it run contrary to the implications of *qiyas*
istinaf	appeal
istislah	the method of *ijtehad* in the Maliki School similar to *Istihsan*
Ithnaashari	of *Ithnaashariyyah*
Ithnaashariyyah	the Twelvers, the main sect of the Shii faith which regard the twelve descendants of Ali as the legitimate and rightful successors of the Prophet Mohammad, and hence their imams
jenayat	felony
jonheh	misdemeanour
kalantar	magistrate

kar-gozariha	legal agencies or tribunals associated with the foreign embassies in Iran before 1925
katib	writer; a clerk of the court
khalaf	petty offence
khana-ye insaf	house of equity
Khatt-e Sharif-e Golkhaneh	Holy Edict of Rose Chamber: an edict which was promulgated by Soltan Abdol Majid of Turkey in 1839 and which launched reform and Westernization in the Ottoman Empire
kolah-e Sharei	a Sharei hat: a trick, a legal fiction, a face-saving device
mahakim-e orf	courts of customary law
mahakim-e solh	district courts
mahkameh	sing. of *mahakim*, a court or tribunal
Majlis, or in full, *Majlis-e Shura-ye Melli*	National Consultative Assembly; the Parliament
malik osh-shoara	the king of poets: the master poet
maslahat khaneh	house of consultation
mazalim	acts of injustice or inequity: a periodical audience granted by kings or state officials in which people brought up grievances and were adjudicated
Moamalat	the division of *ahkam* or Sharia which is concerned with man's relations with and duties towards other men; the civil and criminal code of the Sharia (cf. *Ibadat*)
moasir	contemporary
moddail omum	attorney general, public prosecutor
mofti	giver of *fatva*: a top religious and legal authority, mainly of Sunni world, who passes judgement on the basis of the opinions of a given *mojtahid* or school of jurisprudence
mojtahid	doer of *ijtehad*: the highest authority in Islamic jurisprudence who is entitled to derive new laws of Sharia directly from the Quran and other original sources (cf. *moqallid*)
mokarrar	repeated: the second of two items with the same number or characteristic
molla	learned: a (low-ranking) member of the clergy
moqallid	doer of *taqlid*; one who adopts and follows uncritically the acts and views of a *mojtahid* in *ahkam* and *eateqadat* (cf. *mojtahid*)
mozakki	court clerk
mubadan-mubad	priest of priests: the highest religio-legal authority of the Zoroastrian religion in the Sassanian period in Iran

nazir	observer, overseer
nazr	vow; votive offerings
nezam-e jadid	the new, Western style military system introduced in Iran by the Crown Prince Abbas Mirza in the early 19th century
nezam-nameh	manual: rules of procedure
olol-amr	rulers
orf	customary law
osul	roots: that is, the four foundations of Islamic jurisprudence: the Koran, Sunna, *qiyas* and *ijmaa*
qada	litigation
qadi	judge
qadil-qodat	chief judge
qanun	law
qanun-e jaza	penal law
qanun-e madani	civil law
qiyas	reasoning by analogy; a method used in the process of *ijtehad*
raay	sound opinion
riba	interest
ruznameh	newspaper
sabt-e asnad	registry of (legal) documents
sadr-e aazam	prime minister
sadr os-sodur	the highest religio-legal position of the Safavid court corresponding to *qadil-qodat* and *mubadan-mubad* of the Abbasid and Sassanid courts, respectively
sepahdar	commander of army
sepansalar	commander-in-chief
shahneh	chief of the police
Sharia	the Islamic law
sheykhol Islam	a high religious title signifying spiritual leadership bestowed upon (Grand) *Moftis* or theologians of their rank
Shia	a heterodox Islamic sect which regards Ali and his descendants as rightful successors of Mohammad
Shii	of Shia doctrine or sect
shura-ye davari	judiciary council
shura-ye dowlat	council of ministers
siyasat osh-shariyyah	religious policy; ruling on the basis of expediency
Sunna	the Tradition of the Prophet Mohammad
Sunni	follower of Sunna; orthodox Moslem
taazir, pl. *taazirat*	a discretionary chastisement by the judge, used in the Islamic courts as a punishment for the (minor) offences (which do not entail a *hadd*)

taqlid	a preferential adoption and following of the views and action of a *mojtahid* (cf. *ijtehad*)
taklif	obligation, duty
tamiz	cassation (cf. *divan-e tamiz*)
Tanzimat	a reform programme carried out in the Ottoman Empire in the nineteenth century
Tozuks	rules and ordinances; a set of rules attributed to Tamerlane
tuman	10 rials of Iranian currency, equalling about 0.13 of one US dollar (1977 rate)
ulama	learned: scholars of traditional Islamic sciences
vakil	authorized representative; attorney
vakil or-reaya	attorney of the subjects; public prosecutor, attorney general
vakilol-jaraim	criminal prosecutor
vaqf	*wakf*, religious endowment
velayat-e faqih	the sovereignty of or rule by the *faqih*; a Shii constitutional doctrine
voaaz	preachers
wali	governor
Yasa	rule and pattern: a set of decrees issued by Genghiz Khan and put into effect in his conquered territories, including Iran
yerlighs	ordinances: a set of decrees issued by Ghazan Khan, the grandson of Genghiz Khan
zaheri	of outward: apparent
zina	fornication

4 Competing Ideologies of Conflict Resolution in Sri Lanka – A Multi-Religious Society

Neelan Tiruchelvam

In this paper we shall focus on the different conceptions and domain assumptions about conciliation which wrestled with each other during the critical phase in Sri Lanka's legal history when a state-institutionalized conciliation scheme was being worked out. In doing so we shall pay particular attention to ideas about the organization of the judicial system which may have influenced the principal author of the Conciliation Boards scheme, the foreign and domestic models of conflict resolution consulted by the legislative draftsmen, the different rationalization offered by the protagonists of this scheme during the legislative debates, and the shifting legal ideologies and more specific legal policies pursued by the Ministry of Justice during the years which followed the enactment of this legislation.

I. Historical Development

1. IDEAS IN ORGANIZING THE CONCILIATION BOARD

The architect of the mandatory Conciliation Board scheme was M. W. H. de Silva, the then Minister of Justice in the socialist coalition which was propelled into power at the General Election in 1956. Although relatively unknown in political circles, de Silva assumed this appointment after an extremely distinguished legal career which has been described as "unique in the annals of the legal history of the Island".[1] He was at various periods trial lawyer, law officer of the Crown, legal administrator, and judge, having served as District Judge, Solicitor General, Attorney General, Legal Secretary and ultimately as a Justice of the Supreme Court. He therefore had a deep understanding of the workings of the different units of the legal system, and commanded the esteem and confidence of the Bar and the Bench. An evaluation of M. W. H. de Silva's role as a legal reformer must be preceded by an analysis of the role of the Minister of Justice as it was perceived by the authors of the Constitution and prior incumbents to this office.

One of the more controversial issues confronted by the Soulbury Commission on Constitutional Reform related to the establishment of a Ministry of Justice. While the protagonists believed that the law-enforcement and prosecutorial agencies should come under the supervision of a Cabinet Minister, many opposed such a proposal on the ground that it would heighten executive control over judicial administration and undermine the independence and the impartiality of the courts of law. The Constitutional Commission was forced to compromise. The Constitution did provide for a Ministry of Justice but its powers were curtailed. The Attorney General remained the principal legal adviser to the government and exercised all statutory powers regarding the indictment, prosecution and composition of criminal offences. The appointment, promotion and disciplinary control of the minor judiciary was vested in an independent Commission of Superior Justices. As a result the Ministry of Justice was designed to be "no more than to secure that a Minister would be responsible for the administrative side of legal business, for obtaining from the legislature financial provision for the administration of justice, and for answering in the legislature on matters arising out of it" (*Report of Soulbury Commission on Constitutional Reform*, 1946: Sect. 396). Although the Minister of Justice had administrative responsibility for the working of the several departments under his authority such as the Attorney General's, the Fiscals, the Prisons, etc., whatever power he exercised was of limited policy significance. In practice much of the work of the Ministry was devoted to the processing of numerous applications for appointments as Justices of the Peace, which office, in lieu of a system of National Honours, was disbursed with liberality as a form of a party patronage. Since the functions of the Minister of Justice were more administrative and political than judicial the Constitutional Commissioners conceded that "it would be immaterial whether he were a lawyer". On the other hand they suggested that if there were "a lawyer of distinction among the [Prime Minister's] supporters [he] might possibly wish to offer him the portfolio" (ibid.). The practice had emerged since independence for the party to invite an eminent member of the profession who though not a political activist was really sympathetic to its political platform, to become the Minister of Justice. M. W. H. de Silva's appointment seemed therefore to fit this pattern.

De Silva however had a conception of his role as the Minister of Justice fundamentally different from that of most of his predecessors. He saw himself primarily as a tireless reformist who would direct his energies towards the overhauling of the administration of justice to render it both more efficient and responsive to the needs of poor litigants.

Unlike many of his professional colleagues de Silva was for many years disturbed by popular dissatisfaction with the administration of justice. This is clearly seen in the speech he delivered at the ceremonial welcome accorded by the members of the Bar on his appointment to the Supreme Court. Such occasions were often punctuated by the exchange of pleasantries between the new appointee and the Attorney General, with the former often reminiscing on the illustrious legal career which culminated in his judicial appointment. It was rarely an occasion for serious reflection on the workings of the judicial system. M. W. H. de Silva however did seize upon this opportunity to address these larger issues. He began by drawing attention to what he described as "the very unsatisfactory conditions of litigation in the Island both in the criminal as well as the civil departments". He bemoaned the hardships to litigants caused by the dilatoriness of the courts in processing land disputes, and the pain and anxiety which the accused and their relatives suffered as a result of the long delay between arrest and trial in criminal proceedings. "This state of affairs," he pointed out, is "due to the fact that the arrangements made for litigation in this Island have now proved to be not sufficiently elastic, and not sufficiently adequate, in view of the present state of affairs in the country".[2] He added "that increasing litigation, and the more elaborate proceedings with regard to litigation, have made the present conditions in the Court inadequate to meet the demands of the times". (*Ceylon Law Recorder*, 1946: XV.)

While conceding that there were inherent problems in the organization of judicial institutions which prevented the system from responding to new demands and pressures, he implied that the profession was not entirely without blame for bringing about this state of affairs. He underscored the special obligation on both the judiciary and the Bar to ensure the effective and smooth functioning of the courts of law and urged the Bar to take several positive steps to accelerate the clearance of court dockets.[3]

When M. W. H. de Silva became Minister he was afforded a rare opportunity to implement some of the ideas that he had developed during his long legal career. The then Prime Minister, S. W. R. D. Bandaranayake, who had some familiarity with de Silva's ideas gave him a broad mandate to institute whatever reforms he thought appropriate.[4] De Silva, despite his age, was a tireless worker and his close Ministry associates have pointed out no Minister since independence placed such a high priority on law reform.[5] He was responsible for the formulation of "about fifty proposals and amendments relating to this subject, of which only a fraction was eventually implemented" (*Parliamentarian*, 1956: 673). His primary concern was with the problems of litigiousness and the social costs of an inefficient adjudicatory system specially to indigent litigants. He instituted a voluntary scheme of legal aid to the indigent in the Provincial Courts. He appointed a Commission to examine problems of legal assistance for the poor, which ultimately led to the institution of a legal-aid scheme in 1958. He also closely examined the working of the different courts of original and appellate jurisdiction and searched for new solutions to improve their operation.

It soon became clear that litigiousness could not be reduced by merely tinkering with the procedures of the regular courts of law. What was necessary was a new institutional form stripped of the technicalities and procedural rituals of the regular courts of law (ibid.). At public meetings and in memorandum submitted by the public to the Ministry it was frequently proposed that such a body be set up composed of [indigenous] ayurvedic physicians, teachers, priests, etc."[6] M. W. H. de Silva was familiar with the scheme of voluntary conciliation set up by the police and state agencies since the thirties, and the more spontaneous Conciliation Boards which were established in Panadura and Moratuwa. He appears also to have been deeply impressed by the *Nyaya Panchayats* (Dharma Councils of Five Persons) in India, and secured through the assistance of the High Commission data on their constitution and operation.[7] In a memorandum to the cabinet issued in 1957 he "argued the need for legislation to provide an inexpensive and speedy means of promoting harmony among persons estranged by evil disputes or breaches of certain penal laws by amicably settling these disputes and compounding the offences arising out of those breaches."[8] That the reform was intended to deflect the flow of complaints and disputes from the regular courts of law to a new conflict-resolving mechanism is underscored in other official documents. The explanatory clause in the draft Bill points out that "the Conciliation Boards . . . are intended to serve as a means of reconciling these differences expeditiously and satisfactorily *without invoking the aid of a court of law in the first instance*".[9]

2. THE CEYLONESE SCHEME AND INDIAN MODEL

Once the policy decision was made to institutionalize a new conflict-resolving mechanism, there was some speculation as to the extent to which foreign models were consulted during the drafting process. Although an opposition member angrily charged, during the Senate debate, that the Conciliation Boards Bill which passed as the Conciliation Boards Act, No. 10 of 1958 was an attempt to politicize the judicial system along the lines of the Peoples Courts in Communist countries, there was little concrete evidence to suggest that M. W. H. de Silva made any effort to study the socialist models. Our interviews with his officials in the Ministry also reveal that very little was known at that time of popular justice in the Soviet Union or in China (supra Note 4). We have already mentioned M. W. H. de Silva's interest in the statutory *Nyaya Panchayats*, and it appears that he did examine the West Bengal Panchayat Act, No. 1 of 1957. A copy of the Act was also available to the legal draftsmen during the drafting process. As a result there are some similarities between the Conciliation Boards legislation and the West Bengal Panchayat Act which need to be explored. Firstly, in both societies, although there had been several previous efforts by the state to encourage the extra-judicial settlement of disputes,[10] the effectiveness of these schemes was to a large extent dependent on the esteem and recognition which the tribunal received from the community in which it was located. It was soon felt that the success of such reforms was too important to be left to the vagaries of local community sentiments, and that the new mechanisms for conflict resolution needed to be propped up by the authority and prestige of the state. Under both the West Bengal and the Ceylonese Acts, the state assumed the obligation to establish these tribunals in areas covered by the Act, and to arrange for the recruitment of members.[11] The state indirectly compelled disputants to take their claims to these tribunals by either limiting or barring access to the official courts of law. It imposed sanctions through its judicial machinery on persons who disregarded summons to attend inquiries or to produce documents, or in any other way conducted themselves in a disorderly and disrespectful manner towards these tribunals.[12]

Secondly, as we turn to more specific provisions we see similar recruitment schemes adopted in the Conciliation Boards and the West Panchayat Acts. As regards the statutory *Nyaya Panchayats* in the various Indian states, the question as to whether a system of nomination was to be preferred to a system of selection at the local level has been thought to raise difficult questions of policy. The protagonists of the nominative scheme have pointed out that nomination by a central authority would render it possible for objective criteria such as education, social standing, etc. to be taken into account in the recruitment of *Panchayat* members. Besides it would prevent the interjection of local factionalism and rivalries into the working of these tribunals which might otherwise tend to be overwhelmed by such forces. The opponents however pointed out that the intervention of external authority in the recruitment process would tend to alienate the local populace from these institutions. Most Indian states have leaned in favour of a scheme of local selection, but have qualified it by adopting the procedure of indirect elections (the *Report* cited in Note 12). The West Bengal Act is not however typical of these schemes since it adopts a hybrid procedure combining centralized nomination and local election. The first step involves the election of *Nyaya Panchayat* members by the representatives of *Gram-Panchayats* (Village *Panchayats*) who constitute a *Panchayat* circle (the *Anchal Panchayat*). The persons so selected have to be approved by the state governmental authority for the appointment to become effective.[13] The Conciliation Boards Act also prescribed a scheme combining local selection and central appointment. Each community group in the locality, such as the Rural Development Society, is urged to nominate persons suitable for appointment as Board members. The Minister of Justice in whom the ultimate power of selection is vested, is required to take these nominations into account in making the appointments.[14]

Thirdly, we must draw attention to another substantive provision found in both legislations allowing settlements to be set aside within thirty days. In the Conciliation Boards, the parties notify the Chairman of the Board of their intention to repudiate,[15] while in the *Panchayats* the intervention of a Judicial authority is necessary to set aside the determination.[16]

Notwithstanding the similarities that we have drawn attention to above, the differences between the two models are more striking. Firstly, there are jurisdictional differences in the two tribunals which point to their relative importance in the judicial systems of West Bengal and Ceylon respectively, and to the degree of commitment in each of these societies to the ideal of popular participation in judicial administration. While the civil jurisdiction of the *Panchayats* is limited by a monetary ceiling of 100 Rupees,[17] the competence of the Conciliation Boards to inquire into civil disputes which arise within their localities is unlimited.[18] The criminal jurisdiction of the two tribunals is not, however, different. The enormous civil jurisdictional gap between the Conciliation Boards and the *Panchayats* is somewhat narrowed by the absence of sanctioning powers in the former. The *Panchayats* may on the other hand impose a fine up to 50 Rupees on a person found guilty of a criminal offence, and make awards in civil claims. They may not, however, impose a sentence of imprisonment. The jurisdictional sweep of the Conciliation Boards is such that lack of a sanctioning power would seem less significant. These factors seem to suggest that while the Conciliation Board was envisaged as being an improvement on and a viable alternative to the regular courts of law, the *Panchayat* was designed to be a minor tribunal with jurisdiction over petty disputes and offences. From this perspective the Conciliation Boards Bill seems to reflect a much more radical commitment to the concept of popular justice than the West Bengal Nyaya Panchayats Act.

Secondly, although as we noted that both tribunals enjoy the support and backing of the state in the exercise of their powers, there are important differences in the autonomy and discretion conceded to these bodies in determining the manner in which they should exercise their statutory powers. The West Bengal Act subjects the *Panchayats* to detailed regulation on how applications should be filed, summonses issued, inquiries conducted, and the sanctions and decrees enforced. It is further subject to the supervision and control of the regular courts of law.[19] and its decisions may be set aside by such judicial authorities. The model is that of extreme centralized regulation and that of subordination to local judicial authorities. The Conciliation Board's model is an opposite one: once the tribunal is constituted it is given a great deal of leeway as to the procedure it should follow, and the rules of evidence it should comply with. Even the normative standards which the tribunal should apply are left open. In the act passed in 1958 there were no enforcement proceedings and no judicial or administrative body may intercede during a Conciliation Board's proceedings, nor set aside its determinations. The Ceylonese model, then, is that of extreme self-regulation.

Our discussion, while conceding some influences to the *Panchayats* scheme, leads us to conclude that the two tribunals represent fundamentally different models of conflict resolution. Such a conclusion will lead us to reject the suggestion that the Conciliation Boards represent the transposition of the *Nyaya Panchayat* model to the Ceylonese social milieu.

3. DIFFERENT RATIONALIZATIONS IN THE LEGISLATIVE PROCESS

This discussion hence leads us to the legislative debates on the Conciliation Boards Bill and the different perspectives which emerged on the goals of this legislation. Although the legislation in itself did not provoke a great deal of national controversy, the general feeling among the legislators was that it was an extremely important legal reform.[20] One of the Ministers in the Bandaranayake Government described the Bill as one which would take 'pride of place' among all legislation concerning legal reform.[21] Although legislators of all political shades were generally very enthusiastic about the proposed reform, they seemed to rationalize it differently. For the purpose of our analysis it would seem convenient to distinguish three different schools of opinion which we shall refer to as "reformists," the "specialist legalists" and the "revivalists."

Firstly the "reformists"; those in this school looked upon the legislation as purely a judicial reform intended to enable the British court system to operate more efficiently and effectively. There is no effort here to question the judicial postulates or values which underline the court system; but an attempt to attribute the ineffectiveness of the court system; to the anachronistic procedures which have developed around it, or to inherent weaknesses in the moral characters of the disputants. M. W. H. de Silva seemed most representative of this position. He was anxious to uphold the integrity of the judicial system of which the courts were an essential component. Like the nineteenth-century reformists he felt that the willingness of the rural disputants to rush into the courts for even the most frivolous causes, and the corresponding inability of the court system to cope with the flood of litigation, bred public contempt for the judicial process. One way of protecting the courts from such pressures was to establish a screening mechanism which would shut out those controversies amenable to amicable resolution. What was uppermost in de Silva's mind was the need for an efficient conflict-resolving mechanism to subdue the spirit of litigiousness which seemed to haunt the rural populace. Although implicit in de Silva's observations is a critique of the legal profession, the principal thrust of his attack is not, however, directed towards this occupational group. Although he conceded that the profession is one of the chief benefactors of the litigiousness in Ceylonese society, he did not regard this as being a principal contributory factor towards the malaise in the administration of justice. Nor did he seem profoundly disturbed by norms being weighted in favour of privileged social groups such as the landowners, employers, moneylenders and other secured creditors, as against tenants, employees and debtors.

The "socialist" conception of the Conciliation Boards was however somewhat different. They perceived the legal system in classical Marxist terms as an instrument through which the dominant social class maintains its hold over the remainder of the populace. Correspondingly, legal norms, institutions and processes are geared to serve the objectives and the class interests of the dominant social groups. The legal profession, by reason of the class origins of its members and its fidelity to the existing legal order, is the intermediary through which the interests of the ruling class are safeguarded. During the British colonial period it served the interests of the colonial power and in the post-independent period that of its successor, the western-educated elite. Public antagonism towards the legal system often tends to concentrate on the role of lawyers as capricious exploiters of poor litigants and as the opponents of all social reform legislation. The object of the Conciliation Boards scheme was to reverse this pattern of legal domination. The management of the legal system including that of the judicial process must pass from the elite class of legal specialists to the masses, and specially to those who came from lower levels of the social ladder. The new popular legal institutions and processes would, by facilitating the involvement of emergent social groups in judicial administration, transform the class orientation of the legal system by infusing its operation with a new social consciousness.

Two of the legislators during the debates in the House of Representatives seemed to approach the Bill from this perspective. P. B. G. Kalugalla, one of the Ministers in the Cabinet, began his presentation by extolling the sagacity of the rural peasantry and their capacity to be excellent conciliators. He then underscored his antagonism to the existing court structure and its class orientation by expressing the hope that this legislation would lead to the closing down of all the courts of law in Kegalle.[21] The controversial Minister of Agriculture, D. P. R. Goonewardene, a doctrinaire Marxist, seems to have shared similar perspectives on this problem. His concern was that the legislation did not go far enough. There were para-professionals in the rural communities popularly known as the village "proctors" who had an interest in undermining the operation of this scheme. The provision enabling parties to repudiate settlements provided a loop-hole for such persons to induce parties to disregard the settlements and refer claims to a court of law. To render the scheme more effective, he would confer greater finality on a settlement entered into by the parties (ibid.).

The "revivalists" looked upon this legislation as an attempt to reinstitute the traditional village court which had been suppressed during much of the Anglo-colonial period. Unlike the reformists they were sensitive not merely to the formal differences between the traditional and the western judicial institutions, but also to the fundamentally distinct value postulates upon which the two systems were based (Cohn, 1967: 139–159). The revivalists argued that the transplantation of an individualistic court system on a communal face-to-face society caused great confusion amongst societal members. Many such persons could have no proper comprehension of the purpose of new institutions which seemed strange and alien to them. They soon recognized that the proceedings in these new courts of law tended to be cumbersome and slow. Since the judge had no familiarity with local conditions and great faith was placed on procedural formalities, the villager found that he could with impunity forge documents and provide perjured testimony.[22] The revivalists believed that the debasement of the values of the rural disputants brought about by alien institutions could be remedied by their substitution with legal forms more consistent with the central cultural traditions. Senator Somaratne appeared to be the leading spokesman of the revivalist camp. He provided a brief review of the traditional mechanism for conflict resolution in rural Ceylon, and drew attention to the essential continuity between the traditional and the contemporary models, and believed that the existence of such links would guarantee the success of the scheme. Similar arguments were advanced in the House of Representatives by T. B. Tennakoon.

4. SHIFTING IDEOLOGIES OF THE SCHEME, 1958–65

Each of these perspectives competed with the others for the dominance of the Ministry of Justice policy at various periods of time. M. W. H. de Silva's reformist approach appears to have guided the implementation of the Conciliation Boards scheme during the first decade. The authority which a Minister of Justice normally enjoys over the formulation of governmental legal policy was strengthened in this instance by certain personal qualities of the Minister. He was an authoritarian figure who maintained strict discipline over both the executive and clerical members of his staff[4]. His commitment to a cause which he believed in was total, and he fervently believed that the Conciliation Boards Act was perhaps the most significant legislative reform he had introduced during his association with the Ministry (see references in Note 22). His interest in the Conciliation Boards scheme was such that he even became personally involved in the execution of the various administrative responsibilities prescribed by the Act. He rested the initiative (which the Act seemed to vest in local communities) on the constitution of Boards by urging Governmental Agents and District Revenue Officers to identify two village council areas in each District which were suitable for the establishment of Conciliation Boards. He appears to have relied more on such official recommendations rather than the opinion of local residents in deciding whether a panel should be constituted.[23] Despite his enthusiasm for the scheme the Minister appears to have moved cautiously in both the constitution and establishment of Conciliation Boards. During the first year of the Act's operation no more than twenty Boards were constituted, and their terms of office were limited to two years, which was a year less than that permissible under the Act[23] (cf. Goonesekere & Metzger, 1971: 35, 76). The Minister appears to have summoned and personally attended meetings of the community in a locality in which the Act was to be implemented. At such meetings the suitability of proposed candidates for appointment as conciliators was openly discussed. The local police officers who were usually required to be in attendance during these sessions were also asked to report on the character of various candidates.[24] M. W. H. de Silva's desire to ensure that conciliators would retain the impartiality and detachment of judicial officers and adhere to the precepts of procedural fairness of the British adjudicatory system is seen in his insistence that Members of Parliament be excluded from the list of persons eligible under the Act to make recommendations towards the appointment of Conciliators.[24] It would also appear that active political involvement by a candidate would be considered a disqualification by de Silva.

Since M. W. H. de Silva's resignation from the Cabinet, there were a series of domestic disturbances which led to a lull in the implementation of the Act from 1959 to 1962 (Goonesekere & Metzger, 1971: 75–76). Towards the end of 1961 the then Minister of Justice gave serious consideration to the reimplementation of the scheme.[25] He appointed a Ministerial Committee composed of Chairmen of Conciliation Boards and a Ministry of Justice official to study the Act and make appropriate recommendations towards its revision.[26] Several policy changes on problems as varied as the recruitment of conciliators, remuneration for their services, the panel's relationship to the regular courts of law and other state agencies, and the role of party representatives and members of Parliament, were examined by this Committee. These questions were given further consideration at a meeting between the Committee and the Minister of Justice, Sam P. C. Fernando. A review of the discussion at this meeting provides a valuable insight as to how Ministry of Justice officials perceived and responded to some of the problems of implementing the scheme.[27]

One of the Ministry officials present at the discussion inquired whether an educational qualification should be required of Conciliators. No other participant appears to have favoured such a general requirement. Some, however, felt that the Chairman should be one who already enjoys some position of responsibility in the community. One participant suggested the appointment of an administrative official such as the Revenue Officer. While another participant raised the possible appointment of a lawyer, or at least a Justice of the Peace. The latter proposal was strenuously opposed by almost all other participants including the Minister. The consensus was that it was more important that the Chairman should be an individual who resides in the community in which the Board operates than that he should have some special qualification. Although there appears to have been earlier agitation on the part of conciliators that they should be compensated for their services,[28] the Ministers took a firm stand in favour of the existing scheme of honorary conciliators.

The absence of a special mechanism for the enforcement of settlements reached by Conciliation Boards was perceived as a major flaw in the entire scheme.[28] A closer co-ordination between the Conciliation Boards and the regular courts of law and other state agencies was felt to be necessary to strengthen both the authority of the Boards and the effectiveness of their settlements. One member suggested a fusion of the Conciliation Boards and the Rural Courts as one of the ways in which the objective of closer institutional collaboration can be achieved. Another suggestion which seems to have received considerable support was that the Boards should enjoy the authority to transmit settlements directly to the regular courts of law for enforcement as the decree of such courts. The Minister reiterated the importance of close co-operation between the Police, Rural Organizations and the Boards, while not expressing a view on any of the specific proposals.

Clearly one of the more sensitive issues raised at this meeting was the role of elective political officials such as the Members of Parliament in the working of the Conciliatory scheme. Although the Committee appears to have been sensitive to the possibility that such a reform could lead to the politicization of the scheme, they conceded without much discussion that a Member of Parliament would inevitably have to be consulted before a panel could be constituted in his electorate. This represented an important policy shift, since it signalled a growing transfer of the statutory powers vested in Ministry officials to elective political officials. The Committee was, however, silent on the question of whether the local Parliamentarian should also become involved in the recruitment process. These deliberations, while providing a valuable insight into the state of thinking within the Ministry of Justice, also resulted in four major amendments in 1963.

The first related to an expansion in the operation of the Act from rural to urban areas. This step seemed to signify both government's recognition that "litigiousness" was not peculiar to rural areas, and its increasing confidence in the capacity of the Conciliation Boards scheme to deal with this phenomenon in all areas of the country. Secondly, the amending Act eliminated the requirement that an oath be administered on all persons who offered testimony before the Board. The purpose of this reform was to increase the informality of these proceedings and to reduce the likelihood of harassment of witnesses by hostile Board members.[29] Thirdly, the finality and enforceability of settlements were strengthened in turn by imposing a thirty-day limitation on the repudiation of settlements, and by attaching to settlements entered into by Boards the same enforceability as that of a decree of a court of law. Fourthly, the authority of Conciliation Boards was enhanced by establishing a special procedure for the prosecution of those who acted in contempt of their powers.

To sum up, the overall strategy during the period 1963–65 was then to continue the reformist policies of M. W. H. de Silva. One of the members of the Ministerial Committee emphasized this orientation when he pointed out that their main objective was to ensure "that justice is meted out to those who cannot go to court to settle their disputes."[30] The purpose of the 1963 amendments was to enable the state to pursue these policies more comprehensively and effectively. Subject to an overall simplicity in objectives and goals between this and the 1958–61 period, we perceive two other trends. Firstly, we notice the Ministry successfully resisting moves on the part of some officials to formalize and judicialize the Conciliation Boards scheme by assailing the apparent non-differentiation in education, social standing or official rank of conciliators and other members of the community, and the voluntary and honorary character of their duties. Secondly, we perceive a step towards the politicization of the scheme through a recognition of, and concession to, the growing power and importance of the local Member of Parliament and the representative of the ruling political parties. Even before the formal enactment of the Conciliation Boards Bill there was widespread public apprehension that such a scheme would fall victim to the political factionalism which had overwhelmed many other social and charitable organizations instituted by the state.[31] During the legislative debates on the 1963 Amendments, opposition members repeated the charge that these Boards had become the instruments with which the ruling party harassed its political opponents.[32] Although such charges were vehemently denied by official spokesmen, our discussion points to a relaxation in the Ministry of Justice policy which had previously excluded elected political officials and party representatives from any involvement in the operation of the Act.

5. SHIFTING IDEOLOGIES OF THE SCHEME, 1965–70

The succeeding period of 1965–70 witnessed for the first time the administration of the Act by a conservative government. Many feared that the new Minister of Justice would not display the same enthusiasm as his predecessors for what was regarded by some as a socialist reform. But contrary to such expectations the application of the Act was progressively extended to different parts of the Island. The number of panels functioning at the commencement of this period was almost trebled towards the end of this period.[33] The Minister was even quoted as favouring the establishment of a Conciliation Board in every village in the country.[34]

Despite the proposal to expand the coverage of the Act, there was generally a tendency during this period to treat the Conciliation Board as a somewhat subordinate tribunal competent to deal with only petty rural disputes. It was rationalized that such jurisdictional limitations would enhance the overall effectiveness of the scheme (cf. Note 34). In pursuance of this policy, instructions were issued by the Ministry of Justice to all Conciliation Board Chairmen to refrain from inquiring into complaints involving the Paddy Lands Act, the Rent Restriction Act, and disputes in which either the Crown or a Public Corporation was one of the parties to the controversy.[35] It is, however, important to remember that such a de-emphasis of Conciliation Boards took place in an atmosphere of intense agitation by the profession against the full implementation of this scheme.

We have stated previously that the legal profession was caught flat-footed by the enactment of the Conciliation Boards Act, and that subsequently for several years both practising lawyers and even some lower-court judges continued to ignore its prescriptions (Tiruchelvam, 1971; Goonesekere & Metzger, 1971: 81). But once the far-reaching implications of this legislation on the workings of the court system became clear to more members of the profession, they began to pressure the government to limit the scope of this reform. Several members of the Bar wrote newspaper articles or addressed memoranda to the Ministry protesting against the scope of this legislation and the manner of its operation. Professional Associations such as the Law Society presented memoranda to the Minister reviewing the Conciliation Boards, and proposing several amendments to the principal legislation.[36] They were particularly apprehensive of the broad sweep of the panels' jurisdiction, and questioned the capacity of lay conciliators to inquire into many disputes which were normally dealt with by law professionals. They cautioned that in the absence of proper procedural safeguards and the lack of technical competence on the part of conciliators, these tribunals could degenerate into corrupt and perverse instruments of oppression and thereby threaten the integrity of the entire system of judicial administration. They urged the government to curb the jurisdiction of the Boards, formalize their procedures, and subject them to the supervisory control of law professionals.[37] The Law Commission which was required by the government to recommend amendments to the principal legislation reported along similar lines. One of its principal recommendations was to severely limit the jurisdiction of the Board to inquire into applications in which expeditious relief is claimed, and other disputes such as partition actions, mortgage claims, matrimonial causes, testamentary actions, etc.[38] It also proposed that the scheme be made voluntary, and that settlements should be conferred the effectiveness of courts decrees only for the limited purposes of enforcement.[38]

A negative posture towards this reform was initially adopted by the judiciary in a series of cases in which the jurisdictional limits of these tribunals was controverted. The early judicial reaction was to contain the operation of the Conciliation Boards Act. A constitutional challenge to the mandatory effect of section 14 (1) of the Conciliation Boards Act was upheld by a District Court Judge in a highly publicized decision.[39] The judgement reasoned that to the extent that this provision attempted to bar litigants who had not resorted to pre-trial conciliation from the regular courts of law, it was tantamount to an interference with the exercise of judicial power. In this and two other cases which reached the Supreme Court, the Court avoided the broader issue by upholding the jurisdiction of the courts of law on narrow technical grounds.[40]

The broader question relating to the mandatory effect of this Act was directly confronted in four successive cases in 1967 and 1968. In three of them, the Court affirmed the argument that resort to Conciliation Board was obligatory on all parties who intended to initiate action in the regular courts of law.[41] In the other, Justice Alles held that such a proposition would be tantamount to an erosion of the jurisdiction vested in the established courts of law, and added that a citizen's right to seek redress from a court of law was so fundamental that it could not be taken away even by the legislature.[42] In view of these conflicting judicial pronouncements, the legal position on whether resort to conciliation was optional or compulsory was left uncertain until a Divisional Bench of the Supreme Court clarified the law in 1970. In *Nonahamy v. Silva*, the Court held that a District Court had no jurisdiction to entertain even an application for an injunction where the parties had not previously referred the dispute to a Conciliation Board.[43]

Another significant development during this period of administration of the Act was the increased politicization of the Conciliation Boards scheme. At a debate on the Appropriation Bill, it was charged that several Conciliation panels were reconstituted by the Government apparently because of the left-wing orientation of their Chairmen and other members.[44] It was also charged that the Government had quite blatantly politicized the process by which conciliators were recruited, and had not made even a pretence of applying objective criteria in evaluating the suitability of applicants for appointment as conciliators.[45] Not only did the government delegate the responsibility of recruitment to its local political representative (often the Member of Parliament), but it further provided him with a list of applicants, indicating the political affiliation of each candidate (see Note 45). It was widely believed that appointment to Conciliation Boards was a form of political patronage freely disbursed by the local parliamentarian to his active political supporters.

The *Sun*, a morning daily, in a strong editorial condemned the practice by which "the boards were becoming the political stooges of the party in power" and implored the government to purge politics out of the administration of the scheme so that the Boards may "function with an integrity for which all our legal institutions are justly famous" (The *Sun*, 15 October 1967). The Minister of Justice, however, defended the scheme, arguing that the exclusion of all persons with some involvement in politics would severely limit the pool of qualified candidates for appointment as Conciliators.[46] One Member of Parliament pointed out that the appointment of party sympathizers was the inevitable although unfortunate by-product of a political process in which elected political officials feel obliged to reward their supporters with favours and honours in exchange for the support they had received during an electoral campaign.[47]

We also note that towards the end of this period there was considerable pressure from "revivalist" groups to restructure the Conciliation Boards to revive traditional values and interests, and to serve as the vehicles through which Buddhist precepts could be inculcated in the masses.[48] This movement was spearheaded by a group of newspapers belonging to a consortium known as the Independent Newspapers of Ceylon, which were owned and managed by ultra-nationalistic and mildly conservative commercial interests in the country. (*Europa Year Book*, 1972: 319). These groups painted a romantic image of the harmony and amity in traditional Ceylonese society which they claimed was brought about by "the power of the truth which radiated from the village temple".[49] The dependence of the laity on the moral and spiritual guidance of the clergy was such that the entire community became akin to a "Council of Peace (*Sama Mandalaya*)" (see Note 49). The factionalism and strife seen in the villages for the past two decades, they argued, was the result of the pernicious growth of party politics in rural areas and the increasing detachment between the "village" and the "temple" (ibid.). To correct this trend the "*Maha Sangha*" (the Supreme Monastic Council) should be drawn into the administration of the Conciliation Boards scheme, and "responsible, educated and disciplined" members of the clergy should be appointed as Chairmen of these tribunals.[50] Such a step would result in the restoration of the stability and order which prevailed in the ancient village communities. The government however appears to have taken the firm position that, although members of the clergy would be given equal consideration with other candidates for appointment as conciliators, they would clearly not be appointed as chairmen.[51]

We have attempted through a review of the various steps taken by the Ministry with respect to Conciliation Boards to reconstruct the overarching policy which seems to have guided the conservative government during this period. We have also drawn attention to various pressure groups such as the law professionals, and the ultra-nationalists who were attempting to push the government to adopt various conservative postures towards these tribunals. Although no composite picture emerges clearly from this account, we are able to discern certain distinct trends. The government appears to have downgraded the importance of this legislation as instituting no more than a procedural reform in the administration of justice. Although the number of tribunals were substantially increased, the state severely curbed the jurisdiction of the Boards to exclude those disputes in which the state was either a party, or where its interest were indirectly in issue, as when the dispute involved governmental social welfare programmes. Since the conservative government, unlike the socialist, had no commitment to the absorption of emergent social classes in judicial administration, the Boards were at best regarded as auxiliary mechanisms for the resolution of petty conflict. Even the government's faith in these Boards as efficient managers of minor disputes seemed shaky, as seen in the repeated appointment of party activitists whose effectiveness as conciliators would seem crippled by their political partisanship.

II. Analytical Remarks

1. IDEOLOGIES IN COALITION AND COMPETITION

As we turn to the current period of implementation of the Conciliation Boards Act by the socialist coalition,[52] we find operative a different set of domain assumptions about Conciliation Boards.

These assumptions about the role of Conciliation Boards arose out of the legal ideology of the socialistic regime, i.e. the dominant ideas of the regime on how the inherited legal order may be restructured to accomplish socialists goals and objectives. Although there has been no governmental attempt to issue an explicit and comprehensive statement of its legal ideology, it is clear that the ideologists of the socialist coalition do share a broad set of ideas on the new direction along which the legal system should move.

We shall attempt to explicate these ideas by a careful analysis of the policy statements of the socialist parties and the state,[53] to the extent that they implicate the legal system. There are basically five major value orientations in the socialist ideology[54] of the Ceylonese elite, namely:

(a) nationalism, socialism, state ownership and equality;
(b) democracy, popular participation and social responsibility;
(c) stability and order;
(d) productivity, efficiency and growth;
(e) welfarism, redistribution, and raising living standards.

(a) The nationalism doctrine dictates the severance of the formal political and legal links between Ceylon and her former colonial power, Britain, and her economic dependence on foreign developed nations and "imperialistic" agencies.[55] More specifically it urges that despite the acute foreign exchange crisis, the flow of foreign capital into the country should be under conditions "consistent with the self respect of the nation".[56] The commitment to a socialist development implies more specifically state management of all basic and essential industry;[57] the development of collective forms of property in the means of production, distribution and exchange;[58] and the elimination of economic and social privilege, disparity and exploitation.[59]
(b) The democratic component of the ideology requires the state to resist all trends towards authoritarianism by safeguarding the democratic rights of the people, especially the fundamental right to change the government through the elective process;[60] and by broadening the democratic structure of government to permit popular participation at every level of national life, including the civil administration, the management of the economy and the administration of justice.[61]
(c) The transition from private to public control of the economy should be orderly and should take place with the minimum dislocation of the economy.[62] This commitment to stability and orderly change implicitly rejects the alternative strategy of revolutionary change through a violent social upheaval.[63]
(d) The emphasis on productivity, efficiency and growth to be realized through a rapid development of all sectors of the economy according to a National Economic Plan,[64] increased productivity in both the industrial and agricultural sectors, realized through improved managerial efficiency in the state enterprises.
(e) A commitment to upgrading the living standards of ordinary citizens, by securing full employment,[65] improving the wage structure and conditions of employment of working class (Election Manifesto: 177), and ensuring the equitable redistribution of the social product through welfare schemes.[66]

We must now consider the implications of these value commitments to the legal system. What changes in the conception of the law, or in the organization and management of the institutional complexes and processes which form part of the inherited legal system, were precipitated by the adoption of the strategy of socialist developments that we have described above. There are two distinct and somewhat divergent developments that we may herein describe as "the instrumental conception of law" and "deprofessionalization."

The former refers to the conscious use of the law as the instrument with which the fundamental restructuring of social and economic life is to take place. Implicit in such a conception of the law is the doctrine which dictates that there exists a differentiated body of norms, a complex of institutions and processes, modes of thought and decision making which may be distinctly labelled as "legal".

Such a conception of law further presupposes the existence of a group of law professionals with specialized knowledge of the content of the body of norms, and training in the modes of reasoning associated with this form of normative ordering. The instrumental conception of law also embraces two related ideas. The first stresses fidelity to certain pre-determined processes of political-legal decision making, and points to a certain constancy in form and style in the expression of these policies.

The second emphasizes the law as the principal modality through which societal goals and aspirations may be realized. In other words it points to a commitment to work primarily with the facilitative frameworks, the conflict-resolving mechanisms, the enforcement agencies which are distinctly labelled as legal, to accomplish the state policy objectives. The law therefore is both the effective expression and the principal instrument of state policy.

The concept of deprofessionalization refers on the other hand to the divesting of legal specialists of their monopoly over certain law jobs such as lawmaking, conflict management, advocacy and counselling, and to permitting the performance of these jobs by persons who do not possess specialized legal training. It sometimes takes the form of an effort to contain the operation of formal legal institutions which are usually staffed by law professionals (e.g. the courts of law) by relieving it of its jurisdiction over certain types of problems. The categories of problems are then referred to newly constituted popular or quasi-popular tribunals or allowed to be dealt with by existing mechanisms of informal social control.

Although the doctrine of deprofessionalization appears to be directed at the organization and management of legal institutions it has important implications for the normative components of the legal system. As the institutions and the processes devoted to the finding and application of legal norms become less autonomous from other social institutions and processes, and the personnel who manage these institutions are less differentiated from other societal members, the law's distinctiveness as a special form of normative ordering would correspondingly suffer. And as the repertory of norms, concepts and principles which constitute the legal order lose their autonomy, legal reasoning would in turn become increasingly fused with other modes of political thought and economic reasoning in the community.

We may now demonstrate how each of these strands of thought are accommodated within the legal ideology of the socialist coalition.

We begin by examining the extent to which the instrumental conception of the "law" finds expression in the policy statements of the government. In our elaboration of the instrumental conception of the law, we pointed to two distinct and related aspects of this conception, which we shall herein refer to as the concept of "governmental fidelity to law," and the concept of "law as the principal vehicle of societal change." The concept of governmental fidelity to law finds expression in the socialist coalition's faithfulness to the existing political-legal framework (see Notes 60, 62, and 63); and its commitment to the idea that all governmental activity should be in accordance with pre-established legal standards, to the extent that it would be possible for any individual to predict which governmental agency has the authority to exercise its coercive power in a given circumstance, so that he would be able to plan his affairs on the basis of such knowledge. It is manifested in policy statements which emphasize the need for stability and order in the process of socialist development and denounce the revolutionary alternative of a violent social upheaval;[67] and also seen in the state's commitment to the ideal of "equal protection before the law,"[68] and in its proscriptions against depriving any individual of his "life, liberty or security except in accordance with the law".[69]

In this limited sense of governance in accordance with the law, the instrumental conception of the law points not to a break but rather to an essential continuity between the colonial[70] and the contemporary approaches to the law. It is, however, different with regard to the use of the law as vehicle of societal change. Fundamental transformations had taken place in the conception and function of the state which had important implications for the law. The state, unlike in the colonial period, dominated as it often was by doctrines of *laissez-faire* (Mendis, 1956; K. M. de Silva, 1959; 249), was no longer limited to the collection of revenue and the maintenance of law and order. The commitment to a socialist ideology spelled an unprecedented involvement of the state as the provider of basic social services and welfare measures, as the regulator of the development of all sectors of the economy, and as the entrepreneurial economic actor directly or indirectly controlling the basic means of production and distribution.[71] Correspondingly, the use of law as the principal instrument with which the state accomplishes its multifarious functions places an enormous demand on the resources of the legal system. More specifically the accomplishment of the goals of welfarism and equalitarianism require more social-welfare legislation, providing for the establishment of certain administrative mechanisms for the equitable distribution of the social product.[72] Such legislation has also been directed towards the acquisition and redistribution of surplus land from the wealthy landowners to the landless,[73] control of rent and the allocation of public and private housing units,[74] and the imposition of a ceiling on income.[75] The ideal of rapid economic growth in accordance with a developmental plan is pursued through a series of regulatory laws which attempt, through a system of incentives and prohibitions, to control and direct the development of different sectors of the economy. Examples of such regulatory laws would be industrial licensing laws,[76] fiscal laws designed to control consumption and to encourage savings and capital formations,[77] and price-control laws directed towards the regulation of prices and the even distribution of scarce resources.[78] Similarly the pursuit of the goal of increased state ownership and management of the economy had given rise to new forms of legal associations such as public corporations, co-operatives and collectives.[79] These new legal frameworks have facilitated and defined the increased intervention of the state in internal and external trade,[80] essential industries,[81] and in the plantation and agricultural sectors.[82]

Assumption by the state of the multifarious functions that we have described herein as "provider", "regulator" and "entrepreneur", besides creating an entirely new body of economic laws and the mechanisms for their enforcement, also seems to envisage an important role for the law professionals in their formulation and administration.

They seem to presuppose the involvement of law professionals in the planning of alternative legal schemes for the realization of given policy objectives, in the setting up of a machinery for the implementation of the scheme defining the parameters of its powers, and formulating a system of legal or bureaucratic controls. Correspondingly, the services of such law professionals would also become necessary in the counselling of economic actors on the implications of specific schemes, and in their representation before managers of state enterprises, the courts or other tribunals, deemed competent to deal with the problems which arise in the enforcement of these schemes.

2. SIGNIFICANCE OF DEPROFESSIONALIZATION

The doctrine of deprofessionalization was initially reflected in efforts to restrain the powers of the officials in courts of law, which since independence continued to assert its autonomous power to determine judicial controversies without any external interference, to pronounce upon the validity of arbitrary actions of the executive,[83] and even to invalidate unconstitutional legislation.[84] The exercise of such awesome power by non-elective tribunals, which seemingly obstructed the process of social and economic transformations on "technical" and "legalistic" grounds, was found to be particularly irksome to members of the socialist coalition.[85] It was thought to be especially reprehensible and inconsistent with the nationalistic aspirations of political sovereignty when such power was exercised by a foreign tribunal, such as the Privy Council, which stood at the apex of the multi-tiered pyramidal court structure. Accordingly, one of the early legal reforms implemented by the government was to abolish the appellate jurisdiction of the Privy Council and to vest it in a National Court of Appeal.[86] Consistent with the coalition's desire to weaken the judicial arm of the government and correspondingly concentrate power in the legislative, was its decision to eliminate the "non-elective" second chamber, an essential component of "Parliament" as defined by the previous Constitution.[87] One of the more fundamental postulates of this New Constitution of 1972 is that which by rejecting the prevailing conceptions of separation of power, attempts to restructure the allocation of powers between the different organs of government. Section 4 of the Constitution of Sri Lanka provides "that the Sovereignty of People is exercised through the National State Assembly of the elected representatives of the people," and that the "National State Assembly is the supreme instrument of state power of the Republic." In effect it means that the panoply of state power would be vested in a tribunal which is primarily a legislative institution, the National State Assembly being the lineal successor to the House of Representatives under the previous constitution.[88] And to further remove any doubt on this issue the Constitution adds that while the legislative power would be exclusively exercised by the National State Assembly, the executive and judicial power would be exercised on its behalf by the cabinet and courts of law respectively. Section 5 therefore provides that "the National State Assembly exercises:

(a) the legislative power of the people;
(b) the executive power of the people . . . through the President and the Cabinet Ministers; and
(c) the judicial power of the people through courts and other institutions created by law. . . ."

There were other steps taken by government to weaken the jurisdiction and authority of the courts of law, and to further compound its subordination to the National State Assembly. The Constitution explicitly took away from the courts the power to inquire into or pronounce upon the validity of any legislation.[89] Instead, a Constitutional Court was established as an appendage to the legislature and to advise the latter on the constitutionality of legislative proposals and to enable the legislature to cure any defects by adopting a special procedure to enact the law[90] (see Sects. 54 & 55 of the Constitution of Sri Lanka, 1972). Similarly an Amendment to the Interpretation Ordinance severely restricted the grounds on which the Superior Courts of law could, through the issue of the prerogative writs, inquire into the validity of the executive acts of the government.[91] This legislation, which was subjected to considerable criticism by the national press, the Bar Council, and several trade-union groups, was defended by the

Minister as "an attempt to restrain the court from assuming the role of the legislature" (see *Parliamentarian*[53] (1972): 240).

Apart from the subordination and circumscription of the powers of the courts of law, deprofessionalization was also reflected in the continuing effort to constitute popular and quasi-popular tribunals with exclusive or concurrent jurisdiction over disputes which were normally handled by the regular courts of law (see Tiruchelvam, 1971). The constitution of such tribunals has important implications for the legal profession, since their enabling legislation often placed restrictions on the involvement of lawyers as either judges or as advocates of the interests of parties. The government even considered extending this policy to tribunals which had been constituted in the pre-1970 period. One such example would be the labour tribunals where, although the original Industrial Disputes Act in 1957 conferred on licensed practitioners an equal right of representation with trade-union officials, employer's representatives and other para-professionals,[92] the government gave serious consideration to totally excluding licensed practitioners from such proceedings. Such a step would deprive several younger members of the profession of an extremely important source of income. Fiscal policies such as the imposition of a ceiling on income had the indirect effect of limiting the legal fees chargeable by lawyers and other professionals (supra Note 75). The general economic depression and the resulting decline in commerce and land transactions further eroded the economic base of the profession.[93]

The process of deprofessionalization we have sketched above was accelerated by a continuing confrontation between the government and the profession. Some law professionals perceiving certain tensions between the liberal and socialist components of the state's ideology, deeply believed that it was the special responsibility of the profession to ensure that the former was not consumed by the latter. They correspondingly mobilized several members of the academic community, journalists, trade unionists, and other professionals to form a Civil Rights Movement to combat potential encroachments by the state on the civil liberties of the people. The successive efforts of the government to enact the Criminal Justices Act, the Interpretation (Amendment) Act, the Press Council Act, and the Lake House Acquisition Bill became the focal points of controversy between the Civil Rights Movement and the socialist coalition. The lawyers dominated the

Civil Rights Movement, considering such legislative proposals to be in derogation of the civil liberties and the fundamental freedoms guaranteed by the Constitution, and launched a public campaign through the national press against the enactment of such legislation. The Movement and other individuals even had recourse to the Constitutional Court to impugn the validity of these legislative attempts.[94] We have already alluded to the fact that the socialists in the government had for a long time a negative view of the profession for its persistent opposition to legal reforms and its general indifference towards the legal needs of the poor. The involvement of several prominent law professionals, some of whom had in the past actively supported the socialist parties, in the campaign to obstruct what the government regarded as "progressive legislation," exposed the legal profession to further attack and criticism for being antagonistic to the aspirations of the working classes and the rural peasantry.[95]

There are two other developments that we should refer to in this respect. Firstly, although the state has recently taken several steps to undermine the monopoly of the legal profession over law-related services, it has left undisturbed the authority of the courts of law to guarantee the most sacred right of the people in a pluralistic society, that of constituting their government at pre-determined intervals through an independent electoral process. Stringent election laws vest in the election judges a wide range of sanctions against candidates, their agents and supporters to ensure the legality and the fairness of both the campaign and the voting during Parliamentary Elections.[96] Their powers include the authority to impose the most severe sanction of invalidating the election of a candidate guilty of corrupt practices, such as impersonation, treating, undue influence and bribery. The Constitution of Sri Lanka both reiterated the most basic right of the people to elect their representative to the National State Assembly,[97] and left intact the responsibilities and the powers of the courts of law to safeguard the independence and the freedom of the electoral process.[98]

Secondly, unlike some other societies subjected to similar ideological changes (see Ziadeh, 1968), the state has done very little towards interfering with the autonomy of the professional organizations. Internal divisions and power struggles within the General Council of Advocates have, however, considerably undermined the cohesiveness and the unity of the bar and weakened its ability to protect the interests of the profession. The more reform-oriented groups in the advocates association, frustrated by their failure to dethrone conservative senior practitioners from dominant positions in the governing council, seceded from the parent body to form a rival organization. Once it became clear, however, that the left-wing groups could gain control over the parent body, the two units were fused. The Advocates Association continues to be plagued by intense factionalism, which often has ideological overtones. Curiously however these pressures did not affect the Law Society, the professional organ of the proctors.[99]

It is important to note that deprofessionalization of law-jobs is just one manifestation of the participatory ideology of the socialist government.[100] From this perspective it is clearly related to the debureaucratization trend in the administrative sphere. N. M. Perera, the Finance Minister and perhaps the most articulate doctrinaire socialist in the cabinet, emphasized that the latter was a novel social experiment by which existing forms of bureaucratic management would give way to socialist forms of management (*Budget Speech* 1970–71: 13). The objective he said was to establish mass organizations which would vest the people with some responsibility for "the formulation of plans and their implementation; for efficiency in management, for the curbing of profiteering and the suppression of corruption" (ibid.). The new institutional forms which were established to give expression to these goals were the People's Committees,[101] the Workers Advisory Council and the elected Employee Councils (ibid.: 13). Germane to these developments were the attempts to create Divisional Developmental Councils to decentralize the planning process (ibid.: 199; *Budget Speech*, 1971–72: 199), and the promise to reorganize the armed forces and the police "to identify them with the national and progressive aspirations of the people" (*Parliamentarian*, 51 (1970): 311). The ultimate goals of these institutional forms was the creation of a worker-managed economy with the "Workers Councils being the training ground of the future worker-managers" (*Budget Speech*, 1970–71: 13).

The fundamental importance of popular participation to the socialist developmental strategy of the government was repeatedly stressed by Minister Perera. While explaining the difficulties the government could face in implementing its programme, Perera pointed out, "A mass upheaval such as we have witnessed in many East European countries, in China and in North Korea would have in a sense simplified the task of socialist reconstruction. A revolutionary mass upheaval teaches lessons to the masses in the very process of that upheaval. It awakens people to a high degree of social consciousness. We, on the other hand, are conditioned by an environment charged with old prejudices, old inhibitions and old traditions" (ibid.: 4). To overcome these obstacles it was important to mobilize the whole of the society and "raise its social consciousness on a coherent ideological appeal, that of socialism" (*Budget Speech*, 1971–72: 222). Popular participation at all levels of government as a means of enhancing the popular consciousness assumes, then, a critical significance in a society such as Sri Lanka which had not emerged out of a protracted revolutionary struggle. The working class must recognize, Perera added, that "the struggle to emancipate ourselves from capitalism cannot be accomplished without their assistance and active co-operation".[102]

As the legal ideology of the socialist coalition continued to take shape, it became increasingly important to accommodate the Conciliation Boards scheme within its framework. Policy statements of the government began to rationalize the conciliatory scheme as one of the principal planks of the governmental programme of deprofessionalization, and as being consistent with its broad participatory ideology. To the extent that lawyers were excluded from appointment as conciliators[103] and from the representation of disputants before such tribunals, the reform had to a very significant extent facilitated popular participation in the management of inter-personal conflict. The successful disposition by these Boards of almost half the controversies that were directed to them was found to have a negative impact on the volume of cases handled by the regular courts of law[104] which in turn adversely affected the practice of the legal profession. The new effort to integrate the Conciliation Boards scheme into the socialist ideology of the government is manifested in the principle of state policy in The New Constitution which provides that the, "State shall strengthen and broaden the democratic structure of Government . . . by affording all possible opportunities to the people to participate at every level in national life and in government, *including the civil administration and the administration of justice*"[105] (italics mine).

The government's decision to enhance the powers of the Conciliation Boards and to vest in such tribunals the jurisdiction of the Rural Courts is consistent with the Socialist conception of these Institutions.[106] For the impact of such a reform would be to vest coercive powers in such tribunals and qualitatively transform these from conciliatory bodies to popular "courts of law."

One consequence of such a transformation would be to blast the revivalists' imagery of these boards as the lineal descendants of the traditional *Gamsabhavas* (village council). The socialist coalition in initiating such changes appeared in turn to show less concern for conserving the Conciliation Boards' links with historical antecedents than with manipulating these institutions to be responsive to the social needs and the developmental problems of contemporary Sri Lanka. Correspondingly the government decided to further restructure the Conciliation Boards to enable them to deal with the problems of "indebtedness that hang so heavily on the rural folk".[107]

3. CONCLUDING REMARKS

As shown in the description above, the Conciliation Boards scheme might be said to have achieved a difficult but gradual development with all ideological and practical objections raised by various camps, until their power was further extended by an Act in 1975.[108] However, a vital blow was struck against it soon after.

After the general election in July, 1977, the winning U.N.P. Cabinet led by Junius Jayawardena, who became the first executive President in 1978, carried out radical changes of state policies, including revision of the Constitution of Sri Lanka as passed in August and promulgated in September, 1978. The Conciliation Boards scheme was one among them in the earliest period of the Cabinet. By the use of the power prescribed in the Conciliation Boards Act itself the Minister of Justice issued, as early as within one month of the general election, an order to remove the Chairmen and Members of all the Conciliation Boards without appointing new Chairman and members instead. The function of the Conciliation Boards was thus forced to be suspended, leaving the Constitution Boards Act surviving as it had been. The excuse for such a drastic suspension was alleged to have been political corruption ,accelerated by the Conciliation Boards scheme. (Cf. Marasinghe, 1980: 411)

The heated debates among different rationalizations for the Conciliation Boards scheme, and objections against the Boards aroused especially by lawyers and sometimes by judges, seem to have subsided to a calm. But of course it never meant that the idea embodied in the Conciliation Boards scheme was totally defeated. Rather, the fundamental problem underlying the ebb and flow of the Conciliation Boards could be seen as inseparably connected with a basic problem of Sri Lankan society in terms of law. As made clear in the above discussion, the institution of the Conciliation Boards was an appreciable result of an agreement among camps of different orientations. It should be evaluated as a success on one hand, insofar as different camps reached an agreement, but a failure on the other, in that they failed to reach a formal, reasonable, common understanding in both ideological rationalization and practical administration of the Boards sufficient to continue their function.

Notes

Author's Note: The main part of this article was originally written to be presented to Harvard Law School for a Doctor's Degree.

1 The then Attorney General C. Nagalingam, cited in *Ceylon Law Recorder*, 1946: XIV.
2 Mr. de Silva's address was delivered on 15 January 1946, during a period of acute political activity and intense national consciousness culminating in the promulgation of a new Constitution a few months later.
3 This pronouncement, made almost a decade before he assumed office, provides us with an early indication of de Silva's dedication to the reform of the judicial process.
4 Interviews with S. Canagarayar, the then Assistant Secretary in the Ministry of Justice and G.C.T.A. de Silva, the then Permanent Secretary, on file with the author.
5 Interview with S. Canagarayar, ibid. A bill on the suspension of the death penalty was defeated in the Senate, although it had been passed by the House. See *Parliamentarian*, 1956: 673.
6 A public proposal submitted at a meeting in Yakkala dated 12 July 1956, on file with the Ministry of Justice.
7 Ministry files indicate that a copy of the West Bengal Panchayat Act was made available by the Indian High Commission at the request of the Minister.
8 Memorandum by the Minister of Justice on the establishment of Conciliation Boards dated 26 November 1957, on file with the Ministry of Justice.
9 The explanatory clause appended to the Draft Bill on Conciliation Boards.
10 For Ceylon, see Tiruchelvam, 1973: Ch.3; and for West Bengal, cf. Malaviya, 1956: 340–341.
11 The West Bengal Act in addition renders the awards and sanctions imposed by the *Nyaya Panchayats* as enforceable as court decrees. See Sections 78 and 107. Similar provisions were inserted into the Conciliation Boards Bill in Ceylon by an Amendment passed in 1963.
12 Cf. the discussion on the merits and demerits of the nominative and elective schemes in the *Report of the Study Team on Nyaya Panchayayts*, 1962: 47–54.
13 See Section 70 of the West Bengal Panchayat Act.

14 See Section 3 (3) and (5) of the Conciliation Boards Act.
15 See Section 13 of the Conciliation Boards Act.
16 See Section 93 of the West Bengal Panchayat Act.
17 See Section 80 of the West Bengal Panchayat Act.
18 See Section 6 of the Conciliation Boards Act.
19 See Section 100 of the West Bengal Panchayat Act.
20 See generally the debates on the Conciliation Boards Bill, the Proceedings of the Senate (1957–58), *Hansard*, 1957: 1157–1158 and the Proceedings of the House of Representatives (1957–58), *Hansard*, 1957: 1640–1682.
21 See the Honorable P. B. G. Kalugalla in the Proceedings of the Representatives (1957–58), *Hansard*, 1958: 2897–2899.
22 Compare the comments of British Administrators on the attitude of the Ceylonese villager towards the inherited court structure. See Aelian King, District Judge of Badulla, *Administrative Report*, 1869: 188; R. Morris, Government Agent Kurunagala, ibid.: 120.
23 Information obtained from Ministry files on the implementation of the Conciliation Boards Act.
24 Interview with S. Canagarayar, see Note 4, and interviews with T. G. Siriwardene, formerly Administrative Secretary of the Conciliation Boards Unit, on file with the author.
25 The Minister of Justice at that stage was Sam P. C. Fernando.
26 The Committee was composed of P. P. Siriwardena (Chairman, Aluthgama Village Area), Senator A. D. Jayasekera (Chairman, Kanuwanna Village Area), Mohandiram D. Alagiyawanna (Chairman, Megodapotha Village Area), and D. Wimalaratne (Asst. Secretary to the Ministry of Justice).
27 This analysis of the Committee's recommendations is based on the notes of a meeting on the Conciliation Boards, 11 March 1961, on file with the Ministry of Justice.
28 See Proposals on the Reforms of the Conciliation Boards Act formulated at a meeting of the Ministerial Committee on 27 August 1960, on file with the Ministry of Justice.
29 It was also felt that since the scheme was voluntary (the Boards derived their authority to bring about settlements from the consent of the parties), to compel a witness to testify under oath would not be in accord with the spirit of this legislation. See Recommendations on the Reform of the Conciliation Boards Act issued by the Ministerial Committee (undated), on file with the Ministry of Justice.
30 Senator A. D. Jayasekera at the meeting on 11 March 1961, see Note 27.
31 The article entitled "Do not entrust the herd of cattle to the tiger", The *Lankadipa*, January, 1958.
32 During the Senate Debates on the 1963 Amendments one of the

Senators read excerpts from a letter by a party who had several complaints filed against him for abuse by a person of a different political party. This defendant had been ordered to appear before the tribunal on four different occasions; and on each one of these occasions the Chairman rejected his repeated plea to have the case remitted to a Magistrates Court, and even threatened the recalcitrant party that "he is all powerful," *Senate Debates*, 1963: column 1914.

33 In 1965 there were 128 Conciliation panels functioning, while in 1970 the number of panels had increased to 324. See Table 1 in Goonesekere & Metzger, 1971: 96.

34 See interview with D. J. R. Gunewardene, the then Permanent Secretary to the Ministry of Justice, The *Lankadipa*, November 5, 1966.

35 Interview with T. Gilbert Siriwardena, the then Administrative Secretary to the Ministry of Justice, ibid. It appears that there is no statutory authority vested in the Ministry to curtail the civil jurisdiction of these Boards.

36 See Memorandum by the Ceylon Law Society dated 24 June 1965, on file with the Ministry of Justice.

37 A frequently repeated suggestion in these memoranda is that the Chairman of Conciliation Boards should be a lawyer.

38 See Draft Report of the Law Commission on the Conciliation Boards Act, on file with the Ministry of Justice.

39 See the judgement of District Judge J. G. Swaris in E. Coates & Co. Ltd. v. A. F. Jones & Co. Ltd., The *Times of Ceylon*, 10 September 1966.

40 For the Supreme Court decision in E. Coates & Co. Ltd. v. A. F. Jones & Co. Ltd., see N. L. R. 70(1968): 351 (a dispute between a public servant residing in the area and the government need not be referred to the Board, since it did not entirely arise within the area. See also A. K. Wilasinhamy v. G. L. Karunawathie, C. L. W. 79(1970): 84 (a substitute plaint filed in 1963 in lieu of an earlier plaint, did not require a Conciliation Board certificate, since no Board was constituted in the area when the original plaint was filed). See Goonesekere & Metzger, 1971: 56–57, 63–67.

41 See Samarasinghe v. Samarsinhe, N. L. R. 71 (1969): 151 and Broheir v. Saheed, N. L. R. 70(1968): 276.

42 Wijeyawardene v. Inspector of Police, Panadura, N. L. R. 70(1968): 281.

43 See N. L. R. 71(1970): 217. For the dissenting judgement of Justice A. C. Alles, see ibid.: 223. The effect of Nonahamy's case was to some extent mitigated by Fernando v. Fernando, C. L. W. 80(1971): 14, where the court implied that unless the objection to the jurisdiction of the court was taken at the trial stage of the

proceedings the parties would be taken to have acquiesced in the jurisdictional defect.

44 See the speech of Colvin R. de Silva, at the Debate on the Appropriations Bill, 1967–68, *Hansard*, 1968–69: 1187. He alleged that in one of the Conciliation Boards in Agalawatte the Chairman was removed by the Minister and the entire Board reconstituted for patently political reasons.

45 Colvin R. de Silva, see Note 44, read out a letter to this effect, issued by the Ministry of Justice to a member of the Government's Parliamentary Group but which inadvertently reached a member of the opposition.

46 Senate Proceedings as reported in *Lankadipa*, 14 March 1969.

47 K. P. Ratnam, M.P. for Kayts, the Debate on the Appropriations Bill, 1967–68: 28–39. Cf. Wood, 1961: 68; cf. the revivalists' position in the legislative debates on the Conciliation Boards Bill, supra pp. 205.

48 The newspapers used by these groups included The *Sun* (an English daily), The *Dawasa* (a Sinhalese daily) and The *Rivirasa* (a Sinhala weekly). See The *Europa Year book*, 11(1972): 317, 319.

49 See The *Dawasa*, 11 January 1969 and 27 December 1969.

50 The *Rivirasa*, 10 January 1969.

51 Statement issued by L. H. R. Pieris to the *Rivirasa*, 17 January 1969.

52 This represents the third and the most radical of socialist governments in Ceylon since independence. The first is Bandaranayake's government of 1956 to which we referred earlier in the text. Contemporary historians have varied in their evaluation of the socialist orientation of the Bandaranayake government policies and on the impact of the political programme which it instituted. One scholar believes that the 1956 general elections brought about a social revolution, by which the hitherto dominant western-educated urban elite were dethroned by a more traditionalistic rural petite-bourgeoisie. See Singer, 1964. While others do not perceive a fundamental difference in either the social origins or the policies of Bandaranayake's Freedom Party or the right wing United National Party, they accordingly characterize the Bandaranayake political programme as a mix of clerical and communal chauvinism and feigned reformism and anti-imperialism. See Halliday, 1971.

Among the more important changes initiated by this government were the nationalization of the port authority and all private omnibus companies, and the enactment of Agrarian Reform legislation which provided security of tenure to tenant cultivators of paddy lands. The enactment of legislation making Sinhala the official language of the country precipitated communal tensions culminating in racial riots which rocked the island in 1958.

A series of strikes and other demonstrations, and trade union action by the urban working class in 1956, led to the enactment of the Public Security Act regarded by some as "the most savagely repressive law in the whole arsenal of Ceylonese bourgeoise legislation." For a more extensive account of this period, see Wriggins, 1960.

S. W. R. D. Bandaranayake's assassination by a Buddhist monk in 1959 and the ensuing political confusion led to the second phase of socialist rule in Ceylon under the vanguardship of his widow Srimavo Bandaranayake.

This period was relatively uneventful and no major programmes of radical change were attempted. Of the more controversial legislation enacted during this regime was one passed in 1961 to nationalize the assets of the Anglo-American oil companies. The urban working class, however, during 1962 and 1963 became increasingly restive and militant and closed its ranks against the government to agitate in favour of a series of economic and political demands known as the "common programme". This led to successful overtures being made by the government towards the Trotskyite and Communist parties, with the latter joining the Government Parliamentary Group in 1964. See Farmer, 1965: 189.

Charges of nepotism, corruption and economic mismanagement contributed towards the defeat of the socialist coalition in 1965 and the return to power of the right-wing United National Party for a further period of five years. With exercise of emergency powers during most of these years, a fragile right-wing government was barely able to tide over a period of intense economic and political restiveness. Nationwide dissatisfaction over the cut-back in welfare measures led to an overwhelming rejection of the U.N.P. at the general elections of 1970.

The third phase of socialism was thus commenced on a tide of popular euphoria over the electoral victory of the socialist coalition. Although the new government undertook to institute a wide range of social reforms, including the state control of the export-import trade and the "Ceylonization" of all businesses, and promised to alleviate the economic hardships suffered by the less affluent segments of the populace, a deteriorating balance of trade situation and a generally sluggish economy accelerated the impoverishment of these social groups. The most enthusiastic backers of the government soon became its most virulent critics. The attack against the government was spearheaded by a clandestine group of left-wing intellectuals who had over several years established intimate contact with segments of the non-plantation rural peasantry. It initially took the form of an ideological assault on what was perceived to be the fake socialist policies of the government and its fidelity to the parliamentary system set up by "imperialists". It soon took the shape of violent armed insurrection which broke out in April 1971 and which was suppressed by the government with military assistance from an unusual alliance of nations from both the West and East, and including the United States of America and the Soviet Union. For two distinct perspectives on the Ceylon Insurgency, see Halliday, 1971 and 1972: 258.

53 The policy statements we shall examine include the Election Manifesto (1970); the *Throne Speech*, 1970, 1971; the *Budget Speech*, 1970–71, 1971–72; and the Directive Principles in the Constitution of Sri Lanka (1972), Section 16. Although the ideology of the socialist regime finds its most coherent expression in these statements, we should bear in mind the continuity between some of these ideas and those that were developed during the earlier phases of socialist rule in Ceylon.

54 We should also bear in mind that the socialist ideology is interlaced with several neo-traditionalistic ideas on linguistic and religious revivalism. These ideas find their strongest expression in the Constitutional provisions which decree Sinhala as the official language of the state, and which enjoin the state to protect and foster Buddhism. These policies have clearly had a divisive effect on the nation by alienating its ethnic and religious minorities and have been characterized by many as being anti-socialist and even "reactionary". See Halliday, 1971; cf. Farmer, 1965: 189, 192. Apologists of the coalition would, however, refute this by arguing that Buddhist-Sinhalese, being the religio-ethnic group which suffered the greatest disabilities under several centuries of foreign domination, deserved preferential treatment in the post-independent social order. For a review of doctrinal arguments on the compatibility of Theravada Buddhism and Marxism, see Smith, 1973.

55 The socialist coalition has been repeatedly critical of the terms of the loan arrangements and the "letters of intent" contracted by the U.N.P. with the International Monetary Fund, and has dubbed these arrangements as a "sell out of the national interests . . . to imperialism and neo-colonialism"; see Election Manifesto: 172–173 and *Budget Speech*, 1970–71: 6–11.

56 N. M. Perera, the Minister of Finance, further added "that aid arrangements must be consistent with our self-respect, our independence and our sovereignty", *Budget Speech*, 1970–71: 13.

N. M. Perera, the Trotskyist Minister of Finance, pointed out in his first budget speech that the programme of the socialist coalition was founded upon the thesis that no developing country could leave "development at the mercy of interplay of forces which are motivated solely by the profit instinct" (ibid.: 3). He added that while this doctrine recognized a role for the private sector in the development of the economy, it required the commanding heights of the economy to be firmly under the control of the public sector.

57 In furtherance of the general policy of state interventionism in the economy the government promised to nationalize the banking system, the import-export trade and control and direct the plantation industries through state agencies, and to regulate Agency Houses. See Election Manifesto: 174–175.

58 See Section 16 (2) (e) of the Principles of State Policy, the Constitution of Sri Lanka (1972).

59 See Section 16 (5), ibid.

60 N. M. Perera in his first budget speech pointed out that one of the basic commitments of the government was to establish the foundations for a socialist economy "while preserving the democratic traditions to which we as a people have pledged ourselves", *Budget Speech*, 1970–71: 4–5; cf. also Election Manifesto: 181 wherein it is provided that "all laws and regulations which restrict the democratic rights of the people will be repealed or amended"; cf. Sections 72 and 75 of the Constitution of Sri Lanka (1972) which guarantee that elections to the National Assembly would be free and secret and ensure the continued operation of those laws which protect the orderly conduct of the elections.

61 See Section 16 (5) of the Principles of State Policy, the Constitution of Sri Lanka (1972); cf. Election Manifesto: 173.

62 See the budget speech of N. M. Perera (1970–71: 4).

63 In 1970 N. M. Perera emphasized that the government was embarking on the unique task of attempting a socialist transformation through the ballot (ibid.: 40). This question assumed much more than an academic significance when the J.V.P. (People's Liberation Front), believing that socialism can only be realized through violent revolution aimed at dismantling the existing political-legal framework, set in operation an insurrection which almost toppled the government. In reviewing the havoc caused by the insurgency to the already ailing economy N. M. Perera reiterated his conviction that there could be no short-cut to socialism in a traditional society. He added that those who desired "an instant revolution had succeeded in pushing back revolutionary changes for a considerable time"; see *Budget Speech*, 1971–72; *Parliamentary Debates*, 1971: 171. To buttress this argument he reviewed the circumstances which led the Soviets even after a violent overthrow of the feudal and capitalist overlords to institute a New Economic Programme which retained the involvement of private enterprise in small and middle-scale industries and trade.

64 The Election Manifesto states that the United Left Front seeks to "develop all branches of the economy at a rapid rate and according to a National Economic Plan. . . ." (p. 175). See also Section 16 (2)

(c) of the Principles of State Policy, the Constitution of Sri Lanka (1972); *Budget Speech*, 1970–71: 5.

65 The United Left Front promised that its "program for the rapid industrialization of Ceylon, the extension of irrigation and power resources, the reorganization of the rural economy and the development of fishing would provide employment on a wide scale in both towns and villages"; see Election Manifesto: 177. Subsequent policy statements also underscore the urgency of the problems of unemployment and describe some of the immediate steps which the government proposed to take towards both a short-term and a long-term solution to the problem. See *Budget Speech*, 1970–71: 5, 28–29; Section 16 (2) (b) of the Directive Principle of State Policy, the Constitution of Sri Lanka (1972).

66 In *Budget Speech*, 1970–71, Minister Perera pointed out that one of the more basic policies of the government was its commitment to "those social welfare measures which are an integral part of the nation's social fabric" (p. 5).

67 The leader of the opposition in a bipartisan expression of support to the government for its actions against the insurgency of April 1971, reiterated in Parliament, "We do not approve of the use of violent means to replace a government lawfully elected by the people. . . . We must all co-operate to preserve the democratic way of life. That alone is the way of peace and progress. There is no other way." See *Parliamentarian*, 1971: 216.

68 See Section 18 (1), the Constitution of Sri Lanka (1972) which provides that "all persons are equal before the law and are entitled to equal protection of the law."

69 See Section 18 (1) (b), the Constitution of Sri Lanka (1972).

70 On the colonial period, see Tiruchelvam, 1971; Mendis, 1956, I: Introduction; and C. R. de Silva, 1941–42.

71 Cf. for a general treatment of some of these questions, Friedman, 1971; for a historical account of the expanding economic role of the state in post-independent Ceylon, see Oliver, 1957: 50ff.

72 For the government's commitment to social welfare schemes, see *Budget Speech*, 1970–71: 5; increasing outlays on the subsidizing of food, medical, educational and transportation expenses inevitably made such serious inroads into the surplus available for development that the government was most reluctantly compelled to cut back on some of these measures; see *Budget Speech*, 1971–72; ibid.: 246, 255–259. For an example of social-welfare legislation, see the Food Control Act, No. 25 of 1950, and regulations framed thereunder which set up an elaborate mechanism for the distribution of subsidized food rations.

73 The Land Reform Act imposed a ceiling of fifty acres on the ownership of all forms of land except that belonging to public

companies. See *Budget Speech*, 1971–72; 258, where the Minister of Finance describing the proposed legislation predicted that it would bring about an agrarian revolution in the country.

74 For an account of the several steps that the government proposed to take against what was described as "urban landlordism", see *Budget Speech*, 1971–72: 259; also the Rent Restriction Act of 1972.

75 See *Budget Speech*, 1971–72: 249, 261. This measure was justified on the basis that it was "socially desirable that all salary scales whether in the public or private sector should bear some reasonable relationship to the general patterns of individual earnings."

76 See the Industrial Products Acts, No. 18 of 1949; the Imports and Exports Controls Act, No. 9 of 1955; and the Exchange Act, No. 24 of 1953.

77 See the Compulsory Savings Act, No. 6 of 1971; Department of Inland Revenue Booklet on Compulsory Savings Levy (1971); *Budget Speech*, 1970–71: 249–250; and the Bank Debits Tax Act, No. 27 of 1970.

78 See the Control of Prices Act, No. 29 of 1950. The Minister of Finance promised in 1970 that a comprehensive price-control system would be evolved to combat the cost of living. See *Budget Speech*, 1970–71: 39.

79 See, on public corporations, Amerasinghe, 1972.

80 The government established several State Trading Corporations with a view to regulating the import and export trade and to conferring on the state a monopoly over the importation, exportation and distribution of several commodities such as textiles, subsidiary foodstuffs, tea and coconut products. See the Sri Lanka State Trading Corporations Act, No. 33 of 1970; and *Budget Speech*, 1971–72: 207.

81 To further the state policy of managing all "heavy basic and essential industries" the government decided to set up several industrial development corporations to facilitate the developmental planning and the co-ordination of the production programmes of different sectors of the economy. See *Budget Speech*, 1970–71: 35–36.

See also the Business Undertakings (Acquisition) Act, No. 35 of 1971 which enables the government to gain control of the business operations of "recalcitrant employers and anti-social businessmen [who attempt] to frustrate the application and execution of government programs". *Parliamentarian*, 1971: 134.

82 Although the Trotskyites for almost two decades advocated the nationalization of the plantation sector, once they assumed power, they opted for a more cautious policy of "purposeful intervention", according to which the government through the issue of directives, tax incentives and subsidies, attempts to protect and improve prices paid by importers, to ensure the efficient management of estates and

generally to stimulate investment in the plantation industries. See Budget Speech 1970–71: 204; also the Tea Control Act, No. 28 of 1949; and the Rubber Control Act, No. 29 of 1949.

83 For an account of the circumstances under which the Supreme Court would (in exercise of the supervisory jurisdiction conferred on it by the Courts Ordinance) review executive action, see Cooray, 1968: 105ff. Justice H. N. G. Fernando in Anthony Naide v. the Ceylon Tea Plantation Co. Ltd. (N.L.R. 68 (1966): 558) implied that the legislature could not by ordinary legislation take away the court's power to review administrative actions through the issue of the prerogative writs recognized in Sections 42 and 45 of the Courts Ordinance.

84 See Cooray, 1968: 99–102. See also the judgement of District Courts in Mudanayke v. Sivagnnanasunderam (N.L.R. 53(1952): 25).

85 See the comments on the judiciary during the legislative debates on the Interpretation Ordinance (Amendment) Act of 1971; see *Parliamentarian*, 1972: 238–240; 1971: 134.

86 See the Court of Appeals Act, No. 44 of 1971.

87 See the Ceylon (Constitution and Independence) Amendment Act, No. 36 of 1971; also Jayaratne, 1972: 104.

88 This is clearly seen in the constitution of the first National State Assembly which was composed of all members of the former House of Representatives. See Section 42 (1), the Constitution of Sri Lanka (1972). In addition, the members of the National State Assembly continue to be designated as "Members of Parliament" (Section 29), enjoy the same powers, privileges and immunities as those of the House (Section 38), and continue to regulate the proceedings of the Assembly in accordance with the Standing Orders of the House of Representatives (Section 37).

89 See Sections 48 (2) and 49 (2), the Constitution of Sri Lanka (1972).

90 See Sections 54 and 55, the Constitution of Sri Lanka (1972).

91 See the Interpretation Ordinance (Amendment) Act of 1972. Section 1 construed the phrase "shall not be questioned in a court of law" as barring any inquiry by a court into the validity of any act on which the legislature had conferred this effect; Section 2 strictly defined the circumstances in which a writ of certiorari, mandamus, or injunction may be issued by the Supreme Court to set aside the acts of an executive authority or to compel it to perform an obligation; see *Parliamentarian*, 1972: 240. Section 121 (3) of the Constitution of Sri Lanka (1972) explicitly reserves in the National State Assembly the power to further limit by law the Superior Courts supervisory jurisdiction.

92 See Section 46 of the Industrial Disputes Act, No. 43 of 1950 (as amended by the Act, No. 62 of 1959).

93 During the debates on the Business Undertakings (Amendment)

Bill, the opposition urged the government to accept an amendment rendering it possible for aggrieved parties to appeal against an acquisition order in a regular court of law. The government however rejected the suggestion, arguing that it would defeat the purposes of the Bill, as the process of appeal to the courts of law would take several years of delay. See *Parliamentarian*, 1971: 134.

94 See The *Sunday Observer*, 4 February 1973 for the brief filed by counsel to the Civil Rights Movement before the Constitutional Court impugning the constitutionality of the Press Council Bill of 1972.

95 See the criticisms of the Civil Rights Movement by the Minister of Justice in the debates on the Criminal Justice Commission Bill.

96 See the Ceylon (Parliamentary Elections) Order-in-Council, as amended by the Act, No. 9 of 1970.

97 Section 4 of the Constitution of Sri Lanka (1972) provides that the "Sovereignty of the people is exercised through a National State Assembly of elected *representatives* of the People" (my emphasis).

98 See Chapter XI of the Constitution of Sri Lanka (1972) on the constitution of the National State Assembly, and Section 75 on the continuance of existing laws relating to elections.

99 For a recent clash between the two branches of the profession over a Bar Council ruling on an advocate's right of representation before labour tribunals and the regular courts of law without the assistance of a proctor, see *Ceylon Law Journal*, 2(1971): 314.

100 See supra p. 190, category (b) in the discussion on the value-commitments of the socialist coalition.

101 See the Peoples Committees Act, No. 16 of 1971; and N. M. Perera, *Budget Speech*, 1971–72: 207.

102 Ibid.: 174; Perera pointed out that during the days following the government's decision to demonetize higher-currency notes, those who helped the "tax evaders and hoarders of currency were the workers and [others from the poorest] sections of the people. For temporary gain they helped the rich capitalists escape the rigors of a very useful legislation. . . . Indeed the very people whom we wished to help joined hands with the exploiters". (p. 173).

103 Although there is no statutory provision excluding the appointment of lawyers, in practice the government has strictly adhered to this policy. See the interview with Ratnasiri Wickremanayake, Junior, Minister of Justice, on file with the author.

104 See the statistics on the disposition of disputes by Conciliation Boards, 1964–72, on file with the Ministry of Justice; Goonesekere & Metzger, 1971: 97–100.

105 See Section 16 (6), the Constitution of Sri Lanka (1972).

106 See the speech of the Minister of Justice at the Annual Conference of Judicial Officers, 1972, on file with the Ministry of Justice; see

also the Policy Statement of the Government of Sri Lanka (23 June 1972, *Parliamentarian*, 1972: 351).

107 See *Budget Speech*, 1971–72: 258–259; memorandum by the Legal Research Division on the draft law to relieve rural indebtedness, dated 14 August 1972, on file with the Ministry of Justice; Draft of the Settlement of Debt Act (1972) on file with the Ministry of Justice; and memorandum on the Draft Law by D. L. Mendis, on file with the Ministry of Justice.

108 The Settlement of Debts Law, No. 27 of 1975.

References

Amerasinghe, A. R. B.
1972. *Public Corporations in Ceylon*. Colombo: Lake House.

Cohn, Bernard S.
1967. Some Notes on Law and Change in Northern India. In *Law and Warfare*, ed. Paul Bohannan. New York: The Natural History Press.

Cooray, J. A. L.
1968. The Supreme Court of Ceylon. *Journal of the International Commission of Jurists*, *9*: 96–113.

de Silva, C. R.
1941–42. *Ceylon under British Occupation*. 2 vols. Colombo: Colombo Apothecaries.

de Silva, K. M.
1959. The Colebrooke-Cameron Reforms. *Ceylon Journal of Historical and Social Science Studies*, *2*: 244–256.

Election Manifesto (Common Programme of the United Left Front, Party Manifestos of the United Left Front)
1970. In the *Ceylon Daily News*, Seventh Parliament of Ceylon.

Farmer, B. H.
1965. Nine Years of Political and Economic Change in Ceylon. *The World Today*, *21*: 189–198.

Friedman, W.
1971. *The State and Rule of Law in a Mixed Economy*. London: Stevens.

Goonesekere, R. K. W., & Metzger, Barry.
1971. The Conciliation Boards Act: Entering the Second Decade. *Ceylon Law Journal*, *2*: 35–100.

Halliday, Fred.
1971. The Ceylonese Insurrection. *The New Left Review*, *69*: 55–91.
1972. Politics, April Revolt in Ceylon. *Asian Survey*, *12*.

Jayaratne, B. C. F.
1972. The Abolition of the Senate of Ceylon. *Parliamentarian*, *53*: 104–112.

Malaviya, H. D.
1956. *Village Panchayats in India*. New Delhi: All India Congress Committee.

Marasinghe, M. L.
1980. The Use of Conciliation for Dispute Settlement: The Sri Lanka Experience. *International and Comparative Law Quarterly*, *29*: 389–414.

Mendis, G. C., ed.
1956. *The Colebrooke-Cameron Papers*. 2 vols. Oxford: Oxford University Press.
Oliver, Henry M.
1957. *Economic Opinion and Policy in Ceylon*. Durham, N. C.: Duke University Press.
Singer, Marshal.
1964. *The Emerging Elite: A Study of Political Leadership in Ceylon*. Cambridge, Mass.: MIT Press.
Smith, Ronald.
1973. The Politics of Buddhism. *World Politics*, *16*.
Tiruchelvam, Neelan.
1971. Popular Tribunals and Political Development in Ceylon. Seminar Material on Law and Development. Steiner, Henry, and Unger, Robert, eds. On file with Harvard Law School.
1973. The Popular Tribunals of Sri Lanka: A Socio-Legal Inquiry. On file with Harvard Law School.
1978. 'Popular Courts' on the Eve of British Rule: A Socio-Legal Analysis of the *Gamsabhava*. *Colombo Law Review*, *20*: 26–56.
Wood, A. L.
1961, *Crime and Aggression in Changing Ceylon*. Philadelphia: American Philosophical Society.
Wriggins, Howard.
1960. *Ceylon: The Dilemma of a New Nation*. Princeton: Princeton University Press.
Ziadeh, Faraht.
1968. *Lawyers: The Role of Law and Liberalism in Modern Egypt*. Stanford: Hoover Institute Press.
Government Publications and Periodicals:
Administrative Report.
Budget Speech.
Ceylon Law Journal.
Ceylon Law Recorder.
C.L.W. (*Ceylon Law Weekly*).
Department of Inland Revenue Booklet on Compulsory Savings Levy, 1971.
Hansard.
N.L.R. (*New Law Reports*).
Parliamentarian.
Parliamentary Debates.
Report of Soulbury Commission on Constitutional Reform, 1946.
Report of the Study Team on Nyaya Panchayat, 1962.
Senate Debates.
Throne Speech.

5 People's Law in India – The Hindu Society

Upendra Baxi

I. Introduction

The nature and scope of indigenous law in any society can be studied from a number of perspectives (see Baxi, 1979c). One can study it from the perspective of the state legal system (SLS), for example, ascertaining primarily the enclaves of "customary" or people's law tolerated or legitimated by it and examining the impact of SLS on such enclaves and *vice versa*. But I find such a perspective too limited and too hegemonical. It is limited for the very reasons for which all "top-down" perspectives are limited. "Top-down" perspectives deny existence or value to those areas of social reality and process which are uncongenial to the establishment or official *Weltanschauung*. They also turn out (whether so intended or not) to be hegemonical by favouring the assumption that patterns of legal and social rationality institutionalized in the SLS are inherently superior, if not manifestly so, to those institutionalized in the "folk", "group", "people's" or non-state law. The pre-colonial Asian societies were principally governed by the non-state law. Colonization processes superimposed "Western" legal norms, institutions and culture. Even so, most social life still continued to be under the domain of people's law. In these societies, even after independence and despite massive reassertion of Western legal culture, many vital areas of social life continue to be governed and dominated by non-state legal systems

(NSLS), which as often complement as contradict the SLS. In this paper, I attempt to look at indigenous or people's law in India on its own terms, as providing alternate modes of social action and ordering, and trace briefly the patterns of relationship between SLS and NSLS in what appears often as a struggle for hegemony. In the process, I naturally neglect to list and analyse areas where the SLS had tolerated, legitimated or co-opted congenial elements or aspects of NSLS.[1] This kind of cataloguing, while helpful, may only provide a static, and often distorting, focus as far as the Indian sociojural experience is concerned. This paper deals first with the manner in which the classical Hindu law dealt with the notions of dharma and "custom" and the struggle, under the British regime, on behalf of the "high-culture" law to overcome the people's law. We then examine more specifically the relations between SLS and NSLS in contemporary India. The account is merely illustrative of a process of pluralistic growth and development, which cannot be grasped by an exclusive focus on NSLS.

II. From Dharma to Law: and Back?

1. INTRODUCTION

The interplay between people's law and state law has ancient roots in India, especially in the growth of classical Hindu law. The classical sources of the Hindu law display the dynamic relation of "custom" to the eternal law of dharma as well as the secular law of the Prince. Those sources include: *Dharmasutras* (compiled between about 800 and 500/400 B.C.), *Dharmaśāstras* (circa A.D. 200), commentaries and digests (which appeared as early as A.D. 600). Indeed, the *śāstras* themselves embody numerous customs. *Carita* is specifically recognized as a source of law, though only when it is qualified as *sadācāra* or *sístācāra*, that is "good custom" or "usages of the good". The *śāstra*, of course, did not incorporate all major customs. Thus, the *śāstra* tells us little or nothing about the customs of *mechas*, forest or hill tribes or other untouchables living on the fringe of Hindu society; the jurisprudence did not grow to include them" (Derrett, 1968: 177). Nor do the *śāstras* make much effort to "record or standardize commercial customs, though examples of general commercial usage are to be found" (id.: 159). Customs relating to "land tenure, to tenancies and the like are given little space"; so also customs "relating to marriage were incorporated to a limited degree" (id.: 159–160). Perhaps, since proof of custom overrode the written law, the "jurist's" task was to perfect the latter and not to expatiate on customary deviations" (id.: 161).

But certain basic questions remain: How is one to distinguish (prior to the advent of the Western conception of law and authority) between dharma and law? between dharma, law, custom, and royal power? What kinds of relationships exist among these? What are the relationships between the law-in-books and the law-in-action? What are the distinctive features of the Hindu jurisprudence? These and related questions have no doubt preoccupied eminent scholars in the field, but the late lamented Robert Lingat offers in his *Classical Law of India* (1973), probably for the first time, a systematic array of answers to them. Whether or not all the answers are acceptable, subsequent work in the area will have to take them as starting points for thought.

2. LINGAT'S DISCUSSION ON THE LEGAL NATURE OF DHARMA

Dharma, explains Lingat, is not merely a "set of eternal laws" inherent in the nature of things but it is also "a morality addressed to man in society," a morality which specifies the "totality of duties which bears upon the individual according to his status (*varna*) and the stage of his life (*āśrama*)" (pp. 3–4). The morality of dharma (superior to that of *artha* – wealth, interest – and *kama* – pleasure) is both social and religious: dharma "is essentially a rule of *interdependence*, founded on the hierarchy corresponding to the nature of things and necessary for the maintenance of social order." To deviate from its requirements "is to violate one's destiny and expose oneself to the loss of one's salvation" (p. 211). Dharma is transcendent and immutable; its authority derives from the natural order of things, although dharma has no "constraining power by itself" (p. 258). Thus, says Lingat, the "rule of dharma will remain fixed at the very foundation of the concept of law" (pp. 5–6).

Hence the problem: Can we analytically disengage the rules of dharma from juridical rules? The latter, quite prominent in *Dharmaśāstras* "continue to be incorporated with rules of a purely religious and ritual inspiration." The rule of prescription (though adverse possession) formulated by *Yājnāvalkya*, is virtually of the same nature as that which enjoins upon a *dvija* (a duty of not marrying a woman of *varna* higher than his own.)" Both these precepts "express or rather determine the requirements necessary to maintain the cosmic and the moral order." (p. 135) Fulfilment of both the precepts represent an unquestionable religious duty, and accordingly confer "merit." But are the legal rules expressed in *Dharmaśāstras* direct sources of law or merely indirect ones? In Lingat's sharp formulation: Do they have the "quality of legislation, the authority of which bears directly upon the judge?" or are they "sources of law only in the sense that religion and morality are amongst the sources of law in Europe"? In Lingat's analysis, the latter will not constitute the "*true source*" of law.

Lingat's answer to this question is necessarily complex. *Dharmaśāstras* were obviously not codes "in the European sense of that word," because, prior to the British period, "there never was in India . . . a power to pass legislation, in our sense of that word, at least in matters of private law." Still, the *śāstric* precepts were not entirely without influence. Apart from the authority they had by virtue of their origin, they also offered (particularly "in the judge's eyes") "some framework of juridical reasoning" (p. 141). The precepts, however, were exposed to the Scylla of custom and the Charybdis of royal power and governmental policies. The voyage from dharma to law, Lingat emphasizes, became possible because of the labours of commentators on *śāstric* precepts: it was only with the Mimansa technique of interpretation that "a true juridical science" began in India (p. 143).

One must turn to the art of interpretation (pp. 143–175) to appreciate fully the virtuosity of commentators in interpreting the texts and contexts of the *śāstric* injunctions and precepts, whether through the techniques of manipulating the distinction between a *vidhi* (precept embodying an injunction) and *arthavāda* (additional verbiage offering descriptions, elaborations or reasons for injunctions), or of manipulating the rules for resolving differences between two *śāstric* texts of equal authority (see the discussion of Vijnaesvara's exegesis on adverse possession and prescription at pp. 161–167). It should suffice to note here that the juristic concern with interpretation, overtly analytical and exegetical though it may appear, continually made *śāstric* precepts responsive to social realities, within which they had to function as rules for conduct. Sometimes such interpretation legitimized local customs, the most dramatic example being furnished by Madhyava's interpretation of Manu (IX: 172–173) which prohibits the marriage of a boy with his maternal uncle's or paternal aunt's daughter, common among South Indians. In a *tour de force* of exegesis, Madhyava reinterprets the verse to sanction what it expressly prohibits (pp. 169–171)! It is the same type of creative ability which enables both Vijnaesvara and Jimutavahana to derive from the *Smriti* text "violently opposed theses" resulting into the now well-known "schools" (respectively) of Mitaksara and Dayabaga (pp. 172–175).

Lingat warns us, rightly, not to assume that the commentators' role or function was to "canonize" custom. Customary rules are "often imprecise and incomplete". Interpretation "offers them a framework which demands adjustments and correctives in enunciation, at the same time it allows gaps to be filled". It is this framework through which interpretation could exercise influence upon custom "even when custom has not directed its choice" (p. 172). We see continuing examples of this kind of interaction in Lingat's absorbing analysis of contrasts and conflicts between dharma and custom.

The precepts of dharma and of law stand in sharp contrast to those of custom. *Śāstric* law (religious and juridical) is didactic, religious in conception and consequences. Rule of custom, in principle, "is indifferent to the religious consequences of an act"; customs may be consonant with *śāstric* law, or may be in acute conflict with it. *Śāstric* law as eternal natural law is independent of human volition: "the rules govern the activity of men: they are not influenced by man," whereas custom is a "purely human development". While dharma, and law related to it, has a "transcendent character", custom is a "social phenomenon". Dharma is immutable and universal; custom is territorially limited and variable (pp. 176–177). Lingat shows, however, that these ideal-typical contrasts drawn in literature can mislead us; indeed, he demonstrates that despite these contrasts, the *śāstric* texts disclose "a place for custom in the genesis of dharma" (p. 177).

How does this come about? First, the *śāstras* explicitly recognize *sadācāra* or *sístaācāra*. In a sense, the Good Custom as a source of dharma, "amounts to saying that the conduct of everyone should be ruled by that of *Brahmins*", as only they would best understand how to act in a disinterested way, with a belief that the behaviour is required by "obedience for the divine law" (pp. 179–180). Even though some commentators endeavoured to enlarge this conception to include behaviour of those *not* learned in the *vedas*, the custom which would count as a rule of dharma "must not only be immemorial but also free from all apparent worldly motives, interest, or utilitarian consideration" (p. 180).

Despite all this, second, the *śāstric* texts demonstrate clearly the influence of custom in formulation of precepts and whether directly acknowledged (*e.g.* procedure for hearing of cases) or indirectly manifested through inconsistencies in *śāstric* prescription (*e.g.* condemnation of marriage of a *dvija* with *Sūdra* woman yet providing rules for a share of paternal estate for a son of *Brahmin, Ksatriya* or *Vaisyaya* born of female *Sūdra*!). It may be that the incorporation of custom into *śāstric* injunctions may be selective, and may transform the rules of custom; but neither the fact of incorporation nor the resultant nexus between dharma and custom can be gainsaid.

Third, the theory of *yugas* (epochs), especially as developed by Parasara, would seem to make dharma (and law) more responsive to social realities, often expressed through customs and usages of the group. Hindu cosmogony divides each epoch into four *yugas: krta* (the first golden age) is followed by *treta, dwapara* and finally the *kali* (the present, decadent age). Each period has its own characteristics and its own dharma. What varies, according to Lingat, are not the "moral imperatives" of dharma but rather man's capacities "to obey the moral law" (p. 189).

Be that as it may, Lingat concedes that the theory of *yugas* has "led us little by little to the idea" that although the *śāstric* rules of conduct "retain eternally their redemptive quality, they are not always good to follow" (p. 189). The commentators arrived at this result by asserting that the rule of dharma is not to be followed if it is *loka-vidvista* (odious to the world) or *loka-vikrusta* (reproved by the world). A large number of acts, although enjoined by the *śāstras*, thus become *kali-varjyas* (acts prohibited in the *kali yuga*). The local custom thus triumphs over the *śāstric* norms, though the intellectual activity of the commentators attempts to legitimate this triumph within the framework of *śāstric* law. Lingat, however, feels that the *kali-varjyas* theory has merely a negative character of abrogating old customs. The task is to discover how new customs, contributing to the birth of "new institutions", emerge.

How did new customary rules and institutions arise despite the orthodox position that a practice contrary to *śāstric* precepts is evil and sinful? Lingat shows that most commentators used creatively the doctrine of Good Custom to legitimate whole bodies of customary rules existent in different regions. Moreover, the royal duties extended to the preservation of custom, conventions and usages, not merely of the people in a conquered territory but also with respect to groups of his own subjects. The king is advised that dharma can "only prosper in order": if, therefore, abrogation of custom contrary to dharma is likely to cause disorder, wisdom requires continuance of such custom (pp. 199–200, 224–232).

Lingat concedes that the rule of dharma thus did not become a juridical rule until "it entered into behaviour and was accepted by the population as a customary rule" (p. 202). But he maintains that this "admitted predominance" of custom did not render the *śāstric* rules any the less authoritative. The *śāstric* rules provided the framework for juristic activity; juristic activity, in turn, provided the framework for more precise articulation, adoption and limitation of the rules of custom. Juristic activity put custom in its own place, as it were. A customary rule in contradiction with dharma "is not capable of extension"; the unorthodox rule of custom has no chance of extending its domain". Lingat insists:

> "the rule of dharma has an unlimited power of radiation. It offers itself as a model to every group. It fills gaps in custom and insinuates itself into the customary structure. And once it is established there it is fixed thereafter; it is, and remains, dharma, the group's law." (p. 204)

The crucial differences between the Western legal systems and the classical Hindu legal system, Lingat concludes debatably, is that while the former are founded upon the notion of legality, the latter rests upon the notion of authority. In the former "the primacy belongs to the positive law and in particular to the statute", the other "sources, by no means inconsiderable, are only subsidiary to it"; whereas in the Hindu classical law the *śāstric* precepts were seen to be law "in the sense that the word is used in natural science, a law which rules human activity". Lingat elaborates this point:

> "Everyone knows that no one can escape from the law. As a result, one must try his utmost to conform to it. But it has no constraining power by itself. It puts itself forward, it shows the way one should follow, but it does not impose that way. Society is thus organized on the model of itself, with which it is presented as if it had actually achieved it." (p. 258)

Having said this, Lingat is careful to note that a conception "could have ended in complete divorce between reality and law" but for the fact that the law revealed by the sages was "profoundly based in the traditions and aspirations of the Hindu world" (p. 258). The Hindu system, Lingat concludes, "sustained the unity of the Hindu world, thanks to the authority of the law". The unity was "unrealizable at the lower level, but was realized on the higher level in an ideal participation amongst all Hindus". That ideal "received the dynamic imparted to it by faith, by Hinduism itself, *with the result that custom and written law are inextricably woven together to give rise to law*" (p. 256, italics mine).

III. High Culture Law and Social Mobility

The relation between custom and dharma, between people's law and state law, underwent fundamental change during the colonial period. Both administrative exigencies and high colonial policy made non-interference with religiously based law a desideratum. But such a policy could not immunize the existing laws from fundamental change, especially when colonial authority had to create a national legal system for the governance of the country. Such a system, naturally, "affected the balance between divergent indigenous legal traditions" (Rudolph & Rudolph, 1967: 269). The story of how those changes occurred has been meticulously told by many, but perhaps most authoritatively by Duncan Derrett (1968: 225–320; see also Rudolph & Rudolph, 1967; Jain, 1966; Galanter, 1964). It should suffice here to stress briefly a few distinctive aspects of the transition.

1. BRAHMINIZATION AND ANGLICIZATION OF THE LAW DURING THE INITIAL PERIOD OF COLONIAL ADMINISTRATION

During the initial period of administration, dual systems of courts were established with jurisdiction over all matters, civil, criminal and commercial. The Presidency town courts included royally established Supreme Courts, with English judges and lawyers; the *mofussil* (back-country) courts included *sudder* (chief) courts, manned by judges drawn from the civil service and with Indian pleaders. There was "less formal procedure and less English law" in these back-country courts (Galanter, 1964; Jain, 1966: 81–192). The applicable law also varied. Noteworthy for our purposes is Section 23 of Warren Hastings' Judicial Plan of 1772:

> "In suits regarding inheritance, marriage, caste and other religious usages and institutions, the laws, those of the Shashter with regard to Gentoos, will be invariably adhered to; and on all such occasions, Maulvis or Brahmins shall respectively attend the Courts to expound the law and they shall sign the report and assist in passing the decree."

Regulation IV of 1793 concretized the Hastings Plan by specifically allocating to the governance by Hindu and Moslem law matters pertaining to "succession, inheritance, marriage, caste and all religion usages and institution". These regulations applied to lower or *mofussil* courts, but it was the Act of Settlement, 1781, which extended the principles underlying Hastings Plan to the Supreme Court of Bengal. All matters "arising out of succession to lands, rents, and all matters of contract and dealing between party and party" were to be determined by reference to not just the "laws" of Moslems and Hindus, but by reference to "usages" also. This recognition of custom was extended in Punjab, Madras, Central Province and other parts of British India (Kane, 1950: 42–43; Mahmood, 1977: 10–18).

But how, practically speaking, was this to be done? There were, in Sir Henry Maine's memorable words, "vast gaps and interspaces in the Substantive Law of India". The colonial administrators sought help from the religious cognoscente: *pandits* (the learned in Hindu law) and *maulvis* (Moslem divines) were associated with the courts as experts from 1772 to 1864. In addition, they commissioned, and sometimes produced, digests and compilations of *śāstric* laws: the first such attempt being the work of eleven *pandits* who worked for two years to produce in 1775 a digest, which was later published in an authentic English version as *A Code of Gentos Laws* in 1776. These were followed by compilations, digests, and treatises by (or under the sponsorship of) English scholar administrators like Jones, Colebrook and others (see Derrett, 1968: 242–269; Jain, 1966: 701–770).

In this phase, which Marc Galanter following Max Weber, calls the "expropriation of the law", a most distinctive result, although probably unintended, was achieved. This was the creation of what

Derrett calls the Anglo-Hindu law or the Rudolphs call the cosmopolitan, high-culture law. The textual law, through revival of *śāstric* scholarship and through the association of *pandits* with courts, was elevated above the customary law. No measures were taken by, or since, Hastings to ascertain custom; it was assumed that the indigenous Hindu law was to be found in the *śāstric* texts. Even in cases involving topics not listed in 1793, direction, justice, equity and good conscience, rather than indigenous custom, were to be applied. (Derrett, 1968: 289–306). The choice was perhaps ineluctable: if the government had "backed the customary law instead of *śāstric* law, literally hundreds of different systems of customary law would have emerged" (id.: 317). The result was "the *śāstra* under the British made advances over custom, despite the explicit protection of the latter; and custom has been forced to struggle against what might be called Anglo-*śāstric* law" (id.: 293). The "explicit protection" of custom, to which Derrett refers here, is perhaps the possibility, still left open, of situations when custom may derogate from the personal law or the too-ready reliance in certain cases (particularly in relation to the substantive autonomy of caste-*panchayats*), on local, community customs. But custom still needed to be proved, through alien procedures and alien institutions. Just as the written texts of religious laws, and processes of Western-style interpretation and exegesis led to Anglicization of Hindu Law, so did the neglect of custom lead to the stagnation of Hindu Law during the British period.

The customary rules were subjected, more or less, to the requirement of the common-law burden of proof: custom to be a source of law must be proved to be "immemorial or ancient, uniform, invariable, continuous, certain, notorious, reasonable (or not unreasonable), peaceable, obligatory and it must not be immoral nor opposed to an express enactment . . . or to public policy" (Kane, 1950: 44). Although not involved in every case, these requirements made (whenever involved) proof of custom difficult. Whenever custom was judicially cognized, it was also transformed:

> "From a body of orally-transmitted precepts and precedents, subject to variable interpretation and quasi-legislative innovation at the discretion of village notables or elders, it becomes a body of fixed law to be construed by a professional court. Judicial enforcement of custom rigidifies

> it and strips it of quasi-legislative character: official courts are reluctant to permit the creation of new binding custom (Galanter, 1964; also see Kane, 1950: 44–45)."

The elevation of the high-culture, *Brahminic, śāstric* law has led to elaboration of the claim that "for some time in a variety of ways, indigenous high-culture law aided in establishing a national legal framework" (Rudolph & Rudolph, 1967). By "high-culture law" the Rudolphs mean the "literary law inscribed in classic texts" (the *śāstra* for Hindus, the Koran for Moslems) as expounded to the English judges by *maulvis* and *pandits.* This "high-culture law" flourished and developed during 1772–1864, at the expense of the "popular law of the peasant society" (id.: 269). The "popular" or "customary" law was difficult to ascertain and it was "parochial", whereas the high-culture *Brahminic* law was "cosmopolitan" and "uniform", based on readily ascertainable written texts, and developed through interpretation by legal notables.

But the modernity of the high-culture law did not lie in its substantive norms. Both parochial custom and cosmopolitan high-culture law reflected and embodied "for most part" values that were "antithetical to those in Western law". The Rudolphs bring out the salient value contrasts perceptively.

First, they note that whereas English law valued the individual over "artificial" groups, the traditional Indian law valued the natural associations (family, caste) over the individual. Thus, "traditional" law regulated legal relations among individuals by reference to their group or corporate identity. British law sought to liberate the individual from constrictive group affiliations. Mobility of property increased under British law, for example, by the effective, though by no means simple, device of wills, the legal application of which varied somewhat unevenly from 1792 to 1878 when the Hindu Wills Act 1870 established a general set of rights and requirements (Rudolph & Rudolph, 1967: 289). Changes in the personal law (such as entitling creditors to bring to sale debtors' interest in personal property), and revenue law (making land saleable collateral for defaulting farms and estates) provide other examples.

Whereas high-culture law was "particularistic", English law was universalistic "in principle treating *all men as equal* before it" (id.: 280; italics mine). The qualification is important for, though seldom noted, Englishmen in India enjoyed certain privileges and immunities in the civil justice sector from 1793 to 1843 and in the sphere of criminal law, it was not until 1923 that Englishmen (as well as Europeans and Americans) could be tried by Indian magistrates and judges in the *mofussil.* As an eminent Indian legal historian has pointed out: "It was unjust to give to the Englishmen a right of free resort to the interior, and then to exempt them from the jurisdiction of the local authorities, which were always open to them against the Indian people" (Jain, 1966: 364). Certainly the appreciation of the universalistic orientation of English law on the part of contemporary Indians must have been profoundly affected by this continual derogation from the principles of equality of all men before the law.

Be that as it may, this principle did, as it related to the indigenous peoples themselves, bring a revolutionary change in the modes of dispute-settlement. Both the traditional Indian and the English law value impartiality, but concern for impartiality finds expression in the latter through elaboration and maintenance of rules of procedure and evidence. Thus, for example, English law exhibited a strict concern for the relevance of facts brought before the courts as evidence in support of rival contentions. But the indigenous system saw no objection if a tribunal, "met to settle one dispute, finds itself adjudicating another that lies behind it" (Rudolph & Rudolph, 1967: 257). To be sure, village tribunals have to distinguish between authentic and adulterated testimony. But judgement concerning the credibility of evidence arises from the intimate and direct knowledge the adjudicators have of the dispute before them rather than through an elaborate system of rules of evidence, procedure and pleading.

Finally, Western legal systems are distinguished by adversary proceedings where one party loses and the other wins. Traditional Indian tribunals, according to the limited ethnographical evidence we have, manifest a concern for dispute-settlement through consensus. They do not isolate the dispute from its overall social context. Rather, in and through that context the indigenous tribunals seek a solution which maximizes social harmony or abates group conflict or tension. Reconciliation of parties through compromise and consensus characterizes decisions of those tribunals, whereas (to borrow a striking phrase) the adversary system manifests a "winner-take-all" attitude (Coons, 1964: 787).

The importation of adversary processes for doing justice had important consequences, both enduring and transitional (the latter illustrated by a prevalence of false witnesses and the rise in litigiousness, the extent of which still continues to be debated). The enduring consequences lay in the creation (which still persists) of dual legal systems: the western and the indigenous. According to the Rudolphs, these two systems today exhibit three legal cultures: the parochial, the *Brahminic* and the national. Social change through the law receives impetus as well as encountering formidable obstacles, owing to this multiplicity of legal cultures and the plurality of legal "systems". Indeed, the Rudolphs suggest that the processes of social mobility described as Sanskritization and Westernization find their jural parallel in Brahminization and Anglicization of the law.

It is clear that the modernity of *Brahminic* high-culture law did not arise from its substantive norms, nor in its procedures for dispute-settlement. Both in norms of substance and procedure the *Brahminic* law in operation had more in common with the parochial customary law rather than universalistic English law. How then can it be said that the *Brahminic* law became a "vehicle of modernization?"

The Rudolphs nowhere squarely confront this question. But a handful of very general observations suggest their approach to it. Compared to customary law, the high-culture law was more "uniform" and "cosmopolitan". Unlike customary law, high-culture law was written and its "relative ascertainability, certainty, and consistency" commended it to all, "Indian and British alike, concerned about order and regularity" (Rudolph & Rudolph, 1967: 274). These features of "form and structure", the Rudolphs maintain, made the high-culture law "an amenable if somewhat delusive instrument for Britain's wishing to find and apply a uniform law to Indians" (id.: 279).

No less an authority on Anglo-Hindu law than Derrett has maintained that the law, during the above period, "for all its many anomalies became much more certain and much more uniform" (Derrett, 1968: 316). And to the extent then that "certainty" and "uniformity" are attributes of a modern legal system, the Rudolphs' observations that the high-culture law served as a "vehicle of modernization" must be accepted. But this acceptance must be limited in view of the fact that for any legal system in which the decisional law of courts plays a major role, overall judgements about certainty, consistency and uniformity, even when most circumspectly made, are impossible to verify. This is so not just because these attributes are hard to define and measure both over a time-scale and over rather heterogeneous case-materials, but also because "certainty-consistency-uniformity" are matters of degree, matters of more-or-less, rather than of all-or-nothing. Pockets or sectors within a legal order are more amenable to such judgements than a legal order considered as a whole.

Nor are the above-mentioned the sole or most salient attributes of modern legal orders generally. In fact it might be more correct to say that a quest for (rather than an attainment of) certainty, consistency and uniformity, and accessibility, characterize modern legal systems. Legal growth and legal change are very often accompanied by, and require, departures from certainty, consistency and uniformity. The high-culture law served as an agent of modernization just as much (if not more) because the *śāstric* texts were open to divergent and conflicting interpretations, because the integrity of its authoritative exponents (the *pandits*) was often in doubt, because many *śāstric* norms were impracticable to follow or were obsolete, and because the courts did not (as indeed they could not always) adhere self-defeatingly to the canon that previous decisions ought to be followed (Derrett, 1968: 294–315). Indeed, when we thus look at the system of case law microscopically, the acute contrast drawn between custom and the superior high-culture law, in terms of consistency, accessibility, uniformity and certainty, assuredly becomes faint.

Another glimpse into the Rudolphs' reasons for regarding the *Brahminic* law as a modernizing agent is provided by the reiteration of the view that the high-culture law flourished at the expense of local custom. Legal processes were coloured by Sanscritist perspectives not just by the adoption of *Brahminic* law on the part of the British, and this reinforced its original authority. Not to be overlooked was the fact that the "lower level judges and early incumbents of the modern legal profession were drawn from the upper castes" (Rudolph & Rudolph, 1967: 274). Thus, the Rudolphs suggest, though not quite explicitly, that the Brahminization of law generally helped the processes of Sanscritization in the area of social mobility.

If indeed Brahminization of the law affected processes of social mobility ("lower caste assimilation to higher-caste norms"), then this remains to be demonstrated. True, as the Rudolphs point out, the courts determined legal relations among groups by reference to the higher-culture *śāstric* texts, providing the four-*varna* model or even the simple twice-born model, whereas in reality there was "a multitude of caste groups". But did what the courts say in cases coming before them affect this reality in any significant way? This question is too important to be ignored, but to answer it will require the compilation of social profiles of parties who brought their disputes before the courts during the era of high-culture law. In considering the question whether the introduction of the English system increased litigiousness and whether this contributed to mobility, the Rudolphs favour an affirmative answer on the ground that increase in litigation "may also mean that the litigants are searching for a means to escape the disabilities and coercions of traditional village society" and that such increase "reflects . . . an effort to unravel themselves from the traditional moral and social order" (id.: 267). But the evidence is too slender and varied to transform this statement from a hypothesis into a historical conclusion. If in a few cases Anglo-Hindu law did in fact provide leverage for social mobility, in other cases it also thwarted it, as demonstrated by the refusal of the courts, including the Privy Council, to permit temple entry to the Shanans, which the Rudolphs elaborately note and criticize (id.: 42–44).

Certainly, more than the social biographies of disputants in typical and strategic dispute-situations will be necessary to sustain the above hypothesis. It will also be necessary to describe, analyse and evaluate the impact of the judgements of courts upon the "multitude of caste groups". For fidelity to prescriptions of high-culture law in court decisions is one thing: adherence, in belief and behaviour, by persons and groups affected by these prescriptions through the courts is another. Perhaps pioneering legal sociologist Eugen Ehrlich's distinction between "legal norms" which are constitutive of a social group and "norms for decision" which are norms employed by judicial agencies is most relevant here (1962: 38–60, 120–136).

2. ISLAMIZATION: LAW AND SOCIAL CHANGE IN COLONIAL INDIA

The position regarding Moslem law is strikingly different. Although, in its early phase, custom functioned as a source of law in Islam, "the legal theory of Islam, on the whole, does not recognize custom as an *independent* or *formal* source of law." Custom could only be a "minor constituent of law at the option of the jurist".

But it had "no function or validity as an opponent of law, as it did have under Hindu legal system" (Mahmood, 1975: 101). If this is the correct view of the role of custom in Islamic theory, it would follow that British administrators and legislators were somewhat "misguided . . . by the position of custom *vis-à-vis* Hindu religious law" for the entire period (1781–1901) (id.: 20–21). The reference to "usages" of Moslems may have been partly inspired by the position and practices of Hindu converts to Islam (Malbar, Punjab and Central Provinces) who continued to follow certain aspects of Hindu law as well as the adherence to certain regimes of customary law by "the Mapilla of South India, the Memons of Western India and in particular regions, for example, Punjab and adjoining territories". Fundamental and wide-ranging differences existed in respect of succession in the Marumakkatayam or Aliyasantan customary laws followed in South Kanara and North Malabar.

The juristic advertence to custom amongst Moslems led to a whole variety of responses by Moslem leaders at the beginning of this century, although we do not have studies concerning the actual interplay of "custom" and "law" in Islam during the intervening period. The *ulamas* (Islamic doctors) began efforts

> "For a complete supersession, among the Muslims of all groups and religions, of the non-Islamic customary law, and for the compulsory enforcement of the Islamic legal system. They explained to their people that their religion did not permit them to follow any non-Islamic customs. At the same time they demanded from the Government statutory enforcement of the Shari'a law. These efforts of the Ulama brought to the Indian statute book a number of sectarian, local and central enactments abrogating the non-Islamic customs followed by the Muslims and replacing them by the laws of Islam." (Mahmood, 1977: 21)

The movement culminated in the Shariat Act, 1935; which comprehensively listed all areas where the Moslem personal law (Shariat) was to apply "notwithstanding any custom or usage to the contrary".

The result looks to be the same as with the Hindu law. Just as the high-culture scriptural law virtually prevailed over the "low-culture" customary law, so did the Moslem high-culture law ultimately triumph over the regimes of "un-Islamic" customary law. Or one might vary the metaphor and say that the Great Tradition in Islam ("elite-based, urban, reflective and formalized") triumphed over the Little Tradition (which is "rural-based, consisting of the unlettered and less formalized") (see Yogendra Singh, 1973: 84; Baxi, 1975: 40–52). But the processes by which this was brought about were quite different. The Anglicization processes were at work in the triumph of *śāstra* over custom; the Sharia triumphed over custom because of the leadership of the *ulama* and consistent political pressures. This distinctive phenomenon may be called Islamization. Socio-culturally, Islamization denotes an "increased tendency" among Indian Moslems towards new identity-formation based on an increase in orthodox Islamic principles and cultural life, and conscious rejection of many syncretic elements which had thus far persisted as remnants of their Hindu past (Y. Singh, 1973: 76; Baxi, 1975: 27–28).

It would, indeed, be rewarding to pursue the working of Islamization processes in the period 1900–1950. Abrogation of un-Islamic custom was the basis of new identity-formation for a whole community of people, divided in themselves by a rich heterogeneity of cultural and social traditions. But to what extent have un-Islamic customs been annihilated? Is the social heterogeneity or legal pluralism amongst the Indian Moslems (often given as a ground for the impossibility of arriving at a uniform civil code) only based on the conflicting doctrines concerning the law among the Sunnis (adhering to Hanafi school), on the one hand, and the minority Shafil school, Shia Ithna Ashari school, and sub-groups of the Islamic school of law, on the other? Or is it really attributable, besides differences as to the scope and nature of the revealed law, to actual and significant variances in custom or people's law from the Great Tradition? Is the "triumph" of Islamic law over un-Islamic custom merely a normative victory? Is the distinction between state or revealed law and people's law a universal *a priori* or can one posit situations of total convergence between the former and the latter? Or is it wholly the case that, far "from promoting strict adherence to elements of Sharia, Islamization has allowed the Muslim communities in India to either legitimize local customs and practices or to reconcile them with Sharia?" (Ahmad, 1976: XXXII). These are large theoretical and empirical questions. There is less research on these questions as compared with the work on Hindu law. But both the theses – one proclaiming the rise of the Sanskritizing, high-culture Hindu law and the other vaunting Islamization – merit much closer examination than hitherto accorded to them.

The institution of *kazis*, a typical feature of administration of justice during the Mughul rule in India (Ahmad, 1941; Hussain, 1934), which "survived" in colonial India, highlights another aspect of interaction between SLS and NSLS. The *kazis* performed judicial as well as extra-judicial functions such as acting as notary public, marriage officers, etc. The Hastings Plan of 1772 included *kazis* in matters involving Moslem law; this arrangement continued until 1864. With the reorganization of the judicial system, Act XI of 1864 completely abolished the system of *kazis*. It was reintroduced by an Act of 1880, in deference to the consistent demand by the Moslems. But this measure did not really respond to their desire that "judicial as well as non-judicial matters to be regulated by Islamic law should be tried by *kazis*, and not by non-Muslim judges" (Mahmood, 1977: 63). All that the Act did was to empower provincial governments to enact laws to recognize *kazis* performing non-judicial, private functions (see id.: 64–66).

The community's disappointment at the legislation led to a recourse by the laity to the *ulama*. Tahir Mahmood has provided a valuable account of a number of well-known religious institutions established during the 1867–1921 period, to which Moslems referred disputes involving succession, marriage, divorce, and family relations. Functionaries known as local *muftis*, assigned these jobs of conflict-resolution, emerged in response to the growing demand for Islamic institutions for the administration of the Islamic law. Literally thousands of family disputes were (and still are in some parts of India) referred to these non-state institutions. Religious leaders viewed recourses to state courts with disdain, especially as it meant the administration of Moslem law by non-Islamic judges. The 1880 *Kazis* Act, empowering governments to appoint *kazis* was thus virtually rendered a dead letter (Mahmood, 1977: 67–69).

People's courts, sanctified by religion and legitimated by the community, offer an apt example of popular nullification of the SLS institution of *kazis*. They also remain vitally related to the problems raised a little earlier, concerning Islamization and high-culture law and its hegemony over "custom." There is promise also of interesting correlations between autonomous caste institutions of the Hindus as well as similar institutions of conflict-management among tribal groups in India. People's law often expresses itself more through its dispute handling institutions than through "custom" as a "material source" of law.

IV. People's Law, Development and Justice

1. INTRODUCTION

There has been a general recognition, both in sociology and in jurisprudence, of the fact that most societies are multi-legal; that is, in addition to the state law they display kindred regulatory system of norms, institutions and culture performing functions similar for social groups that the state law aspires to perform for the entire society. But this recognition is usually obscured by the fact that jurisprudents and sociologists are not comfortable in characterizing the group regulatory systems as "law" or "legal systems". This in itself represents both logical and ideological problems which cannot be explored here (see Baxi, 1979c).

Indian society too is multi-legal, comprising congeries of NSLS in dynamic interaction with SLS. But we still need to know the extent of reciprocal relations of exchange and support among these systems and the extent of their autonomy. Moving away from the "pure" types of village and customary law, we need to focus on the interaction between the numerous local and national systems, and the mutuality of cross-systematic influence/impact, including a systematic description of key points of tension and conflict between the systems (cf. Cohn, 1965; 103–109; Khare 1972; see also Chakravarty, 1975; Sharma, 1979).

In addition, we need to *explain* the persistence of the plurality of the legal systems. To understand reasons for persistence of the "village" law and justice is also to understand some of the limits of effectiveness of planned social change through the instrumentality of the national legal system. Description and explanation of NSLS/SLS interaction naturally raise the problem of evaluation: Is the discovered pattern of relations (maybe of complementarity or conflict) between the good or bad in terms of the attainment of the constitutionally proclaimed social order?

2. DESCRIPTION

A most general picture of dispute institutions in rural areas may still not vary from the outlines provided by Srinivas. Writing in 1962, and reflecting upon field researches dating back to the early fifties, Srinivas in a brief analysis recalled anecdotally and rather at a general level his own impressions of dispute settlement procedures studied over a period of two years (1962: 118–119; see also Srinivas, 1952; 1976).

His findings were: (i) "something like case law exists, though it is not systematized" (Srinivas, 1962: 112), (ii) some disputes (e.g. partition of family properties) tend to "drag on" for weeks (id.: 113), (iii) the intimate knowledge of the dispute and the disputants by parties and village elders provided a "pre-existing image" so that "even the 'same' facts are fitted into different configurations", although the pre-existing image is seldom unchangeable, (iv) rudimentary indices of probative value of witnesses through reputation and unwritten rules analogous to the hearsay rule enable a narrowing of competing versions or "true facts", (v) ulterior influences and factors such as favouritism or nepotism occasionally influence the outcome (id.: 115), and finally (vi) the village tribunals are orientated to the ideal of justice (*nyaya*, dharma), moralistic and religious considerations, and influenced by "public opinion" to a degree. A more detailed conspectus would, however, have to acknowledge a wide variety of dispute institutions and processes in India.

At least three main types of NSLS exist in rural India. Very generally, these are caste-based NSLS, community-based NSLS, and innovative/reformist NSLS. The distinction between caste and community NSLS is (as we will shortly see) relative. It is based on the view that "most individuals in rural India have two sets of predominate social relations, one that ties them to a village community which may be viewed as a vertical set of ties and one that connects them horizontally to their *biradari* (community) and *jati* (sub-caste)". Each set of special relations has "norms that can be considered legal and individuals and groups possessing the socially recognized authority to apply physical force to enforce them within the local communities" (Cohn, 1965: 82). The community NSLS extend beyond the caste to the village unit itself, though patterns of caste dominance or of power distribution here intrude sometimes to a point that a village *panchayat* becomes the very extension of dominant group government. The innovative/reformist NSLS are dispute institutions like the "People's Court" (*Lok Adalat*) at Rangpur, which are sponsored by acculturating agents or agencies with ideologies which centre upon the principle of generation of *lokshakti* (people's power for social transformation) and which deny or circumscribe the state power (Baxi, 1976b).

In addition, there is in some parts of India, an interesting nexus between caste *panchayats* and religious institutions. The various Hindu *matas* (religious organizations) especially in the South, seem to have an overarching jurisdiction over some aspect of caste *panchayats*. But their role is largely advisory and in discharging it the *matas* generally respect the authority of caste *panchayats*. The patterns of interaction between caste *panchayats* and various religious institutions have recently been studied by K. Ganambal (1973); but on the whole this area has been neglected by sociologists and anthropologists. It is therefore difficult to assess the spread of the interaction of religious institutions in their adjudicative role with other types of NSLS.

The dominant form of the organization in each case is a set of dispute institutions (*cf.* Abel, 1973: 217) called *panchayats*. *Panchayats* normally are a group of five people who hear and decide disputes mostly when they are summoned to do so but frequently on their own. However, in each type of NSLS, the subject matter varies. Very generally, caste (*jati*) *panchayats* deal with conflicts of interests and values within *jati*-groups, including factional alliances within those groups. Village or territorial *panchayats* deal with conflicts of interest cutting across caste factors, though those very factors may often play a crucial role in the "resolution" of a particular conflict.

Jati panchayats vary enormously in structure and scope. Bernard Cohn has, with insight, grouped the structures and scope of *jati panchayats* in terms of territorial units as well as patterns of caste dispersal and domination. This classification yields three types of *jati* NSLS:

(a) Villages with a small population of a single caste;
(b) multicaste villages with single head (authority figure);
(c) multicaste villages with a dominant caste (Cohn, 1965: 83–98; see also Srinivas, 1962: 118–119: Ganambal, 1973: 106–204).

It is clear that *jati* NSLS may have a wide territorial reach in terms of aggregation of *jati* circles, so that it is not unusual to find as many as fifty villages falling within the scope of *jati* NSLS. The limits of the territorial reach are conditioned only by "the means and the speed of transportation" and "by the kinship radius of the convenors" (Mandelbaum, 1966: 271). There is equally clearly a federal component in *jati* NSLS and different levels of hierarchy (*e.g.* Cohn, 1959). The nature of the conflict or its importance to *jati* solidarity patterns may, however, involve the use of the highest collectivity of *jati* NSLS (*panchayats* comprising as many as 20-25 villages).

Jati panchayats also show interesting variations in the organization of power and authority. While these remain to be systematically studied, a mix of any of the following variables offers some clue to authority and sources of legitimation. The close correlation between age and wisdom provides one mix; the *panchayats* are often led by, or even composed of, such men. Esteem, reputation, integrity, and charisma provide another mix. Economic base, as related to social status, also invests power and authority in certain men. So does the status of being a faction leader (cf. Chakravarty, 1975). Although not so prevalent now, we cannot altogether ignore the hereditary or royal allocations of role and authority (cf. Cohn, 1965: 85–90).

Jati NSLS primarily involve disputes and conflicts which are related to the maintenance of *jati* ranking (in terms of ritual axis of pollution and purity) and solidarity. Ritual lapses, marital relations, commission of pollution acts, sexual deviance, *inter se* land disputes, credit transactions, patron-client (*jajman*') relations – all these fall typically within the range of *jati* NSLS. As in SLS, the *jati* NSLS involve application of pre-existing norms (see Srinivas, 1962: 118–119; contrast: Cohn (1965:91) who says "there is, *apparently*, little question of what 'the law' is in *panchayat* proceedings." Italics mine) as well as instant norm creation and norm innovation. The distinction between norm-creation and norm-interpretation is, in most decisional processes, never *so* sharp as some *wish* it to be. The breach of pre-existing "customary" law is always a major ingredient in the convening of *jati panchayats*. Indeed, *jati* NSLS sometimes make law prior to occasions of adjudication. For example, it has been frequently noted that untouchable *jati* groups, in their desperate bid for social uplift, have adopted regulations "for whole sections of a caste forbidding practices believed to be responsible for their *low* status . . . Chamars are prohibited from removing dead cattle" (Cohn, 1965: 108; and the literature there cited).

There is general agreement that the processes of dispute handling, however complex, in *jati* and village *panchayats*, share common features of informality, flexibility, democraticity, and decision-making (at least always in style if not in substance by consensus). The state law strives to attain justice *inter partes* through "impartial" judges and elaborate procedures for ascertaining "truth." Indigenous dispute institutions promote justice with notorious informality through village notables who know disputants personally. The adversary systems (broadly speaking) of state law seek to individualize justice; village law and justice seek collectivized justice. Village law and justice seek social, group harmony, whereas state law, followed to its end, rests on the "winner-take-all" principle. The flexibility of *jati* and village *panchayats* consists in a wider sense of relevance, not the strait-jacket notion of relevance. The village elders, it is often observed, assembled to hear one dispute will "discuss another which lies behind it" (Cohn, 1959; Rudolph & Rudolph, 1967). This is partly a function of democraticity – that is free-wheeling public participation in the hearing process – of the proceedings, an element fast disappearing in state law systems. Indeed, the democraticity has been confined to random public "say" but it has a distinctly egalitarian character, Mandelbaum observes, at least in relation to *jati panchayats*:

> "The egalitarian aspect of the traditional panchayat seems to pose a paradox. The need for unanimous consent and the right of every man to be heard appear dissonant to the leitmotif of hierarchy. . . . The answer seems to be that most define a *jati* council as a council of peers . . . even a poor man will speak if he feels moved to do so." (1966: 291)

While the substance of this account is correct, it remains ideal-typical, too. The theoretical right of every caste-man to invoke *jati panchayat* and speak freely at its sessions is often nullified in practice by the high costs involved in convening a *panchayat* meeting (see *e.g.*, Sharma, 1979). And the prevalence of the so-called tradition of consensus in India needs very critical examination. On most vital issues, the appearance of consensus may well be a mask for domination. The consensual style of decision often serves effectively the dominant interest. One may assume that in most situations consensus would be "pre-fabricated", "contrived" or "manipulated" (Baxi, 1976a). Yet, all in all, indigenous justice, its structure and process are thus at fundamental variance with those of professionalized justice.

The *jati* and village *panchayats* have a repertoire of sanctions which include fine, public censure, civil boycott, ostracism, and varied public-opinion pressures by village notables and sometimes by predominant groups in the area. The *jati panchayats* additionally, have the very potent sanction of "outcasting" and "excommunication."

> "Fines are levied for a wide variety of offences. For petty thefts, cash fines of small amounts are levied. Higher fines are levied for adultery and other sexual offences. Rape is regarded as a very serious offence and a special punishment is imposed in addition to fines. The culprit has his face smeared with soot, a bucket containing mud is placed on his head, and he is made to walk around the *cheri* (area) in this guise, while a drum is beaten along the route. This is considered the most degrading form of punishment." (Beteille, 1965: 63–64)

One striking example of a new kind of sanction is provided by the *Lok Adalat* (People's Court) at Rangpur. When disputants are sent an "invitation" to join the meeting of the *Adalat*, the last paragraph of the notice reads: "You surely know (appreciate) that expensive and frequent visits to law courts are not in the interests of us poor farmers". One may conceptualize this kind of admonition as a sanctioning device itself. Indeed, in the intersubjectivities of the villagers, such a statement might imply that if a party does not even appear before the *Lok Adalat* the *Adalat* itself may encourage court action or, at any rate, it may not discourage such action. Conceptually, then, the *threat of recourse to the instrumentality of the state legal system is itself stressed and apperceived as a sanction, whose very probability generates compliance*. This is a rather unique phenomenon wherein the NSLS appropriates the intimidating paraphernalia of the SLS to sustain and enhance its continual efficacy, viability, legitimacy and even hegemony. Of course, parallel processes may be perceived in conflict resolution through out-of-court settlement, private arbitration and other forms of mediation. But the striking peculiarity of the *Lok Adalat* is invocation of formal litigation as a self-conscious sanctioning process to an extent that the range of choices for alternate means of resolution is endeavoured to be effectively eliminated or at least minimized. This indeed is the very definition of "force." To the extent that the threat of recourse to litigation *actually operates* to reduce parties' choice of action, we have surely an operation of sanction (Baxi, 1976b: 83–86).

The effectivity of sanctions is an empirical question which has not been closely examined in relation to NSLS. Recalcitrance is both conceivable and likely; its incidence is however unknown. Isolated examples also suggest that the dominant group members or resourceful persons can by acts of defiance occasion changes, bypassing, or even momentary collapse of sanctioning processes. But overall, the strength of collective conscience or sentiment in the village (and caste) contexts cannot be gainsaid.

3. EXPLANATION

There is considerable evidence of multilegalism or autonomous existence of two or more dispute-resolution systems – at levels of norm, behaviour and culture. How is this to be explained?

B. Cohn (1959) maintains that "the way a people settle disputes is part of its social structure and value system". The indigenous and the "official" legal systems differ rather drastically in both these aspects. The constitutionally desired social order seeks to foster (in part) through the legal system the value of equality, whereas "the North Indian society operates on the reverse value hypothesis: Men are not born equal and they have widely differing inherent worth." Cohn comments:

> "The adversary system has developed to equalize persons in court. To an Indian peasant this is an impossible situation to understand. The Chamar knows he is not equal to the Thakur. . . . The Thakur cannot be convinced in any way that the Chamar is equal, but the court acts as if the parties to the dispute were equal."

Moreover, Indian villages are "multiplex" societies; and the "network of relationships" thus involved cannot be "summarily cut by a decision of the courts";

> "Two Thakurs disputing over a piece of land are not only buyer and seller with a contractual tie, but in classificatory kinship terms are brothers or uncle and nephew. . . . So decisions of the courts based on ideas of contract do not fit in the value system and social structure of the Indian village."

Nor do the notions of relevance engendered by law or procedure and evidence, and the winner-take-all principle of the adversary system, accord with the "traditional" preference for settling disputes through consensus and with liberalism in the notion of relevant matters shown by the indigenous tribunals.

Beteille somewhat similarly finds (1965: 154–165) that in the Tanjore village the village *panchayat*, under statutory protection and political patronage, is less effective than the *de facto cheri panchayat*, without either. The village *panchayat* is relatively weaker because it is an attempt involving an "imposition of a democratic formal structure on a social substratum which is segmental and hierarchical in nature". In contrast, the effectiveness of the *cheri panchayat* is due to "its social homogeneity and the pervasive nature of the moral bonds which unite its members". The "vitality" of this *panchayat* lies in its "correspondence" with the structure of the "community which it represents".

Kidder (1973) proposes an explanation which stresses the limitations of the SLS as arising from "the social structure of the judicial system rather than in their incongruity with indigenous values". Kidder analyses in some considerable detail the bureaucratization of the system of judicial justice leading to a *de facto* maximization of the judicial pursuit of compromise through a *de jure* adversary system. One central factor is delay in judicial disposal. Kidder finds that:

> "In Mysore state . . . the 'average duration of contested original suits' disposed of during 1966–67 by judicial decree was slightly over seventeen years."

In some instance, delays extend over a little over two decades. But this delay, and the frustrations attendant upon it, seem to be regarded by most litigants "as being the intentional product of a shrewd" adversary; for other litigants, delaying procedures were a part of a war of attrition aimed to terminate in a compromise. Nor does the ultimate resolution favourable to the plaintiff (who thus compromises) mean a "final victory" for him. Kidder notes:

> "One landlord spent five years getting an eviction decree on his tenant only to have the 'defeated' tenant disappear with the key. He then learned from the police that the tenant could easily keep him out of the house for at least two years just by manipulating police eviction procedures. Meanwhile,

the landlord could not even collect rent on the property."

Over-recourse and non-recourse to courts is thus related to what Kidder calls "the failure of the adjudicative ideal". In this view this failure is better explained by reference to the structure of "adversial relationships" rather that through value-incompatibility hypotheses like Cohn's. This is so because the pattern of compromise and delay is neither "expected" nor "valued" by the court-users and because such a pattern is far from unknown in practice to American and British litigants.

The opposition between "cultural" and "social structural" approaches has been a familiar theme in legal anthropology (Moore, 1966). In the present context, Kidder's analysis does not quite join issue with Cohn's. As Kidder himself states, his research was conducted "in the courts of Bangalore, Mysore state, with supplementary observations made in lesser courts in outlying districts". How much the "outlying districts" approximate to Cohn's Senepur village remains a matter of conjecture. Be that as it may, it must be emphasized that recourse, non-recourse and over-recourse to courts must be affected by a myriad of factors. The language of the law, physical distance from court-sites, economics of litigation, the nature of contention *inter partes*, are also some of the relevant variables here.

Cohn asserts that in a culture-conflict situation the "Indians in response thought only of manipulating the new situation and did not use courts to settle disputes but to further them" (Cohn, 1959: 155). Such a view, according to Kidder (with whom I agree), misjudges "the importance of conflict as a constructive force in social interaction" and also ignores "the opportunity which is created by systems of formal adjudication" (Kidder, 1973: 31).

The importance of conflict as a "constructive force in social action" has been imaginatively explored in two recent works by Anand Chakravarty (1975) and Miriam Sharma (1979). These studies depict the relation between the nature of dispute and their processing with reference to power relations and transformations of power relations and structure in rural India. Growth of new patterns of leadership and authority becomes significantly related to dispute behaviour and ways of channelling and controlling it. Ability of a faction leader to deliver "justice," by attacking bias or inertia or hostility on the part of other leaders (who lead or influence community adjudication) seems an important source of legitimation of leadership and authority (Chakravarty, 1975). This is what seems to be happening when we look at dispute from a social structure standpoint. When we look at dispute processes from the actor's point of view we find some tendencies towards "forum shopping." In other words, disputants in most cases do seem to retain the final option as to whether they will resort to a third-party intervention and if they so do whether the third party agency would be a caste *panchayat* or a village one or *nyaya panchayats* or official courts (Sharma, 1979). Of course, the choice is circumscribed not only by the "cultural" or "political" factors but also by "economic" ones. For, very often, recourse to any third party intervention costs money (even calling of *biradari* or *panchayat* is in some cases expensive); and recourse to SLS agencies, police and courts, often requires substantial investment for all the parties involved (Sharma, 1979; Chakravarty, 1975 mentions at many places the examples of bribery and extortion by agents of NSLS).

4. EVALUATION

The existence of multilegalism in dispute settlement is a problem calling for explanation only because of some underlying value premise, not very often made explicit. The relationship between the "local law-ways" and "lawyer's law" (Cohn, 1965) can be (i) marked by complementarity and reciprocal reinforcive coexistence and (ii) characterized by conflict and tension, resulting in a miscarriage of justice-values embodied in either or both. One's unarticulated perception of this relationship (which inevitably must be a mixed rather than a pure type) and the bearing of it on the attainment of values of the constitutionally desired social order, is certain to influence the evaluation process.

True, one can exalt or denigrate "local law-ways" in particular instances. The incident of a cowherd who committed the mortal "sin" of secretly cohabiting with the Brahmin's young *third* wife and who compounded it by leaving the landlord's house by the front door (instead of the usually permitted back door entry and exit), resulting in the youth's castration and murder, is a shocking instance of the lynch-justice of the local law-ways (Gough, 1955; Cohn, 1965: 90). Contrast this, however, with the almost idyllic manner of dispute settlement in a single-caste small village of Malana, involving a kind of participatory democracy in reaching substantive outcomes in dispute situations (Cohn, 1965: 83).

Contrast this, too, with the all-India legal system demanding almost heroic patience and fortitude for the just plaintiff who is rewarded with a judgement which he finds so difficult to enforce, as in the landlord's case described by Kidder.

But conflicts of value go even deeper than those contrasts between state and non-state law indicate. R. S. Freed (1972: 423–435) has presented one aspect of such conflicts in her study of village life in North India through the case of Maya. Maya, a married but illicitly pregnant girl, was killed by her father because he believed that his *dharma* as father obligated him to do so for the spiritual well-being of her soul. The sooner her sinful phase in the cycle of births and deaths was terminated, the better would her prospects be in the endless cycle of birth and rebirth. He reasoned also that Maya, if allowed to live, would be excommunicated from the village society, and end up as a cheap urban prostitute, a life full of unmitigated misery. Everybody both in her in-laws' village and his own agreed – so much so that two of the kinsmen of Maya's father who were police constables did not do anything to activate the legal process. The police visited the village twice but did nothing. Village law was here in sharp antithesis to state law, and the latter, more or less yielded to the former. *Dharma* thus conceived is the legitimating principle of this NSLS which diverges sharply from the democratic belief system sustaining the SLS.

On the other hand, well-organized local legal systems may often almost altogether "oust" the state legal system and provide an almost idyllic alternative as is shown by *Lok Adalat* in Rangpur, North Gujarat – a tribal belt of about 100 villages mostly irradiated by the *Sarvodaya* (lit. uplift of all) ideology of *bhoodan* and *gramdan* (voluntary gifts of lands and villages for redistribution of common use).

Almost all disputes in the region are referred to the *Lok Adalat*. In the last 25 years, it has settled more than 25,000 disputes. The very fact that the case is brought before it is often enough a valid ground for adjourning proceedings in official courts. Adjudication is done with substantial public participation: each session is attended by 300–400 villagers. The Court's decisions are rarely disobeyed. This is because of their intrinsic fairness and community involvement. In some ways, this Court achieves a quality of justice still sought for by the state legal system; for example, it more effectively protects women's equal rights of inheritance, matrimonial property, etc. The Open Court's criminal justice system already provides for effective compensation for the victims of crime which is still on the legislative anvil of the state legal system. Its rehabilitative techniques are much more advanced in some respects: a murderer is "punished" by having to look after the widow and minor children of the victim for a term of years under close supervision of the local community, whereas his imprisonment in the official legal system would have rendered both families destitute.

The *Lok Adalat* experiment also illustrates other dimensions of relationship between the state and non-state legal systems. Often, dispute institutions generate and sustain broad-based leadership patterns which promote developmental activities both economic and social. It was through his role as a mediator in village disputes that the leader of the *Lok Adalat*, Shri H. Parikh (an eminent *Sarvodaya* worker), attained legitimacy and a degree of charisma. In turn, he used *Lok Adalat* to translate his vision of socio-economic reform by making it a vehicle of reform-oriented adult education. He made the adjudicatory occasions into educational ones, both through actual decisions and plain preaching on many themes – family planning, ill-effects of overconsumption of alcoholic drinks, honesty in credit transactions, civil liberties, irrationality of belief in witchcraft, equality of women, agricultural innovation, etc. Today, the area of about 1000 villages has witnessed remarkable socio-economic changes partly fostered and sustained by this kind of didactic adjudication. In this sense perhaps more has been achieved by mobilization of lay justice for development than by insistence on adoption of professional justice, as is illustrated by the state's abortive attempts at formalizing village justice through the statutory *nyaya panchayats* (Baxi & Galanter, 1979).

The *Lok Adalat* is not an isolated phenomenon, although it may be in several respects unique. On a lesser scale, quite a few such experiments exist. Moreover, not too dissimilar functions (of promoting welfare, development, status mobility) have been and are being performed by *jati panchayats*, as noted by several sociologists and anthropologists. When they perform such functions, as they increasingly do, both in adjudicatory and other contexts, the *jati panchayats* supplement the role of state in bringing about social change, although they do so on the basis of caste loyalty and patronage.

It would be misleading to assume that the conflicts between state and local legal orders are merely conflicts of values; there are also conflicts of interests. Adoption of constitutional values naturally calls for sacrifice of personal or group interests, which are clearly not acceptable to those in positions of higher class, status or power. Some would even say that what are spoken of as values are nothing more than rationalizations of interests of vested-interest groups.

Whatever be one's views on the latter aspect, one example of conflict of interests is manifested in the decisions of some *panchayats* of the so-called "denotified" tribes (which were designated by the British masters as "criminal tribes" as early as 1773, a labelling which persisted for whole groups and a stigma which was removed by the repeal, in independent India, of the Criminal Tribes Act 1933). A recent study of Simhadri (1979) indicates that the Yerukulas, a former criminal tribe in Andhra Pradesh, "commit crimes not only to earn their livelihood but also to pay fines and bribes to *Panchayat* and police and a good proportion of their booty in theft and burglary goes towards the maintenance of these agencies". While tribal *panchayats* ordinarily discourage commission of crimes, Simhadri finds instances where the *panchayat* itself suggests that a criminal could engage in theft in the ensuing dark days (new moon days) in order to earn money "to pay fines" (1979: 124). We have in this kind of situation a clearly antagonistic relation between SLS and NSLS. But the antagonism does not appear, as in the case of Maya, to be at the level of values; it exists at the level of interests. Ordinarily, theft is discouraged. But if theft is the only or the best way in which to pay fines to and through *panchayats* (and the executions in some situations by the police), the superior interests of the group prevail over the interests and values sought to be promoted by the SLS and even the NSLS. And the very agents of the SLS whose duty is to uphold its values and interests temporarily become co-opted in the NSLS, which obviously serves their material interests better.

The limits of state power, authority and law are not set just by values and interests but also (and perhaps no less decisively) by the level or organization of efforts. Most "developing" countries are poor (appallingly so, as in the case of India, where a large number of people do not have means of bare subsistence). We immediately perceive that the level of poverty affects adversely the reach of state law and the quality of its justice. Investment in administration of law and justice is not (and probably cannot be) a high priority item in national budgets of poor societies at the very time when they have to resort to the machinery of law to foster social change in developing societies.

All this means, of course, that there are not enough courts, constables and lawyers – carriers of official law – in poor societies. Thus, for example, in India (according to one estimate) there are only 183 lawyers per one million of the population as against 507 lawyers in the United Kingdom, 1,595 in the U.S.A., 947 in New Zealand, 638 in Australia, and 769 in Canada. Indeed, some areas in India have no lawyers at all, and *inter se* distribution of lawyers within India reveals even more striking disparities (Galanter, 1968b: 201). As regards police in 1971; according to the official estimates there was one policeman for every 800 persons in India, but the distribution is uneven between the rural and urban centres. The average jurisdiction of a police station is about 200 square miles covering 100 villages and a population of approximately 75,000 persons. It was estimated in the 1950s that police stations were, on the average, about 8 miles from any village (Bayley, 1969: 79).

SLS, pervasive in urban areas, is only slenderly present in rural areas. The low visibility of SLS and its slender presence renders official law (its values and processes) inaccessible and even irrelevant for people. Other factors (such as the language of the law, which is alien to about 95% of the people) compound the distance between SLS and people.

All these variables make the relationship between SLS and NSLS a very complex affair. Failing in empirically informed evaluation, one can have hazardous recourse to aprioristic or ideological bases (*e.g.* in terms of Gandhi's ideal of *Ram-Rajya*) or elaborate evaluative framework from comparable experiments (*e.g.* Henderson's analysis of traditional conciliation and the growth of democratic legality).

Henderson's critique of the Japanese statutory conciliation system (*Chotei*) may well be extended *mutatis mutandis* to the indigenous dispute-settlement processes in India:

> ". . . the excessive use of conciliation stunts the growth and refinement of the body of rules necessary to sustain complex community life; it dulls the citizens' sense of right, essential to the vindication of law. It may also allow old rules and social prejudices, which new legislation has sought to

> abolish, to influence the outcome of disputes; or it may allow a new regime to ignore the law in favour of its policy. . . . In other words, conciliation is neither conservative nor progressive in principle; it is simply unprincipled. It may favour the powerful over the weak, in the name of bargaining; it ordinarily forces plaintiffs to discount their claims; it may operate to compromise large scale group interests which might be better handled by forthright reform legislation. In short, conciliation is only on adjunct to, not a substitute for, a legal order; and if relied upon excessively, it is not merely non-legal – it has antilegal results. . . . It takes a legal framework to protect the voluntary character of conciliation; and if it is not voluntary, conciliation will likely become in practice simply a standardless use of forces." (1965: 241)

The basic ideal-typical contrasts thus emerging are clear and common enough: namely, that indigenous dispute-settlement processes may allow room for "prejudiced" rather than "principled" determination; that it may be swayed by power differentials between parties; that in some ways it is "antilegal." And at an ideal-typical level, the case for structuring and confining local law-ways through the national legal order is clearly a compelling one.

But such a conclusion needs to be checked against a model of SLS, accentuating different aspects (behaviour rather than value, reality rather than myth). Are judicial and legislative decisions pre-eminently grounded in "principle" rather than in "prejudice"? Are the national law-ways substantially free from "old prejudices" cancelling the objectives of social change through law? Do no power differentials between adversaries affect legal initiations and outcomes? Does not the volume of out-of-court settlements in civil cases, and of plea-bargaining in criminal matters, contrast sharply with the adjudicative adversary ideal? And can one ignore the growing bulk of evidence of "lynch-justice" in police stations and jails?

These are big questions, but sociological studies of national legal orders have begun to point to the great gap between rhetoric and reality, between proclaimed objectives and dysfunctional processes and results. The lesson to be drawn from these partial and ongoing explorations is not that there are no significant differences between SLS and NSLS *but that these differences are of degree rather than of kind.*

5. TRIBAL LAW AND JUSTICE

India has a substantial tribal population. According to the 1961 census the population of the scheduled tribes (as these are constitutionally designated) was 30 million; the 1971 census places the population figure at 41 million. Half of the scheduled tribe (ST) population is concentrated in three states of India: Madhya Pradesh, Orrissa, and Bihar. Few states and Union territories have a predominant ST population.

It is beyond the scope of this paper to attempt, even in bare outline, the evolution of tribal policies during the colonial regime or in independent India. It should suffice here to mention that there are hardly any tribal groups which have not been exposed to contact and penetration of non-tribal people. The Constitution seeks to safeguard the cultural unity and identity of tribal groups through provisions in fundamental rights, autonomous statehood or self-governance arrangements and institutions and a whole variety of limitations on the nefarious activities of the non-tribals, especially moneylenders (Hidayatullah, 1979). At the same time, the Indian State has undertaken a wide range of tribal development and welfare programmes including land and agrarian reforms. It has consistently resorted to strategies (constitutionally sanctioned) of reservations in education, employment and legislation and allied aspects of compensatory (or reverse) discrimination and other measures, designed to eliminate exploitation of ST population.

The overall results are difficult to assess. In most situations it would appear, the ST populations remain subject to exploitation and underprivilege, despite a plethora of ameliorative measures (see *e.g.* Patel, 1974); in other situations we find autonomy and maintenance of cultural heritage (as among the Santals; see Somers, 1977). The situation is so infinitely varied across ST communities, that it is rash to generalize concerning the tribal situation in India; nor does the state of art justify much scientific assessment of the overall situation (ICSSR, 1974). It is in this context that we note some persistent aspects of tribal customary law in India.

The tribal communities are not above the state law. But for all practical purposes they are governed by complex regimes of customary law, administered by community-dispute institutions. There is naturally a wide variation in the regimes and institutions of people's law, study of which continues to remain a pressing priority on the agenda of legal anthropology in India (Das, 1974, 2: 383). The normative and institutional regimes of people's law vary according to the stage of social and economic development. Nomadic food-gathering tribes (*e.g.* Chenchus of Andhra Pradesh and Andaman Islanders) have simple societies, with rudimentary division of labour, with no established authority for enforcement of norms. Elaborate and complex moral norms exist, some may even be called distinctively legal (*e.g.* the strong sense of individual property) and disputes recurrently arise (especially in relation to sexual morality and property). Yet in these societies there are no recognizable dispute institutions. Community disapproval of violations of well-established norms provides the most effective sanctions. This is explained by the fact that the "fluidity of social units permits the easy separation of those who cannot agree" and also by the unusual situation posed by the fact that "the rewards of a wilful and successful flouting of the accepted standards of behaviour are not great in a society where no one can materially benefit by infringing another man's rights" (Fürer-Haimendorf, 1967: 32).

When we move from food-gathering groups to tribes which practice shifting cultivation, we come across the fact of "greater permanency of the local groups" and correspondingly "greater need for social controls" over activities of those who may threaten the order of the group (id.: 38). Fürer-Haimendorf, relying on his study of the Reddis of Andhra Pradesh (1945a), shows that the emergence of dispute institutions and mediatory roles is related to common ownership of land, with rights of cultivation given to the person or group actually clearing the forest and tilling the land for a period. "Common ownership of a tract of land is . . . the main basis of group's cohesion, and the sense of unity finds expression in common ritual activities" (id.: 39). While there is no centralized authority for settlement of disputes in both the groups, for the tribes as a whole, "several neighbourhood settlements form a group and the elders of these settlement meet to constitute an *ad hoc* council whenever a serious breach of customary law disturbs the harmony of the group" (id.: 44). Such councils are final and authoritative arbiters of the conflict but they are informal bodies which arrive at participatory decisions in public meetings. Punishment usually consists of fines – a result of the advent of money economy; but ostracizing and excommunication are often employed.

Both these types of tribal groups, the food-gatherers and cultivators, share a basic egalitarianism. Theirs is primarily a "society of equals" not only "in resources". Only "one standard of conduct is expected of them all, and there is nothing to favour the crystallization of conflicting moral attitudes." Enforcement of conformity is not very problematic. But in societies "accepting or even favouring differentials in power and wealth such enforcement is a relatively "less simple matter". (id.: 55)

This is shown by the situation of Apa Tanis on Indo-Tibetan borderlands. The Apa Tanis are settled agriculturalists who have developed "highly efficient system of rice cultivation on permanent irrigated fields." The Apa Tanis recognize private property in land; and have a rigid stratification, with immutable barriers between the nobleman (wealthy people) and commoners. Their dispute institutions are not *ad hoc* bodies but have a formal composition. The councils comprise representatives of each clan of the village. There is a clear distinction between "public" and "private" wrongs in Apa Tani jurisprudence. Theft is considered to be a wrong against society, necessitating public trial and punishment, whereas for private disputes self-help (*avemong*) is permitted. Village councils will activate themselves only on such occasions where private disputes develop a tendency to affect public peace. The interference by the council takes the form of peaceful negotiations. (id.: 1945b, 74–83)

In his study of Konyak Nagas, Fürer-Haimendorf finds two types of Naga villages; the "democratic" and "chiefly" villages (id.: 84–104). There is a clear recognition in both types of villages of "authorities empowered to exert control and impose sanctions." In "democratic" villages, village councils, comprising hereditary or elected heads of families settle disputes in a distinctively judicial capacity. Most breaches of customary law are punished by fines, although banishment is often awarded as a punishment (in cases, for example, of repeated course of thefts). There is scope for self-help, particularly in cases where a person is a victim of deliberate physical injury. The kinsmen of the victim are entitled to avenge; but even so, village councillors often intervene in "quarrels which have not yet led to violence." The Konyak village councils also enforce many taboos as "necessary precautions against many magical dangers". The councillors aim at harmony, which often means that the powerful clans may obtain outcomes they prefer against the relatively weak adversary.

But this bias towards the strong clans is not so thoroughgoing in "democratic" villages as it is in the "chiefly" villages. There exists a "fundamental difference in the conduct expected from the commoners and those appropriate to members of a chiefly clan." For example, monogamy is "mandatory" for the commoners, but the members of chiefly clans are permitted to have many wives.

The situation of Raj Gonds, who are settled plough cultivators over the centre of peninsular India which is much larger than the British Isles, is strikingly different. One reason is that the Gonds "widely dispersed in space" are conscious of a "unity inherent in a social framework which allocates to every Gond a precise place in society" (Fürer-Haimendorf, 1967: 177). During the fifteenth to the seventeenth centuries, the Gonds exercised significant political power, although the Gond ruling dynasties have lost their sovereign status, the Gond *Raja* (King) retained a traditional role of considerable importance.

Social control is exercised among the Gonds through village-level *panchas* (groups of five men), drawn mainly from the influential and important circles of the village. The *panch* may meet on its own to prevent the consequences of an action that is regarded as "polluting," or it may meet to settle a specific dispute brought before it by the parties. The most interesting feature of the *panch* meetings, which are relatively informal and open to the public, is that:

> "every meeting . . . tends to elucidate, reiterate and interpret the unwritten law of the tribe, and there are instances when the assembled men spend more time on discussing the principles involved than on investigating the rights and wrongs of the specific disputes to be settled" (id.: 122).

Of course, the *panchas* try to arrive at a solution of disputes which is acceptable to both parties but "Gonds consider it necessary to elucidate what tribal custom prescribes, if the *panch* is to strike a balance between the conflicting claims of two litigants" (id.: 122; see also for the Khasi system of criminal justice, Deb *et al.*, 1970: 206).

In a recent study (1979), Fürer-Haimendorf has elaborated

further on the Gond concept of justice and related social values. In a particularly important discussion of sanctions, he indentifies three forms of excommunication, the most severe being *tapu*, imposed on those "who have lost their normal ritual status by such a polluting act as the sharing of a meal or having sexual intercourse with a non-Gond of a low status." The second degree of excommunication is a form of outcasting; and the third, the least severe, amounts merely to exclusion from worship at ancestral shrines. In the last two forms, no purification ceremonies are required but the first form condemns the excommunicant to a ritually polluting status. He must undergo "an elaborate purification ceremony, which traditionally could only be conducted by a *raja*." Excommunication of the first two forms really reinforces the identity of the group and its authority structures. A Gond refusing to comply with the decisions of the *panchas* is "no longer a Gond" (1979: 165). Fürer-Haimendorf finds that a decision to excommunicate "is binding on Gonds wherever they live." This result differs from the Nagas: while "Naga justice is concerned only with the comparatively small in-group of a single village, Raj Gonds see themselves as a part of much wider society extending ideally to the far flung regions where groups of their community dwell" (id.: 166).

Fürer-Haimendorf warns against regarding excommunication as a mere punishment against an offence. Rather, it is "an act of self defence on the part of society". In other words, excommunication does not take the form of physical banishment as in some other tribal societies; "Gonds place only social distance between tribal society and those who will not abide by its laws." He suggests a "deep conceptual difference" between this kind of sanctioning process and those which entail infliction of physical pain or territorial ouster or exile. Excommunication represents a "non-violent desinteressement in those who flaunt society's rules" (id.: 167).

There are many interesting and distinctive features of Gond conceptions of justice. First, as noted, unlike Nagas, the Gond "recognizes . . . the existence of social and moral order extending over the whole of Gond society and in no way limited by geographical boundaries." Second, while a limited amount of self-help is permitted, there is among the Gonds a general disapproval of "retaliation as a means of obtaining justice." Among the Gonds there is "no room for institutionalized reprisal of the type current among the tribes of Arunachal Pradesh." Third, the importance of enunciation and maintenance of customary norms is often balanced with the need for restoring "the disturbed social harmony." Often, the *panchas* endeavour to promote a settlement which may give to parties less than what might be due to them on a strict standard of customary law. Fourth, a "characteristic feature of justice administered by Gond *panchayats* is the absence of any provision for the award of compensation for injuries suffered;" compensation is awarded only for the actual expenditure incurred. Fines, when levied, usually accrue to *panchas* and not to the victorious party. Fifth, discussion on "general rules applicable and hypothetical cases involving similar legal problems" occurs frequently in Gond *panchayat* sessions. Thus, "the law as recognized by tradition and public opinion is periodically restated and reformulated, and adjustments necessitated by changed conditions can be ventilated and gradually evolved." (id.: 169–171) Sixth, the principles of Gond justice allow no joint responsibility of kinsmen as prevails amongst most of the tribal societies of north-east India, where the misdeeds of one man may be avenged by an assault on any of his close agnatic kinsmen". There is no custom of blood feud, common amongst the Nagas and Nishis. The Gond "is . . . expected to break off all social contact with even the closest of kinsmen, not excluding a full brother, who has fallen in a state of pollution" (id.: 174). Finally, the assumption amongst Gonds is that the village council will always administer justice "according to the dictates of prudence and customary law, and that force will never be allowed to prevail". No doubt, this is an ideal picture. Nevertheless, "in theory, public opinion does not allow individuals to fight out their quarrels by themselves, and any major outbreak of violence normally results in proceedings before a competent *panch*" (id.: 177).

The Santals of Bihar (notable for their "Hoon" rebellion in 1885 against fraudulent moneylenders, rapacious tax collectors, including landlords, and cruel and corrupt police) have been, during the course of long history, an "encapsulated" tribe, which has been able to maintain, despite intensive contact, its own cultural identity and heritage. The headman, mostly hereditary, performs a key leadership role among the Santals at the village level. The role of the headman is indeed very complex as he is not just the key adjudicator of disputes but he is also an administrator, among others, of the village and also an articulating link between this community self-regulation and governmental development programme: he in fact acts also as a village *pradhan* (bureaucratic agent) (Somers, 1977). But in terms of our present concerns the headman's role specifically requires (i) protection of collective rights, (ii) protection of individual rights, (iii) ensuring performance of collective duties, (iv) containing deviance and ensuring commitment to Santal community and culture (id.: 193). The headman works through village leaders and in collaboration with his counterparts in other villages. The "Santal headman is a recognized catalyst in the process of attaining consensus". He represents the "customs and expectations of the ancestors whose rules of behaviour are considered correct"; the customs of ancestors are considered "guiding principles". Headmen have often resigned their position when they seem to the "administrative elders" or to the people unable to perform this role. In many ways Santal culture happily combines egalitarianism and participatory decision-making with deference for age and seniority, and for the catalytic role of the headman.

This cursory overview presents a profile of the rich variety of regimes and institutions of indigenous customary law. The nature and function of dispute institutions are related to the variables of social organization, agrarian enterprise, cultural values and even cosmogony. Anthropological studies do not, by and large, analyse the nature and scope of interaction between indigenous tribal institutions and those of the state law. We have a few titbits of information concerning interaction between the two legal systems. Introduction of cash fines represents not only the monetization of tribal economy, but also the impact of SLS "stock-in-trade" restitutive sanction. The prevention of the practice of head-hunting among Nagas, and the actual disuse of this sanction, is a direct consequence of the imposition of state law as an initiator of change in the indigenous law. The reference to SLS by the indigenous systems in most situations of murder is a fair measure of acceptance of the hegemony of the SLS in certain areas over NSLS. But as the Santal situation illustrates the SLS has a negative face for most tribals, perhaps this is not a problem of differing cultural modes but rather one of the manifest corruption and cruelty of its non-tribal agents – the police, prosecutors and in some cases even the courts. (Also see Baxi, 1976b, 1979c on the Rangpur experience; Elwin 1943).

We also learn from these studies about the differences and

similarities in conceptions of justice and its relation to power. The moral and jural double standards of Konyak Nagas are perhaps atypical; but the SLS in its enforcement of law and administration of justice is not much removed from the stratified justice of Konyak Nagas. In any case, the concern for harmony, favouring the resourceful over the underprivileged through a careful elaboration of the law found amongst the Raj Gonds, offers almost a paradigmatic description of the Indian state legal system. It is doubtful if there exists for the entire tribal population of India any distinctive conception of justice; there seem to exist however, distinctive types of conceptions of justice among them (Fürer-Haimendorf, 1967). These need to be examined in relation to conceptions of justice manifest in the village legal systems and these manifest in the SLS.

The impact of the constitutional solicitude for the scheduled tribes over the internal political and judicial processes of the tribal systems also remains to be examined. Anthropological studies have reiterated that the "clear and expectable" direction of tribal change is towards acceptance of *jati* characteristics (Mandelbaum, 1966: 593). To what extent do the constitutional rights and privileges support and arrest this trend? In other words, how do tribal groups make conscious choices to identify themselves as members of *jati* rather than tribe, and what awareness of constitutional benefits goes into the calculus of their choice? There have been notable examples where tribal groups identified themselves with a *jati* only to revert to the original tribal identification (*e.g.* the Bhumij of Bengal studied by Surajit Sinha, 1959: 12–30). To what extent, if at all, do the *jati* models of law, adjudication and justice influence such exercises in identity realignment?

The foregoing indications and questions underscore the need for a sustained systematic examination of the relation between people's law and state law, and the underlying value and ideology considerations. No genuine understanding of the social change dynamics through legal pluralism is possible without such efforts.

Note

1. The Indian legal system (ILS) recognizes people's law as "custom" at many points. The Indian Constitution itself, in Article 13, recognizes that "custom or usage" may have "force of law in the territory of India" and seeks to abrogate it only to the extent it can be said to contravene the guaranteed fundamental rights granted by Part III. In a controversial decision, the Supreme Court of India has rejected the contention that power of excommunication from a religious sect is thus unconstitutional. Excommunication based on religious grounds does not violate freedom of religion or of conscience guaranteed by Articles 25 and 26 (see Saifuddin Saheb v. State of Bombay, A.I.R., 1963 S.C.). Thus an important sanctioning mechanism of the NSLS stands legitimated. The Constitution also continues in force "custom or usage having the force of law" before the Constitution came into force; although the text of Article 372 does not explicitly refer to custom, the above result has been achieved by judicial interpretation which has asserted that all custom having the force of law shall, subject to the provisions of the Constitution, have the force of law. Thus, not just people's law in India but people's law in Britain in so far as it was extended to India in the colonial period continues to operate with a constitutional legitimation. Article 31, which until 1977 guaranteed a right to property, recognized implicitly large number of customary agrarian tenures and property relations.

   The ILS recognizes large enclaves of people's law. Customary marriages and divorce are, for example, recognized by the Hindu Marriage Act (Derrett, 1963; 1970; Diwan, 1978, 1979). A similar diversity of customs and usages in regard to marriage and divorce exists among the many Indian Moslem groups (see, *e.g.* Ahmad, 1976; Husain 1976; Mahmood, 1972b; 1977). Systems of family property in land are protected through customary regimes, as in Punjab and Haryana (Diwan, 1978). The law relating to negotiable instruments continues to recognize the indigenous, customary "instruments" such as the Hundis. As recently as 1978, a Government of India Committee urged codification of the law of indigenous negotiable instruments. Industrial law accepts at places the notion of a "customary" bonus. Agrarian reform measures, particularly the tenancy legislation, relied on customs and usages in defining the area of "personal cultivation" which can be retained or resumed by the landowner as against the tenant. Even though untouchability is abolished, as a matter of fundamental right, customary rights of scavengers are still operative in certain parts of India (Baxi, 1979b).

It would be rather tedious, and somewhat unproductive, to list areas in which ILS specifically recognizes people's law. It is, however, important to note that the ILS derives considerable support and legitimacy by recognizing and maintaining regimes of customary or people's law. At places, it co-opts people's law; at others it restricts the scope of the operation of the people's law; at places it seeks to supplant it; and, finally, at places it simply chooses to coexist symbiotically, as it were, with people's law.

References

Because of their basic relevance to the discussion, certain references not cited in the text are included in this list.

Abel, R. L.
1974. A Comparative Theory of Dispute Institutions in Society. *Law & Society Review 8*(2): 217.

Ahmad, I., ed.
1976. *Family, Kinship and Marriage among Muslims in India.* New Delhi: Manohar.

Ahmad, M. B.
1941. *The Administration of Justice in Mediaeval India.* Karachi: Manager of Publications.

Baxi, U.
1975. Uniform Civil Code and Reform of Muslim Personal Law: A Crisis of Commonsense? In Mahmood, 1975.
1976a. Access, Development and Distributive Justice: The Access Problems of the 'Rural' Population. *Journal of the Indian Law Institute* 18: 375.
1976b. From *Takrar* to *Karar*: The *Lok Adalat* at Rangpur. *Journal of Constitutional & Parliamentary Studies* 10: 53.
1979a. Popular Justice, Participatory Development and Power Politics: The *Lok Adalat* in Turmoil. Mimeo.
1979b. *Untouchability, Constitution, Law and Plan.* In *Removal of Untouchability.* M. K. Ghandi, ed. Ahmedabad: Gujarat University Press.
1979c. People's Law, Development, Justice. *Verfassung und Recht in Uebersee* 12: 97.

Baxi, U., & Galanter, M.
1979. Panchayati Justice. In M. Cappelletti & B. Garth, eds., *Access to Justice*, Milano: Giuffre Editore 3: 341.

Bayley, D. H.
1969. *The Police and Political Development in India.* Princeton, N.J.: Princeton University Press.

Beteille, A.
1965. *Caste, Class, and Power: Changing Patterns of Stratification in a Tanjore Village.* Berkeley: University of California Press.
1972. *Inequality and Social Change.* Delhi: Oxford University Press.
1974. *Studies in Agrarian Social Structure.* Delhi: Oxford University Press.

Bhargava, B. S.
1949(?). The Criminal Tribes: A Social and Economic Study of the Principal Criminal Tribes and Castes in North India.
Chakravarty, A.
1975. *Contradiction and Change: Emerging Patterns of Authority in a Rajasthan Village.* New Delhi: Oxford University Press.
Cohn, B. S.
1959. Some Notes on Law and Social Change in India. *Economic Development & Social Change*, *8*: 79.
1965. Anthropological Notes on Disputes and Law in India. *American Anthropologist*, *67* (Special Issue: Ethnography of Law): 82.
Coons, J. E., Jr.
1964. Approaches to Court-Imposed Compromise: The Uses of Doubt and Reason, *Northwestern University Law Review*, *58*: 787.
Das, V.
1974. Sociology of Law. In ICSSR, 1974, 2: 367.
Deb, R., et al.
1970. Patterns of Criminal Justice among some Tribes. *Journal of the Indian Law Institute*, 12: 205.
Derrett, J. D. M.
1957. *Hindu Law: Past and Present.* Calcutta: Mukerji.
1963. *Introduction to Modern Hindu Law.* Bombay: Oxford University Press.
1968. *Religion, Law and State in India.* London: Faber & Faber.
1970. *A Critique of Modern Hindu Law.* Bombay: N. M. Tripathi Private.
1976a. *The Death of a Marriage Law: Epitaph for the Rishis.* New Delhi: Vikes Publication House.
1976b. *Essays in Classical and Modern Hindu Law.* Leiden: Brill.
Desai, I. P.
1976. *Untouchability in Rural Gujarat.* Bombay: Popular Prakashan.
Dhagamwar, V.
1974. *Law, Power and Justice: Protection of Personal Right under the Indian Penal Code.* Bombay: N. M. Tripathi Private.
Diwan, P.
1977. *Muslim Law in Modern India.* Allahabad: Allahabad Law Agency.
1978. *Customary Law of Punjab and Haryana.* Chandigarh: Publication Bureau, Punjab University.
1979. *Modern Hindu Law.* 4th ed. Allahabad: Allahabad Law Agency.
Ehrlich, E.
1962. *Fundamental Principles of the Sociology of Law*, transl. W. L. Moll. Cambridge: Harvard University Press.
Elwin, H. V. H.
1943. *Maria Murder and Suicide.* Bombay: Oxford University Press.

Epstein, A. L.
1969. *Matupit: Land, Politics and Social Change among the Tolai of New Britain*. Canberra: Australian National University Press.
Epstein, T. S.
1962. *Economic Development and Social Change in South India*. Manchester: Manchester University Press.
Felstiner, W. L. F.
1974. Influences of Social Organizations on Dispute Processing. *Law & Society Review*, 9: 63.
Freed, R. S.
1972. The Legal Process in a Village in North India: The Case of Maya. *Transactions of New York Academy of Sciences*, 33(2nd Ser.): 423.
Fürer-Haimendorf, C. v.
1943. *The Chanchus: Jungle Folk of the Doccan*. London: Macmillan.
1945a. *The Reddis of the Bison Hills*. London: Macmillan.
1945b. Notes on Tribal Justice among Apa Tanis. *Man in India*, Vol. 26.
1948. *The Raj Gonds of Adilabad*. London: Macmillan.
1967. *South Asian Studies: A Study of Values and Social Controls*. London: Weidenfeld & Nicolson.
1979. *The Gonds of Andhra Pradesh*. London: G. Allen & Unwin.
Galanter, M.
1964. Hindu Law and the Development of the Modern India Legal System. Mimeo. Prepared for the Annual Meeting of the American Political Sciences Association, Chicago, Illinois.
1968. Changing Legal Conceptions of Caste. In M. Singer & B. Cohn, eds., *Structure and Change in Indian Society*, Viking Fund Publications in Anthropology, No. 47: 299.
1969. Introduction: The Study of Indian Legal Profession. *Law & Society Review*, 3: 201.
1972a. The Aborted Restoration of "Indigenous" Law in India. *Comparative Studies in Society and History*, 14: 53.
1972b. The Abolition of Disabilities: Untouchability and the Law. In *The Untouchables in Contemporary India*, J. M. Mahar, ed., Tucson: University of Arizona Press: 227.
Ganambal, K.
1973. *Religious Institutions and Caste Panchayats in South India*. Delhi: Controller of Publications.
Gough, K.
1955. The Social Structure of a Tanjore Village. M. Marriott, ed., *Village India: Studies in the Little Community*, Chicago: The University of Chicago Press.
Gurvitch, G.
1947. *Sociology of Law*. London: Kegan Paul, Trench, Trubner.

Henderson, D. F.
1965. *Conciliation and Japanese Law: Tokugawa and Modern.* 2 vols. Seattle: University of Washington Press.
Hidayatullah, M.
1979. *The Fifth and Sixth Schedules to the Constitution of India.* Gauhati, India: Ashok Publishing House.
Husain, S. A.
1976. *Marriage Customs among Muslims in India.* New Delhi: Sterling Publishers.
Hussain, W.
1934. *Administration of Justice during Muslim Rule in India.* Delhi Idarah-i Adabiyat-i Delhi.
ICSSR (The Indian Council of Social Science Research).
1974. *A Survey of Research in Sociology and Social Anthropology.* 2 vols. Bombay: Popular Prakashan.
India, Government of
1978. *Report on Indigenous Negotiable Instruments Chundis.* New Delhi: Banking Laws Committee.
Iswharan, K.
1964. Customary Law in Village India. *International Journal of Comparative Sociology*, 5: 228.
Jain, M. P.
1966. *Outlines of Indian Legal History.* 2nd ed. Bombay: N. M. Tripathi Private.
Jossi, P. C.
1975. *Land Reforms in India: Trends and Perspectives.* Bombay: Allied Publishers.
Kahre, R. S.
1972. Indigenous Culture and the Lawyer's Law in India. *Comparative Studies in Society and History*, 14: 71.
Kane, P. V.
1950. *History of Dharmaśāstras: Ancient and Mediaeval Religious and Civil Law in India.* 5 vols. Poona: Bhandarkar Oriental Research Institute.
Kantowsky, D.
1960. Indische Laiengerichte: Die Nyaya Panchayat in Uttar Pradesh. *Verfassung und Recht in Uebersee*, 1: 140.
Kidder, R.
1973. Courts and Conflict in an Indian City: A Study in Legal Impact. *Journal of Commonwealth Political Studies*, *11*: 121.
1974a. Formal Litigation and Professional Insecurity: Legal Entrepreneurship in South India. *Law & Society Review*, 9: 11.
1974b. Litigation as a Strategy for Personal Mobility: The Case of Urban Caste Association Leaders. *Journal of Asian Studies*, 33: 177.

Kushawaha, R.
1977. *Working of Nyaya Panchayats in India: A Case Study of Varanasi District.* New Delhi: Young Asia Publications.
Law & Society Review.
1969. A Special Issue Devoted to Lawyers in Developing Societies, with Particular Reference to India. Vol. 3, No. 2-3.
Lingat, R.
1973. *The Classical Law of India.* Berkeley: University of California Press.
Mahmood, S. T.
1972a. *Islamic Law in Modern India.* Bombay: N. M. Tripathi Private.
1972b. *Family Law Reform in the Muslim World.* Bombay: N. M. Tripathi Private.
1976. *An Indian Civil Code and Islamic Law.* Bombay: N. M. Tripathi Private.
1977. *Muslim Personal Law: Role of the State in the Sub-Continent.* New Delhi: Vikes Publication House.
Mahmood, S. T. ed.
1975. *Family Law and Social Change: Essays in Honour of A.A.A. Fyzee.* Delhi: Sanskaran Prokashak.
Mandelbaum, D. G.
1966. *Society in India.* 2 vols. Berkeley: University of California Press.
Moore, S. F.
1966. A Social Structure Approach to Legal Reasoning. *Southern California Law Review*, 39: 615.
Morrison, C.
1969. Social Organization at the District Courts: Colleague Relationships among Indian Lawyers. *Law & Society Review*, 3: 251.
1972a. Kinship in Professional Relations: A Study of North Indian District Lawyers. *Comparative Studies in Society and History*, 14: 100.
1972b. Munshis and Their Masters: The Organization of an Occupational Relationship in the Indian Legal System. *Journal of Asian Studies*, 3: 309.
1974. Clerks and Clients: Paraprofessional Roles and Cultural Identities in Indian Litigation. *Law & Society Review*, 9: 39.
Patel, M. L.
1974. *Changing Land Problems of Tribal India.* Bhopal: Progress Publisher.
Pillai, K. N. G.
1977. Criminal Jurisdiction of Nyaya Panchayats. *Journal of the Indian Law Institute*, 19: 436.
Pospisil, L.
1958. Social Change and Primitive Law: Consequences of a Papuan Legal Case. *American Anthropologist*, 60: 832.

1971. *Anthropology of Law: A Comparative Theory*. New York: Harper & Row.
Robins, R. S.
1962. Judicial Panchayats in Uttar Pradesh. *American Journal of Comparative Law*, 11: 239.
Rudolph, L. H., & Rudolph, S. H.
1967. *The Modernity of Tradition: Political Development in India*, Chicago: The University of Chicago Press.
Saran, A. B.
1974. *Murder and Suicide among the Munda and the Oraon*. Delhi: National Publishing House.
Sharma, M.
1979. *The Politics of Inequality: Competition and Control in an Indian Village*. Honolulu: University Press of Hawaii.
Sher Singh, Sher.
1965. *The Sansis of Punjab*. Delhi: Sterling Publishers.
Simhadri, Y.
1979. *The Ex-Criminal Tribes of India*. New Delhi: National Publishing House.
Sinha, S.
1959. Bhumij Kshatriya Movement in South Manbhum. *Journal of Anthropological Survey of India*, 10: 9.
Somers, G. E.
1977. *The Dynamics of Santhal Tradition in a Peasant Society*. Cambridge: Schenkman.
Srinivas, M. N.
1952. A Joint Family Dispute in a Mysore Village. *Journal of the M. S. University of Baroda*, 1952: 7.
1962. *Caste in Modern India and Other Essays*. Bombay: Asia Publishing House.
1976. *The Remembered Village*. Delhi: Oxford University Press.
Stokes, E.
1959. *The English Utilitarians and India*. Oxford: University Press.
Verma, S. C.
1979. *The Bhil Kills*. Delhi: Kunj Publication House.
Yogendra Singh.
1973. *Modernization of Indian Tradition: A Systematic Study of Social Change*, New Delhi: Oriental Press.

Glossary

artha	wealth, interest
arthavāda	additional verbiage offering descriptions, elaborations or reasons for injunctions
āśrama	the stage of one's life
avemong	self-help
bhoodan	voluntary gifts of lands for redistribution of common use
biradari	community
Brahman, Brahmin	a member of the highest priestly caste
carita	custom
cheri	area
chotei	Japanese system of conciliation
dharma	essential quality of the cosmos, right behaviour
Dharmaśāstras	The Hindu Codes
Dharmasutras	Collections of right behaviour
dvija	a duty of not marrying a woman of *varna* higher than his own
dwapara	the third *yuga*
gramdan	voluntary gifts of villages for distribution of common use
jajman	patron
jati	sub-caste
kali	the present, decadent *yuga*
kali-varjyas	acts prohibited in the *kali yuga*
kama	pleasure
kazis	judges in Muslim communities
krta	the first golden *yuga*
Ksatriya	a member of the second, royal and warrior caste
Lok Adalat	People's Court
loka-vikrusta	reproved by the world
loka-vidvista	odious to the world
lokshakti	people's power for social transformation
matas	religious organizations, mostly temple administration
maulvis	Muslim divines
mechas	forest or hill tribes or other untouchables living on the fringe of Hindu society
mofussil	back-country

muftis	functionaries assigned the jobs of conflict-resolution
nyaya	dharma
panch	the five persons of a council
pancha	a council of five persons
panchayat	a council of five persons to decide on matters of a Hindu caste, village or other body
pandit	the learned Brahmin
pradhan	a bureaucratic agent
raja	king, ruler
Ram-Rajya	the Ideal Rule
sadācāra	good custom
Sarvodaya	the welfare of all – Ghandi's idea
śāstras	rules, treatises of law-books
sístācāra	usages of the good
Smritis	Dharmaśāstras
sudder	chief
Sudra	a member of the lowest worker caste
tapu	form of excommunication
treta	the second *yuga*
ulama	an Islamic doctor
Vaisyaya	a member of the third, mercantile and professional caste
varna	status, class
vedas	the entire body of Hindu sacred writings
vidhi	precept embodying an injunction
yuga(s)	age(s), epoch(s)

6 Reception of Law in Thailand – A Buddhist Society

Preedee Kasemsup

This article will be a discussion of the reception of Western law in an Eastern country, the problem of indigenous legal elements in the legal system of a non-Western culture, and the relationship between the indigenous elements and the received elements in the legal system. In the nineteenth century, with the expansion of European economic, political and military powers, we saw the two great legal systems of Europe, Common Law and Civil Law, received in most of the countries of the other world, either voluntarily or involuntarily. With the reception of Western law, problems arose concerning the relationship between the received elements and the role of jurisprudence in the receiving countries. In discussing these problems, one has to guard against the deeply ingrained concepts and categories of the Western jurisprudence, lest one should be accused of producing treatises "suitable for a manual of an ethnocentric political science rather than for comparative law" (Hooker, 1978: 32). As preconceived ideas and categories are harmful to scholarly investigation, a well-arranged conceptual scheme is indispensable for accurate analysis. We shall first attempt to lay out such a scheme.

I. Theoretical Framework

1. CONCEPT OF LAW

In any article concerning the problem of legal pluralism and reception of Western law in non-Western cultures such as the Thai, the proper meaning of what we call law should be provided for correct analysis of the problem. For that purpose we have to trace the normal development of law and its relationship with other social institutions, that is, usages, customs, morals, etc.

By the word "law" in this article we mean a norm or a system of norms, the violation of which by necessity calls forth human responses known as sanctions. Law possesses a distinctive nature, seriousness, in that its violation is so serious that the violation will not be left unchallenged by either the victim or the community at large. The norms are adhered to strictly. The seriousness and strictness are thus inherent in the nature of law, and give security for enforcement of sanction, the most distinctive feature of law in Western jurisprudence. In case of violation of these norms, the victim generally would not remain passive but would react actively to the violation in defence of himself, seeking redress, self-help or revenge. In a primitive community, the inviolability of the legal norms may have been supported by the belief in a supernatural power which expressed itself in the concept of taboo. Later on when the community was more developed, its members organized themselves to support and ensure the authorized enforcement of the legal norms instead of allowing the parties to use unrestrained self-help to protect their rights and interests. The judicial institution and process were established in the community to settle disputes. In brief, we may say that the norms of behaviour in the community of the early period emerged in the form of usages and customs, and gradually developed through repetitive practices over a long period of time, until the community felt that there was an obligation to follow such practices as they were right. Part of the usages and customs that remained unaccompanied by sanction through deliberate and organized enforcement, became differentiated from law accompanied by sanction as simple custom. The legal nature of the norms was derived not so much from the mere existence of sanction, however, but rather from the very nature of the norms themselves, which makes enforcement inevitable for its developed seriousness and strictness.

2. CATEGORIES OF LAW

(1) Stage of *Volksrecht*

When the word "law" is understood as stated above, it is certain that in every community, however primitive, law is always found to exist. The kind of law was simple and its rules were known to all members as derived from their communal life. The growth of the rules were spontaneous and their development was slow and gradual. This type of law is known in German as *Volksrecht* which is translated into English as "people's law."

(2) Stage of *Juristenrecht*

When the community expanded and grew more complex, conflict situations that demanded solution took place more frequently, and the institution and procedure for conflict resolution gradually appeared in the form of law. As a result, *Volksrecht* was refined and articulated in details; their application to various situations accumulated precedents; and the conception of the hierarchy of legal rules was gradually established. Over a long period of time, the originally simple contents of *Volksrecht* became enriched and complicated, so as not to be understood by laymen. This stage of law is known as *Juristenrecht* in German or "lawyer's law" in English. *Juristenrecht* as a legal system was understood only by the persons who were specially trained in it. A new profession known as jurists or legal nobles began to emerge. Their knowledge and skill were what we call legal science or jurisprudence. The reasoning employed in the jurisprudence may be called, to use Edward Coke's words, "the artificial perfection of reason" which the layman's common-sense alone cannot understand nor command. Being specifically rational and systematic, it was capable of being studied and taught only in law schools as well as being transplanted into countries having different cultural backgrounds. Roman law and English law were the remarkable examples of the law that developed to the stage of *Juristenrecht.*

In the legal systems that appeared through the two stages of *Volksrecht* and *Juristenrecht*, customary law was still living. Customary law was not formulated by human deliberation. Being inherited from the ancestors, it was sacred and permanent with practical application to most of the needs of the community. However, they had to face the need to devise new rules for specific purposes. The new rules were understood, even when successfully devised, as a temporary measure to meet the special needs of the day. Even if they were kept valid for a long time, the community still considered them as not true law or Dharma, but merely a kind of law of inferior status to the legal rules of *Volksrecht* and *Juristenrecht.* They were called *lege* or *jus scriptum* in Roman law and "provisions" or "statutes" in English.

(3) Stage of *Satzungsrecht*

Since the community developed further to another level, in Europe from middle-ages to modern era, systematic law-making became prevalent and the number of made-laws has increased. The reluctance in law-making in the preceding ages faded away with the emergence of the concept of sovereignty propounded by Jean Bodin in the sixteenth century. The distinctive feature of the modern sovereign state lies in its power to make law without any limitation. The concepts of sovereignty and legislation were enthusiastically acclaimed as a great achievement of the modern era. The modern concept of law therefore differs radically from those of the preceding ages. The law is to be made by the sovereignty of the state, comparable to the miraculous power of God. Once a law is enacted, the problems of the purpose, function and limit of law should disappear from the concern of jurisprudence. The concern should be concentrated upon "legislated law (*Satzungsrecht* or *Gesetzesrecht*)". The European modern legal system is completely dominated by this type of enacted law, and the idea of different types of legal rules coexisting side by side in a legal system prevalent in preceding ages was no longer acceptable.

The new theory of law known as legal positivism has dominated European legal thinking since late nineteenth century. As a matter of fact, however, the jurisprudence based on legal positivism is not capable of developing the theory of the purpose, function and limit of the law, nor is it conducive to research into the relationship of law with morals and culture. Thus it can not develop true juristic method, that is, application and interpretation of law in such a way that the legal system is able to accept some influence of social morality and cultural tradition to refine the law compliantly with the identity of the community.

(4) Summary view

Among the three stages of legal development, the first one of *Volksrecht* was the period when legal rules began to come into being and developed gradually, as if without any human purposive effort. It would not be too far-fetched to follow F. Hayek's terminology to describe the legal rules in this category as forming "spontaneous order" (1976, 1: Ch.2), although they may also be called "grown" elements in law. The legal rules in the second stage of *Juristenrecht* developed further into those that were articulated and systematized by the purposive effort of the jurists who played the role of the midwife for the birth of those rules. This human effort was, however, not of the mother herself. It was only an outcome of human intellectual ability to discover and rationalize legal rules created by someone else. The third stage of *Satzungsrecht* was different from the preceding two stages. The legal rules in this stage were devised by the deliberation of human will and design, and could be classified into exogenous order and called "made law" or "made elements in law."

This differentiation of three types of legal rules might be thought an oversimplification of the complicated historical facts. But, the purpose of such differentiation is first to trace the basic stages of development of law, and then to employ the results as a conceptual framework to analyse the problems under consideration. The concepts of *Volksrecht, Juristenrecht*, and *Satzungsrecht* obtained from Western history may be employed in the analysis of the contemporary legal systems in non-Western cultures.

3. RHYTHM OF LEGAL DEVELOPMENT

With regard to the relationship between law and morals, only those absolutely convinced of legal positivism could deny the inseparable connection between both. Wang Pe-Chi, a learned and deep-thinking contemporary Chinese scholar, wrote with perceptive wisdom that "their relationship is in fact like the relationship between a body and its shadow, which can never be separated." The less the distance between law and morals in society, the more stable the society may be, and the more contented its members may feel. However, law is by nature a conservative force under normal conditions, and morals always the leading force of human behaviour. Law must not lag behind morals. It is the duty of the jurists to try to keep the law as close to morals as possible, although the problem is one of the most fundamental and difficult in jurisprudence; Jhering once compared it to Cape Horn, where few jurists could avoid shipwreck in the journey of jurisprudence.

On the other hand, we can find two spirits of the age, spirits of *jus strictum* and *jus aequum*, always contending against each other in the last 2,000 years of European history. The spirit of *jus strictum* is the inclination of the legal profession to adhere strictly to the letter of the law, holding the contents of the law so sacred and perfect as to be applicable to all the problems of society. There is no need to consider other factors beyond the domain of law. We can find evidences of such a spirit in the society where the development of law and legal science reached full maturity, as in France after the Napoleonic Code, in Germany in the form of *Begriffsjurisprudenz*, and in England in the complacency of common law before the emergence of equity. When the legal system is fortified by the spirit of *jus strictum*, it lacks the flexibility required for just and proper solution of conflicts.

On the contrary, the jurists who are sensitive to the defects in the legal system are inclined to introduce para-legal concepts into the legal system in order to make it responsive to the demand of justice and further to reform the system itself. Such inclination of the jurists has been known as the spirit of *jus aequum*. It appears to us that the birth of *jus gentium* and *Praetor legem* in the time of Romans or equity in England in the seventeenth century was the expression of this spirit.

The era dominated by the spirit of *jus strictum* was always followed and supplanted by an era dominated by the spirit of *jus aequum*; but the hands of the clock tended to swing back to the era of *jus strictum*. The eras of *jus strictum* and *jus aequum* tend to alternate again and again over the long history of legal development. In the history of law and jurisprudence in Europe, the study of Roman law revived in Italy in the eleventh century, and the following Glossator and Post-Glossator Schools represented an era of *jus strictum*. But the later period of around 300 years through the period of modern natural law would be taken as an era of *jus aequum*. After the Napoleonic Code, however, modern times entered again into the era of *jus strictum*, dominated by the spirit of legal positivism.

4. THE ROLE OF JURISPRUDENCE

The decisive factor causing this rhythm of legal development in Europe was, we can say, nothing but the legal science born by jurists. In the history of Roman law, the early *jus strictum* era was developed to the later *jus aequum* era by the jurists who employed the concepts of *jus naturale* and *jus gentium*. The former Roman law, which had contained some characteristics of primitive law, was developed step by step into the classical Roman law which formed a more advanced, mature legal system suitable to the great Roman Empire. This was possible solely because the efforts of the jurists led to the birth of a systematized jurisprudence, bequeathed later to the world as a great cultural heritage. After the introduction of Greek moral concepts such as *humanitas* and *bona fide* into the Roman law, Roman law was developed to a rational, flexible legal system consistent with the sense of social morality of the era. At the same time, however, jurists and legal science began to search for further details and certainty of the law. The inclination went so far as to finally cause the legal system to become rigid, thus returning to the era of *jus strictum*.

A similar role of jurists and legal science could be found in later eras, as clearly observed in the Common Law System, where the legal profession acted as the agent of change in a similar way. The English legal profession at the Bar developed common law, making it an advanced and mature legal system suitable for the Empire under diverse circumstances. Then, through their search for further details and certainty of the law, the English legal profession led the common law into the era of *jus strictum*; common law became inflexible and unresponsive to the need of the society. As a result, equity had to be invented, through the Court of Chancery, to cure the rigidity and unresponsiveness of the common law. The invention of equity in England was also one of the great works of the legal profession.

To sum up, it cannot be denied that the important driving force of legal development was the jurist whose intellectual ability devised the glorious academic discipline called jurisprudence. Any analysis of the historical development of law that disregards the vital role of jurisprudence would never be able to give an adequate account of the subject under consideration. The analysis of legal reception which makes the same mistake would be sure to fall into the same failure.

II. The Traditional Thai Legal System

1. HISTORICAL SURVEY

The Thai legal system, before coming into contact with and being thereby greatly influenced by Western law and culture, had a feature common with those of other countries of the East. The feature is generally labelled as "traditional" or "pre-modern." In order to analyse the Thai legal system in the theoretical framework mentioned above, a brief historical survey will be made.

(1) The Thai nation: Its cultural setting

The modern Thais, the Shans, the Laotians and many other hill-tribes in the south of China, belonged to the same race known as

"Thai". Even though there is still some disagreement among experts, it is generally accepted that the original settlement of the Thais was in the south of China. Chinese historical documents had records about the Thais since 600 B.C. and their mention was more frequent in later periods. Many historians note that the Thais, who were scattered over a vast northern area, were moving south gradually and spreading out. On their way they had to adapt themselves to the requirements of new circumstances. They also came under the influence of other tribes with which they came into contact. After reaching the Indo-Chinese peninsula they further mingled extensively with the Khmers, the Mons and other tribes.

Despite these contacts with different tribes, some distinctive features of the Thais have been tenaciously retained. The customs about marriage and family are the most remarkable, differentiating them from their two great neighbours, China and India, and leaving some imprints on the present Thai legal system, to be described later.

In A.D. 1238, the Thais that had settled in the north of present Thailand, with increasing population, declared independence from the Khmers, to establish the Thai state for the first time at Sukhodaya. From that time on, we can speak of the history of Thailand in three periods.

(2) The Sukhodaya period (1238–1350)

A graphic description of the life and custom of the Thai people, and law and administration in the first Kingdom, are found in the famous Sukhodaya inscription, purportedly made during the reign of King Rama Kamhaeng the Great of Sukhodaya. The Thai community of this period was a simple tribal one. The status of the monarch was rather that of a tribal chief, not qualitatively different from his people. In the words of the learned Prince Dhani,

> "The monarch was of course the people's leader in battles, but he was also their father in peace-time, whose advice was sought and expected in all matters and whose judgement was accepted by all. He was moreover accessible to his people, for we are told by an old inscription that in front of the Royal Palace of Sukhodaya there used to be a gong hung up for people to beat upon whenever they wanted personal help and redress" (Dhani, 1965: 162).

During this period trade was developing. Property right, especially ownership of land and right to succession, were recognized. Simple judicial processes like dispute settlement in the family was in existence. Animistic religious beliefs existed side by side with Buddhism. The law in this period could be called *Volksrecht*, in which custom and morals were indistinguishably mingled.

(3) The Ayudaya period (1350–1767)

After a century or so of the Sukhodaya Kingdom, the power moved to the Ayudaya Kingdom, and continued there for over four centuries. This was the period during which the power of the Thai nation was firmly established in this part of the Indo-Chinese peninsula. The Kingdom developed gradually to become one of the most important administrative centres in this area. Geographically, Ayudaya was situated near the sea and the main international trading routes. The society became more complex through trade and commerce as well as by expanding territory and increasing population. These necessitated the reorganization of the administrative system. The loosely-organized administrative system was no longer suitable. An important reform of the administration occurred in the reign of King Trailok (1448–1488), based on the administrative system of the Khmer Empire which was itself strongly influenced by Hinduism. The administration was more centralized and the centre was divided into four ministries: Palace, Interior, Finance and Agriculture. The monarchy was gradually transformed from that of a patriarchal kinship group during the Sukhodya period to a divine kingdom influenced by the Khmers and Hinduism.

The legal system became more complex. The judicial system and procedure became fixed and institutionalized. Robert Lingat believed that Hindu legal culture represented by the Code of Manu had been known in Thailand since the Sukhodaya period. However, we may state that the Hindu legal culture and the Code of Manu had a greater influence on the Thai legal system and society during the Ayudaya period than at any time before.

The Kingdom of Ayudaya was destroyed by the Burmese army in 1766. But the Thai recovered their power within a short time.

(4) The Bangkok period (1767–)

As the destruction of the Ayudaya Kingdom by the Burmese army was almost total, the early Bangkok period was the time of restoration of every aspect of Thai society. In terms of legal history, the Bangkok period inherited the law of the Ayudaya period without any change. The restoration of Thai law finally culminated in the Code of Rama I or the Code of the Three Great Seals. It was a compilation of the verified written law of Thailand, and a decisively important event in Thai legal history, enabling posterity to see the Thai traditional legal system and concept of law.

The Code of the Three Great Seals promulgated in 1805 by King Rama I was enforced until the beginning of the reign of King Rama IV, when Thailand began to modernize her government by the reception of Western law. But its basic ideas have still remained alive as the *corpus juris* of Thai law. Its nature and mode of application is explained later.

2. THE THAI TRADITIONAL LEGAL SYSTEM

(1) *Dharmasastra*: Its juristic character

The traditional Thai legal system possessed a special characteristic, of which anyone wishing to study it ought to take special note: there was a written *corpus juris* in the form of the *Dharmasastra* which assumed a dominant place in the system. It was well known that this *corpus juris* had its historical and cultural source in the Indian Code of Manu. According to Lingat, a recognized authority in the field, the Thais had already accepted the *Dharmasastra* "as the supreme rule of equity for the administration of justice among their countrymen" (1949: 24) even before the establishment of the first Siamese Kingdom of Sukhodaya in the thirteenth century. Be that as it may, the Indian Code of Manu and the Thai *Dharmasastra* were in many ways different. The special characteristics which distinguished them were that while the former was a mixture of moral and religious exhortations and legal norms, the latter was, according to Lingat, a truly civil, legal code (ibid.: 23–25). The original Indian code contained in greater part the mythology and a practical manual of moral and religious advice, and in smaller part provisions which were truly legal. It could not be considered, therefore, as a code of law in the strict sense of the word. On the other hand, the Thai *Dharmasastra* had, apart from the exordium, categorized sections and classified components in a relatively systematic manner almost comparable to early legal codes in Europe. If we read its provisions with care, we might be surprised to find that this premodern code of law contained, incredibly, some modern elements;

each provision of the code stated what to do or not to do, and listed punishments with extremely laconic precision. Unjuristic expressions, such as superfluous justifications or vague admonitions which abound in the Indian and Burmese texts of similar origin, were rarely allowed to creep into the Thai code. However, we have to admit that it was not a code in the modern sense, in spite of its juristic character. It was not a comprehensive statement of law to govern the all-inclusive area of human relations. It is inaccurate to say that "the entire field of ordinary civil and criminal justice was covered by written law." (Wichiencharoen & Netisastro, 1968: 89). Moreover, in trying to understand the Thai traditional legal system, we must guard against the preconceived ideas of modern jurisprudence, for the Thai traditional concept of law is different from it, as stated below.

(2) Two domains of law: Written and unwritten

Many knowledgeable persons with some acquaintance with the legal systems of the East, particularly China, show considerable surprise at the fact that there is a wide area of unwritten law, especially that related to civil law, which is of general application, in spite of its being unwritten. Some show their surprise that the legal systems of the East are occupied invariably, and mainly, by the provisions of criminal law (cf. Jamieson, 1970: i). One has to bear in mind that the traditional legal systems of the East, especially the Thai, were products of the characteristic concept of law of the East. The people of the East conceived the idea that the relationships between people in a community should comply with the well-established tradition of usages, customs and morals, and therefore do not make a clear distinction between the concepts of usages, customs and morals on the one hand and law on the other. With the passing of time, it became necessary to enforce sanctions against the violation of the existing norms. There emerged the process of adjudication that should lead conflicts to solution either by way of persuasion, reconciliation or compulsion. Within the narrow circle of the close-knit community, only when compulsion could not be effected was the assistance of the external political authority needed to enforce compliance or to punish intransigents. When the King adjudicated a conflict case, it was normal practice to announce that the adjudication should be taken as precedent for all future similar conflicts. In this way the written rules in the Thai traditional legal system came into being, with the form of Royal Ordinances or Royal Decrees.

a. The domain of written law

When the number of the written legal rules formulated as above became great they were compiled to form an integral part of the main *corpus juris*, known as the *Dharmasastra* or Code of Manu. The legal rules so incorporated into the *Dharmasastra* are called the *Rajsastra*, being the law of secondary rank, a derivation from the rules and principles of Dharma as stated in the *Dharamasastra*. The legal rules originally appearing in the *Dharmasastra* were known collectively as *Moola kadi*, meaning literally "the roots of the matter", while those in the *Rajsastra* were known as *Saka kadi*, literally "the branches of the matter".

But the nature of the written law was not like that of Western law; this is most conspicuously exemplified by the Uttalum case.[1] It may help understanding if a provision of the law of *Laksana Rad Fong* (Reception of Complaint) directly relevant to the Uttalum case is referred to (Procedure 4, Section 1).

> "Whoever is an 'Uttalum' person, having no gratitude to his parents, his paternal grandparents or his maternal grandparents, bringing a complaint against his parents, paternal grandparents or maternal grandparents, shall be severely punished by flogging. He shall be considered an ungrateful son, a bad example to be followed by no one, and his complaint shall be dismissed."

b. Autonomous legal domain

The above punishment of flogging was merely the procedural measure to dismiss the disputed case which the Thai traditional legal system conceived as an internal affair to be resolved by family members. Such a practice meant that the Thai traditional legal system considered the family as an "autonomous legal domain." Any matter concerning the family had to be settled within the family by the members, and the King and Royal Court would not involve itself in such affairs. The family has been a very important but much-neglected traditional legal institution.

The autonomous legal domain, or the autonomous domain of unwritten law, meant the role and status of the members of a community, governed by usages and customs established since ancient times. Such a form of social control sprang from the "spontaneous order" in Hayek's terminology, deriving its authority from strongly sensitive bonds among the members. Any conflict and deviational behaviour of the members should be handled entirely within the said autonomous domain. The written legal rules in the Thai traditional legal system contained no rules concerning such autonomous domains.

Apart from the family, another autonomous legal domain recognized was the *Sangha* (Brotherhood of the Buddhist Monks or Ecclasiastical Order).

The norms of conduct to regulate the members of the family were usages, customs, morals or even religious teachings, which all the Thai people knew very well. Each member knew his or her role and status in accordance with the norms of the domain concerned. A familiar comment on the conduct of a person who was considered as grossly overstepping his proper role or status was "What a father he is!" or "What a husband he is!" Such a comment presupposed a certain idea of what a good father or husband ought to be like. Such norms of conduct in the family, whether they were called usages, customs or morals, were enforced within the family. The Uttalum case was related to the norms of a son-in-law to ensure his proper behaviour toward the members of his wife's family.

The law of husband and wife which formed part of the *Dharmasastra* showed clearly the acceptance of such a practice. In the Code of Rama I, Section 57 stated:

> "The man who has taken another person's daughter or niece as his wife shall pay proper respect to the wife's parents, elders and relatives as if they were his own, and shall not act improperly. If he quarrels with or beats his wife, intends to use weapons against her, her parents and relatives (who have tried to persuade him to desist), or refuses the persuasion and beats them, causing bodily harm, he has committed a serious improper act, and his wife's family shall return to him the property brought by him and expel him from their house without compensation. If he still loves his wife and wishes for forgiveness, saying that he has been wrong, he shall be ordered to beg forgiveness of her parents. When he has done so, he shall be allowed to continue to cohabit with his wife.
>
> If a man beats his wife's parents or elders, causing them grievance about bodily harm, or commits robbery, he shall be considered a rude, dishonest and unreasonable person, and his wife's parents shall confiscate all his property, give it

> to the wife, and expel him from the house to prevent further harm. If the wife still loves him and wishes to follow him, she shall be allowed to do so, but not be given any property. When she has children, the property shall be given to them, as she has lost her gratitude to her parents."

The contents of the said Section referred to the duty of the child towards his parents, elders and relatives as already existed in customs and morals. This customary and moral rule was extended to be applicable to the son-in-law who, according to the normal practice, went to live with his wife's family. This Section also stipulated the types of conduct which were considered such serious violations of the customary and moral duty that the authority had to become involved.

Another important provision was, Section 58, concerning good conduct, which was to ensure in another way that the intransigent son-in-law would conduct himself properly toward the elder members of his wife's family. It declared:

> "The man who has taken another person's daughter as his wife shall pay proper respect to his wife's parents, elders and relatives. If he does not do so and always gets drunk, beats up his wife, refuses to listen to her parents' advice to desist, becomes rude to them, and hits them even though unintentionally, he shall beg forgiveness from them. Her parents shall require from him a bond of good behaviour. This shall be applicable to his wife's elder brothers and sisters and uncles and aunts *mutatis mutandis.*"

The customary and moral rules enforced in the autonomous legal domain were based on the idea that the parents or the elder members of the family had the authority to ensure that each member of the family conduct himself properly. This was the essence of the internal enforcement procedure within the family.[2] The said rules backed by such organized sanction were, therefore, legal norms according to the theoretical framework mentioned earlier.

(3) Comparative analysis of the two domains

a. Written law

The Thai written law consisted, in a formal classification, of the *Dharmasastra, Rajsastra* and Royal Ordinances. The *Dharmas-*

astra included sacred, permanent and immutable legal rules derived from Dharma. It was perhaps comparable to natural law in the Western terminology. Those known as the *Rajsastra* and Royal Ordinances were neither sacred nor immutable as they were devised by human authority. Royal Ordinances or Royal Decrees were originally issued to meet the requirement of the times, to provide practical details for resolving actual conflicts. When their validity was successfully testified by repeated application, they were collected, revised and compiled into the code called the *Rajsastra*. The *Rajsastra* and Royal Ordinances could be amended or repealed when thought inapplicable, and were understood as a secondary natural law inferior to the *Dharmasastra*.

It was a special characteristic of the Thai written law that it was not considered as arbitrarily created by human authority. It contained the elements of both natural law and man-made law, similar to the *lex humana* of St. Thomas Aquinas, and was not a product of the legislative process according to the modern legal theory. Lingat confirmed for this reason in his famous lecture in 1949 that "The (Western) notion of law is entirely foreign to the traditions of the people in the Far East." Although the modern Western notion of law is foreign to the Thais, the ancient and mediaeval notion is probably similar to the Thai.

Deriving from the permanent Dharma, the direct source of the Thai written law, were decisions on the actual conflicts that came before the authority. If we survey various important categories of law in the Code of Rama I, we find that the exordium of each chapter described the cause of the formulation of the law. It was unequivocally stated that the conflicts were adjudicated, and that the content of the decisions juristically abstracted should be followed in later decisions. We may thus say that the traditional Thai legal system was based on the notion of law for conflict-resolving, like case law in the West. But the Thai did not accepted the theory of binding precedents, because what were being followed were not the precedents adjudicated, but provisions in the Royal Ordinances. The important consequence of this practice was that only the types of conflicts that had been expected to be received by the *corpus juris* might have been brought before the authority, and that the cases brought would have been decided in accordance with the relevant legal provisions. In other words, the Thai *corpus juris* prescribed only the types of conflicts that the court would receive for adjudication. This is different from the

Western legal system, especially in the field of private law where the general principle of rights, duties and liabilities allows private persons to bring any case before the court. This made Western jurists come to the somewhat distorted conclusion that the Thai written law was neither systematic, comprehensive, nor general in its structure; they neglected to mention private law in various areas (cf. Hooker, 1978: 3). Truly, the Western code did consist of general rules and principles to govern almost the whole of life; the Thai *corpus juris*, in contrast, approved the other system of unwritten law to regulate private spheres.

b. Unwritten law

As mentioned earlier, the autonomous legal domain, developing gradually and spontaneously over a long period of time, covered various spheres of community life in the family and Brotherhood of Buddhist monks. Its law was well-known to all the members through usages, customs and morals, and well-observed by the internal enforcement process. It was, in fact, wider in prevalence than written law. If we compare it to the ocean, written law may be compared to isolated islands scattered in the ocean. The fact that the Thai traditional legal system allowed unwritten law to regulate the internal affairs of domains in accordance with their spontaneous rules can be said to show great wisdom in the form of *Volksgeist* of the communities.

The evolution of the modern European law led to the attempt to employ state power to regulate almost every sphere of life, including the most sensitive domain of family. This was a fallacy of legal positivism and constructivism that prevailed in the West for a long time. If we are aware of the danger and harm caused by the excessive use of the law as a form of social control, we may be able to appreciate the high value of the rationality and wisdom underlying the Thai traditional legal system, to overcome the ethnocentric jurisprudence of the nineteenth century.

3. LEGAL SYSTEM AND JURISPRUDENCE

(1) The process of legal formation

The *Dharmasastra* was originally a collection of just and equitable, as well as sacred and immutable, principles, formulated by the propounder with full wisdom into Dharma, rather than coming about by arbitrary human power. It could only be enforced by the Royal authority in a human community. The role of the King, therefore, was not as the creator of law, but as the administrator of law to enforce temporary measures to keep social order.[3]

Thus the Royal Ordinances issued by the King which had come into force from time to time since the Ayudaya period (Lingat, 1949: 17, 28) were never referred to as Dharma, owing to their man-made nature. Still, having been devised by the King as the agent for the propounder of the *Dharmasastra*, they could be regarded as a derivation from the *Dharmasastra*, and they were compiled into the *Rajsastra* after being collected and revised; and the *Rajsastra* came to acquire the same authority and status as the *Dharmasastra* over a long period of time. According to Lingat's words, Royal Ordinances "became henceforward permanent rules not because they emanated from the Kings, but because they were illustrations of the eternal law and partaking in its authority" (ibid.: 27). The last recension of the Royal Ordinances was carried out by King Rama I, and resulted in the famous Code of the Three Great Seals.

The above process of incorporating the man-made law into the sacred *Dharmasastra* may be said to be the most ingenious device invented by the Thai traditional law, the product of the indigenous jurisprudence. It is through this process that various sources of seemingly conflicting laws were integrated into a seamless, single whole. This is quite different from the Western jurisprudence where the conflict between positive law and natural law has been conspicuous since the Christian middle-ages.

(2) Text and interpretation

The cause of the recension of the Code of the Three Great Seals was a case brought before the Royal Court: A married woman had committed adultery and petitioned the Court for divorce. The Royal Court granted her divorce; the unsatisfied husband appealed to the King. King Rama I was of the opinion that the Court's decision was unjust, as the wife, who was in fact guilty, had won the case. The King ordered the judges of the Court to be investigated to see whether they were guilty of partiality, as the husband contended. If the judges could not have justified their decision, they would have been severely punished. The judges in fact justified their decision as strictly based on the letter of the law. The King then asked to examine the official copy of the legal text, and found it stating clearly that if a husband is not to blame when his wife asks for divorce, her request shall be granted. The King was not satisfied with the matter and could not accept that the sacred and eternal *Dharmasastra* might contain so unjust a legal rule. He rationalized that the text might have been copied incorrectly by someone in a later generation. He appointed a Royal Commission to restore the pure original state of the *Dharmasastra*. The result was the Code of the Three Great Seals promulgated in 1805.

From the above event, we can infer that the provisions in the Thai *Dharmasastra* could be referred to with the highest legal authority, which even the King had to respect. Although the King had the power to issue Royal Ordinances to be enforced throughout the Kingdom, the Thai traditional concept of law considered them as merely detailed rules to supplement the *Dharmasastra*. It followed logically that the King could not issue Royal Ordinances contradictory to the provisions of the *Dharmasastra* and that the law must be adhered to with the spirit of *jus strictum* by the legal profession.

(3) Legal education and legal profession

There are some problems relating to knowledge of the law, written or unwritten: whether the general public or only government officials concerned should know the law, and what position the legal profession occupied in the traditional Thai legal system.

The *Dharmasastra* prescribed that it is the duty of the King to study the *Dharmasastra*, and there was a custom since ancient times that every day the King had a certain time to listen to the *Dharmasastra* read by an official.[4] Pallegoix, a Catholic priest who came to live in Thailand in the nineteenth century, said in his book: "The King always keeps the *corpus juris* in his sleeping chamber, so that the Royal official can read to him at least 2-3 pages of it every day. Every senior judge and provincial governer must have a copy of the *corpus juris* ready for use." (1977: 336) Another learned scholar also wrote that the Thai *corpus juris* was the manual of officials for the performance of their duties.

Due to its conflict-resolution-oriented character, the written law was necessary for the official and judge to consult before giving decisions. But the knowledge of the written law was confined to the group of experts or officials concerned; the general public could not be expected to know it at all. Even today, the older generation with a strong conservative view is still reluctant to let their children learn law. The profession of lawyer is not highly regarded in the belief that a good person does not need to know the written law, nor to go to the court, if he conducts himself in compliance with usages, customs and morals. Moreover, the Thai traditional legal system contained a provision prohibiting any person from intervening in another person's case. Any person who helped another unrelated person was deemed to be punishable[5] for the offence of inciting conflicts. The tradition of the Senatorial advocates who were praised as the Priest of Justice in Rome, or that of the Barrister in England, could not be established under the Thai traditional law. The ideal of a learned patrician in the East was that of a gentleman who makes peace, not an able advocate who wins cases for others in the court.

(4) Religion and law

The influence of religion on law and administration of a country is an undeniable fact, but the extent of the influence depends upon the country's cultural background. In understanding the influence of Buddhism upon the Thai traditional law, we must carefully guard against misunderstanding. Buddhism is truly known as the national religion of Thailand, but the *Sangha* has, throughout its long history, never established itself as an authority to rival the secular one. This is quite different from the case of Christianity since the middle-ages in Europe, where the Church has been an institutional power to rival the state. There has never been any bitter conflict between the *Sangha* and the state with respect to jurisdiction over the country. In reality, Buddhism has no theology to support a claim for the authority to take control of the worldly affairs, and to enforce its teachings on the public. However, the adherence to the Buddhist teachings has formed a common bond between the ruler and the ruled over several centuries; the spirit, social philosophy and moral teachings of Buddhism have exerted great influences upon the way of life and traditional Thai law.

The widely-known special nature of Buddhism is that it is a religion to praise peace and gentle treatment of man as deserving admiration. Although Buddhism has not fully succeeded in turning most countries into peace-loving ones, with all its prevalence over the vast area of South-Eastern Asia it has at least succeeded in tempering considerably the cruelties perpetrated by man against man, as found in many instances in the Thai traditional law. One such instance was a provision during the Ayudaya period, prescribed for a case of robbery: If a robber murdered the victim, the robber should be handed over to the family of the deceased so that they might punish him as they wished; but if they do not intend to punish him cruelly, they can choose to have him pay a ransom in exchange for his liberty, or beg for redemption of his sinful act by becoming a monk, or else they may forgive him and set him free[6]. This provision still retained a trace of the law of self-revenge on the one hand, but it attempted on the other to find a milder measure to avoid the possibility of causing another death. Such an attempt was influenced by Buddhism, because the Hinanaya Buddhist considers killing to be the gravest sin of man, and accordingly there is an established teaching that only forgiveness can terminate the vicious circle of killing.

According to another provision,[7] if a man is felling trees away from the highway and the axe-head looses from its handle and kills another person, the law deems it to be the *kharma*[8] of the victim and the tree-feller shall perform meritorious acts for him; but if the axe-head *and handle* loose from the feller's hands and cause death, it is the fault of the tree-feller, and he shall pay compensation at the rate prescribed by the law. The performance of meritorious acts for the victim was used here to effect reconciliation between both parties according to the Buddhist idea.

Divorce by consent was prescribed in the Royal Ordinance on the Law of Husband and Wife, Section 67 as follows:

> "If a husband and his wife no longer feel physically and psychologically attracted to each other and wish to get a divorce, the divorce shall be granted. They shall not be compelled to cohabit, as the previous merits which had sustained their cohabitation have been exhausted."

This provision also expressed the Buddhist belief that being husband and wife in this life is the result of the common merits performed by them in their previous lives. The length of the period of cohabitation depends therefore on the amount of the common merits performed. If the latter is great the former will last for long time. Defiance of the belief is impossible.

The King sometimes attempted to employ the law as an instrument to enforce compliance with religious precepts in the Kingdom. One such attempt occurred during the reign of King Rama I: A Royal Proclamation required the public to comply with the five norms of good behaviour prescribed for laymen by Buddhism,[9] and further prescribed punishment to be imposed in case of violation. However, it is not known how this provision was enforced, nor whether it achieved the desired result. It is believed that the fate of this law was no different from that of any other laws that tried to enforce compliance with religious precepts on the public.

The *Sangha* is governed mainly by a Buddhist *corpus juris canonici* known as *Vinaya* (Holy Precepts), forming one of the three parts of the Buddhist Holy Scripture, the *Traipidhaka* (Tripitaka), originating from Buddha himself. *Vinaya* is unalterable in nature, but is in fact supplemented by the commentaries of a long tradition, and by commentaries on the commentaries, together with usages and customs developed within the *Sangha.* These various sources constitute the subject-matter of Buddhist jurisprudence. The jurisprudence has been studied, taught and imparted from generation to generation, and is judiciously cultivated in the two Buddhist universities and all monastery schools in Thailand. The administration of the Buddhist law is considered as an internal affair of the *Sangha*, another autonomous domain like the family. However, in cases where secular support is needed, a secular law-suit may be resorted to. This is evidenced in the Declaration of the Buddhist Ecclesiastical Order dated 15 July 1903 (Bangkok Era 121) by the name of the Great Patriarch, Prince Vachirayan Varorasa who was the great reorganizer of the Order in modern Thailand (Vachirayan Varorasa, 1971: 40, 41). It stated:

> "All Buddhist monks are, apart from being bound to comply with the *Vinaya* as our own personal law, also under the jurisdiction of the secular law either as particular law applicable to a limited class of people or as general law binding on the general public. They must also comply with good custom that is not contradictory to the two kinds of law above-mentioned. In brief, the *Sangha* is bound by law from three different sources. The Act on the Organization of the Buddhist Ecclesiastical Order therefore ought to be studied by every monk so that he may understand it and conduct himself correctly."

4. CONCLUDING REMARKS

Originally, the Thai traditional law was probably a body of simple customary rules which could be classified into *Volksrecht.* With the reception of Indian cultural influences, the written law element was formally introduced into the Thai legal system, and the Thai judiciary came to be dominated by Hindu Brahmins from India.

The Thai jurisprudence also evolved itself along this line of law under the influence of Indian law and culture. When the evolution reached the stage of maturity, the law was probably taught and imparted by Court Brahmins as a variation of *Juristenrecht*. The Hindu belief that the Code of Manu was sacred and unalterable, representing the principles of justice and equity, was also kept alive. This belief, combined with the concept of Hindu *Devaraja* and Buddhist *Dharmaraja* (Divine and Righteous Kingship), led the Thais to hold the idea that the monarch is merely the upholder of law and not its creator, for his authority was human. The *Dharmasastra* was the basic written law of Thailand and filled with such legal provisions and principles.

Apart from the *Dharmasastra*, there were many other rules enacted by the Kings to enforce temporary measures for the administration of the country. They were issued in the form of Royal Ordinances, and after repeated application were compiled into a body of texts known as *Rajsastra*. The *Rajsastra* was neither sacred nor immutable and could be altered by the King, who issued other Royal Ordinances, or his successors. Thus the Thai traditional legal system implied a concept of hierarchical pluralism of the *Dharmasastra* and *Rajsastra*. Such a concept of law in Thailand was similar to that in Europe in ancient times and the middle-ages, but different from that in modern times (cf. McIllwain, 1955: 364–365).

Last but not least, it should be particularly noted that the reception of the *Dharmasastra* into Thai law did not, contrary to the case of modern codes, produce any disturbing effects on the existing customary rules, for the Hindu idea of law was by no means hostile to usages and customs. On the contrary, the *Dharmasastra* served as an ideal criterion for criticizing and improving the customary rules of law by its very moral nature, thereby producing salutary effects on the positive law, in that the Hindu notion of law facilitated Thai law, transforming it from a simple law to a sophisticated system of mature law, as Stoicism did for Roman law.

We can see that the spirit of Thai jurisprudence from the time of King Rama I to the era of the reception of Western law showed a strong tendency toward *jus strictum* as typically understood by the background story of the compilation the Code of the Three Great Seals. When we survey the judicial decisions during this period, we can conclude that the Thai legal profession had an admirably high degree of judicial sophistication.[10] This had a great positive influence on the legal development at the time Thailand began to receive Western law.

III. Reception of Modern Western Law

Even though some serious doubts have been expressed about the use of the words "modern" and "tradition" in the study of contemporary law, I believe that there is no reason to shun such useful terms, for the modern Western world is an undeniable fact and the aspiration of the Third World to modernize is also understandable.[11] The process of legal modernization of non-Western countries by Western law is truly a serious problem to us.

1. THE EMERGENCE OF MODERN WESTERN LAW

By modern Western law we mean the legal systems of European countries in the nineteenth century after a long history of evolution. It first revealed itself in the legal system of the Romans, and evolved further through the middle-ages and the Renaissance to the emergence of modern states. This was inclusively called "the classical era of natural law" by Bodenheimer (1981: 31–33). In the Age of Enlightenment in the eighteenth century the application of the creative ideas produced in the preceding ages was seen, as epitomized in the famous French Civil Code, which established the modern system of law.

It was this modern system which was carried along to the East by merchants and naval forces. The impression of the modern system on the Eastern mind was deep and soul-searching. Several superior qualities of the Western legal system made the Eastern mind feel the necessity of reception. We shall illustrate briefly some characteristic points of them.

1. The modern Western legal system was based on the particular system of jurisprudence originated in the Roman genius, refined by the Glossator and Post-Glossator Schools, and enriched and rationalized by eminent jurists of the classical era of natural law. In witnessing the emergence of legal rationality we may say, in Max Weber's terminology, that, with the advent of the nineteenth century, Europe completed the long process of legal development. The heterogeneous pre-modern law was, by means of the modern

doctrine of natural law and the idea of Enlightenment, transformed into a really modern law, rational, efficient and humane. The driving force of this transformation was the jurisprudence of Roman times, nourished with the developing Western ethos by the legal profession. It is only in Western culture that the jurist and his craft have enjoyed a place of honour in society. The jurisprudence developed by the legal profession made the Western law easier to enforce, teach and furthermore to be implanted in other countries.

2. The emergence of the modern nation state, with the doctrine of sovereignty, made it possible for the modern concept of legislation to become the driving factor in the formulation of law by human authority. As modern law could always be reformulated, modern European states were able to improve their administration more effectively. The society which had been slowly growing could be reshaped in its various fields in a relatively short period. The modern Western society was progressive and full of hope and confidence in the virtue of human legislation.

3. The modern European states developed an efficient administrative and judicial system and expanded their operations into every part of their territories, however remote from the centre.

4. Since the beginning of the modern period, the idea of liberalism and individualism led to the reform of private law in accordance with the principles of equality, the dignity of man, freedom of contract, the inviolable right to property, and others. This further led to rapid progress in economic life, from poverty without amenities, to affluence. The individual began to really enjoy freedom and dignity respected by the state.

5. After the traumatic experiences of religious wars, and the Inquisition from the fifteenth to the seventeenth centuries, Europe was able, by virtue of its spiritual and intellectual resources, to redeem itself through a series of enlightened and enlightening reforms, which included the abolition of the slave trade and cruel punishments. Thus the society and law in Europe in the nineteenth century became fully rational, humane and efficient, and totally different from that of previous ages.

In summary, the modern European legal system, accompanied by mature jurisprudence, was rational and systematic, and easy to impart to other countries. It was quite reasonable that the non-Western countries received it as a whole, whether voluntarily or not. Nevertheless it should be understood that a variety of problems occurred in the process of reception, and are pressing even today in the receiving countries.

2. PROCESS OF RECEPTION

When the independent countries in the East like China, Japan and Thailand began to feel the pressure of the West, they realized the necessity of modernizing themselves after Western models. In the modernization process, they had to face the problem of determining which part and to what extent of the Western culture, including law, they should receive, as well as what of their own culture they should retain. The problem sometimes led to bitter divisions of opinions in many countries, especially in China and Japan, where struggles between the conservative and progressive took place. As each country has cherished certain cultural traditions which its people feel obliged to retain at all costs, the problem was so much more serious.

After the period of half a century, Japan proved to be the most successful country, and became counted among the most developed, while China, even after the great dislocation caused by political, economic and social upheavals, has still not succeeded in modernization. However, even in Japan which is said to have completed her modernization, the problems of reception of Western law and preservation of traditional culture have still remained. In order to solve the problem, the resounding motto given by one of the great reform leaders in the last decade of the Manchu Dynasty, Chang Chi-Tung, "Chinese learning for foundation, Western learning for application" sounds relevant even today. It probably represents a common consensus of the East.

As for Thailand, there were contradicting desires to preserve the national cultural tradition and at the same time to achieve an enormous progress. The most important personage representing the both desires was King Mongkut (1851–68). The King employed his great intellectual capacity and authority over the people to determine the course of the country. We are now proud to say that His Majesty succeeded in the task. His philosophy in this matter was well expressed in his letter to Mrs. Anna H. Leonowens in 1862, who was invited to Thailand to work as a governess in the Royal Court for his children.

> ". . . And we hope that in doing your education on us and our children (whom Englishmen call inhabitants of a benighted

> land) you will do your best endeavour for knowledge of English language, science and literature, and not conversion to Christianity; as the followers of Buddha are mostly aware of the powerfulness of truth and virtue, as well as the followers of Christ, and are desirous to have facility of English language and literature more than new religions." (Leonowens, 1870: V-VI).

It is to be noticed that the word "religion" means national culture in the cultural context of Thailand. The concern to retain national culture as expressed by the King is agreed to in general as an idea highly beneficial to Thailand, allowing modernization to proceed smoothly without disruptive violence. A real modernization was carried out during the reign of King Rama V (1868–1910). In a German encyclopaedia, Thailand under his reign was depicted as follows:

> "The progressive-minded King created a modern army and navy, built the railway system, established ocean-going shipping lines, and turned his kingdom into a modern state in all respects like any European state without blindly imitating the European institutions. As such, even though Thailand did not introduce the constitution or the representative government, it had to be accepted that Thailand was one of the best governed states in the world. This was because the King had performed all the moral duties required of him in accordance with the ideal of an Oriental monarch." (Ploetz, 1960: 971)

3. FROM ENGLISH, THROUGH FRENCH, TO GERMAN LAW

In Thailand, English common law was first received during the reign of King Rama V. English legal principles were taught in the Law School of the Ministry of Justice which was established by Prince Rabi, known as the Father of Thai Law. They were also employed by the Thai court in adjudicating disputes when considered necessary and suitable. In practice, the reception of English law was piecemeal, on a case-by-case basis. The cases where the Thai court could employ English legal principles were those where traditional Thai law was never found, or was obsolete and unsuitable in the circumstances. Traditional Thai law as described in the Code of the Three Great Seals and others still formed the main source of the Thai legal system.

After about half a century of such reception of English law, at the end of the reign of King Rama V, an important change occurred in the development of Thai law. The Thai government decided to create a complete code by appointing a Legislative Council in 1897 to draft the Criminal Code, and another in 1909 to draft the Civil and Commercial Code. The completed Civil and Commercial Code, Part I and Part II, which was drafted by French legal advisors, was promulgated in 1923. The decision to draft it, and its promulgation, represented a most important change in the development of the Thai legal system, for it meant altering the model of reception from English common law, which had been chosen half a century earlier, to Continental French law, which is strikingly different in juristic methods and thinking. In fact, it was promulgated to test the reaction of the legal profession itself. Eventually the Code was repealed two years after its promulgation, to be replaced by a new one.

The new Civil and Commercial Code, Book I and Book II, was drafted on the lines of the Japanese Civil Code, which was modelled after the German Civil Code. Here was another important moment of change, for the model of the new Code was altered from French to German, which differed from each other in several important points, although they belonged to the same Civil Law System.[12] Its promulgation in 1925 was at the beginning of the reign of King Rama VII. The Civil and Commercial Code, Book III and Book IV, was promulgated in 1928 and 1930 respectively. The Civil and Commercial Code, Book V and Book VI, was promulgated in 1934 in the reign of King Rama VIII. The Code, completed under the reign of three successive Kings, was a great edifice of codification, and still valid today.[13]

4. JURISTIC IMPLICATION OF THE RECEPTION

In connection with the reception process described above, it must be remarked that one very important aspect of the difference between the French Civil Code and the German Civil Code was, though rarely noticed, attributable to the spirit of the age. The French Civil Code was promulgated at the turning point between the eighteenth and nineteenth centuries, while the German Civil Code appeared roughly 100 years later. The spirit of the former was the product of the jurisprudence of the two preceding centuries, when the great system of natural law was fully developed and embodied in the Napoleonic Code. Law became an articulated, fixed system, with the emphasis on certainty of the law, that is, the spirit of *jus strictum*. It meant that the spirit of jurisprudence became similar to that of the Renaissance. Law became a machine of logic, ready to be employed by lawyers indiscriminately. Their only role was to press the button of deductive logic and to let the machine automatically work out the prearranged conclusion. Law was in this way divorced from morality.

At the end of the nineteenth century, the pendulum of the legal spirit had swung the opposite way. The belief in the perfection of the legal system began to yield to the pursuit of desired purposes and the protection of individual interests. Natural law with changing content was propagated; sociological jurisprudence was invited. The sign of the age pointed clearly to a new spirit of *jus aequum*. The German Civil Code included some ideas of this spirit in its provisions, for instance, on good faith, public order, good morals, and prohibition of abuse of right (Wang, 1956). A code composed of such substantial elements may truly be called, to use Roscoe Pound's terminology, a "maturity of law" (1926: Ch.1).

IV. Conclusion

The reception of Western law in the East in the nineteenth century meant the reception of legal systems at different stages of development in a totally different culture. The Eastern countries were not only receiving new systems of law but also totally new ways of thinking of law, such as the idea of state sovereignty with its accompanying legislative power. Receiving those new ideas, the Thais availed themselves of a dynamic power and instrument of change, and succeeded in transforming their society and legal system from traditional to modern.

In this process, however, they inadvertently abandoned their age-old traditional conviction in the immutable law of justice and equity over which no human law could prevail. It was unfortunate that the reception occurred in the nineteenth century when the spirit of *jus strictum* was dominating the age, with only a little of the spirit of *jus aequum* supplemented in later codifications as in the German Civil Code. The Western positivistic jurisprudence was hurriedly imparted to the East. The spirit of *jus strictum* was fortified by an over-confidence in the omnipotence of law and the fallacy of modern constructivism (cf. Hayek, 1976, I: 14–15). It was not possible for the new-born legal profession, trained under such a jurisprudential spirit, to develop a fruitful organic connection between the received Western law and the indigenous cultural milieu. If we understand the jurisprudential spirit in legal development in the three main categories mentioned earlier: *Volksrecht, Juristenrecht* and *Satzungsrecht*, and employ them properly in treating various systems of law, it would be possible to develop a method of interpretation and application of law sufficiently to take full account of the jurisprudential techniques and cultural backgrounds.

The modern fallacy of the omnipotence of law must be overcome, and the limitation of law as an instrument of social control must be recognized. The Thai traditional legal system had the wisdom of the autonomous legal domain: an area where the written law of the state dare not tread, for the sensitive and delicate nature of internal relationship is one with which the rough hand of the law is not appropriate to deal. This, along with other similar social institutions in the East, is a product of a true wisdom after many centuries of experience. The wisdom was old in its origin, but is still relevant to contemporary problems of our society. The time may be ripe for a new synthesis, and the old wisdom may be put into its rightful niche with refreshed energies for the future development of society.

Notes

Author's Note: I want to express my sincere appreciation to my young colleagues and friends at Thammasat Law Faculty who assisted me devotedly in various ways in preparation of this article – among others, Mr. Pichet Maolanond who helped me from the beginning and Mr. Kittisak Prokati and Mr. Kamolmit Wuttichamnong both of whom assisted at the final stage.

1 The Uttalum case is one arising from the complaint brought by an intransigent son against his parent.
2 In his public lecture delivered at Thammasat University on 14 August 1950, Lingat correctly mentioned adjudication of the disputes within the family without resorting to the Royal Court, during the Ayudaya period.
3 It should be understood that the Royal Ordinances issued by a King were effective only during his reign; see Lingat, 1935: 52–53.
4 The *Dharmasastra* prescribes that the King shall listen to the custom, usage, and equity every day.
5 Law on the Reception of Plaints, Section 2.
6 Royal Ordinances, Section 3, which was issued to replace old laws during the reign of King Rama I.
7 Royal Ordinance on Miscellaneous Laws, Section 153.
8 *Kharma* means literally "an act," but the implication here is that even though the person's death is sorrowful, no one can be blamed for it. The victim's death must therefore be the result of some sinful act which he himself had committed previously.
9 Royal Ordinance on Old Law, Clause 36.
10 Instances of the decisions of the Thai Royal Court can be found in *Collection of Royal Decisions on Cases of King Rama I* in part of the Code of Rama I.
11 The words "modern" and "traditional" have not settled meanings and are still subject to controversy in academic circles (see Chiba, 1980). Despite some objections, I think they are still useful in enabling us to understand the problems to be discussed.
12 The switch from the French type to the German type was narrated vividly by Phaya Manavarajsevi in "*Recorded Interview of Phaya Manavarajsevi*," mimeo, on file at Thammasat University.
13 The first Thai Penal Code was promulgated in 1907 and replaced by the present one of 1956. The process of Thai codification was completed with the promulgation of the last two books of the Civil and Commercial Code, the Code of Civil Procedure and the Code of Criminal Procedure in 1934 (1478 B.E.).

References

Because of their basic relevance to the discussion, certain references not cited in the text are included in this list.

Abbot, Low Moffat.
1968. *Mongkut: The King of Siam.* New York: Cornell University Press.

Bodenheimer, Edgar.
1981. *Jurisprudence.* Cambridge, Mass.: Harvard University Press.

Chakkrapani, Luang.
1956. *The Story of Chao Phya Mahithorn.* (in Thai) Bangkok: Tironasan.

Chiba, Masaji.
1979. Three-Level Structure of Law in a World of Many Cultures. In *Law and the Future of Society*, Archiv für Rechts- und Sozialphilosophie, Beiheft Neue Folge, Nr. 11.
1980. Doubts on the Utility of "Traditional vs. Modern": From an Asian Point of View. *Law and Development*, 1978/1979 Issue: 34–45.

Chula Chakrabongse, Prince.
1982. *Lords of Life: A History of the Kings of Thailand.* Bangkok: DD Books.

Coedēs, G.
1966. *The Making of South East Asia.* London: Routledge & Kegan Paul.

Crosby, Sir Josiah.
1973. *Siam: The Crossroads.* London: Hollis & Carter.

Department of Fine Arts, Ministry of Education.
1978. *The Code of Rama I* (The Law of the Three Great Seals).

Dhani Nivat, Prince Kromamun Bidyalabh.
1965. *A History of Buddhism in Siam.* Bangkok: The Siam Society.

Durant, Will.
1957. *The Reformation: A History of European Civilization from Wycliffe to Calvin, 1300–1564.* New York: Simon & Schuster.

Engel, David M.
1975. *Law and Kinship in Thailand during the Reign of King Chulalongkorn.* Michigan Paper on South and Southeast Asia, No. 9.

Gluckman, Max.
1975. *African Traditional Law in Historical Perspective.* London: Oxford University Press.

Hayek, F. A.
1976. *Law, legislation, and Liberty.* 3 vols. London: Routledge & Kegan Paul.

Hooker, M. B.
1975. *Legal Pluralism: An Introduction to Colonial and Neo-Colonial Laws*, Oxford: Clarendon Press.
1978. *A Concise Legal History of South-East Asia.* Oxford: Clarendon Press.
Hsii, Immanuel C. Y.
1975. *The Rise of Modern China.* Oxford: Oxford University Press.
Jackson, Bernard S.
1975. From Dharma to Law: Comments. *American Journal of Comparative Law*, 23: 490–512.
Jamieson, G.
1970. *Chinese Family and Commercial Law.* Hong Kong: Vetch & Lee.
Khoo, Gilbert.
1970. *A History of South-East Asia since 1900.* Oxford: Oxford University Press.
Kocourek, Albert, & Wigmore, John.
1979. *Evolution of Law*, Vol. 1: *Sources of Ancient and Primitive Law.* Littleton, Colorado: Fred B. Rothman.
Laloubire.
1967. *The Kingdom of Siam.* (in Thai) 2 vols. Bangkok: Advanced Media.
Landon, Kenneth P.
1968. *Siam in Transition.* Westport, Conn.: Greenwood Press.
Leonowens, Anna Harriette.
1870. *The English Governess at the Siamese Court.* London: Trübner. Repr. as *Anna and the King of Siam*, Bangkok: Chalermnit, 1979.
Ling, Trevor.
1979. *Buddhism, Imperialism and War.* London: Allen & Unwin.
Lingat, Robert.
1935. *History of Siamese Law.* (in Thai) Bangkok: Thammasat University Press.
1949. Evolution of the Conception of Law in Burma and Siam. *Journal of Siam Society*, 38: 8–31.
1973. *The Classical Law of India.* London: University of California Press.
Lord, Donald C.
1969. *Mo Bradley and Thailand.* Grand Rapids, Mich.: William B. Werdmans.
McIllwain, Charles H.
1955. *The Growth of Political Thought in the West.* New York: Macmillan.
Nitisastra Paisal, Prince Phya.
1933. *The Story of the Courts.* (in Thai) Bangkok: Ministry of Justice.
1959. *History of Thai Law.* (in Thai) Bangkok: Thammasat University Press.

Pallegoix, Jean Baptiste.
1977. *The Story of Siam*. transl. S. T. Komolbutr. Bangkok: Advanced Media.
Pichit Preechakorn, Prince Krom Luang.
1929. *Collected Works of Prince Krom Luang Pichit Preechakorn*. (in Thai) Bangkok: Sophonpipatthanakorn.
Ploetz, Karl.
1960. *Auszug aus der Geschichte*. 26te Aufl. Würzburg: A. G. Ploetz.
Pound, Roscoe.
1926. *Law and Morals*. Chapel Hill, N.C.: North Carolina University Press.
Quaritch Wales, H. G.
1965. *Ancient Siamese Government and Administration*. New York: Paragon.
Rabi, Prince.
1925. *Lectures on Jurisprudence*. (in Thai) Bangkok: Sophonpipatthanakorn.
Seidenfaden, Major Erik.
1963. *The Thai Peoples*, Book I. Bangkok: The Siam Society.
Spiro, Melford E.
1970. *Buddhism and Society*. New York: Harper & Row.
Suksumran, Somboon.
1977. *Political Buddhism in Southeast Asia*. London: C. Hurst.
Suranai Prasus, Prince Luang.
1956. *Development of Legal Education in Thailand*. (in Thai) Bangkok: Thammasat University Press.
Syamananda, Rong.
1977. *A History of Thailand*. Bangkok: Thai Watana Panich.
Vachirayan Varorasa, Prince, The Great Patriarch.
1971. *Collected Works of Prince Vachirayan Varorasa: Volume on the Buddhist Ecclesiastical Affairs*. (in Thai) Bangkok: Maha Makut Buddhist University Press.
Wang, Pe-Chi.
1956. *Modern Legal Thought and Indigenous Chinese Culture*. (in Chinese) Taipei: Ministry of Justice.
Weeramantry, C. G.
1975. *The Law in Crisis*. London: Capemoss.
Wichiencharoen, A., & Netisastro, L. C.
1968. Some Main Features of Modernization of Ancient Family Law in Thailand. In: *Family Law and Customary Law in Asia*, D. C. Baxbaum, ed. The Hague: Martinus Nijhoff.
Yut Sang-Utai.
1980. *Legal Textbooks in Thailand*. In: *Publication in Commemoration of Professor Yut Sang-Utai's Funeral*, Bangkok: Thammasat University Press.

Glossary

Begriffsjurisprudenz	conceptual jurisprudence
bona fide	in good faith
corpus juris	a compilation of law
corpus juris canonici	a compilation of canon law
Devaraja	Hindu concept of Divine Kingship
Dharmaraja	Buddhist concept of Righteous Kingship
Dharmasastra	the Basic Code of Human Norms
humanitas	humanity
Juristenrecht	lawyer's law
jus aequum	equitable law
jus gentium	international law
jus naturale	natural law
jus scriptum	statute
jus strictum	strict law
kharma	act bringing upon oneself inevitable results, either in this life or in a reincarnation
lege	*jus scriptum*
lex humana	human law
Moola kadi	the roots of the matter
Praetor	Roman Magistrate of Civil Justice
Rajsastra	the Law of the King
Saka kadi	the branches of the matter
Sangha	the Brotherhood of the Buddhist Monks
Satzungsrecht	made law
Traipidhaka	Pali Canon consisting of three parts
Vinaya	Holy Precepts
Volksrecht	people's law

7 Three-Level Structure of Law in Contemporary Japan – The Shinto Society

Masaji Chiba

I. Introduction

1. CONTEMPORARY LEGAL SYSTEM OF JAPAN

Japan is a modern country. She has an elaborate system of enacted laws and judicial courts under an advanced constitution. A variety of laws appear to be operating through well-organized machineries and functionaries for administration and adjudication.

Such a legal system was founded in her modernization process which commenced full-scale operation after the Meiji Restoration in 1868. The first modernized system of Japanese law was not of indigenous origin but was received from developed Western countries. The model of reception was primarily taken from Germany, mainly Prussia, then a rising absolutist empire under the reigns of Wilhelm I and II, and additionally from France and some others. The systematic legislation modelled after Western law was mainly achieved in the decade following the enactment of the first constitution in 1889. With the modernized form of law having been established, the Japanese legal system steadily developed until it was comparable in appearance with its mother law in Western countries. Japanese law before the end of World War II is without doubt grouped into the Civil Law system.

After World War II, Japan was forced to accept a Common Law system directly from the U.S.A. It is true that the Common Law system made an important contribution to the required democratization of Japanese law and society, but the Civil Law system seems to have been too firmly rooted in Japanese law as well as in the Japanese science of law to have been replaced wholly by the Common Law system. Some scholars criticize this reform of the law, from absolutist to democratic, as unsatisfactory, while others appraise it as a harmonious though not perfect coexistence of both systems.

However opinion may be divided, Japan has a well-organized and well-functioning legal system which may be compared with no other country in the non-Western world.[1]

2. COMPLEXITY OF LAW IN JAPANESE SOCIETY

Contemporary Japanese law is composed of systematic enacted law accompanied by case law that is thought to be a result of the application of the former. Legal specialists such as administrators, judges, lawyers and legal scientists as well as laymen usually resort to law books, and additionally case records, to gain first-hand information about valid law. Foreign specialists who want to know Japanese law as well refer to those measures directly or through the writings of Japanese specialists. Such written sources are, indeed, indispensable to identify what Japanese law is.

But they are insufficient to represent the reality of Japanese law as it functions in society. It is rather a general practice to use such expressions as "Exceptionally . . ." or "In reality . . .," when speaking of law. What is "exceptional" or "real" law, may be not always be accepted as valid by legal specialists. It may, however, function in society as if it were valid law. Some people make choices in individual cases between two or more competing, conflicting ways of behaviour, attaching more weight to the as-if-valid law than to the valid one. They may sometimes be disapproved of by official agencies, but at other times be approved, implicitly or explicitly, with no official sanction applied by the people, or even by official agencies. From the legalistic point of view, specialists may do without consideration of such as-if-valid law. From a behavioural point of view, on the other hand, people cannot do without varying degrees of consideration of it, for such consideration may bring gain to them, and no one can prohibit others from thinking of their own loss or gain without any prerogatives to do so. Other measures than written law are thus needed to grasp and evaluate such behavioural law, whether negative or positive.

The concepts of "living law" and "law in action," which were developed by the Sociology of Law and Realistic Jurisprudence respectively, may be among such measures. Truly they are of great use in collecting needed information about law other than "positive law" and "law in books." But they are of little use in presenting the behavioural and cultural differences of law in various countries. On one hand both concepts were devised in Western countries indifferent to the cultural characteristics of law among other peoples, and on the other, Japan is situated in a non-Western area with her own characteristic culture. Japanese law as actually functioning in society is too complex to be represented accurately by concepts so indifferent to cultural characteristics.

Some legal theorists, especially motivated by anthropological requirements, have tried to devise new analytical tool concepts of law to denote cultural differences among peoples. Unfortunately however, their efforts have had no results that we can immediately rely upon. A noted but unresolved controversy between Max Gluckman and Paul Bohannan on the tool concept – whether to use English or the native language to express and analyse observed raw materials,[2] shows the significance of devising culture-born concepts of law, as well as the difficulties. We are still faced with the requirement of devising enough new tool concepts to accurately represent cultural differences in law.

An analysis of contemporary Japanese law as functioning in society through the two working hypotheses raised in the Introduction is therefore expected to disclose the nature of a non-Western law and, at the same time, verify the hypotheses. Before the discussion, the Japanese legal history is briefly reviewed to give some background to the contemporary legal system, with special attention to indigenous factors and their relation to received factors.

II. A Brief Review of Japanese Legal History: Development of Indigenous Japanese Law

1. BEFORE THE MEIJI RESTORATION IN 1868

Although the origin of Japanese society and government is not exactly known, law and government had been shaped since the third and fourth centuries in their indigenous form "not distinguished from other social rules" and "not influenced in any way by foreign civilization" (Noda, 1976: 20–21).

(1) First reception of Chinese law

As the government strengthened its power during two centuries which followed, Japan began to enter her first international relationship, whether in peace or conflict, with the Korean Peninsula. Traffic to and from the Korean countries paved the way for Japan's direct contact with China, which had achieved much more influential dynasties and advanced systems of enacted law, and which had also created various systems of ethical thought, including Confucianism, as well as receiving the religious system of Buddhism. The law, Confucianism and Buddhism were hastily imported to Japan and played a decisive role in moulding Japanese indigenous culture into more systematic forms.

The first systematic reception of Chinese law was promoted by Shotoku Taishi (Crown Prince Shotoku) who has been admired as a leading intellectual statesman throughout Japanese history. *Kan'i Juni-kai* (the Twelve Grades of Officials) instituted by him in 603 strengthened the authority of the *Tenno* (Emperor) to appoint officials in the new twelve grades adopted from a Chinese system embodying Confucian ethics. More significant was the *Kempo Jushichi-jo* (the Seventeen-Article Constitution) promulgated and enforced in 604. Its significance lay not only in the label "Constitution," adopted in such an early year,[3] but also in its value system, which brought about remarkable influences on Japanese intellectual history thereafter.

Fourteen of its seventeen articles prescribed the duties of officials. Coming before these, the first three articles declared the basic principles of Prince Shotoku's political ideal. The first article began with the symbolic sentence of the Constitution: "*Wa* (harmony) is to be most valued, and an avoidance of wanton opposition to be honoured." The second article demonstrated the leading idea through which harmony could be achieved: "Sincerely reverence the three treasures, viz. Buddha, Dharma and Sangha." But in this world, the ideal should actually be realized through the relation between the lord and the subject, because the third article ordered: "When you receive the commands of *Tenno*, fail not scrupulously to obey. The Lord is Heaven, the official is Earth."[4]

As is apparent from this construction, the Seventeen-Article Constitution declared a political ideology rather than positive legal regulations; it was a mixed product of the indigenous *Tenno* system and received Buddhist and Confucian ethical ideals (cf. Nakamura, 1970). However, mixed factors were assimilated with one another as years went on, thus comprising an indigenous politico-social postulate in later years – the principle of the *Tenno*-governed state and the ideal of *wa* among the membership of the group. During a long period after, the authority of *Tenno* and the idea of *wa* may have sometimes lost their validity, just as declared in the Seventeen-Article Constitution, but they have still kept their influence upon Japanese politics and society, recurring in Japanese history, especially at times of national crisis.

Their first recurrence was invoked when the heads of influential clans attempting to usurp the Office of *Tenno* were destroyed by a legitimate prince and an assisting court noble in a *coup d'état* in 645. The political reform, called Taika Kaishin, was followed by a most thorough legal reform, in order to provide firmer ground for a centralized state. The model of the legal system was taken from the Chinese one – the codes systematized under the T'ang dynasty. The system comprised four parts: *ritsu* (sanctioning laws), *ryo* (admonitory laws), *kyaku* (supplementary laws), and *shiki* (particularized rules); it was thus called the *ritsu-ryo seido* (system). The new Japanese legal system, which was finally compiled in the Taiho Ritsu-ryo in 701 after several decades of trial legislation, was a faithful imitation of Chinese codes.[5]

This might be seen to be one of the most comprehensive examples of the reception of law in human history. In reality, however, as Yoshiyuki Noda states:

> "The system of *ritsu-ryo* did not stay in favour for long. The cultural milieu of Japan differed considerably from that of China, which made it difficult for the laws to be assimilated. Most of the provisions soon fell into disuse, and around the legislative texts *more and more usages of an administrative or judicial nature developed*, with the result that *the basic text soon became obscure or was forgotten.*" (1976: 24; italics mine.)

The Japanese reception of Chinese law was thus an exercise that brought few substantial effects. And the systematic reception of foreign law by Japan was not tried until after the Meiji Restoration. Seen from this point of view, the Japanese legal system thereafter has been primarily of an indigenous nature.

(2) Later development

Such reception of law should be carefully assessed in relation to indigenous Japanese law. For instance an area where the received Chinese system was best preserved was that of legal regulations in the Imperial Court. The main part of the Imperial regulations concerned the status and office of the various *kuge* (court nobles) working for *Tenno*, being thus called *kuge-ho* (court nobles law). However, its relative importance was very limited, because although *Tenno* cherished a unique indigenous authority over it, the influence of *Tenno* and the *kuge* had to decline as the *bushi* (warriors) became dominant, until the latter finally established the *Bakufu* (Shogunate) for *Tenno* at Kamakura in 1185. The legal postulate of *buke-ho* (warriors law) which founded the Bakufu may be another example. The influential warriors used to be appointed by *Tenno* to various grades in the *kuge-ho*; however they may have been real rulers and the appointments may have been nominal. The China-modelled grades were an embodiment of Confucian ethics. The ethics without doubt encouraged the rising value system and ethical code among the warriors. Their real ethics, however, were not the same as in Confucianism but a unique one called *bushido* (the code of warriors). And the ruling warriors succeeded in creating indigenously a variety of legal systems of their own, generally grouped under the rubric of feudal law. Noda again states:

> "Generally the law of the era [early feudal periods] is of customary nature, and morality occupied an important place in it. . . . The system of morality of the *bushido* rests in Confucianism but, in contrast to the moral concepts of the preceding era when Chinese ideas were followed blindly, the *bushido* was formed in a spontaneous manner in the daily life of the *bushi*. However, it must not be forgotten . . . Buddhism penetrated into the daily life of the people, and its influence was very great on the *bushi*." (1976: 30–31)

The Japanese reception of Chinese law was thus rather an interacting process between received law and indigenous law as the Japanese saw it. We may reasonably characterize the resulting development of Japanese feudal law as indigenous, especially when compared with her reception of Western law in modern times.

The indigenous law which prevailed throughout feudal, pre-modern Japan is characterized by differentiation of social classes.

The major classes were *bushi* or *buke* and *shomin* (commoners). The former was regulated by the elaborate warriors' law, written or unwritten, divided into the general law of the Shogunate and the particular laws of individual feudal domains. The latter comprised peasants, under the official control of the warriors law – who customarily developed community law and land law, and town dwellers – who also developed town law and merchant law in their circles. The remarkable minority classes were the court nobles, who preserved the *ritsu-ryo* system and its variations, and the priests, whether Buddhists or Shintoists, who enjoyed relative autonomy within each sect. The law of those people in regard to marriage, family, inheritance, contract, and personality and conflict management was differentiated according to their classes. Finally, some discriminated classes should be mentioned who without doubt developed their own independent customary law, a few survivals among which will be referred to later as minorities.

However variously it may have been differentiated, Japanese law during these periods[6] is characterized by some features commonly found in all varieties when compared with foreign laws. Among them are some legal postulates which remained functioning through the later years of modernization. Main ones are the authority of *Tenno* and the ideal of the *Tenno*-governed state; the highly valued ideal of *wa* in human relationships; the principle of *kazoku-seido*[7] (family system) and its fictitious extension among social groups; and the system of *mibun kaiso-sei* (status hierarchy, or the hierarchical order of the family or person by status), and related authority of persons of higher status, with the obligation of the lower to observe their *bun* or *bungen* (restrictions attributed to one's status). They will be described in later pages insofar as they function in contemporary Japanese society.

2. ALLEGED MODERNIZATION OF LAW IN THE MEIJI SYSTEM

(1) Systematic reception of Western law

The Meiji Restoration means, literally, the restoration to the Meiji *Tenno* of the sovereign power over all of Japan from the Shogun Tokugawa who had been the *de facto* ruler of the country. Among various urgencies the Meiji government faced, the most pressing was the need to furnish the new centralized country with a modern legal system in order to achieve a rapid development of the country from feudal to premodern modern, as well as to afford ground for the desired revision of the unequal treaties which Japan had been compelled to conclude with Western countries. Without any indigenous system of law comparable to the Western, the Meiji Regime rushed to receive the advanced system from Western countries.[8] The result was, as Noda reasonably stated, that ". . . the modern state law has no connection with the former Japanese law. The modern law considers itself rather as an heir of Western law" (1976: 39). The same author argued, on the other hand,

> "All this does not mean, however, that early Japanese law has no place in an extensive or profound study of contemporary law. There may be a marked difference between the modern and the old law at the level of state law, but *at the level of living law there was no break in continuity.* The latter evolved spontaneously and unconsciously. Historical continuity interrupted in the conscious continues in the subconscious, and this subconscious factor plays an important role in the social life of the Japanese people today. . . . *The relationship, between the old and the new law is one that has not yet been fully studied*, and the historical study of Japanese legal thought itself is still a virgin field." (ibid.: 39; italics mine)

The author is right in declaring the existence of indigenous factors still functioning in contemporary modernized Japanese law as living law, but he left unattempted its further exploration, except for limited mention of the validity of custom and *jori* (reasonableness) and discussions on *giri* ("the manner of behaviour required of one person to others in consequence of his social status"), (ibid.: 217–224, 159–183). According to our terminology, the indigenous law has appeared in three forms. First, some considerable phases were adopted in the new state law and have functioned in the system of received "official law." Second, other phases have been rejected as official law, some of which became simple custom or lost influence on law at all, while many others actually still function effectively, though unofficially, regulating people's behaviour in concert or in competition with the official state law, and occasionally even preponderating and forming "unofficial law." And last, still other phases survive in various ideas such as authority, ideals, values, often with the validity of supporting the above official or unofficial law in idea and ideology, thus forming "legal postulates." The discussions which follow attempt to identify these three forms of indigenous factors in contemporary Japanese law.

Contemporary Japanese law was founded by the overall legal reform following the Meiji Restoration. But, as is well-known, it suffered a considerable change after World War II, which caused or promoted disappearance of some indigenous factors that had survived in the Meiji received system. Some comments on the period before World War II may be useful for a more correct understanding of the situation.

First, main legislations after the Meiji Restoration[9] are listed.

1880 The so-called Old Penal Code and a criminal procedural code were promulgated to come into force in 1882.

1889 The Constitution of the Empire of Great Japan (the Old or Meiji Constitution), which was replaced by the present one later in 1947, was promulgated and enforced.

1890 The Old Code of Criminal Procedure was promulgated to come into force for the preceding criminal procedural code until replaced by a new one in 1922.

1890 The Code of Civil Procedure was promulgated to come into force in 1891; still valid today with some revisions.

1890 The Civil Code was promulgated separately twice with the schedule of enforcement in 1893. But as it provoked strong opposition and debates, the scheduled enforcement was postponed to enable a thorough revision of the Code.

1890 The Old Commercial Code was promulgated with the schedule of enforcement in 1891, but not enforced because of opposition similar to that of the Civil Code.

1896, 1898 The revised Civil Code was promulgated, the parts concerning property in 1896 and those of family and inheritance in 1898, coming into force in 1898, the former parts being still valid and the latter parts replaced by the present one enacted in 1947 after World War II.

1899 The revised Old Commercial Code was promulgated and went into force, although some parts had gone into force in 1893 and 1898.

1907 The present Penal Code was promulgated to come into force in 1908 replacing the old one, still valid with some revisions.

(2) Received and indigenous factors: Especially of the Constitution

Some remarkable features of Japanese reception of Western law by the above codification are found in the underlying listed facts.

First, the reception was not simple adoption from a single model. For instance, the Constitution was truly modelled after the absolutist Prussian one. But it was adopted after a thoughtful consideration by Japanese political leaders who compared the various Western constitutions with one another, ultimately, unanimously adopting a conservative policy. Such a policy as a result of comparative consideration was approved by many "prominent men of the Western world" at that time (Takayanagi, 1963: 9).[10] This means secondly that the Japanese reception of a constitution was not imposed, but voluntarily achieved by her own choice, even though the choice was made in unavoidable international circumstances. The comparative consideration, and the voluntary nature, left room for the survival of indigenous factors. In fact, indigenous legal postulates since Shotoku Taishi were actually fundamental in formulating the Constitution under the authority of *Tenno*, with the ideal of *wa* based on the principles of the family system and status hierarchy.

Thus, the Japanese reception of Western law in the Constitution was an interacting process between received and indigenous factors, sometimes an amalgamation or coexistence, sometimes a collision or struggle between them. The power of *Tenno* declared in the Constitution and prescribed in other laws will pointedly illustrate this process.

In the Constitution, the indigenous authority of *Tenno* was armed with a received absolutist character. *Tenno* was the only ruler holding sovereign power. The people were subjects without sharing any powers. As a result, the Diet, not being the representative of the people, was no more than an organ to assist *Tenno*, without any power of its own. In fact, the Diet was able to enact statutes which the government had to obey. But there were two powers of *Tenno* beyond the Diet.[11] One was to issue Imperial Ordinances, whether to modify the prescription of the statute or to establish any measures besides the statute for national well-being as *Tenno* saw fit. The other was the prerogative of the Supreme Command which developed the military law independently of the government. Thus, the absolutist power of Tenno[12] was truly prescribed after the received Prussian model. But the indigenous authority of *Tenno* had not wholly been covered by the received system. It required another form to embody itself into a valid, normative system. The concept of *kokutai* (national polity or national structure) was developed for this reason.

Briefly, the essence of *kokutai* was the reign of *Tenno*, as declared in Article 1 of the Meiji Constitution, that "The Empire of Japan shall be reigned and governed by a line of Emperors unbroken for ages eternal," and, as expressed by a foreign observer, "the deep spiritual relationship between the *Tenno* and his people" (Oppler, 1976: 49), which required an ethical code. The Meiji political leaders promptly prepared the required code. It was *Kyoiku Chokugo* (The Rescript on Education) issued by the *Tenno* in 1890, the first year after promulgation of the Constitution, in order to oblige the people to follow a national code of ethics centring around *chu-ko* (fidelity to *Tenno* and piety toward parents).[13] It was drafted by Eifu Motoda, Confucian mentor to Meiji *Tenno*, and Kowashi Inoue, one of the draftsmen of the Constitution. Its character was described by an American specialist in Japanese history:

> "There was an unmistakeable reaction to the rapid pace of Westernization, and a desire to return to the purity of 'Japanism.' It served to indoctrinate generations of school children, through periodic public readings of the rescript and through required memorization, but it was repudiated in 1948 by the second post-war Diet." (Lu, 1974, II: 70.)

The Japanese people were much more familiar with the Rescript than the Constitution. For they could repeatedly recite the words and sentences every time and everywhere together in the company of others,[14] and the Rescript stated systematically the daily ethics which they were in reality performing or ideally aiming to perform. The Rescript was the supreme constitution of the Japanese ethical system, while the legal Constitution was the supreme code of the Japanese legal system. The leading postulate of both systems was one and the same: *kokutai.* The principles, values, ideals and authority underlying the Rescript was thus nothing but the legal postulate of Japanese law under the Meiji Constitution. It was systematized by a Confucian idea. But the essence was indigenous, for it was a recurrence of the principle of the *Tenno*-governed state and the ideal of *wa* among the membership as formulated by Shotoku Taishi about thirteen and a half centuries ago.

(3) Indigenous factors in the family system

Similar processes took place in other legislation. Most noted among them was the Civil Code, which was forced to be rewritten when it was faced with strong opposition to the promulgated system of family and inheritance. The opposition was born among traditionalists, who insisted on preserving "indigenous culture," whether aware or unaware of its amalgamation in reality with Confucian, abolutist, or other foreign factors.[15] There is a noted symbolic phrase of the opposition: "Once Civil Code enforced, Subject's Fidelity and Filial Piety are to Perish." This was the title of a rather short but most provoking article written by Yatsuka Hozumi, professor of constitutional law at the University of Tokyo. Hozumi "was the founder of the school of constitutional scholarship which enshrined Japanese tradition at the cost of the Western idea of law" (Minear, 1970: 6). He attempted "rare excursions into the field of civil law", but, provoked by the promulgated Civil Code which he was convinced must undermine the constitutional spirit of *kokutai*, he wrote the article to "urge the revision of the proposed civil code away from Western individualism toward Japanese familism" (ibid.: 178). The result of the revision was that he and his camp were not satisfied with the enforced Civil Code, to whose drafting his brother Nobushige Hozumi, an evolutionist professor of jurisprudence at the same university, contributed greatly. But, they were successful in their promotion to establish the new indigenous *ie-seido* (family system) in the Code, which was characterized by the ideal of *wa* and authority of the family-head,[16] along with the individualistic system of property taken from Western models.

Indigenous factors struggled against received factors so successfully that they let the authority of *Tenno* and the *wa* of family survive beyond the rushing modernization of law after Western models, in both legal systems and ideal postulates. Still many other indigenous factors have also survived. Those still functioning in contemporary Japanese law will be enumerated later in detail. The others, which lost *raison d'etre* and function during the legal reform soon after World War II and during preceding years, are briefly mentioned below.

3. INDIGENEITY OF THE MEIJI LEGAL SYSTEM

Supplemented and revised, the alleged Japanese modern legal system basically founded after the Meiji Constitution, kept developing beyond the Meiji era under the reign of Meiji *Tenno*, through the following Taisho era under the reign of Taisho *Tenno*, 1912–26, and the first half of the Showa era until the end of World War II under the reign of the present *Tenno* Hirohito. As the basic system remained unchanged, we call this legal system the "Meiji legal system," although it was valid throughout the Taisho and Showa eras. The received modernity of the Meiji legal system included indigenous factors which were adopted randomly among various laws and ordinances.

(1) Discrimination of tenants, women and labourers

The national policy to protect large landlords economically, politically, and legally, which was to maintain a feudal system (cf. Smith, 1959), was begun in the relatively early year of 1873, when a revolutionary modern tax law was enforced to promote a capitalistic economy in Japan. Its effect "was to recognize legally a large landlord class (many of them petty owner-cultivators), a sizeable group of part-owners and part-tenants, and a smaller class of tenants, roughly in the proportion of 45:35:20" (Havens, 1974: 32). The proportion of the latter two classes increased so much that it could be said that "more than three fourths of the farmers in Japan are either partially or totally tenants, paying rentals amounting to half or more of their annual crops" at the time when defeated Japan was ordered to plan a land reform by the occupying Allied Powers after World War II (Lu, 1974, II: 209). The farm land they were cultivating under tenancy was owned by large landlords, usually absentee or non-operating, who formed a very limited number of the landlord class compared with the petty owner-cultivators. This came about in a significant sense because of the legal protection of the large landlords since 1873 (cf. ibid.: 73–74). The domination by large landlords extended beyond economic privileges to include political ones. Adopting a very limited suffrage, the first election law for the House of Representatives under the Meiji Constitution conferred the right to vote to a small number of larger landlords, leaving the smaller ones and the tenants unrepresented. Furthermore, as high taxpayers, some of the largest landlords in a prefecture enjoyed the privilege of electing members to the House of Peers from among themselves.[17] The landlord system in pre-war Japan was thus an indigenous one under the Meiji legal system, and it could not be a modern one in the true sense.

Another indigenity concerned the legal discrimination of women. For instance, according to the Civil Code adult women were deprived of their legal capacity on marrying, on the grounds that they should be obedient to their husbands, so as to preserve the *wa* of their families. Women were not given the right to vote even after their arrival at adulthood, as men had been (see Note 17). Women were also not admitted into a university, except under limited conditions, for they should prefer womanly virtues to higher education. Adultery by married women was criminalized in the Penal Code, while that of married men was not.

Labourers were worse off than tenants and women in legal protection. Their equal position in concluding employment contracts was formally protected by the Civil Code. But it was found in Japan after World War I that such a classical civil right in contract was of no help to the fundamentally weak position of labourers against capitalists. Some of the labourers had begun to organize labour unions, and their leaders formed proletarian political parties with a few supporting politicians. But their collective movements encountered intensive official oppression and in some instances faced criminal punishment. Even their opinions were criminalized by a law specifically enacted in 1925[18] to protect *kokutai*, and the labourers were obliged, according to *kokutai*, to co-operate in realizing *wa* with the capitalists, among whom *Tenno* was the largest land owner with an inviolable authority "for ages eternal" as declared in the Constitution. The labourer was, as far as his proper right to work was concerned, thus outlawed.

The legal discrimination against tenants, women and labourers was achieved by the received form of law in conjunction with indigenous ideas and materials. Such discrimination was, however, justified only by the absolutist *Tenno* regime. It was destined to be abolished when the present Constitution was enacted with its ideas of liberalism and democracy. Tenants could acquire their own land through the post-war land reform law. Women's equal rights were secured in many aspects of law. And by new labour laws, labourers could enjoy the right to work, organize their unions, and strike. They were all emancipated in the official law.

(2) *Jinja* and *Matsuri*

Another important factor is the social institution of *jinja* (Shinto shrines) and its *matsuri* (rituals in and festivals for a *jinja*).[19] The ideological foundation of the institution is Shinto which is anglicized to mean "the native religion of Japan, primarily a system of nature and ancestor worship." Shinto is socio-culturally divided into three main forms: *Kyoha* Shinto (Sectarian Shinto), *Jinja* Shinto and *Kokka* Shinto (State Shinto). The first is a religion comparable with other established religions in the world with definite creeds, ceremonies, priests and subdivided orders. The second is a folk belief with activities centred on a *jinja.* A *jinja* enshrines an *ujigami* (Shinto god or gods) in a *buraku* (hamlet) accompanied by regular rituals for the god and festivals of the population. But it is not founded on established creeds or orders. Instead, it is supported ideally or ideologically by the inhabitants of the locality where the shrine is located. Being called *ujiko* (the children of an *ujigami*), the inhabitants are willing or obliged to donate specified and/or voluntary money and services for the needs of their shrine to maintain it fiscally, take part in its rituals, and celebrate their festivals for it. This type of *jinja*, an indigenous factor of Japanese culture, outlines the customary rights and duties of the inhabitants to enshrine, worship and feast their shrine.[20]

The third is a political institution unique in Japanese history. The position of *Tenno* as the hereditary ruler of Japan was justified, on the one hand, from its first foundation, by the myth that *Tenno's* authority had been directly bestowed by the Creator, who is the ancestor of the Japanese people, and armed, on the other, by the legal institution that *Tenno* was the superior priest, able to worship the Creator and following gods, as well as being the only sovereign for that people. This is called the principle of *saisei-icchi* (the unity of Shinto and state). It underlay the Seventeen-Article Constitution by Shotoku Taishi in 604 influenced by the Buddhist idea. In 907 the *Engi-shiki*, a form of the *ritsu-ryo*, was enforced to make the first systematic arrangement of the country's shrines. It limited the number of official shrines to 2861, some of which were especially esteemed for their enshrining of the Creator and closely related gods, or persons who had done distinguished service during the pacification of early Japan. After three centuries or so, when Yoritomo Minamoto founded the first Shogunate in Kamakura, he enforced a hierarchical rearrangement of the shrines to give the shrine of his clan in Kamakura the highest status in order to preside over the other shrines. It also allowed a vintage shrine in each feudal domain to preside over the others within the domain. This was another *saisei-icchi* by the ruling warrior.

The Meiji government established the third, most systematic rearrangement of the shrines by law. It was a thoroughgoing, hierarchical system of the shrines all over the country. Most remarkable were, first, the above-said local shrine in a hamlet, which had been left out of the official legal hierarchy, was now incorporated into the lowest status of the system, with the outcome that other shrines in the same hamlet had to compete, supported by the enshrining inhabitants, for official recognition of the status, or to be merged when defeated in the competition (cf. Fridell, 1973). Second, the Ise-Jingu supported by *Tenno* to enshrine the Creator and the God of Rice, recovered the formal supreme status over all the shrines, people and land, which had been previously usurped by the shrine of the Shogun during the feudal ages. Third, new *jinja* were established or officially recognized in concert with Japan's political expansion. Whenever she acquired a new external territory (see note 11) and as she planted settlements in mainland China and the South Sea Islands under the Japanese mandate by the League of Nations, a presiding shrine was settled in each area to enshrine the Creator and closely related gods under the central Ise-Jingu, as well as several attending shrines to preside over the native gods. Other special ones were Yasukuni-Jinja to enshrine the war dead and similar ones in each prefecture.[21] Finally, the governments, both national and local, were legally obliged to support *jinja* financially from public funds along with private funds, and responsible officials were required to make formal worship of the *jinja*.

This was the Meiji State Shinto system. It was most exalted type of State Shinto. Because it incorporated another form of *Jinja* Shinto and its ideological justification was supported by the doctrine of *Kyoha* Shinto, the Meiji State Shinto was meant to unify the three main forms of Shinto in a system. The leading postulate was *saisei-icchi* in *kokutai*. This was disclosed to be absurd when the Meiji system collapsed, and the Japanese government was ordered to abolish such a State Shinto system by the occupying Allied Powers after World War II. The present Constitution declares emphatically the separation of religious organizations from the state.

4. LEGAL REFORM AFTER WORLD WAR II

(1) Disappearance of indigenous factors

With the defeat in World War II, Japan was forced to make sweeping reforms in law and politics, in other words, radically transform a Prussian type of absolutist *Tenno* regime, a Civil Law system, to an Anglo-American type of democratic government, a Common Law system. The surrender on 15 August 1945 was immediately followed by occupation by the Allied Forces under the command of the American General Douglas MacArthur. Orders from his General Headquarters and reactions from the Japanese government prepared the draft of a new constitution in Spring 1946, and submitted it to the then Diet under the Meiji Constitution. After discussion from early Summer to October, the new, present constitution was promulgated on 3 November 1946, and enforced on 3 May 1947. An extensive legal reform followed the Constitution, and from it emerged a new democratic system. Political reform was to prepare, support or realize this. Social reform was both provoked and encouraged by the legal and political reform.[22]

The legal reform was primarily modelled after the American system under the international circumstances at that time. As a result, the contemporary legal system under the Showa Constitution is a mixture of both Civil and Common Law systems. This is the first aspect to be pointed out in relation to the received character of law after the war, for the reception of Western law with such a wide range may appear to have left little room for survival of indigenous law.

Truly, many indigenous factors so significant in the Meiji legal system disappeared due to the reform. Among these, the *Tenno* was deprived of his supreme status "eternal for ages" (Article 1, Meiji Constitution), "sacred and inviolable" (Article 3, ibid.), to be "the symbol of the State and of the unity of the people, deriving his position from the will of the people with whom resides sovereign power" (Article 1, Showa Constitution). Further, the prevalent family system comprising the legally constructed extended family with the family-head regulating the members, fortified by the postulate of *wa*, was replaced by a modern system of the nuclear family which, at the same time, swept away the discrimination of sex in the family. The related basic policies declared in the new Constitution were embodied in the revised part of the Civil Code concerning family, marriage and inheritance.[23] Two other aspects of the discrimination of tenants and labourers were also invalidated by the land reform and legalization of the labour movement. The State Shinto was destined to be abolished for its "dangerous manifestation of hypernationalism" (Reischauer, 1977: 219), causing all the shrines to be freed from the official control of the government, and the Shinto ideology to be separated from the state as a genuine religion, resulting in the total disappearance of Shinto from within the official legal system. So a great deal of indigenous law was lost by the legal reform after the war.

(2) Surviving indigenous factors

On the other hand, indigenous factors were not entirely lost, nor were their influences. Many of them survived the sweeping reform accomplished by foreign pressure and received law.

This is clearly seen first of all by the Japanese understanding of this radical reform. From a strict legal point of view, the reform meant a change of the Japanese polity from the absolutist *Tenno* state to a democratic peoples' state, which in itself might be called something of a revolution. As a matter of fact there was strong opinion among both Japanese people and the occupying General Headquarters to instil a revolutionary nature to the reform, and accordingly to establish a new constitution without any connection to the former one. But the formal procedure to make the new constitution valid was finally chosen not by declaring establishment of a new constitution separated from the former one, but by amending the latter in accordance with existing procedures. This was the reason that the new proposals were deliberated by the old Diet under the Meiji Constitution, which voided itself when it was replaced by the new Constitution. The new Constitution was accepted by the people with its nature of continuity from the old Constitution. Another reason for the general confidence in the new Constitution was ascribed to the continuation of the *Tenno* from the old Constitution, which will be discussed below for its indigeneity, even though his position and power were apparently radically changed.

The problem of the continuity of the Constitution was also raised in another issue, which was whether the new Constitution was enacted voluntarily by the Japanese people, or forced on them by the Allied Powers. Those who believe the latter have ground for their opinion in the fact that the victors in the war were able to dictate terms to the defeated. Their opinion has a corollary that insists upon the necessity of voluntarily re-revising the new Constitution. Theirs is an opinion desirous of an indigenous constitution.[24] In contrast, the former has rebuffed it saying that the Constitution was realized by the voluntary will of Japanese people to liberate themselves, irrespective of the apparently forced procedure of the revision. They find some indigeneity in the so-called received Constitution. These opposing factions evidence the nature of the Constitution, that it not only comprises received factors, but also includes indigenous factors, be they potential or actual. It is the objective of the following discussions to identify the various modes of indigenous factors in, and related to, the legal system under the Showa Constitution.

III. Indigenous Law Adopted in the Contemporary State Law

1. INDIGENOUS OFFICIAL LAW

Indigenous factors are found in the official legal system, being dispersed among a variety of the received forms of the state law. Those which disappeared during the legal reform had been valid mainly in the fields of public law or those of private law, the principles of which had been supported by the old Constitution, such as *ie-seido*, discrimination by status, State Shinto, etc. In other words, they were characterized as absolutistic, or at least supporting the absolutist *Tenno* system. However, indigenous factors in a general sense must not be represented by these alone. They must include some others, indifferent to the absolutist regime or significant for their character other than in the absolutist sense. These kinds of factors, although mostly belonging to the fields of private law or technical public law, had been adopted in the Meiji legal system, and survived the Showa legal reform.

Furthermore, the Meiji system had opened the gate through which indigenous factors could be legalized when their validity was disputed in actual cases. The gate remains unchanged in the present system. The general clause concerning legalization of custom in three laws is a principal example. It is first provided in Article 2 of the *Horei* (Proper Law Act), promulgated and enforced in 1898, to give custom the validity of the law under some conditions, but without an allegation of either party. In contrast, Article 92 of the Civil Code allows custom to regulate a transaction with the allegation of both parties. The last one has a limited application in a smaller circle of commercial matters, but surpasses another important law, Civil Code. The gate has functioned dynamically in making explicit certain indigenous factors by legalizing a variety of customs. The general clause concerning the legal validity of custom is therefore a point of tangency where the Japanese state law can absorb custom, that is, a functioning unofficial law.

The Showa Constitution does not authorize any other kinds of official law, "official legal systems prevailing in Japan which are sanctioned by authorities other than the state and which are officially authorized by the state itself." This is a remarkable feature of the whole structure of law in Japan when compared with the other five countries in this survey. For there are found in those countries some religious, local, or other authorities, whose proper jurisdiction is officially authorized by the state, with corresponding legal systems which are administered by these authorities as independent of the state law. This feature of Japanese law may also seem strange to Western countries where established systems of religious law authorized by the state have prevailed. It is thus a unique feature of the Japanese structure of law. Under the Meiji system, two subsystems might be regarded as official law: colonial law and military law, both of which were abolished together with the Meiji Constitution. Truly they were beyond the reach of government control by Diet, Cabinet or the Court, but remained within the reach of *Tenno's* control under the Meiji Constitution. They were duly classified into state law, though with relatively separated jurisdictions, and into no official law other than state law.

2. CONSTITUTIONAL LAW

(1) The *Tenno* System

The *Tenno* is truly deprived of not only the absolutistic authority he had enjoyed under the Meiji Constitution, but also his entire legal power and political influence. Under the Showa Constitution, his official capacity "in matters of state" as "the symbol of the State and of the unity of people" is neither a right nor a power; his official capacity is nothing more than itemized "acts," for which *Tenno* himself is not responsible but the Cabinet obligated to give "advice and approval" to *Tenno* (Article 3, cf. Articles 4, 6, 7). Such a position and capacity of the *Tenno* may convince most people of a successful democratization of Japan, or the dissolution of the *Tenno* system.

Still, the *Tenno* is situated in the Constitution. Moreover, the *Tenno* provisions occupy such an important part of the Constitution that they are covered in the first eight Articles. One of them guarantees the "dynastic" succession of his Throne "in accordance with the Imperial House Law[25] passed by the Diet" (Article 2). Another one guarantees the possibility of establishing a Regency when needed (Article 5). The *Tenno* is systematically instituted in the Constitution, the basis of the whole Japanese official law. His position and capacity are really provided legally to entail some kinds of rights and duties in a broad meaning of the Hohfeldian scheme, while some strict legalists insist upon no legal rights of *Tenno* being written into the Constitution. There is good reason why some people are convinced of the continuity of the *Tenno* system, which might mean the failure of democratization in Japan.

Accordingly, the *Tenno* system under the present Constitution might be dubious in its character, as Noda states that "the present regime is neither monarchic nor republican, but it can be interpreted either in a monarchic or republican sense . . ." (1976: 70). Such an apparently equivocal nature, however, is to be considered the essence of the *Tenno* throughout Japanese history. The *Tenno* system under the Meiji Constitution should be understood as rather an exceptional construction, disguised by the Prussian type of absolutist regime. Historically, the *Tenno* has enjoyed supreme authority only formally or nominally, while the authority has been always protected legally, despite the fact that the ways of protection have been varied. In this sense, the *Tenno* has kept his legal position continuously from the era of Prince Shotoku, through the feudal ages with the Shogunate and Meiji era with the absolutist Constitution, up to the Showa era with the present Constitution. This is the indigenous *Tenno* system of Japan, flexible enough to adapt itself to changing circumstances. The *Tenno* system under the Meiji Constitution was a variation of its essence, as is the present one.

(2) National Holidays

One law among those belonging to the Constitution, brief but most closely related to the daily life of the people, is the National Holidays Act promulgated and enforced in 1948. It provides twelve holidays.

1 January	*Ganjitsu* (New Year's Day)
15 January	*Seijin-no-hi* (Coming of Age Day)

11 February	*Kenkoku-Kinen-no-hi* (National Foundation Day)
Spring Equinox	*Shunbun-no-hi* (Vernal Equinox Day)
29 April	*Tenno-Tanjo-bi* (*Tenno's* Birthday)
3 May	*Kempo-Kinen-bi* (Constitution Day)
5 May	*Kodomo-no-hi* (Children's Day)
15 September	*Keiro-no-hi* (Respect for the Aged Day)
Autumn Equinox	*Shubun-no-hi* (Autumnal Equinox Day)
10 October	*Taiiku-no-hi* (Health-Sports Day)
3 November	*Bunka-no-hi* (Culture Day)
23 November	*Kinro-Kansha-no-hi* (Labour Thanksgiving Day)

Among the twelve, the only one that can be regarded as mostly received in nature, is Constitution Day, for it was instituted after World War II to commemorate the enforcement of the Constitution with the received postulate of democracy. The other two, Respect for the Aged Day and Health-Sports Day, might appear to be similar to it, for they were additionally instituted in 1960, deliberately to promote care for the aged and the health of the people respectively. However, the basic idea to respect the aged had been established as a national feeling with the social principle of seniority and Confucian ethics since the feudal ages, and the practice of various sports in autumn, especially in the month of October, had long prevailed among the people. Within these two holidays are found indigenous factors.

All the others are rooted in indigenous traditions in history and society. New Year's Day, Vernal Equinox Day, Autumnal Equinox Day, and Labour Thanksgiving Day originated from folk customs inseparably connected with purely indigenous, Confucian, Buddhist and/or Shintoist practices. Their justification having been recognized, they were instituted as National Holidays under the Meiji Constitution though with different names. In contrast, Coming of Age Day and Children's Day are new under the present Constitution, but initiation ceremonies and festivals for children had been established folk customs much like the above-mentioned four. The remaining three, National Foundation Day,[26] *Tenno's* Birthday and Culture Day, were legally initiated under the Meiji Constitution for their fundamental significance in celebrating the anniversary of the nation's foundation, *Tenno's* birthday and the commemoration posthumously of the achievements of the Meiji *Tenno*. They may have been promoted by received practices, but their matrices were derived from the indigenous national understanding of the nature of *Tenno* and the nation, with the exception of Culture Day, which was converted after the war from the birthday of the Meiji *Tenno* to a day of culture and peace as declared in the new Constitution.

The National Holidays are thus by and large an indigenous elaboration assimilating received factors of varying degrees.

(3) *Gengo*

Gengo, also called *nengo* in Japanese, is the name of an era under the reign of a *Tenno*. This practice was originally received from China. Taika was the first *gengo* officially adopted in 645 when the Throne was defended by a loyal prince and a noble. From that time on until the Meiji Restoration it was used as the only way of reckoning the year, officially or otherwise, and so took on an indigenous character. Under the Meiji Constitution, its use was officially instituted with the principle of "A *Tenno*, a *Gengo*" by a specific law, while two other systems also became prevalent: the indigenous way of *Kigen*, whose first year begins at the year of the accession of the first *Tenno* Jimmu and runs continuously through succeeding reigns,[27] was favoured more by the government; and the received way of the Christian year favoured to a lesser degree among the people. After the war, the *Kigen* system collapsed, for it was inseparable from absolutist ideology. *Gengo* also lost legal protection due to its connection with the *Tenno* system, though it is still used both officially and unofficially. The use of the Christian year has increased in popularity.

Faced with this fact, those who preferred the indigenous *gengo* to the received system, whether nationalistically or not, attempted to protect *gengo* by law. They were successful in instituting it officially into law in 1979. The specific law, however, provides nothing more than the principle of "A *Tenno*, a *Gengo*" without any official obligation to the government and the people to use the *gengo* system. Whether *gengo* will continue in its present usage along with the alternative choice of the Christian year, or become obligatory by law in the future, remains to be seen. Nevertheless, there is no doubt that this indigenous practice has recovered a position in the official law.[28]

(4) Court ranks and honours

The old Twelve Grades of Officials instituted by Shotoku Taishi initiated the Japanese official system of status hierarchy. Such a system was formally held even during times when the power of the *Tenno* was exercised by the Shogun. It was reformulated under the Meiji Constitution into a most inclusive national system called the *ikai kunto* (imperial court ranks and honours), the first of which was long held by Admiral Heihachiro Togo. It was destined to be abolished together with the official *Tenno* system for its violation of the democratic principle of human equality before law.

Some years after recovering independence, a similar system of court ranks and honours revived, the highest of which was granted to the late Premier Shigeru Yoshida. Its constitutionality is advocated by the government against popular opinions otherwise.

(5) Some others

a. Paternal unilateralism of nationality

The Nationality Law, promulgated and enforced in 1899 and wholly revised in 1950, adopted a paternal unilateralism to give newborn children Japanese nationality, while it opened the way of nationalization for those of foreign nationality. But until recently the principle was never questioned because the indigenous way to recognize the social qualification of newborn children had been primarily that of paternal unilateralism, supported by the *ie-seido* under the Meiji Constitution. Although it is still legal, doubts as to its reasonableness have arisen. The reason is mainly the increasing number of children born to women of Japanese nationality married to foreigners whose children are denied Japanese citizenship due to this principle. The indigenous principle is destined, as I expect, to yield itself sooner or later to a received one of bilateralism by giving those children Japanese nationality.

b. Exclusion of foreign teachers from schools

No law has ever explicitly prohibited Japanese schools from hiring foreign teachers. Actually many foreigners have been hired by schools of various levels. But, as far as the national and public universities are concerned,[29] the foreign teachers have been part-timers except in rare cases of full-timers at minor universities. This is because the government has adhered to a restrictive interpretation of the qualifications of foreign teachers at national and public schools. Japanese nationality is demanded of the teachers at national and public schools on the grounds that they, as public servants, exercise public power for education. This absurd interpretation originated in an indigenous insularism and reinforced by the absolutist idea under the former Constitution, survived even under the democratic present Constitution. A new law was finally enacted in 1982 to open the way for the universities concerned to hire foreign teachers, although the law still prohibits the latter to take part in university administration.

c. Protection of minorities

Japan has been noted for national homogeneity, not only culturally but also racially, with the exception of a few minority groups.[30] The most noted is the Ainu whose homes are scattered in Hokkaido. They are known for traditional poems based on their own religious system. But their indigenous law has never been remarked upon nor surveyed by Japanese scholars, although its existence is evidenced by two facts. One is the brief description of B. Z. Seligman that "the patrilineages are territorial corporate groups, formerly owning defined areas where they held the sole rights of hunting, fishing and collecting" and related explanations (Munro, 1963: 157, cf. 141–158). The other, relevant to the discussion here, is the Hokkaido Native Tribe Protection Law, promulgated and enforced in 1899, to specifically validate the personal and collective ownership of their traditional lands. The effectiveness of the Law is dubious, for as a matter of fact the indigenous law of the Ainu seems to have been almost lost.

Another example is *buraku* or *burakumin* (hamlet people, or people of special hamlets), a matter of contemporary controversy. They are said to be the descendants of outcasts of the feudal ages.[31] After the Meiji Restoration they were legally emancipated. But, as practices of social discrimination before the law have not disappeared, the Act of Special Undertaking for *Dowa* (de-discrimination) was promulgated and enforced in 1969 to promote national and local governments to undertake various measures effective in annihilating discrimination of *burakumin*. The law is to protect a constitutional principle by regulating an unconstitutional, unofficial law of discrimination.

3. CRIMINAL LAW

The received criminal law was so different from the Japanese indigenous criminal law that it outlawed some indigenous crimes and punishments on the one hand and adopted some unprecedented ones on the other with its fundamental principle of *nullum crimen, nulla poena sine lege* and Aristotelian-Christian ethics. However, many indigenous remnants were found in it. Some of them, such as heavier punishment for crimes against the Imperial Families,[32] and punishment for adultery by wives but not by husbands, were abolished in the postwar legal reform because of their absolutistic or undemocratic nature. Still others survived the legal reform. It goes without saying that such traditional crimes as theft, injury, murder and some others were adopted in the received Penal Code for their universality, with some arrangements for modern criminal procedures. Below are a few limited examples to be specifically mentioned.

(1) Heavier punishment for the murder of an ascendant

The Meiji Penal Code adopted indigenous ethics to respect one's ascendants more than others, as had been naturally accepted in the traditional family system. Article 200 provided a harsher punishment for the murder of one's ascendants than any other. After the post-war legal reform, it was faced with strong criticism, for feudalistic morality was suspected. But a prevailing conservative opinion, advocating its universal humanity, won over criticism, allowing the Article to survive. A Supreme Court decision in 1950 upheld the conservative opinion when a case to test the constitutionality of the Article was defeated eight to seven on appeal. But in 1970 the Article was declared by the Court to be unconstitutional on the grounds that it violated the constitutional principle of "equality before law." The Article has not been formally deleted yet, but an indigenous law has been lost through official judicial review.

(2) Punishment to protect *inkan* or *hanko*

Articles 234–239 of the Penal Codes provide punishment for the forging and use of *inkan* or *hanko* (seals and their impressions) of official organs and private persons without authority. This is to protect the widespread practice of using a seal to show one's acceptance of legal responsibility or declaration of intention as Westerners would do so by giving their signature. Official registration of a *jitsuin* is required to make it the legitimate seal of a person. But the provisions of the Penal Code protect not only the registered seal, but also unregistered seals which may be used so arbitrarily that protection by law may often pose difficulties.

4. FAMILY LAW

Instead of the *ie-seido*, a new family law was prescribed for a received type of nuclear family in 1947, resulting in Westernization of the Japanese family system. Nevertheless, some indigenous factors survive, as seen in the examples below.

(1) *Naien*[33]

Upon receiving the Western system founded upon Christian

ethics, the former Civil Code adopted the *de jure* marriage as the only legitimate way, differing greatly from the indigenous way of the feudal ages. Seeing that there had been provided no system of official registration, a feudal marriage might be regarded as *de facto* marriage. Seen from another fact, however – that it had in general required social recognition by holding established ceremonies and that such customs had been regarded as of a legal nature in the society – it may have been *de jure* marriage. Therefore, the received way did not totally replace the customary way of marriage. As a result, under the new system many unregistered wives remained totally unprotected by law in cases where their husbands would not register their marriages. Their marriages are called *naien* (*de facto* marriage). The Supreme Court handed down a new interpretation in 1915 that an unregistered marriage was legally significant as a pre-engagement of a marriage to be registered. In addition, the government was during World War II compelled to take legal measures to admit the legitimate status of the wives who lost their husbands in the war before their marriages were registered. After the war, such interpretation in favour of the unregistered wives has been further expanded the better to protect them and their children (cf. Tanaka, 1976: 157–162).

(2) Divorce by consent

The former Civil Code and the revised one also opened two ways of divorce: by consent of the involved parties and by a decree of the court. The latter way was received and the number of such cases has been increasing, especially after the war. The former is a variation of an indigenous way and still accounts for the overwhelming majority of actual divorce cases. The right to declare divorce was in feudal ages enjoyed exclusively by the husband, or the head of his family, leaving his wife with no rights at all.[34] The first Civil Code assumed a marriage as the movement of a spouse from his or her born *ie* (a family) to his or her spouse's *ie* and, accordingly, a divorce as the return of the divorced spouse to his or her born *ie*. The procedure of divorce by consent of the parties, as was provided in the Civil Code, was devised to legalize the feudal way of divorce, as well as to accept the Western principle of individualism and equality of sex. The present Civil Code regards both marriage and divorce as personal contracts between the individual parties, and the democratization after the war tended to discourage the exclusive right of a husband to divorce. Still, the way of divorce by consent may function to legally approve such a right.

(3) Privileged inheritance of family memorials of ancestors

The individualistic Civil Code, overruling the former one which adhered to primogeniture, approved equal inheritance among all the children. But "there is one important exception to" it (Smith, 1974: 34). Article 897 conferred the privilege to inherit "genealogical records, utensils of religious rites, and tombs and burial grounds" to "the person who is, according to custom, to hold as a president the worship of the memory of the ancestors." This was to preserve an indigenous law, for "Such a person may be designated by the previous head of the house, or he may be the person who by custom would have been the legal successor in the past." (ibid.) Here is embodied the indigenous postulates of perpetuity of a family.

The examples enumerated above were adopted into official state law with an interpretation as being democratic, not as patriarchal or primogenitary. On the other hand, they may function in reality to preserve some attributes of the customary family system. Here are cases where the unconstitutionality of the provisions concerned are suspected by some critics. The following is a good example of this kind.

When the new Civil Code secured equal inheritance for all the children, many farmers did not necessarily welcome it for they feared their farm lands would be divided by the inheritance into plots too small to be financially productive. A group of reactionalists, who wanted to revive ideologically a former type of perpetual family, gave support to these farmers by drafting a proposal in 1949 whose aim was to approve farm land to be inherited *en bloc* by the child who was responsible for continuing the farming. But they were unsuccessful, for the draft has never passed into law because of strong opposition criticizing its unconstitutionality as an attempt to revive the old *ie-seido*. (cf. Wagatsuma, 1977: 141–144)

As a result, it is known at least that indigeneity adopted in the official law is not static but dynamic in the possibility of constant transformation in terms of the official provisions on the one hand, yet it functions positively to preserve indigenous practices as well as negatively to encourage a reactionary movement on the other.

5. CIVIL LAW

The principal law regulating the civil life of Japanese people concerning their legal personality, property, contracts and related phases, is provided for in the former part of the Civil Code which has been valid since its first legislation under the Meiji Constitution, while the latter part on family, marriage, and inheritance was revised after the War as stated above. Supplemented by other minor laws, it functions to cover all phases of civil life. Described here is such a legal system related to Japanese civil life.

Truly civil law was received from Western countries. However, without sufficient indigenous development of important legal practices to assimilate or be smoothly replaced by received systems, no reception could have been successful. Such a rapid assimilation or replacement of law as that which took place in Japan's modern history must be evidence of the preceding indigenous development. As a matter of fact, such important legal practices as of legal personality, possession, ownership, pledge and hypothec, contract, tort, damage, etc. had been developed with relative similarity to those in developed Western countries (cf. Wigmore, 1967–79). Their differences lie in that they were limited to some small circles of the population under feudal control by the Shogunate and lords. Many more indigenous factors may be enumerated among a variety of items in civil law than in public and criminal law. Below are some noteworthy examples to be compared with other countries.

(1) Customary rights in adjoining relationships

The Civil Code includes thirty Articles of various adjoining relationships. Among them, four Articles (217, 219[III], 228 and 236) make provisions for the parties to follow "local customs" which are different from the Code's provisions in regard to the bearing of expenses for necessary work concerning water, fences, buildings and boundaries. Still other customs may be adopted by the general clauses of Article 92 of the Code and Article 2 of the Proper Law Act as already mentioned.

(2) *Iriai-ken*

Japanese farming in feudal ages depended to a large extent upon the common use of pastures and forests, whose legal character is now understood to be almost the same as that of the *Gesamteigentum* of a German *Genossenschaft*, rather than the Roman type of possession or ownership as provided in detail in the Civil Code.[35] The right of the members of a village community to a common land has been called *iriai* or *iriai-ken*. Because the received law included no appropriate models for the right, and the

Japanese legislators did not have enough detailed information concerning the practices to devise a new system of the indigenous right, only two general clauses were inserted in the Civil Code to meet urgent needs. The first was to apply local customs of that area as well as the provisions of joint ownership (Article 263), and the second local customs as well as those of easements (Article 294). Such treatment resulted in clashes, often leading to violence or struggles for generations, between the owners, including the state, who were protected by modern official titles, and the farmers who dependend upon their common lands in customary practices with insufficient legal protection. Many cases have been brought before the courts. But the courts' decisions, based ordinarily upon a legalistic interpretation, have tended to be unfavourable for farmers, disregarding a few opinions of scholars for farmers. The right of common has declined due to such insufficient official protection. Still it has survived, even with some transformation of older practices. In 1966, a new law called the Common Land Modernization Act was enacted for the purpose of improving farmers' rights to common lands by reformulating their outdated practices into more modernized rights. The indigenous right of common has thus been changing dynamically.

(3) *Eikosaku*

There is an indigenous kind of practice adopted in the Civil Code; it has as many as ten articles, but in reality it seems almost lost. This is the *eikosaku* or *eikosaku-ken* (perpetual land lease) which means a farmer's cultivation or cattle-raising on another's land under a special type of contract with periods of duration from twenty to fifty years, according to the law. It was originally devised to reformulate an indigenous type of land use that had prevailed in feudal Japan among landless peasants. These peasants had been subordinated to landowners with an ascribed status without any definite limitations to their obligation to landowners or duration of their status. The provisions of the Civil Code aimed in a way to elevate the status of such peasants by reducing their indefinite duties to definite ones, while their subordinate status was preserved for the benefit of landowners. The provisions are thus of feudalistic character in a sense. The practice has almost disappeared, especially after the land reform, and criticisms have been raised among specialists calling for the deletion of the provisions from the Code.

(4) *Ne-teito*
The Civil Code provided two ways of securing the payment of a debt: *shichi* (pledge) mainly on movables, and *teito* (hypothec) mainly on immovables. By these provisions, *ne-teito* (fixed collateral), a widely prevailing practice to deposit security on immovables for an unlimited number of debts within a limited amount, lost official validity. But its practical usage was so effective that the Supreme Court approved it as valid in a suit as early as 1901.[36] After a long period of approval in case law, a most extensive supplement in the Civil Code took place in 1971 to add new provisions of the *ne-teito* with twenty-one articles (Articles 398–2 to 398–22).
(5) *Joto-tampo*
There is another practice of security which took a similar course to *ne-teito*. It enabled a debtor to keep the offered movable and used by himself, unlike *shichi* where the offered movable should be handed over to his pledgee. In order to escape from invalidation of this kind of contract on the ground of its formal violation of the *shichi*, they arranged, for instance, to make a formal contract to transfer the right to the security with a special agreement to return it after payment of the debt, with or without compensation. Such a fictitious legal contract, by the name of *joto-tampo* (mortgage) facilitated the practice under law. Since 1906 the Supreme Court has approved in case law the validity of the *joto-tampo*, disguised in other kinds of formal contract, in order to meet social needs. A special legislation for it is recommended by specialists and requested by persons concerned, but not realized yet.
(6) Some others
One, relating to *inkan* or *hanko* (seals and their impressions), has been already mentioned in the previous description on criminal law.
a. Mimoto hosho
This is somewhat similar to the previously mentioned *ei-kosaku* in its historical transformation. When a person was hired in the feudal ages as a labourer, whether for home work, shop work or manual work, a guarantor was required to vouch for his origin, morality, religion, family, history and so on, as well as to secure his possible negligence, tort and damage. Being called *mimoto hosho* (vouching for a person as a whole), it was an indispensable institution to maintain the social structure based on feudal status. In the Meiji era the practice survived, and the contract of *mimoto*

hosho was approved as legally valid by court judgements. In 1933 a law called the Personal Reference Act was enacted to standardize the contract by limiting some specific obligations of a guarantor, though with some feudalistic survivals. After the War, having been viewed as unsuitable for the capitalistic, democratic society, the law is almost officially unused, though the practice still often nominally followed.

b. Kazoe-doshi

In Japan, one's age was and still is often counted in calendar years unlike Western countries that count it in full years. The Age Counting Act, which was enacted in 1902 with a single principle sentence, provided to "count one's age from the day of birth." The provision is apparently understood to have adopted the received way of counting in full years. It can also be interpreted as having left room to count age in calendar years, that is, *kazoe-doshi*, if they count the year when one was born as the first year and the next year beginning from January 1 as the second. The latter interpretation was, in reality, much more prevailing. The Age Expressing Act in 1950 converted the method into one using full years, still leaving room for using the customary way in exceptional cases.[37] This is evidence that received law does not always consistently realize itself, due to pressure from indigenous factors.

c. Shakkan-ho

The measurement that Japanese people had used for a long time was *shakkan-ho*, of Chinese origin, and based on *shaku* for length and *kan* for weight. Two other systems were received after the Meiji Restoration: the metric and the yard-pound. After several decades of mixed use of the three systems, the government adopted before the War the policy of depending upon the metric system. In 1959 the Measurement Law was promulgated, to go into force the following year. It limited the legitimate system to metric only and prohibited production and sale in the measures of other systems except those specifically admitted as special units. In actuality, the metric system has been gradually extending its coverage to many phases of Japanese life. Still, *shakkan-ho* is used prevailingly, among others, in the measurement of lands, buildings, cloth, liquids, etc., where the Japanese traditional styles of life are preserved. The practical need for it was so ardently demanded that the government legally recognized it in 1977, although exceptionally and partially, under the metric system of the Measurement Law.[38] This is a good example of an indigenous practice which competes with the law and then becomes valid by way of a legal technique.

Through the examples enumerated above from civil law, a trend may be found: the indigenous factors adopted in the official civil law are not static, but in dynamic transformation, declining, persisting or reviving. The declining are feudalistic factors supported by an absolutist policy, such as the perpetual land lease and vouching for a person as a whole. The persisting are useful ones, whether in feudal ages or modern, such as the adjoining relationships, fixed collateral and mortgage. The reviving are the other three examples. But the modes of the revival are varied. Their revivals are not as they were before the war nor in feudal ages. Even a declining tendency is found in the three reviving ones, for the counting of one's age in calendar years is adopted in no more than exceptional cases, the traditional measures are limited, and the right of common has been reformulated. Still, they occupy formal positions in the state law. In brief, the indigenous factors adopted in the received legal system are in transformation or reformulation, adapting themselves to changing circumstances.

6. COMMERCIAL LAW

Commercial law as designated here includes not only the Commercial Code of 1899, but also some others related to it, as in the case of civil law. Fundamental preparations in the latest feudal age for receiving Western capitalistic commercial law had also been pushed forward indigenously, as was recognized by an author who even stated on the other hand that "the development of a legal structure for economic enterprise began only in the Meiji era" (Michida, 1963: 507–508). Apparently the Japanese commercial law is mostly composed of received factors. But, as has been pointed out, the Commercial Code declares in Article 1 that commercial custom should apply to commercial matters when there is no provision in the Code. The modernity-oriented commercial law thus could not totally expel indigenous factors. What is more remarkable is that some specialists in Japanese economic history tend to exemplify the existence in later feudal ages of many indigenous commercial measures compared to capitalist ones in Western countries, such as wholesaling and retailing, money-lending, bills of exchange, money orders, partnerships, maritime law, etc. These practices have been so inseparably assimilated with received factors that their indigeneity cannot clearly be discerned. Other than these, the following two are seen as clearly indigenous.

(1) *Inkan*

The popularity and seriousness of the *inkan* or *hanko* have been described. But, being most used in the commercial world, they are furnished with a specific law, although it comprises only one sentence. This is the Law for the Cases Requiring Signing, promulgated and enforced in 1900. The law reads that "*kimei natsuin* (showing one's name and impressing one's seal) shall replace signature even when the latter is required in the Commercial Code." The applicability of the provision extends in actuality to all phases of civil life beyond that related to the Code. "Showing one's name" does not necessarily mean giving one's signature, except in those cases specifically requiring the *written* name. Impressing a stamp of one's name is usually sufficient for many purposes. Thus one's signature may very often be replaced by impressing stamp and seal.

(2) *Noren*

In 1962, a provision was added to the Commercial Code as Article 285–7, along with many others. This is the first appearance in the official law of the indigenous practice of *noren* (goodwill). *Noren* originally meant a sign curtain at the entrance of a shop, and after that, an intangible form of goodwill. It differs from Western goodwill in its close connection with the familial or quasi-familial ties among the sharers of the same *noren*. The owner of a shop with a good reputation and many regular clients may authorize some of his children or loyal apprentices to open their own shops, using the *noren* of his shop, and even allotting some of his clients to the new shops. Then his shop occupies the status of *honten* (main shop), while the authorized shops assume the status of *bunten* or *shiten* (branch shops). Such a familial or quasi-familial tie between *honten* and *shiten* is in the same vein as in the *dozoku* to be mentioned below. The first Commercial Code had no provision that specifically applied to the indigenous *noren*, assuming that the provisions of the trade name could cover it. Faced with many disputed cases, the courts established before long a precedent to protect the *noren* as a legal right. The supplement of an article in 1962 was specifically enacted to make explicit how to assess its economic value, assuming its legal validity. The *noren* in the Commercial Code is thus a limited but revived indigenous institution.

7. PROCEDURAL LAW: CONCILIATION

Having been quite foreign to Japan, the modern court system as well as procedural law was wholly received from Western countries in order to make the system operate. In criminal procedure, there was no room for adopting indigenous practices. The Otsu Case may be an illustration of this, for it exemplifies that even an appeal to a national crisis or the authority of the Imperial Family finally failed to outweigh the observance of the modern penal principle (cf. Note 32). In civil procedure there is a significant exception in that it adopted an indigenous practice, called *wakai* (conciliation) or *chotei* (mediation).

As is noted in an article written by Takeyoshi Kawashima, it was an influence of Japanese indigenous law that:

> ". . . Japanese not only hesitate to resort to a lawsuit but are also quite ready to settle an action already instituted through conciliatory processes during the course of litigation. . . ."
>
> ". . . in the traditional ways of settling disputes the solution was, in principle, reached through agreement by both parties. The notion that a justice measured by universal standards can exist independent of the wills of the disputants is apparently alien to traditional habit of the Japanese people." (1963: 50)

The influence was so deeply rooted in Japanese society that four mediation laws were enacted to deal specifically with problem cases of leased land and buildings in 1922, of tenancy in 1924, of loan in 1932, and of family affairs in 1939. Their lawmakers' intention was that "the disputes themselves were to be 'washed away' (*mizu ni nagasu*) by reconcilement" "instead of co-ordinating the conflicting vested interests" (ibid.: 53–54). Such an idea of legal conciliation developed out of the legal reform after the War into a general mediation system applicable to all cases between persons, although the main laws concerned are divided into two: Law of Mediation of Civil Affairs in 1951 and Law of Mediation and Determination of Family Affairs in 1947.

But such a general institution of mediation cannot function to preserve the "premodern" Japanese preference alone.[39] The Family Court, with jurisdiction of mediation and determination of family affairs, was instituted under the strong influences of the modern idea of family declared in the new Constitution. The present mediation system has assimilated received factors as well as preserving indigenous ones.

IV. Indigenous Law Prevailing Unofficially

1. INDIGENOUS UNOFFICIAL LAW

As clearly seen in the examples enumerated in the preceding chapter, various indigenous factors are adopted within the state legal system. From a legalistic point of view, they may be explained as having been adopted for their effectiveness and desirableness. But the question arises: Why are they so effective and desirable? They are not simply factural practices, but must be approved and supported as being justified social norms. Indigenous factors adopted into official law concerning each example may not ordinarily be all the components of related social norms; part of them are selected, modified or reformulated by governmental policies of varying degrees.

As a matter of course, the other factors that are not adopted may continue to function as social norms outside the realm of official law. Some or many of them may be conformable or indifferent to the effectiveness of official law, while others may function to supplement, compete with, modify or undermine state law, thus becoming unofficial law.

The validity of unofficial law is not discerned so definitely however, for, unlike that of state law, the source of the validity is not clearly identified or presented. The validity may originate, in one group of cases, in personal preference or judgement without any relevance to pressure from outside. Or in another group of cases, they may be effective by a blind choice without any conscious intention. But there may be yet another group of cases where they are "customarily sanctioned by a certain circle of people in popular conceptions and actual behaviour patterns."

Unofficial law is in reality significant for the function of the state law, and can be conceptualized in terms of this significance. Its concept may not yet be furnished with the elaborated component variables sufficient to be used as a tool concept. It might be rather easy to define the word in a conceptual, logical work. But such a work may fall prey to the danger of excluding the real referents which must be described accurately by the concept, for the referents are not yet clearly observed. Furthermore, the referents may vary with localities, groups, time, cases, etc. What must be done first is to collect the materials which are thought to be relevant to the referents.

2. PUBLIC LIFE

Public life refers to the social sphere of the Japanese people as far as related to the constitutional, administrative and procedural regulations of the official law.

(1) The *Tenno* system

The official *Tenno* system as stated in the preceding chapter is deeply rooted in the indigenous practices which accompany more varieties of the unofficial function of *Tenno* than are provided officially in Article 7 of the Constitution.[40] For instance, when *Tenno, Kogo* (Empress) and often other Imperial Family members go out on trips or attend meetings, the official functionaries in charge are privileged to enforce security measures that may result in multiplying the routine duties of public servants concerned and regulating the freedom of private persons. This has been often criticized as "building a wall between *Tenno* and the people." In commemoration of a *Tenno*'s visit, some people are obliged to preserve rooms, buildings, and important furnishings that he used, and trees that he planted; to display or distribute Imperial gifts to their families or close friends; to have specified persons promoted in court ranks and honours; and so on. In reality, *Tenno* cannot function without exerting any political influence, however slight, when seen from a broader perspective. The most striking case of this was the decision of the present *Tenno* to surrender to the Allied Powers (cf. Lu, 1974, II: 175–176). The decision was made under the former Constitution of an absolutist character. But, in reality, *Tenno* had usually been so reluctant in making his own decision that no other case has been known where his decision was voluntarily expressed. His decision to surrender is understood to have been made not by the power granted to him in the Constitution, but by his authority derived from the indigenous *Tenno* system throughout history. It was because this authority was appreciated to be "accorded with the will of the majority of the Japanese people, . . . likely to spare further bloodshed, . . ." that the *Tenno* system was finally determined to be retained at the surrender with all opinions otherwise (Oppler, 1976: 51).

(2) *Jinja*

Jinja, with the function of *matsuri*, was truly deprived of its official legal nature which had been protected in the Meiji legal system, resulting in abolition of the State Shinto. At the same time the rapid development of Japanese society toward modernization and urbanization caused a falling tide of the *Jinja* Shinto. But this did not necessarily result in the disappearance of the indigenous practices of *jinja*.

The *Tenno* is still recognized as a Shinto priest to perform Shinto rites for the Gods of his Imperial Family. The principal shrine, Ise-Jingu, is the highest-ranked shrine in Japan. It is supported mostly by the people. But *Tenno*, representing the Imperial Family, also supports it from the Family funds authorized by the Diet, including expenses for his *matsuri* at Ise-Jingu, interpreted as an event of his family, not the state. *Tenno* thus enjoy certain indigenous rights and duties of *jinja* and *matsuri*.

Because of its close connection with *Tenno*, who is respected by people with a special authority, Ise-Jingu forms a remarkable target of national worship. Not only many private persons feel it their duty to visit the shrine, but also Cabinet ministers are socially obliged to visit it. The Prime Minister and other Ministers also feel obliged to offer worship to that shrine and another shrine called Yasukuni-Jinja, which a Christian Premier, Masayoshi Ohira, visited as well. Such practices violate, as many scholars maintain, the constitutional prohibition that "the State and its organs shall refrain from religious education or any other religious activity" (Article 20). They hold, however, their own justification, as is clear in the following case.

There has been such a strong opinion to legalize the supporting of Yasukuni-Jinja at national expense that the conservative party in power counts it as one of their policies. Their justification of its constitutionality lies in that the *jinja* is not a religious facility but a cultural one, based on folk beliefs unrelated to religion. This kind of justification was finally approved by the Supreme Court in 1977 in a noted case of the Tsu City *jichin-sai* (a ceremony to purify a building site). The issue was whether the *jichin-sai* held by Tsu City with its public fund was an unconstitutional religious event or simply a constitutional convention. The Supreme Court decision was to terminate the conflicting opinions in favour of the latter.[41] The essence of this interpretation is that which was adopted by the Meiji regime to enable them to compel people to worship the *jinja*, whatever religion they might believe in. Assuredly found in this is that the Japanese conception of religion would be difficult to understand from the Western point of view and that a kind of unofficial law may be functioning to undermine a provision of the Constitution to separate State from religion.

Jinja Shinto is furthermore alive with its own unofficial law at each shrine in a community. Truly, in a sense, the declining of the shrine and its *matsuri* may be mainly affected by the recent modernization of Japanese society, as well as the official rejection of their support. But they are still surviving, although restructured with a tendency that "diffuseness is born of the delocalization of Shinto belief and practice" (Morioka, 1975: 70). A revival of the *matsuri* is further found among big shrines famous for their spectacular events. And there are many *miyaza* (guild of a shrine) and local organizations to support community shrines. These shrines survive by a strong mutual tie among the inhabitants privileged to the shrines in the indigenously formed rights and duties to support their *jinja* and *matsuri*.[42]

(3) Established administrative discretion

The administrative authorities are empowered to exercise discretion with regard to the matters within their jurisdiction. The discretion is to be exercised in accordance with the explicit provisions or principles in the legal system. Among numerous cases, discretionary practices are sometimes conventionally established to supplement, compete with, modify or even undermine the law. Examples are found among those of the tax office with regard to the assessment of the income of people and corporations, and of tax upon them; those of local governments to entrust private *chonai-kai* (town-block associations) with some official business in order to make direct contact with their citizens;[43] those of the prosecutor's office not to prosecute a person who committed a misdemeanour for the first time; and many others.

Some people might object to regarding these practices as a kind of law on the grounds that they are an application of law. But in actuality, many persons, not only private but often public, regard them as the standards of judgement, and adopt them as if they were official standards. From a behavioural point of view, they are a law functioning together with, or alternatively with, the official law.

An important characteristic common to all of them is that they were not established traditionally but rather have been established since the reception of Western law. They are an indigenous outcome of the reception, or as Hooker has it, "indigenous adaptation" (1978: 4–5). In truth, the above-mentioned *Tenno* system is another indigenous adaptation. We find here that indigeneity should be viewed in the mode of reception as well as of the contents of the received law – in other words, through assimilation processes.

3. FAMILY LIFE

(1) The procedure of a marriage

A marriage is officially recognized by registration. But, as in other non-Western countries, Japanese society has cherished various ways of social recognition of a marriage functioning in addition to, and often against, the official requisites of *de jure* marriage. Some of these ways are declining, but others are persisting or metamorphosing. Among others adopted into official law are *Naien*, and divorce by consent. Other important examples are referred to below, except those almost disappearing after the Meiji era (cf. Yanagida, 1957: 161–181).

a. Nakodo

A senior couple, or possibly two, is chosen for a marriage as *nakodo* (go-betweens). Their functions range from the nominal one of simply sitting at the main table of the wedding ceremony and reception party, through a substantial one such as introducing the bride and groom for the first time, called *miai*, arranging the marriage, and holding a party, to a far-reaching one in establishing a fictitious parental relationship with the couple, called *oyabun* and *kobun.*

b. Approval by relatives

Although to a lesser degree than the go-between, advance approval of a marriage by close relatives is usually needed. This might be regarded as a survival of the old council of relatives, which was granted some prerogatives in the official family system under the Meiji Constitution. But it is an indigenous practice much older than Meiji.

c. Yuino

Yuino (betrothal gifts) are to be exchanged at the conclusion of a marriage contract. The gift items have included rings since Japanese modernization, but the principal ones and their formality are so specifically fixed traditionally that special shops or sections of department stores sell such items and teach the formality of them.

d. A ceremony and a party

A ceremony combined with a reception party is required of a marriage. To hold the ceremony and the party is a duty of a new couple or the parents of the couple. It further includes some rights and duties of the participants. There is a general rule established, although not always in a definite form, of the extent and seating order of the guests. In the case of a marriage in a traditional community, the size and procedure of the meeting may be required to be in accordance with traditional practices.

Those stated above and some others not mentioned here may not be always universal in Japan. But they are so effective that the failure of a party in performing their duties is often thought to justify the right of another party in raising indignation, and in serious cases to cancel a marriage contract which was legally concluded. As a matter of fact, people tend to observe the practices, however legally unrequired.[44] For the people, they form an unofficial law. The people are as a rule required to perform those unofficial duties, while a marriage is formally completed by official registration.

(2) *Muko-yoshi*

The *muko-yoshi* (groom foster-son) is an indigenous practice indispensable for the traditional, patriarchal and primogenitary family system of Japan. For it supplies a family, who has a daughter but not a son, with a male heir adopted from another family in place of the daughter who was expected to be a female heir. This was legally adopted in the former family system, under the Meiji Constitution. Under the present official family system, the practice, which has lost official legal validity, is still prevailing. By its persisting need, the legislators put an article in the new Civil Code to officially justify this practice, although latently. Article 750 reads "Husband and wife assume the surname of the husband or wife in accordance with the agreement made at the time of marriage." It originally aims to let the parties choose their surname by themselves according to an individualistic principle. But in actuality, the cases where the surname of the wife is chosen are almost always marriages for the intention of the traditional type of *muko-yoshi*. Those practices are nothing but evidence of the ideal of a perpetual family across generations, as a foreign observer pointed out that "these similarities between old and new provisions actually tend to keep alive the house concept in the mind of the population" (Steiner, 1977: 113).[45]

The practice of *muko-yoshi* presents an important feature of indigenous law. It is sanctioned, although latently, by official law together with the modernized type of marriage, the idea of which may contradict *muko-yoshi.* As far as this fact is considered, the contents of official law is both received and indigenous. This means an indigenous adaptation of received law. Received factors and indigenous factors cannot be separated in reality, but coexist in an assimilation process.

(3) *Tandoku sozoku*

A similar indigenous adaptation is found in *tandoku sozoku* (sole-heir inheritance) which was officially deprived of legal validity for its primogenitary ideology. One may still often want, and be expected, to inherit a legacy without sharing it with the other joint heirs, whether the reason be primogenitary or not. Available to them are the provisions of the Civil Code for voluntary refusal of inheritance to be made in exceptional cases. These provisions thus function for purposes both received and indigenous.

(4) *Ie*

Although some more indigenous, unofficial laws may be found, that of *ie* (family or household) should be treated here for its basic importance.

The Japanese family is in an ideal type regarded as a particular entity represented by the authority of the family head for continuity across generations "stand(ing) somewhat midway between the Confucian and the feudal types" characterized by "some conception and practice of 'feudal' rights and duties" (Kawashima, 1963: 106).[46] It fostered various rights and duties of the family members, the fundamentals of which were specifically identified as *kaho* or *kaken* (the constitution of a family). The *kaken* of such families of reputation as nobles, warriors, landlords and the big merchants often took written forms, collections of which were now and then published before the war as models for ordinary families. Furthermore, various social organizations in Japan were structured after such a familial constitution, to be mentioned in another section.

Of course, the change of *ie* after the war has been rapid and great, especially in urban areas (Koyama, 1962; Dore, 1962). Assuming the "greatly weakened" "notion of the 'transcendental' unity of the family group across the generation," "attitudes of 'collectivity-orientation' can still survive in a new form" (Dore, 1962: 184, 185) as is exemplified by the change of ancestor worship

(Smith, 1974: 211–226).

The indigenous unofficial law of family is still observable as far as the "obligations . . . of the family group" (Dore, 1962: 185) or "the right and duty to conduct" the rites for ancestors (Smith, 1974: 222) are observed.

(5) *Dozoku*

The *ie* principle has afforded a basis for formation of an extended family called *dozoku* (common kin) as is noted in various literatures (cf. Nakane, 1967; Kitano, 1962). When a family head is succeeded by a primogenitary heir, his brothers have to establish separate families of which they become the heads. But their families are not truly independent of the former. In the calling of *bunke* (branch families), they are obliged, with the ideal of *wa*, to help as well as depend on the former called *honke* (main family). When the families of those brothers are further divided into their children's, the *honke* is called *so-honke* (the head family of the related *honkes*). Certain relationships of *bunke* with their *honke* and between one another are required to be kept by the duties and rights of the families of a kin group concerned, in a genealogical hierarchy.

Such a system of *dozoku* was a most basic structure of Japan although with a variety of names. It originally developed in a locality. Being so persistent, the ties between the families of a *dozoku* function beyond the boundary of the locality. Its form and principles have permeated many other kinds of social organization. The before-mentioned main-branch tie in *noren* and *oyabun-kobun* relationship are among its remarkable variations.[47] Other variations will be mentioned later. Without doubt such *dozoku* structures are declining. It "still remains true, however, that the patrilineal relationships which are maintained tend, where appropriate, to be structured in traditional main-branch family patterns" (Dore, 1962: 180).

4. CIVIL LIFE

(1) *Giri* relations

Giri, which is defined as "a category of Japanese obligations" (Benedict, 1954: 317) or "the manner of behaviour required of one person to others in consequence of his social status" (Noda, 1976: 175), is one of the best-known Japanese cultural features of behaviour. In order to differentiate a certain pattern of behaviour from the underlying value system, the term "*giri* relations" is here used to denote that behaviour pattern, leaving the term "*giri*" to be used for the value. The principal constituent of *giri* relations is a reciprocal duty to pay the debt later on with equivalence to the gift or favour received on a preceding occasion. Observance of one's *giri* has been respected as one of the most fundamental ethics (cf. Benedict, 1954: 133–176) and very often led people to behave even against individual freedom and rights as protected by official law (cf. Noda, 1976: 179–180).

Among various *giri* relations, gift-giving is most noticeable. It is reciprocally obliged between specifically related parties, whether families, collectives, or individuals, such as those related by blood and marriage, living in a neighbourhood, working at a place of work, belonging to the same group, or connected with a particular tie, such as between the go-between and the new couple, *oyabun* (fictitious parent) and *kobun* (fictitious children), voucher and the vouched, patron and the person under the patronage, teacher and pupil, and so on. The hidden responsibility for reciprocal gift-giving may be discharged at particular occasions such as *chugen*[48] (mid year present) and *seibo* or *oseibo* (year-end present), marriage or death of a person, birth of children, diseases and disasters, completion of a new building, and so on. A gift from one party to another with no preceding significant relationship may provoke the obligation of the latter to reciprocate.

The substance to be exchanged is not necessarily limited to material goods. Especially between the parties of different social status, the inferior may be obliged to reciprocate goods or services for the favour, benevolence, or convenience given by the superior. In these cases, the apparent imbalance of material gifts exchanged are in fact balanced when psychological gifts are taken into consideration.[49]

Truly Japanese *giri* relations are considered premodern as demonstrated in the stories of Benkei, ever loyal to his lord (Benedict, 1954: 138–139) and of the Forty-Seven *Ronin* (lordless warriors) (ibid.: 199–205), and they may be featured by an "affectional, emotional" nature (Noda, 1976: 17 –17). But they are without doubt a manifestation of the universal principle of reciprocity, the most famous of which was disclosed among the Torobriand Islanders by Bronislaw Malinowski (1926). The premodern characteristic of Japanese *giri* relations are declining during post-war years.[50] Still, they are functioning, intermingled with universal and indigenous nature (cf. Noda, 1976: 183).

(2) The order of the seats

The order of the seats constitutes official law with regard to the public status in public and international law. Here discussed as unofficial law is that of ordinary persons in their civil life.

The order of the seats is more or less conventionalized in every country, often with stronger pressure than equality before official law. The characteristics of the Japanese one are found in two factors. The status hierarchy forms a guiding principle on the one hand, and the obligation to observe the order is laid on the people connected with a persistent tie in a community, on the other. For instance, every side of the square *irori* (fireplace) of a traditional house is specifically assigned to a different status: the head of the family, his wife, their guests, or other families and servants, the misuse of which by the bride might have constituted sufficient reason for divorce. In formal parties such as funerals and wedding ceremonies, the order is observed with utmost care so as not to injure the prestige of persons gathered, or the *wa* of the community.

The customarily established order is today transforming. The indigenous need is still functioning to preserve it in concert with its universality, while its nature as an unofficial law is to be further examined in various cases.

(3) *Murahachibu*

Most Japanese communities had a customary punishment for their members called *murahachibu* (expulsion from a community) as a means of last resort. Originally, it is said to mean, for a village community, to withhold all help to a member except in two cases of death and fire.[51] The word has been extendedly used to mean any dismissal of a member from any social group, or rejection of him by the other members of a community, which may not be accounted as unofficial law.

Leaving aside many instances before the war, a noted case took place in an agricultural community in early 1950s. The community kept their own customary constitution, as usual in other communities, to vote unanimously in an election for a certain candidate by advance agreement. A girl, who had been inspired by the free vote guaranteed by the new Constitution, told this unconstitutional advance agreement to a man outside the community and, as a result, brought public indignation of the community action in mass communication. The outraged community decided to exercise *murahachibu* against her family for her violation of their "constitution." With no help offered by the community during rice-planting, her family was compelled to call personnel from outside at much greater expense. The family suffered more troubles occurring from the *murahachibu*. Although such a typical case has not been publicly reported since then, the practice and supporting in-morals cannot be said to have been terminated.

(4) Conflict management

The Japanese aversion to modern legal treatment of conflict is well-known (cf. Kawashima, 1963; Noda, 1975: 132). This fact allows us to assume some unofficial procedural law of conflict management as prevailing more effectively than official procedure, although its realities and characteristics have yet to be explored.

Some of their features are presupposed. The intervening third party, both privileged and responsible, is a person influential on the contending parties, such as a senior, superior or officers. The criteria for management are adopted from conventional morals prevailing in the community, not from official law.[52] The procedure is initiated by the advice of surrounding third parties rather than both parties. The decision is reached not by any differentiated form of conciliation, mediation, arbitration or award as in modern legal systems but by a mixture of them all. The aim of the management is rather to recover the peace between the parties and of their circle than to declare legal rights and duties of the parties.

Such a way of conflict management might be labelled as "aversive to modern legal treatment" when adopted by people prior to the official legal procedure; but in fact it is used alternatively to the latter, to be rather characterized as coexisting with modern legal treatment. Similar practices are found not only in primitive societies (Abel, 1974) and Asian countries (Noda, 1975: 128–129; Htin Aung, 1969), but also in Western countries, as "Settled out of Court" is practised in reality (Ross, 1970). Of course, differences among those countries can not be disregarded. But it also cannot be simply labelled as "premodern," for it is an established practice in modern societies as well.

(5) Some others

a. Lunar calendar

The solar calendar was received after the Meiji Restoration to take the place of the former lunar calendar which was given the name of *kyureki* (old calendar). The lunar calendar has gradually decreased in general popularity. Still, it has kept prevalence in some limited circles. Among others, fishermen need it for their dependence on ebb and flow of tide due to the moon; farmers enjoy its availability for its amalgamation in their agricultural calendar; and people may be reminded of some special events relating to it such as the Lunar New Year, Bon Festival, *matsuri* of their shrines, etc.[53] They could use the solar calendar for these purposes by converting the days concerned. This possibility of conversion should have promoted people to desert the old way, but it also must have enabled people to perpetuate its use.

b. Shakkan-ho

Shakkan-ho (old measurement by *shaku* and *kan*) still enjoys a wide prevalence as an unofficial law, although some of the units are almost out of usage.[54] The before-mentioned partial revival in official law shows the prevalence.

The units of *shakkan-ho* may be converted into metric ones. However, rare justification would be needed to consider it more convenient to use a *ken, tsubo* or *sho* than to use about 1,818 metres, about 3.3 square metres, or about 1.8 litre. The reason why the usage of *shakkan-ho* is required in limited circle is similar to that of the lunar calendar.

c. Annual events and rites of passage

A family has traditionally established regular events recurring every year: for instance, New Year, Girls' Festival,[55] Spring Equinox, Boys' Festival,[56] Bon Festival, Autumnal Equinox, festival of the community shrine, Celebration of Children of Three-Five-and-Seven Years of Age,[57] Year End, etc. A set of such events is called *nenju gyoji* (annual events) (See Smith, 1962 for an example). A person also passes important threshholds of life as he or she grows. These are particularly commemorated in traditional ways, beginning from birth, through visits to the community shrine thirty-three days after birth, Celebration of Children of Three-Five-and-Seven Years of Age, marriage, retirement, *kanreki* (sixtieth birthday), *beiju* (eighty-eighth birthday) to a hundred years old. They are a variation of the rites of passage noted by the study of Arnold van Gennep (1960).

Some difficulties are found in asserting that both annual events and rites of passage are indigenous unofficial law. Firstly because many of their events originated in old China. Secondly because, received Western events have been added to or have replaced them, such as the new academic and fiscal year from April 1st, summer vacation, Christmas, visit to a famous shrine for the community shrine, entrance into primary school for local boys' groups, Coming-of-Age Day for local initiation ceremonies, silver wedding and gold wedding, etc. Thirdly, because they changed and are still changing, generally speaking, toward voluntary practices rather than enforced ones. Still, they preserve some indigenous nature. And such cases are found, as the people concerned observe those private events as an official duty in society, often attaching greater weight to them than official legal duties. Furthermore, in other countries to be compared with Japan, religious duties often may constitute unofficial law or legal postulates in the form of annual events and rites of passage. Japanese ones will be useful as a comparable material, even if their nature of law may be dubious.

5. ESTABLISHED COMMUNITIES

In Western society, civil life is understood to be the personal life of an independent citizen. In Japan, however, the personal life of a citizen seems very often accompanied or regulated by collective pressures, typically by family and community. The pressures by a family have already been described. Below are shown those by a community.

(1) *Buraku*

The *buraku* (hamlet)[58] has formed the basis of Japanese local communities of different types. In urbanized areas, it is usually called *chonai* (town-block) or *chonai-kai* (town-block association). It is structurally a *Gemeinschaft*-like community, constituted of regular families the members of which are oriented to group unity, internalized or compelled. It is functionally a self-regulating organization with its own system of norms and sanctions, including *murahachibu*, some of which are elaborated into the traditional law of the community called the *kempo* (constitution) or *shikitari* (convention) of a *buraku*.

Being one of the most remarkable features of Japanese social structure, the *buraku* has been frequently studied by both Japanese and Western scholars, with many useful results.[59] Leaving its description to these works, a comment is here added.

The *buraku* is a systematic organization, including subsystems, which may often function as the *buraku* itself. The subsystems may be *iriai* groups for joint usufruct of pastures and forests, *ujiko* groups for support of their shrines, *wakamono-gumi* (youth associations) and other age groups, or voluntary associations such as those for agriculture or fishery, religious activities, fire service, guard and the like, which were formally instituted by received kinds of motives but have been materially replaced by the traditional group structure.

So an inclusive nature of the *buraku* was the ground of its strength. In recent years when the "disorganization of agricultural communities" is observed along with the corresponding wide and rapid urbanization of the country, *buraku* could not stay as it was. Its trend toward disorganization is seen in the increasing departure of those subsystems from a *buraku*. It still functions, however, as a self-controlling collective body in one form or other, although the changing structure has yet to be investigated.

(2) *Iemoto* organization

The structural principle of the *dozoku* has been applied to various social organizations. A notable application is *iemoto* (the main family of a school of traditional arts); correctly *iemoto seido*, it is detailed in the study of Francis L. K. Hsu (1975).

Iemoto seido has been the distinguished feature of Japanese organizations for training and enjoying Japanese traditional arts. Its central figure is *iemoto*, head of a particular school and conferred with an absolute authority on the art and control of the school. His or her disciples are called *deshi*, who are classified into a hierarchical order according to their skills in the art, and from among the highest of which the successor to the *iemoto* is selected, although a child of the *iemoto* is often expected to be the successor. Such a structure is maintained by a system of traditional norms and sanctions, which may bc valid to the school members even if it violates freedom and equality under official law.

The *iemoto seido* is mainly preserved in schools for personal accomplishments such as *sado* or *cha-no-yu* (tea ceremony), *kado* or *ikebana* (flower arrangement), public entertainments such as the *no* play, *kabuki* play, various kinds of *hogaku* (Japanese music) and *nihon buyo* (Japanese dancing), and old military arts such as *kendo* (fencing), *karate, kyudo* (archery), *eiho* (art of swimming), and so on. It also shows further variations as in *sumo* (Japanese wrestling) or applications as in *haiku* (seventeen-syllable poem) and *waka* (thirty-one-syllable poem).

(3) *Shuha*

The application of the *dozoku* principle in the religious world is found among organizations of Buddhist *tera* (temples).[60] Each temple in a *shuha* (sect) is ranked on a level of the hierarchy controlled by the *honzan* (main temple) of the sect, being called a *matsuji* (subordinate temple). With some "minor and inevitable discrepancies, it is clear that there is a strong resemblance or basic pattern common to the secular [*dozoku*] and the Buddhist organizations" (Morioka, 1975: 92). The structural difference of the *shuha* from the secular *dozoku* is said to originate in the reflection of the Tokugawa regime "constructed with the *Shogun* at the top, *daimyo* (local lords) under him, *daimyo*'s retainers next and, finally, commoners at the very bottom" (ibid.: 93–94).

Their norms and sanctions have formed an established system of canon law concerning the authority of the main temple in the orthodox creed and secularistic administration of the sect, rights and duties of the subordinate temples, and especially important succession regulations of the presiding priest of the main temple, whether hereditary or selected by qualified priests. Furnished with the offices of administration and adjudication, the *shuha* code truly enjoys some privileges independent of the state law by courtesy of the constitutional separation of state from religion, and might be classified into an unofficial law. As far as the contemporary situation is concerned, however, it may be duly regarded as belonging to official law on the ground that it is authorized as an embodiment of the constitutional freedom of belief, and that its adjudicative authority is finally to be sanctioned by the official court of the state.[61]

(4) Deviant groups

Another variation of the *dozoku* is found among a peculiar kind of group. There are groups in Japan, as in other countries, which are sociologically labelled as antisocial or pathological. But they are characterized by a special trait, not wholly antisocial or pathological but partly social or normal. Each group is basically structured by the hierarchical order of *oyabun* and *kobun*, the latter differentiated into *kyodaibun* (fictitious brothers), fictitious principle of the *dozoku*, and supporting norms and sanctions. The trait of its normative system lies rather in its leading value system, which justifies the deviation from, and very often violation of, the official state law, when circumstances require, in order to maintain the group structure and members' *kao* (face). It does not necessarily aim to resist legal order, but is compelled rather to respect its traditional value system than the official law. Three ideal types are differentiated among those groups.[62]

A first type is the *rotensho* (stall keepers) as they call themselves for their lawful occupation, or *yakuza* (delinquents) as people regard them because of the apparent difficulty in discerning them from the next type. They are, in appearance, lawful sellers of daily commodities at local festivals, markets and other kinds of social events, moving here and there in a certain district or over the country, although originally belonging to a particular *kumi* (grouping) of a *dozoku* structure. But they are so strongly bound by their duties of *jingi* (covenants) of their own as to sometimes resort to unlawful behaviour.

A second type is called *Bakuchi-uchi* (professional gamblers). Their substantial source of income is unlawful gambling, even though some of them pretend to have a lawful profession. Their value system requires them, as a moral duty, to protect their *nawabari* (territory of influence) as among the stall keepers, and not to let it become threatened or violated by gamblers from other territories; they must also, whenever possible, expand their influence over other territories. *Nawabari* thus often causes violent struggles between them, not easily discernible from those in the next type.

The last one is *boryokudan* (gangster organizations). They also pretend to have a lawful profession, but are faithful to their supreme imperative to protect, and wherever possible to strengthen and expand, their structure and *nawabari* by any measures, however unlawful, including murder.

V. Indigenous Legal Postulates

1. INDIGENOUS LEGAL POSTULATES FUNCTIONING IN SOCIETY

Some social norms are seen as indigenous unofficial law because of their actual influences upon the state law as described above, but still another indigenous factor is found which can exert similar influences upon the state law. Behaviour in accordance with this factor may not necessarily be established in society so tangibly as to be defined as "customarily sanctioned by a certain circle of people in popular conceptions and actual behaviour patterns," but it is approved and supported by a circle of people for its ideal or ideological embodiment of, or dependence on, any specific principle, value, ideal or authority so firmly established as to influence application of social norms and legal rules. Such specific principles, values, ideals or authorities are called here indigenous legal postulates, as far as they are significant to the validity and effectiveness of both the official state law and unofficial laws. They function to justify any official or unofficial law in idea or ideology and, at the same time, to disqualify other official or unofficial laws opposing them.[63]

It may be desirable first to define more clearly the concept of the indigenous legal postulate sufficiently for it is to be applied as an analytical tool; but this is difficult at present for lack of necessary data. Furthermore, what is required is not to delineate the concept hastily or too rigidly but rather to maintain it as broadly as possible, so as to collect the important materials which are to differentiate the Japanese situation of law from Western and non-Western varieties. M. B. Hooker recently concluded convincingly:

> "The texts discussed in this brief survey . . . show the variety of reference which the term 'law' bears in South-East Asian cultures, but despite this variety the texts as a group have a number of features in common. First, they all describe both a social system and an ideal moral or ethical order conceived as a unitary whole. Second, the foundation of these orders is not the principle of legality but rather the implementation of an ethical order. Third, all texts omit a number of areas of legal obligation in whole or in part." (1978: 108)

In other words, "the concept of law that the texts present is a regulation of human behaviour that is a part of the nature of things" (ibid.: 98) and therefore implies moral or ethical postulates, whether called principles, values, ideals, authorities, or any other. However it might seem, the concept of an indigenous legal postulate is operationally useful to collect related materials in Japan, to acquire detailed facts, and to elaborate a more precise view of it.

To undertake a difficult task, it seems useful to differentiate between the two ideal types of the postulates. The first includes those with a particular applicability to any specific indigenous law, being thus inferrable from the observed practices. The other type has a wider, more general applicability to different indigenous laws as well as to other social norms. The former may be called the "specific indigenous legal postulate," while the latter the "diffuse indigenous postulates."[64]

2. SPECIFIC LEGAL POSTULATES

(1) *Tenno* adoration

Concerning the national unity and polity, the influence of *Tenno* is moral and legal. His status has suffered ups and downs throughout history. Sometimes his authority was supreme in appearance, as in the regimes of Shotoku Taishi and Meiji *Tenno* where the ideal of the *Tenno*-governed state was realized. But his political power in actuality was at best only formal or even nominal. Under the present Constitution he is officially deprived of any power of political influence. With all such variations of the official status, the *Tenno* has had his peculiar influences upon the moral and legal life of Japanese people, even though some critics disapprove. And the influences have been validated by the people's adoration of *Tenno*. "*Tenno* adoration" is inferred as the postulate for the indigenous *Tenno* system, official or unofficial.

(2) *Ie* idea

Ie had for long been the main basis of Japanese society, controlled by the family head and led by the postulate of *wa*. But since post-war democratization and legal reform, the components of such a collective *ie* have lost their official validity, and at the same time are declining in their social influences. On the other hand, such practices as privileged inheritance of family memorials of the ancestors, *muko-yoshi*, sole-heir inheritance, and the attempt at legislation for inheritance of agricultural lands *en bloc*, exemplify some surviving elements of the idea of collective *ie*. Any idea of *ie* as a whole, although the concept of "perpetuity" may be more appropriate than *wa*, can be said to be still functioning.

(3) *Buraku* spirit

Buraku, which had been another basic element of Japanese society, has truly been losing its actual influences upon its members during the post-war years. The "disorganization of the *buraku*" might be reasonably recognized as a general trend, and the code of *buraku* might be losing its general validity. It is true, however, that the spirit of *buraku* is still very often functioning as the collective postulate of a local community, and that the word is fictitiously used to emphasize the collective unity of social groups, often critically called an "insular narrowness." Paternal unilateralism of nationality and exclusion of foreign teachers are but a few examples of the latter. "Buraku spirit," real or fictitious, is inferred as a vague but functioning legal postulate.

(4) *Dozoku* principle
Dozoku is an expansion of an *ie.* But, consisting of apparently independent families, a *dozoku* is characterized by a more systematical structure centring on the authority of the main family over the branch families, ordered in a genealogical hierarchy. When fictitiously applied to social organizations with no blood-relation, such as *iemoto* organizations, *shuha* and deviant groups, the leading principle is developed as a postulate to support their explicit rules. Despite the strong opposition of post-war democratic ideas, the *dozoku* principle stubbornly survives.
(5) *Mibun* order
The above four postulates are characterized by some common features. Collectivity-orientation, which is so often pointed out by foreign Japanologists, may be one of them. Status hierarchy is another, the most important structural principle meaning that collectivities are structured by a hierachy of ordered members, leaving the authority with the upper, and subordinate *mibun* (status) to the lower.

Status hierarchy has, generally speaking, undergone a considerable change; for instance, the unit of the members changed from family to person, grounds of status changed from ascription to achievement, the order of succession of member status is no longer determined by heredity but by selection among the qualified, and official protection was abolished.[65] Nonetheless, people still show a general tendency to respect status hierarchy as a stable structure in various societies. Those who are recognized as superior in origin, rank, reputation, seniority, or property tend to have more chances of obtaining higher posts, with less consideration for their own personal ability. Not only in *dozoku* and *dozoku*-like communities, but also in vouching for a person, *giri* relations, and order of the seats, the difference in the status of the parties are frequently represented in their actual attitudes. And court ranks and honours have revived officially under the present Constitution. But, as it would be a more diffuse conception than the traditional status hierarchy postulated for contemporary practices, the term *mibun* order is here chosen for status hierarchy.
(6) *Kami* conception
The basic postulate for the *jinja* and *matsuri* is the indigenous conception of *kami* (god) in Shintoism. It is polytheistic. It includes, besides the Creator and related gods, a variety of men, whether distinguished or ordinary, for all the dead are welcomed

as gods and even natural settings are worshipped in some *jinja*. Not only strictly religious supernaturals but also certain secular superiors can be included in *kami*, as *Tenno* was worshipped as a god. Shinto also could include political State Shinto and folk *Jinja* Shinto as well as strictly religious *Kyoha* Shinto. Such a conception of *kami* is still alive, with the possibility of interpreting Shinto and its practices as either religion or folk custom. According to its conception, it essentially doesn't matter whether an official position in law is given or not, for it is a peculiar *kami* conception, so diffuse and all-inclusive, without any rigid criteria.

3. DIFFUSE INDIGENOUS POSTULATES: AMOEBA-LIKE WAY OF THINKING

The above inferred postulates are further generalized into a less specific two. Four of them, *ie* (idea), *buraku* (spirit), *dozoku* (principle), and *mibun* (order), function among the people of limited circles and assign certain behaviour patterns to them relativistically as circumstances require. They are accordingly included in "emphasis on group affiliation" and "particularlistic relations" formulated by Edwin O. Reischauer (1977: 127, 142) or "social relativism" characterized by "social preoccupation and interactional relation" by Takie Sugiyama Lebra (1976: 9). They may form a relativistic postulate to have people adapt flexibly to changing circumstances. The other two postulates, *Tenno* adoration and *kami* conception, share a common character of a superior authority with their own individualities. They are an embodiment in idea of "a very strong self-identity" stressed along with "the group orientation and relativistic ethics" by Reischauer (ibid.: 146). They may form a limiting postulate to have people maintain their individuality, however flexibly they may adapt themselves to circumstances.

The six specific postulates have their own significance. But in reality they function in concert. Thus a general diffuse postulate is assumed as supporting the above-mentioned postulates: a postulate to enable people to behave as flexibly as possible, to adapt themselves to changing circumstances, as well as to maintain their individuality. Such a postulate is tentatively called the "amoeba-like way of thinking" for its similarity to the flexible movement of an amoeba with its individuality maintained. It has of course operated for the indigenous laws that are supported by the six specific postulates. It has supported, too, the other indigenous laws in varying ways: supporting some indigenous laws adopted in the official law as in adjoining relations, right of common, fixed collateral, mortgage, seals, and goodwill; allowing the substantials of some others to more or less permeate the official law, as in National Holidays, *gengo, de facto* marriage, divorce by consent, *kazoedoshi, shakkan-ho*, groom foster-son, sole-heir inheritance and conciliation; validating still others out of the realm of official law, as in the procedure of a marriage, *giri* relations, order of the seats, *murahachibu* and lunar calendar; or leaving a few others, once adopted into official law, to decline, as in perpetual land-lease and vouching for a person.

When the amoeba-like way of thinking operates to allow very flexible movements, the resultant behaviour may be seen at a glance as "unlimited inclusiveness" without definite criteria, as a Japanese leading political scientist criticized (Maruyama, 1961), which might induce the loss of identity. It is still possible to survive with innate individuality maintained. Such a postulate is assumed as diffusely operating for the indigenous laws.[66]

VI. Conclusion

The above descriptions and discussions do not aim to make evaluation or devaluation of indigenous law, individually of its various parts or wholly of its concept, but to make known its wide existence, interrelated to and interacting with received law. Its evaluation or devaluation should be done in a later stage of study on reasonable methodological considerations. Without them, unconscious ethnocentric ideas would creep in, whether of Western countries (Trubek, 1972: 16) or non-Western countries, called "negative ethnocentrism" (Abel, 1974: 228). For convincing evaluation or devaluation, further empirical investigation may be required to identify more facts and reclassify known items, including those which may be found in the future.[67] Nonetheless, the above descriptions and discussions seem to present some concluding suggestions about the characteristics of the whole structure of law in contemporary Japanese society.

First of all, there is no system of official law other than state law. Especially remarkable is the absence of official religious law as in Christian, Islamic, Hindu, Buddhist and Judaic countries. Various religious orders, including Shinto ones, have truly had their own canon laws, but these laws have never enjoyed an official position authorized by the state law as an independent system. On the contrary they have, in general, been included in the state law, whether in a subsystem as the past State Shinto or in the contemporary form of free religious institutions. Underlying those facts is the Japanese vague conception of religion, which is clearly seen by the conception of *kami* and Shinto. The non-existence of official laws other than state law may be viewed as a result of an overwhelming prevalence of the state law, or strong influences of unofficial laws separately functioning outside of the realm of the state law. The author tends to accept the latter view.

The reason is supplied by a second characteristic: a wide prevalence of indigenous unofficial law. It exists in different relations to the official state law; adopted in the latter either in whole or in part, or rejected formally by, but permeating substantially with, the latter, or else functioning outside of the realm of the official law. It is still alive by flexibly adapting itself to changing circumstances, and is supported by indigenous legal postulates. The amoeba-like way of thinking, the most general of the postulates, must function even to admit some deviation from established criteria owing to its relativistic capacity as seen by wide administrative discretion and the existence of formally unlawful deviant groups.

Thirdly, to specifically emphasize a point mentioned in the above second characteristic, indigenous law is not confined to any one level of the whole structure of law. Many indigenous laws spread over both levels of official and unofficial law supported by legal postulates, thus over a total of three levels. Some others rejected by official law may be supported by the other two levels. The common idea, "state law received, and customary law indigenous," is found to be incorrect; what exists is the interrelation and interaction between received and indigenous law.

A fourth characteristic is that indigenous law is never stable, but changes dynamically to adapt itself to given circumstances, whether affected by received law or as the result of its own development. Japanese indigenous law received Chinese law in earlier ages but achieved its own development over a long time, up to the Meiji Restoration. Even after the rushed reception of Western law, it has maintained essential indigenous factors, although one might not want to recognize some as indigenous law. Our problem is not to discern indigeneity completely from reception, but to conceptualize accurately different stages of indigenous transformation in an assimilation process with received law. The favoured dichotomy, "traditional law versus modern law," is likewise found too simple to observe this process of mutual influence (cf. Chiba, 1980).

Lastly, the above whole system of law is not uni-structured but multi-structured, consisting of different systems; roughly, two systems from legalistic and behavioural points of view. Strictly seen from the legalistic view, unofficial law has to disappear from the front stage of law, together with the postulates behind it; and seen from the behavioural view alone, the concept of law has to lose an essential component. Each observer is free to choose between them. But those who want to identify the law of the people as giving them in reality the criteria for their behaviour cannot depart from the behavioural view, where reconstruction of the concept of law and methodology for it is required in order to include the legalistic concept as well.

Notes

1 Five books are recommended for reference in English to contemporary Japanese law: Ishii, 1969 for description of legislations in the Meiji era; von Mehren, 1963 for collection of articles on post-war legal reform; Noda, 1976 for comparative and philosophical perspectives; Tanaka, 1976 for inclusion of useful materials; and Coleman & Haley, 1975 for bibliography.

2 The controversy was latently originated when Bohannan reached the idea of differentiating "folk system" from "analytical system" in his monograph (1957). After exchanging attacks and rebuttals, Gluckman and Bohannan had a direct debate during a conference (Nader, 1969).

3 The label is the same as that of the basic law of the modern state. But the meaning used in the Shotoku law is different from our modern usage; it means virtuous precepts of a philosophical and religious, rather than a legal nature.

4 The English translation of the Constitution is by W. G. Aston (1896) with minor revision by the present author.

5 The text of the Taiho Ritsu-ryo was lost except for fragmental quotations in some other books. The text of the oldest extant Japanese *ritsu-ryo* is the Yoro Ritsu-ryo promulgated in 718.

6 Five book are available in English for detailed research of these Japanese laws. Wigmore, 1967–79 is a voluminous collection of material related to law of contract, property, persons and procedure. Henderson, 1975 is another collection of various contracts in villages. Henderson, 1965, vol. I is a description with materials on characteristic conciliation by indigenous conflict institutions. Hall, 1979 and Hess & Murayama, 1980 present particular laws.

7 The Japanese term *kazoku-seido* (family system) has three different meanings: it refers firstly to a household or kinship in human society, secondly to the particular system practised throughout Japanese history, and thirdly to the patriarchal family system which was established under the Meiji Constitution. I use *kazoku-seido* for the second meaning and *ie-seido* for the third according to general usage.

8 For this reason, most of the authors who treat the general history of Japanese law start by describing Japan's reception of Western law (cf. Ishii, 1969). For a more concentrated discussion of the reception, see Takayanagi, 1963 and Noda, 1976. Henderson, 1965, vol. II and Minear, 1970 treated more limited topics.

9 The word *roppo* (literally six codes) is generally used to mean all the codes and laws of Japan. For the six codes – Constitution, Civil Code, Commercial Code, Code of Civil Procedure, Penal Code and Code of

Criminal Procedure – were thought to include the important law at the period of codification. To be noticed first is that three other fields of law had developed elaborate systems which were not counted among them: the local system, military control and international relations. This was because the local system was thought to be settled not for the benefit of people, but for the benefit of sovereign control of *Tenno*; because military law was separated from governmental control on the ground that its nature was under the surpreme command of *Tenno*; and because international treaties were to be concluded only by the authority of *Tenno*. It is noticed that some fields of law which had occupied important official portions of the legal system in the Western models, were not given corresponding positions in the Japanese system at all, for instance, religious law such as Canon Law, community law in a borough, *Gemeinde*, or *commune*.

10 According to Takayanagi, such prominent scholars were found among those who had given direct advice to the Japanese draftsmen of the Constitution: Herbert Spencer, James Bryce, Albert Dicy of England; Rudolf von Gneist and Rudolf von Jhering of Germany; Lorenz von Stein of Austria; Le Bon of France; and James Bradly Thayer and Oliver Wendell Holmes, Jr. of the U.S.A. (1963: 7–9).

11 Later, when Japan acquired external territories: Taiwan after the war with China in 1894–95, South Sakhalin after the war with Russia in 1894–95, and the Peninsula of Korea by absorption in 1910, another power emerged. That was the power of *Tenno* to rule the *gaichi* (external territories). The jurisdiction over the external territories was separated from the *naichi* (homeland). Each of the external territories was formally governed by the Governor-General, who was directly appointed by and legally responsible to *Tenno*, although the law issued by the Governor-General in the name of *Tenno* which was called *gaichi-ho* (law of external territories, colonial law) was by and large copied from the law of the homeland.

12 The absolutism was in a sense not more than formal. The powers of *Tenno* were in actuality exercised by the highest officials in the name of *Tenno*; the Imperial Ordinances were issued according to the preference of the prime minister, sensitive to his own political interests; and the military laws were laid down by the leaders of the army and navy. This was a reason why Japanese politics before World War II was controlled by a limited circle of privileged political and military leaders.

13 For further details, see Passin, 1965: 149–160. The text of the Rescript is:

Know ye, Our subjects:

Our Imperial Ancestors have founded Our Empire on a basis broad and everlasting, and have deeply and firmly implanted virtue;

Our subjects ever united in loyalty and filial piety have from generation to generation illustrated the beauty thereof. This is the glory of the fundamental character of Our Empire, and herein also lies the source of Our education. Ye, Our subjects, be filial to your parents, affectionate to your brothers and sisters; as husbands and wives be harmonious, as friends true; bear yourselves in modesty and moderation; extend your benevolence to all; pursue learning and cultivate arts, and thereby develop intellectual faculties and perfect moral powers; furthermore advance public good and promote common interests; always respect the Constitution and observe the laws; should emergency arise, offer yourselves courageously to the State; and thus guard and maintain the prosperity of Our Imperial Throne coeval with heaven and earth. So shall ye not only be Our good and faithful subjects, but render illustrious the best traditions of your forefathers.

The Way here set forth is indeed the teaching bequeathed by Our Imperial Ancestors, to be observed alike by Their Descendants and the subjects, infallible for all ages and true in all places. It is Our wish to lay it to heart in all reverence, in common with you, Our subjects, that we may all attain to the same virtue.

14 Even the youngest primary-school children were required to memorize the Rescript to be able to recite it in unison, without understanding the meaning of it. As a result, the Japanese people who were educated by the system under the Meiji Constitution, could and still may recite the Rescript correctly with one voice. They enjoyed the same equal national identity when they recited it as when they sang the national anthem.

15 For further details of the debate on the Civil Code, see Mukai and Toshitani, 1967.

16 Many references are found relating to the family system. For a brief description of the system, see Toshitani, 1976: 36–39.

17 The movement for electoral expansion had been strong since the first election law. After a few revisions of the expansion, a "universal" suffrage was realized by the law of 1925, though still denying women the right to vote.

18 Cf. Noda, 1976: 61–62. This law aimed not only at oppressing labourers and their movements, but also at annihilating any *thought* or activity, however moderate, against *kokutai*, which was symbolized by the idea of the eternal *Tenno*, private ownership, and *wa*.

19 Main studies by the present author on *jinja* are collected in Chiba, 1970 in Japanese. Among references available in Western languages, see Bunce, 1955 for a general description; Hibino, 1928: 98–147, Coville, 1948, Holtom, 1963 for ideological aspects; Yanagida, 1957: 291–316, Harada, 1959, Nishitsunoi, 1959, Beardsley, 1965: 310–347, Hori, 1968, Kreiner, 1969, Morioka, 1975: 13–72 for socio-cultural

aspects; Matsudaira, 1937 for a socio-political aspect; Fridell, 1973 for a legal aspect.

20 Of course, there developed wide variations. For instance, there are the *jinja* of a clan, *dozoku* (to be mentioned later) or family, on the one hand, and the *jinja* established and supported by political rulers such as *Tenno*, Shogun, or feudal lords, on the other. And the ideal or ideology of "all the inhabitants as *ujiko*" has been declining as society has been modernized and urbanized (cf. Morioka, 1975).

21 Still another sort of god was enshrined. They were those whose services were appreciated as most distinguished to the peace of the land and development of local economy. Examples were mainly found among leading warriors, pioneers and lords in feudal ages, and military personnel in the Meiji era and after.

22 For political dynamics in the process of occupation after the War, see Ike, 1957; Quigley and Turner, 1956; Maki, 1962; Burks, 1964. For the drafting of the present Constitution and related legal reform in general, see Takayanagi, 1963; Tanaka, 1976: 630–685; Oppler, 1976.

23 The demanded revision of the Civil Code, which was to be done at the same time as that of the Constitution, was not achieved as expected because of the laborious preparation needed. In reality, the revision was promulgated later on 9 December 1947, to come into force on 1 January 1948. A law was enacted for a temporary purpose to fill the vacant period from 3 May 1947, to 1 January 1948. It was the Law concerning Temporary Adjustment of the Civil Code Pursuant to the Enforcement of the Constitution of Japan. (cf. Steiner, 1977: 104–107)

24 Among many items in the Constitution which they want to re-revise, principal ones are the revival of some old systems under the Meiji Constitution, such as *Tenno's* legal and political power, a collective family system, and rearmament, which is forbidden in the present Constitution. Seen from this angle, they are grouped into conservative trends confusing indigeneity with conservativeness.

25 Promulgated and enforced in 1947 as an entire revision of the old one under the Meiji Constitution. It provides the qualifications for the succession of the Throne and the order of the qualified candidates, limitations on marriage of the Imperial families, Regency, Imperial reverences, and the Imperial Council.

26 It is a later additional establishment in 1966. The date of 11 February is the same as of the former one, which was based on a myth ideologically supported by the absolutist Meiji regime. For this reason, the addition meant a success of a reactionary movement as well as an expression for national identity.

27 The first year of this system, based on an unproven myth, begins 660 years earlier than the first Christian year.

28 The recovery was of the same nature as the addition of National

Foundation Day, supported by both humane affection and reactional tendency.

29 As private schools, including universities, are out of governmental control in this point, the problem arises concerning national and public universities which have a greater demand for foreign teachers than schools of lower grades.

30 Correctly speaking, Japanese homogeneity is no more than a myth in disregarding some existing minority groups, including Koreans.

31 Among the references to the *buraku*, Reischauer, 1977: 36 is the briefest description. The most detailed one may be De Vos and Wagatsuma, 1972. Readers are advised to be most prudent not to be included in the controversy today, when they want to know or say something about them. For the problem is now a political one as is seen by the special legislation in recent years to improve the status of the *buraku*.

32 A noted case took place in 1891 to test the Japanese reception of the principle of *nullum crimen, nulla poena sine lege* in relation to this punishment. It was the Otsu Case, where the Russian Crown Prince was injured by a policeman on a road in Otsu during his visit to Japan. Political pressure was so great that the heavier punishment clause of the Penal Code, which explicitly concerned Japanese Imperial Families alone, was to be applied to a foreign prince against the principle in order to mitigate possible Russian indignation. But without regard to political pressure, the then Supreme Court finally punished the accused policeman in accordance with the clauses applicable to the case of injury of ordinary citizens. The decision is highly evaluated as evidence of reception of such an important criminal principle. (cf. Tanaka, 1976: 626–627)

33 Among many references, see Watanabe, 1963: 365–366, 371 for a brief explanation, and Civiska, 1957 for a more detailed one.

34 Of course, some measures of redress for wives were created. For instance, restriction on the husband's unreasonable exercise of his right was possible by his *honke* (main family to branch families), *shinzoku-kai* (council of the relatives), any related person of higher status, or any other influential third party. The most notable was the *enkiri-dera* (a Buddhist temple for divorce). Several Buddhist temples in Japan, the most famous of which was Tokei-ji in Kamakura, were found to have functioned as refuges for wives who sought divorces. In such cases of appeal, the temples enjoyed social prerogatives to harbour the wives and to intervene in the case in favour of the wives. The law of *enkiri-dera* was without doubt a kind of equity in Japan. But it is still open to further discussion to determine whether it belonged to official or unofficial law.

35 Both the Civil Code and Japanese legal scholars had for a long time referred to the right of common only among farmers. After the war,

two other kinds of the right of common were disclosed to have been functioning – among fishermen on fisheries and hotel owners on hot springs.

36 At the same time, urged by rapidly growing industry and commerce, important statutes were enacted to legalize blanket hypothecs on both movables and immovables, specifically applicable to factories, railroads, mines and some others in 1905 and after. Among them, the Mortgage Debenture Trust Law in 1905 may be noted for its purpose "to make possible the use of the same collateral as security for several different issues of bonds on an equal footing" (Michida, 1963: 527).

37 By the Act, the people are encouraged to calculate in full years, and the governments, national and local, are obligated to do so, although exceptionally they are permitted to use calendar years when necessary.

38 The administrative decision to approve the *shakkan-ho* in part was made in 1977. The legal form for the decision was arranged by an ordinance in 1978 and enforced a year later. However the ordinance does not specifically declare the adoption of *shakkan-ho*, but simply approves production and sale in divisions of 10/33 and 25/66 of a metre. In reality the former is equivalent to a *shaku*, a general length measurement, and the latter to a *kujira-jaku*, a measurement mainly for Japanese cloth.

39 Kawashima assumes that such Japanese attitudes aversive to legal treatment for a "premodern" nature will be sooner or later lost. But I find in them indigenous cultural traits of the Japanese people not to be attributed to the special character of a limited historical period. See Haley, 1978 for a criticism of the myth Kawashima holds.

40 The "acts" which *Tenno* performs with the advice and approval of the Cabinet are promulgation of law, convocation of the Diet, dissolution of the lower House, proclamation of general election, attestation of the appointment and dismissal of high officials, attestation of amnesty, awarding of honours, attestation of diplomatic documents, receiving foreign diplomats, and performance of ceremonial functions.

41 Tanaka, 1976: 735–737 describes two decisions of lower Courts on the case.

42 Sonoda, 1975 describes in English how much the traditional rights and duties of the privileged inhabitants are elaborately developed.

43 The town block association was originated in feudal Japan to create self-control of community affairs with a variety of names. During World War II, it was officially utilized by the government as the lowest level of means to a totalitarian mobilization. After the war, it was forbidden for the government to have any connection with it. But in reality, these practices are still alive. See Quigley and Turner, 1956: 55–56, 367–369 for explanation.

44 I myself had to be absent from the funeral ceremony of my father

who had died unexpectedly, in order to perform the role of go-between at the wedding ceremony and party of a young couple on the same day, for my absence from the latter would have necessitated a postponement of the marriage. I had sent my wife to the funeral, held in a remote city, in my place to perform my duty to my father, but this obliged me to request a lady to sit with me at the wedding in place of my wife, for the go-between is required to be a couple.

45 The *muko-yoshi* that was discussed by Befu, 1962 was such a kind with the purpose of succeeding an occupation, important in business circles but of a special type. The *nyufu* (incoming husband) that was mentioned by Steiner, 1977: 112–113 was the husband married to a daughter who succeeded the family head due to the absence of a male heir, while *muko-yoshi* is the husband of a daughter who transferred her status of the heir to her husband.

46 I hold that the Confucian or feudalistic character of Japanese family is not the essence of Japanese culture throughout her history, but one of its variations. Cf. Note 39.

47 There was an extended variation of the *noren* relation, called *zaibatsu* (finance clique). The calling was given to a form of a cartel for its *dozoku*-like structure. The form was decentralized by the post-war legal reform because it had made a substantial contribution toward pre-war expansionist economy and politics. (cf. Burks, 1964: 45–48) But, some groups of big industries in contemporary Japan are said to be functioning, owing to the strong ties among the group members, as if *zaibatsu* groups.

48 *Chugen* means originally the fifteenth day of the seventh month of the year in lunar calendar, connected with the *Bon* festival, a Buddhist practice to worship one's ancestors who are believed to come back home once a year on this occasion.

49 The last case might be accounted as an *on* (a category of incurred obligations) relation, which is coupled with the *giri* relation (cf. Benedict, 1954; Lebra & Lebra, 1974). *On* is an unlimited obligation which cannot be exhaustively repaid, while *giri* is a limited one which can be reciprocally repaid.

50 According to Befu (1974: 212–217), the typical *giri* is observed in rural society between households, while its modern variations in urban society are found between individuals or between an individual and a collective party, and often with ulterior motives.

51 Remember that the farmers depended so largely upon the mutual help of co-members for farming in the village community without developed capitalistic division of labour that they would have made them give up farming and living in the community if help was entirely withheld.

52 *Rakugo* is a traditionally elaborated form of comic story of ordinary people in their traditional daily lives. Two types of persons frequently

play an important role in its many stories. They are the "esteemed retired elder in the neighbourhood" and "owner of tenant long-houses" who give useful advice about all daily affairs, including suggestions concerning conflict management. Today, their role is largely replaced by seniors or superiors in profession, and the like. Sometimes, a resident policeman or teacher is asked to intervene in a private matter of conflict. A go-between is thought to be responsible for managing conflicts between the spouses whom he helped get married.

53 These days are very often observed as social holidays in local areas. Public offices may be disturbed in their routine work due to the absence of too many workers. Their heads are socially forced to excuse their absence.

54 For length, the standard *shaku*, about 0.303 metre, is used mainly by carpenters together with *sun*, one-tenth of a *shaku*, *bu*, one-hundredth of a *shaku*, and *ken*, six *shaku*. *Ken* is still the standard length for Japanese buildings as the long side of a *tatami* (room mat) as well as the breadth and height of the *shoji* (paper screen) and *fusuma* (sliding door). *Shaku* has a variation called *kujira-jaku* (whale-*shaku*) for Japanese cloth. For dimensions, a *tsubo*, a square *ken*, is the basic unit for buildings and land, for the latter of which a *tan*, 300 *tsubo*, and *chobu*, ten *tan*, are also applied. The units for weight are losing general usage as well as those for distance. In contrast, for capacity, a *sho*, about 1.8 litre, is frequently used together with *go*, one-tenth of a *sho, to*, ten *sho*, among others, for sake, and *koku*, one hundred *sho*, among others, for lumber.

55 Held on March 3rd to celebrate and pray for the happy growth of girls by displaying a traditional set of beautiful dolls.

56 Held on May 5th to celebrate and pray for the happy growth of boys by displaying brave dolls and raising carp streamers.

57 On November 15th, three- and five-years-old boys and three- and seven-years-old girls are brought in formal wear to their community shrines, or more recently to any famous shrines.

58 Be careful about the use of the word *buraku*, for it also refers to a group of alleged outcast people.

59 Fukutake, 1962, Cornell, 1962, Beardsley, 1962, Johnson, 1967, and the classical monographs of Embree, 1946 and Beardsley *et al.*, 1957.

60 It is not found among Shinto shrines. The reason may be that while a Buddhist temple is connected with individual families, every Shinto shrine is connected with a local community as a whole.

61 Extended freedom enables the *shuha* to enjoy autonomy, on the one hand, and causes internal conflicts between temples or factions, on the other. This is seen by the social and political activities by a *shuha* of the Nichiren denomination in the names of Soka Gakkai and Komei-to, as well as critical strife in one of the biggest sects, Higashi-

Honganji-ha of the Shin denomination, between the presiding priest, brother of the Empress, and administrative office.

62 See De Vos and Mizushima, 1967 and Iwai, 1974 for details.

63 Of course, the official state law is supported by its own legal postulates ranging from such general legal ideas as justice and equity, to such positive legal principles as public policy, *nullum crimen, nulla poena*, as in the Western countries from which Japanese law was received.

64 The differentiation is a relative one and some other types between may be identified in the future. But discussions here are made first of the two types.

65 Remember that such systems of official discrimination as court ranks and honours, limited suffrage, and privileged large land-owners had been legalized under the Meiji Constitution.

66 The idea of the amoeba-like way of thinking was first put forward in Chiba, 1975 and conceptualized in Chiba, 1982. It is used here for its usefulness for comparison, although I know that it is still to be further elaborated.

67 Furthermore, philosophical discussion should be added to reach a final conclusion. A general premise for the discussion is, as I am convinced, esteem for one's own culture, respect for the others' culture, and efforts to create universal standards to facilitate peoples to understand, communicate, and co-operate with one another.

And I know that another basic problem in methodology is left yet to be discussed. For, there are two difficulties, frankly speaking, in asserting the existence and functioning of unofficial laws in Japan. First, those indigenous institutions appear to have lost their formal structure since the beginning of the so-called modernization process which started over a century ago, and in particular after its amazingly rapid development in industry in the last few decades. As a result of the modernization it has become difficult to identify each of the unofficial laws empirically. Second, my findings stated here were obtained through my own field research and from other scholars' achievements, but most of the data obtained were collected before the rapid changes following the recent economic growth. Some might argue, relying on this fact, that Japanese indigenous unofficial laws have disappeared. Such an opinion may be true in a sense, but false in another sense. The change of unofficial laws cannot mean their total disappearance. On the contrary, we find many examples of traditional practices, however informal or disguised, with serious relevance to official law. In addition, their ideal factors appear to have become more conspicuous in many cases, in place of empirical formal factors, as arguments on Japanese attitudes toward law provide evidences of their existence and functioning so influential as to be embodied into unofficial laws.

References

Abel, Richard.

1974. A Comparative Theory of Dispute Institutions in Society. *Law & Society Review*, 8(2): 217–347.

Aston, W. G., transl.

1896. *Nihongi: Chronicles of Japan from the Earliest Times to A.D. 697.* London: George Allen & Unwin.

Beardsley, Richard K.

1962. Community and Kinship Organizations. In Silberman, 1962: 68–98.

1965. Cultural Anthropology: Prehistoric and Contemporary Aspects. In Hall & Beardsley, 1965: Ch.2.

Beardsley, Richard K., Hall, John W. & Ward, Robert E. eds.

1957. *Village Japan.* Chicago: The University of Chicago Press.

Befu, Harumi.

1962. Corporate Emphasis and Patterns of Descent in the Japanese Family. In Smith & Beardsley, 1962: 34–41.

1974. Gift-Giving in Modernizing Japan. In Lebra & Lebra, 1974: 208–221.

Benedict, Ruth.

1954. *The Chrysanthemum and the Sword: Patterns of Japanese Culture.* Tokyo: Charles Tuttle (1st ed. Houghton Mifflin 1946).

Bohannan, Paul.

1957. *Justice and Judgement among the Tiv.* London: Oxford University Press.

Bunce, William.

1955. *Religions in Japan: Buddhism, Shinto, and Christianity.* Tokyo: Charles Tuttle.

Burks, Ardath W.

1964. *The Government of Japan.* 2nd ed. New York: Thomas Y. Crowell.

Chiba, Masaji.

1970. *Matsuri no Hoshakaigaku* (A Socio-Legal Study of Shinto Rituals and Festivals). Tokyo: Kobundo.

1975. A Comparative Analysis of Attitudes toward Individual Rights among Westerners, Africans and Japanese. Presentation to the ISA RCSL Annual Meeting, Hakone, Japan. September, 1975.

1979. Three-Level Structure of Law in a World of Many Cultures. In *Law and the Future of Society, Archiv für Rechts- und Sozialphilosophie*, Beiheft Neue Folge Nr. 11.

1980. Doubts on the Utility of 'Traditional' vs. 'Modern': From an Asian Point of View. *Law and Development*, 1978/1979 Issue: 34–45.
1982. The Unofficial Jural Postulates Underlying Attitudes toward Law. *Zeitschrift für Rechtssoziologie*, 3(1): 59–73.
Civisca, Luigi M., S. J.
1957. The Validity of *Naien. Monumenta Nipponica Monographs*, 17. Tokyo: Sophia University.
Coleman, Rex, & Haley, John O. comps.
1975. *An Index to Japanese Law: A Bibliography of Western Language Materials. Law in Japan*, an annual special issue, 1975.
Cornell, John B.
1962. *Buraku* Social Organization and Community Life. In Silberman, 1962: 36–67.
Coville, Cabot.
1948. Shinto, Engine of Government. *The Transactions of the Asian Society of Japan*, 3rd Series 1: 1–23.
De Vos, George A., & Mizushima, Keiichi.
1967. Organization and Social Function of Japanese Gangs: Historical Development and Modern Parallels. In Dore, 1967: Ch.9.
De Vos, George A., & Wagatsuma, Hiroshi.
1972. *Japan's Invisible Race: Caste in Culture and Personality*. Berkeley, Calif.: University of California Press.
Dore, Ronald P.
1962. The House. In Silberman, 1962: 167–186.
Dore, Ronald P., ed.
1967. *Aspects of Social Change in Modern Japan*. Princeton, N.J.: Princeton University Press.
Embree, John F.
1946. *A Japanese Village: Suye-mura*. London: Kegan Paul, Trench, Trubner.
Fridell, Wilbur M.
1973. *Japanese Shrine Mergers 1906–12*. Tokyo: Sophia University Press.
Fukutake, Tadashi.
1962. Village Community ('*Buraku*') in Japan and its Democratization. In Smith & Beardsley, 1962: 36–40.
Haley, John O.
1978. The Myth of the Reluctant Litigant. *Journal of Japanese Studies*, 4(2): 359–390.
Hall, John C.
1979. *Japanese Feudal Law*. Washington, D.C.: University Publications of America.
Hall, John W., & Beardsley, Richard K., eds.
1965. *Twelve Doors to Japan*. New York: McGraw-Hill.

Harada, Toshiaki.
1959. The Origin of Community Worship. In *JARS*, 1959: Ch.21.
Havens, Thomas R. H.
1974. *Farm and Nation in Modern Japan: Agrarian Nationalism, 1870–1940*. Princeton, N.J.: Princeton University Press.
Henderson, Dan Fenno.
1965. *Conciliation and Japanese Law: Tokugawa and Modern*. 2 Vols. Seattle: University of Washington Press.
1975. *Village "Contracts" in Tokugawa Japan*. Seattle: University of Washington Press.
Hess, Albert G., & Murayama, Shigeko.
1980. *Every Day Law in Japanese Folk Art: Daily Life in Meiji Japan, as seen through Petty Law Violations: Woodcuts, c.1878*. Darmstadt: Scientia Verlag Aalen.
Hibino, Yutaka.
1928. *Nippon Shindo Ron: Or the National Ideas of the Japanese People*. transl. A. P. Mackenzie, Cambridge: University Press.
Holtom, D. C.
1963. *Modern Japan and Shinto Nationalism: A Study of Present-Day Trends in Japanese Religions*. Rev. ed. New York: Paragon.
Hooker, M. B.
1978. *A Concise History of South-Eastern Asian Law*. Oxford: Clarendon Press.
Hori, Ichiro.
1968. *Folk Religion in Japan: Continuity and Change*. Chicago: The University of Chicago Press.
Hsu, Francis L. K.
1975. *Iemoto: The Heart of Japan*. New York: Halsted Press.
Htin Aung,
1969. *Burmese Law Tales: The Legal Element in Burmese Folk-lore*. London: Oxford University Press.
Ike, Nobutaka.
1957. *Japanese Politics: An Introductory Survey*. New York: Alfred A. Knopf.
Ishii, Ryosuke.
1969. *Japanese Legislation in the Meiji Era*, transl. William J. Chambliss. Tokyo: Toyo Bunko.
Iwai, Hiroaki.
1974. Delinquent Groups and Organized Crime. In Lebra & Lebra, 1974: 383–395.
JARS (Japanese Association for Religious Studies & Japanese Organizing Committee of the Ninth International Congress of the History of Religions).
1959. *Religious Studies in Japan*. Tokyo: Maruzen.

Johnson, Erwin H.
1967. Status Changes in Hamlet Structure Accompanying Modernization. In Dore, 1967: Ch.5.
Kawashima, Takeyoshi.
1963. Dispute Resolution in Japan. In von Mehren, 1963: 41–71.
Kawashima, Takeyoshi, Nagai, Michio, & Bennet, John W.
1962. A Summary and Analysis of the Familial Structure of Japanese Society. In Silberman, 1962: 101–111.
Kitano, Seiichi.
1962. '*Dozoku*' and '*Ie*' in Japan: The Meaning of Family Genealogical Relationships. In Smith & Beardsley, 1962: 42–46.
Koyama, Takashi.
1962. Changing Family Structure in Japan. In Smith & Beardsley, 1962: 47–54.
Kreiner, Josef.
1969. *Die Kultorganization des japanischen Dorfes.* Wien: Wilhelm Braumüller.
Lebra, Takie Sugiyama.
1974. Analytical Reappraisal of the Japanese Concept of *On*. In Lebra & Lebra, 1974: 192–207.
1976. *Japanese Patterns of Behaviour.* Honolulu: The University Press of Hawaii.
Lebra, Takie Sugiyama, & Lebra, William P. eds.
1974. *Japanese Culture and Behavior.* Honolulu: University Press of Hawaii.
Lu, David John.
1974. *Sources of Japanese History.* 2 vols. New York: McGraw-Hill.
Maki, John M.
1962. *Government and Politics in Japan: The Road to Democracy.* New York: Frederick A. Praeger.
Malinowski, Bronislaw K.
1926. *Crime and Custom in Savage Society.* London: Routledge & Kegan Paul.
Maruyama, Masao.
1961. *Nippon no Shiso* (The Thought of Japanese). Tokyo: Iwanami Shoten.
Matsudaira, Narimitsu.
1937. *Fêtes saisonnières au Japon.* Paris: Maisonneure.
Michida, Shinichiro.
1963. The Legal Structure for Economic Enterprise: Some Aspects of Japanese Commercial Law. In von Mehren, 1963: 507–546.
Minear, Richard H.
1970. *Japanese Tradition and Western Law: Emperor, State, and Law in the Thought of Hozumi Yatsuka.* Cambridge, Mass.: Harvard University Press.

Morioka, Kiyomi.
1975. *Religion in Changing Japanese Society*. Tokyo: The University of Tokyo Press.
Mukai, Ken, & Toshitani, Nobuyoshi.
1967. The Progress and Problems of Compiling the Civil Code in the Early Meiji Era. *Law in Japan*, 1: 25–59, Don Fenno Henderson, transl.
Munro, Neil Gordon.
1963. *Ainu: Creed and Cult*. B.Z. Seligman, ed. New York: Columbia University Press.
Nader, Laura, ed.
1969. *Law in Culture and Society*. Chicago: Aldine.
Nakamura, Hajime.
1970. Ideal of the Universal State. *Philosophical Studies of Japan*, 8: 1–24, Japan Society for the Promotion of Science, comp.
Nakane, Chie.
1967. *Japanese Society*. Penguin Books.
Nishitsunoi, Masayoshi.
1959. Social and Religious Grounds in Shinto. In *JARS*, 1959: Ch. 22.
Noda, Yoshiyuki.
1975. The Far Eastern Conception of Law. In *International Encyclopedia of Comparative Law, 2*, ed. René David. Ch.1, 120–136. Tübingen: J. C. B. Mohr, and The Hague: Mouton.
1976. *Introduction to Japanese Law*, transl. Anthony H. Angelo, from French. Tokyo: University of Tokyo Press.
Oppler, Alfred C.
1976. *Legal Reform in Occupied Japan: A Participant Looks Back*. Princeton, N.J.: Princeton University Press.
Passin, Herbert.
1965. *Society and Education in Japan*. New York: Teachers College, Columbia University.
Quigley, Harold S., & Turner, John E.
1956. *The New Japan: Government and Politics*. Minneapolis: University of Minnesota Press.
Reischauer, Edwin O.
1977. *The Japanese*. Cambridge, Mass. The Belkap Press of Harvard University Press.
Ross, H. Laurence.
1970. *Settled out of Court: The Social Process of Insurance Claims Adjustment*. Chicago: Aldine.
Silberman, Bernard S., ed.
1962. *Japanese Character and Culture*. Tucson: The University of Arizona Press.
Smith, Robert J.
1962. The Life Cycle. In Silberman, 1962: 187–213.

1974. *Ancestor Worship in Contemporary Japan.* Stanford: Stanford University Press.
Smith, Robert J., & Beardsley, Richard K., eds.
1962. *Japanese Culture.* Chicago: Aldine.
Smith, Thomas C.
1959. *The Agrarian Origins of Modern Japan.* Stanford: Stanford University Press.
Sonoda, Minoru.
1975. The Traditional Festival in Urban Society. *Transactions of the Institute for Japanese Culture and Classics*, Kokugakuin University No. 35: 1–34.
Steiner, Kurt.
1977. Post-war Changes in the Japanese Civil Code. *Washington Law Review*, special reprint volume 1977: 97–123.
Takayanagi, Kenzo.
1963. A Century of Innovation: The Development of Japanese Law, 1868–1961. In von Mehren, 1963: 5–40.
Tanaka, Hideo, ed.
1976. *The Japanese Legal System: Introductory Cases and Materials.* Tokyo: University of Tokyo Press.
Toshitani, Nobuyoshi.
1976. Japan's Modern Legal System: Its Formation, and Structure. *Annals of the Institute of Social Science*, No. 17: 1–50.
Trubek, David M.
1972. Toward a Social Theory of Law: An Essay on the Study of Law and Development. *Yale Law Journal*, 80(1): 1–50.
van Gennep, Arnold.
1960. *The Rites of Passage.* transls. Monika B. Vizedom & Gabrielle L. Caffee, Chicago: The University of Chicago Press.
von Mehren, Arthur T., ed.
1963. *Law in Japan: The Legal Order in a Changing Society.* Cambridge Mass.: Harvard University Press.
Wagatsuma, Sakae.
1977. Democratization of the Family Relation in Japan. *Washington Law Review*, special reprint volume 1977: 124–145.
Watanabe, Yozo.
1963. The Family and the Law: The Individualistic Premise in Modern Japanese Family Law. In von Mehren, 1963: 364–398.
Wigmore, John Henry, ed.
1967–79. *Law and Justice in Tokugawa Japan: Materials for the History of Japanese Law and Justice under the Tokugawa Shogunate, 1603–1867.* 10 vols, 10th vol. unpublished. Tokyo: Kokusai Bunka Shinkokai & Japan Foundation.
Yanagida, Kunio.
1957. *Japanese Manners and Customs in the Meiji Era.* transl. Charles S. Terry. Tokyo: Obunsha.

Glossary

bakuchi-uchi	professional gambler(s)
Bakufu	Shogunate
beiju	eighty-eight years old
Bon	the Buddhist All Souls' Day
boryokudan	gangster organization(s)
buke	warrior(s)
bun, or *bungen*	restrictions attributed to one's status
bunke	branch family(-ies)
bunten	branch shop(s)
buraku	hamlet; discriminated hamlet
burakumin	people of a *buraku*
bushi	*buke* (warrior(s))
bushido	the code of warriors
chanoyu	tea ceremony
chonai	town block
chonai-kai	town block association(s)
chotei	mediation
chugen	mid-year present(s)
chu-ko	fidelity to *Tenno* and piety toward parents
daimyo	local lord(s)
deshi	disciple(s)
dowa	de-discrimination
dozoku	common kin
eiho	art of swimming
eikosaku, or *eikosaku-ken*	perpetual land lease
enkiri-dera	a Buddhist temple for divorce
fusuma	sliding door(s)
gaichi	external territories
gengo	the name of an era under the reign of a *Tenno*
giri	the manner of behaviour required of one person to others in consequence of his social status
haiku	seventeen-syllable poem(s)
hanko	a seal and its impressions
ho	law
hogaku	Japanese music; jurisprudence
honke	main family(-ies)
honten	main shop(s)

honzan	the main temple
ie	family; household
iemoto	the main family of a school of traditional arts
ie-seido	Japanese family system under the Meiji constitution
ikai kunto	imperial court ranks and honours
ikebana	flower arrangement
inkan	*hanko*
iriai, or *iriai-ken*	right to a common land
irori	fireplace(s)
jichin-sai	ceremony to purify a building site
jingi	covenants
jinja	Shinto shrine(s)
jitsuin	the legitimate seal of a person
joto-tampo	mortgage
jori	reasonableness
kado	*ikebana*
kaho, or *kaken*	the constitution of a family
kami	Shinto god(s)
Kan-i Juni-kai	Twelve Grades of Officials
kanreki	sixtieth birthday
kao	face
kazoe-doshi	age in calendar years
kazoku-seido	family system
Kempo	Constitution
Kempo Jushichi-jo	Seventeen-Article Constitution
kendo	traditional fencing
Kigen	Year after the Accession of the First Tenno Jimmu
kimei natsuin	showing one's name and impressing one's seal
kobun	fictitious children
Kogo	Empress
kokka	state
kokutai	national polity of the *Tenno* regime
kuge	court noble(s)
kujira-jaku	whale-*shaku*, a special measure for length
kumi	a grouping, community
kyaku	supplementary law(s)
kyodaibun	fictitious brothers
kyoha	Shinto sect(s)
Kyoiku Chokugo	The Rescript of Education
kyudo	Japanese archery
kyureki	old, lunar calendar
matsuji	subordinate temple(s)
matsuri	rituals in, and festivals for, a *jinja*

miai	an interview with a view to marriage
mibun	status
mibun kaiso-sei	status hierarchy
mimoto hosho	vouching for a person as a whole
miyaza	*ujiko* group(s) with a specific relationship to the *ujigami*
mizu ni nagasu	to wash away
muko-yoshi	groom foster-son(s)
murahachibu	expulsion from a community
naichi	homeland
naien	*de facto* marriage
nakodo	go-between(s)
nawabari	territory of influence
nengo	*gengo*
nenju gyoji	annual events
ne-teito	fixed collateral
nihon buyo	Japanese dancing
noren	goodwill
nyufu	incoming husband
on	unlimited incurred obligation
oseibo	year-end present(s)
oyabun	fictitious parent(s)
rakugo	comic story(-ies)
ritsu	sanctioning law(s)
ronin	lordless warrior(s)
roppo	six codes; the Japanese codes and laws
rotensho	stall keeper(s)
ryo	admonitory law(s)
sado	*cha-no-yu*
saisei-icchi	the unity of Shinto and state
seibo	*ose ibo*
seido	system
shakkan-ho	the traditional measurement
shichi	pledge
shiki	particularized rule(s)
shikitari	convention
shinzoku-kai	a council of the relatives
shiten	*bunten*
Shogun	the president of the hereditary Shogunate
shoji	paper screen(s)
shomin	commoners
shuha	Buddhist sect(s)
so-honke	the main family of the related *honkes*
sumo	Japanese wrestling
tandoku sozoku	sole heir inheritance

tatami	room mat(s)
teito	hypothec
Tenno	Japanese Emperor
tera	Buddhist temple(s)
ujigami	Shinto god(s) of a hamlet
ujiko	children of an *ujigami*
wa	harmony
waka	thirty-one-syllable poem(s)
wakai	conciliation
wakamono-gumi	youth association(s)
yakuza	delinquent(s)
yuino	betrothal gifts
zaibatsu	finance clique(s)

8 Conclusion

Masaji Chiba

Each of the individual reports from the six countries in the preceding chapters presents a description of the state of affairs in the country in terms of the common purpose of our joint study. The state of affairs differs from country to country, and the particular concerns and personal backgrounds of the authors are, of course, not the same. For these reasons the presentations may appear at a glance to be too divergent in their content to permit any reasonable conclusions common to all. By examining each report carefully, however, invaluable suggestions related to the working hypotheses stated in the Introduction are found to be scattered throughout or, at least, underlying each of the descriptions. Especially remarkable points of such suggestions will be sketched out below as the editor considers relevant to the working hypotheses. Some important relevant points of each report will be first summarized as follows.[1]

I. Main Implications of Each Report

The report from Egypt, a typical Sunni-Islamic country, by El Sayed Yassin presents a representative process of the transformation of the whole structure of law of the non-Western country which received Western law in modern times in the development of its own indigenous law. Egypt had established in ancient times her own official law based on the Pharaonic principles with some influence from Roman law. Unofficial law must also have prevailed in the form of custom though its differentiation from official law may have been obscure. A drastic change took place when Egypt first received Islamic law as a result of the "Islamic conquest" of the country. The reception of Islamic law was so far-reaching that it totally replaced the former official law, and the received law became assimilated to such an extent that it may itself now be called indigenous law. At the same time, however, various traditional non-Islamic customs were so deep-rooted as to have survived the dominant official jurisdiction of Islamic law, some of them even having been incorporated into the official law while others continued as unofficial law outside of the official domain. The whole structure of Egyptian law from that time was a process of developing interaction between the assimilated official Islamic law and the continuing unofficial indigenous laws. The second major change began with the proposal of Napoleon to apply his Napoleonic code to Egypt. While the proposal was not successful as such, the reception of French law went on rapidly in various fields of law. Seen from a formal point of view, contemporary Egyptian law might be said to form a representative example of a received system. From the substantial point of view, however, the official law, to say nothing of the unofficial law, includes, especially as to personal status, various religious laws and traditional customs, that is, indigenous law in the broader or narrower sense. Based on the descriptions of the author, the whole structure of contemporary Egyptian law cannot be viewed as a simple received system, but rather as a complex of integration, conflict, and interaction between indigenous law and received law at both official and unofficial levels. While the author does not mention which law is dominant, his characterization of Islamic law as "ever-changing" strongly suggests that the reception of Western law has not resulted in the latter's conquest of Egypt, as implied by Jhering,[2] but rather in a function of "everlasting" Islamic law – in other words, a transformation of Egyptian law itself.

The historical development of law in Iran, the only Shiah-Islamic country, seems to have been by and large similar to the Egyptian process. Iranian received official law was first established when Shiah Islam won domination over the country, perhaps either reclassifying the existing official law into unofficial law or simple custom, or adopting some of it as well as other customs into the official Islamic law. Long since that time, the everlasting nature of Islamic law has kept its dominance persistently, even with all the formal reception of Western law for the purpose of modernizing the country. In this sense, the process is similar to the Egyptian. On the other hand, there are some evident contrasts between the histories of Iranian law and Egyptian law found in the descriptions of each of the authors.

First, judging from the descriptions, contemporary official law in Iran appears to have incorporated various factors of indigenous Islamic law into its system in both civil and criminal law though with some minor differences, while that in Egypt has incorporated mainly factors of personal status. Second, the initiative in such an apparently active reception of Western law seems in Iran to have been always displayed by political leaders in a "top-down" way – major political decisions and constitutional principles first being declared, and supporting statutes then being legislated. Third, and perhaps most remarkable, legislative and administrative tactics were devised in the Iranian process of Western-oriented legislation in order to mitigate, compromise, or rather evade contradicting requirements of Western law as evidenced by "experimental legislation" or "evasive practices" which, in fact, are to undermine the modern constitutional principles of received Western law. Finally, the resistance of the Iranian traditionalists, led by *ulamas*, to the policy of reception of Western law has been so severe and effective as to make the author complain of the failed policy of the reception, as the received law was no more than a superfluous copy without the intended revolutionary development of the whole structure of Iranian law.

The above contrasts between Iran and Egypt might be not entirely valid, as the descriptions on which they rely are written from the different viewpoints and concerns of each of the authors.[3] Still, it would be reasonable to conclude that the reception of Western law in Iran has met with considerably more conflict from the rejecting Islamic law than has been the case in Egypt, where integration has been emphasized, even if partially. It would be interesting to explore to what extent the differences in religion, Shiah and Sunni, have affected the differing results in the reception of law.

The first two reports from Islamic countries are made from the perspective of pursuing the transformation of Islamic law, which had long been the exclusive official law through periods of reception of modern Western law, with lesser emphasis on unofficial laws and underlying legal postulates coexisting interactingly, conflictingly or indifferently. The next two reports from countries of Indian culture are made, in contrast, with greater emphasis on legal postulates or unofficial law functioning to support or oppose official law.

Neelan Tiruchelvam presents a report from Sri Lanka, a multi-religious country with an intricate history in reception of law.[4] Generally speaking, every legal institution is supported by one or more ideologies in the author's term, which include legal postulates in the editor's term, and cannot therefore be free from more or less criticism from opposing ideologies. Such an institution was the Sri Lankan Conciliation Board, which worked for no more than 20 years after its institutionalization in 1953. It was devised for the benefit of the general public unfamiliar with official legal procedure, as a special measure to improve the lagging administration of justice soon after the independence of the country. At its institutionalization, reference was made to three existing models: the revived people's council in India, the created people's court in communist countries, and the traditional village council in Sinhalese society. The discussion of the author is focused on disclosure of the ideologies maintained by the advocators of the three models. Several facts are particularly noticeable in the author's description. First, the Conciliation Board had to take difficult steps during its lifetime which were far from the rose-coloured efficiency visualized at its birth. Second, the Board was finally suspended in 1973, after twenty years of such difficult steps, when all of its members were discharged and no successors were appointed. Third, the difficulty was apparently caused in the main by the persistent opposition of lawyers to the deprofessionalized nature of the Board. Finally, curious but true, the official law which institutionalized the Board remains valid even though the Board is suspended in practice. These facts must be related in a complex way to various social, economic and political backgrounds. It is in consideration of these backgrounds that a problem is specifically raised in terms of our purpose. That is how the unusual destiny of the Conciliation Board is relevant to the basic attitudes of Sri Lankan people toward official law and institutions, as a complex reflection of the different consciousness of law, received or indigenous, official or unofficial.

The report by Upendra Baxi aims mainly to disclose the contemporary state of "people's law" in India, the typical Hindu country, which has been one of the important subjects of his recent studies. He begins his discussion with an examination of the profound concept of Dharma, which has formed the basic indigenous legal postulate for the Hindu society to give unity to the whole range of working customs and written law in a higher level. According to the author, such a unifying postulate is required, considering the plurality of Indian law, constituted as it is of people's law and state law or, more exactly, a multi-legal structure including both various group regulatory systems and Anglo-Hindu high-culture law. People's law, that is unofficial law in our terminology, is best represented by the regulations of *Panchayat*, which has been practised among people in Hindu society and which has been adopted into the official legal system since World War II. The whole structure of Indian law, which had kept its totality through the unification of Dharma although it included various types of law of both official and unofficial character, underwent a remarkable metamorphosis when it received English law in modern times. While some rare parts of it have remained without influence from the reception, others have fully or partially yielded to English law to form a new system of official law, which now features a mixture of indigenous Hindu law and received English law. Besides this official law, the whole structure includes still other types of law, among which two are specifically remarked on: originally received Islamic law on both official and unofficial levels, and indigenous tribal law of the mountain peoples in the North.[5] The official state law is formally, or rather theoretically, guided by modern Western principles, but because of the striking difference between Western principles and Hindu principles, the official state law is not so efficient in practice as to totally replace unofficial people's law. At the same time, the author notes an interplay between the two theoretically different systems of law, which is ideationally made possible by the functioning of Dharma. In this connection, special attention should be paid to the fact that the interplay between state law and people's law, and the existence of a unifying factor, are emphasized through all the multiplicity of the whole structure of Indian law. The identity of Indian law is assumed here as having been maintained through its apparent metamorphoses and multiplicity and, without any basic legal postulate presupposed, the survival of such an identity through history would be unable to be theoretically elucidated.

Those who take Western law and jurisprudence for granted as the only authentic law would be astonished by reading the next report by Preedee Kasemsup from Thailand, a typical Buddhist country. The author wants at the outset to formulate a theoretical framework for his following arguments with high regard to suggestion of German theorists and data from Western legal history. He then attempts to apply that devised framework to his analysis of Thai law in its historical development through the reception of Western law in modern times. Frankly, his attempt might be seen as less than successful. The failure may in a minor part be caused by the insufficiency of the author in formulating and/or applying the framework. But, I strongly feel that the major cause is a fundamental difference in the inherent nature between the framework, obtained from Western models and used as an analytical tool, and the Thai law to which the tool was applied. His descriptions suggest just such a difference. For instance, the Thai people have cherished their own indigenous law since its first appearance in history. Some of it was embodied in the level of official law sanctioned by Kings of the succeeding Kingdoms. But the official law was never the kind that would be understood by Western models. It was written law classified into two main types: *Dharmasastra*, which expressed the sacred and immutable principles of Thai law, and *Rajsastra*, which was the revised compilation of Royal Ordinances issued by the Kings to enforce the principles. These types of written law were furthermore accompanied in the whole structure of Thai law by the unwritten laws of the "autonomous legal domains", which, except for those few specifically adopted into official law in judicial judgements, remain unofficial. The whole structure, then, is found to be composed of the hypothesized three levels of law: legal postulates of the principles of *Dharmasastra*, official law of positive provisions in *Rajsastra* and Royal Ordinances, and unofficial law of autonomous legal domains. The boundaries between the three levels are not as rigid as in the case of Western law. Rather they are so flexible that the time-honoured *Rajsastra* could be elevated into *Dharmasastra*, and, as exemplified by the noted Uttalum case, positive official law could be revised in serious consideration of the autonomous legal domain. Remarkably enough, furthermore, the reception and administration of modern Western law has been undertaken with full recognition of its different nature from Thai indigenous law.[6] Based on these facts and with reference to the "everlasting"

Islamic principles and unifying Indian Dharma concept, I would suggest as a hypothesis that some basic legal postulate has been working throughout the historical development of the whole structure of Thai law to confer it with an indigenous identity, although the author does not manifestly state so in his report. If this is true, his presentation of the nature of Thai law as different from Western law should be appreciated as a success for our purpose.

The reason why I specifically emphasize the possible functioning of a basic legal postulate for Thai law is that a similar postulate is suggested in my own report from Japan, the unique Shinto country. Japan is often said to be perhaps the only non-Western country to have smoothly accomplished required modernization (or Westernization) in many phases of society, including industrial development and legal systematization. On the other hand, the Japanese are also noted for their characteristic culture, whether praised for an elegant refinement in their traditional sense of beauty, humane attitudes and hard-work ethic, or criticized for their insular narrowness or economic egoism. As far as law is concerned, it is well-known that the Japanese tend to prefer a peculiar attitude toward it which is difficult for Western people to understand and which cannot be reasonably explained by Western conceptions of law and legal theory. In my report, I have attempted to elucidate the basis for such ambivalent Japanese attitudes by presenting the whole structure of Japanese law, comprising official state law systematized in a received form, and indigenous unofficial laws ideationally supported by their corresponding legal postulates. The unofficial laws identified may appear to be less conspicuous than those reported from the other countries, with the exception of Sri Lanka,[7] and the legal postulates may not be as manifestly established as those in Islamic and Indian cultures. Scientifically reliable methods must be further elaborated to accurately identify and classify such indigenous unofficial laws and legal postulates. But it is an evident fact that Japan has preserved its indigenous law along with such an apparently successful modern legal system. The problem is this seemingly well adjusted parallelism of official law and unofficial law, or received law and indigenous law. While it would be methodologically easy to assume one phase or the other as the only one justifiable, the whole structure of Japanese law still covers both phases in reality. In order to elucidate the parallelism reasonably, it would be useful to presuppose a basic legal postulate which has permitted the Japanese to maintain their identity in terms of law through their entire historical development, including the reception of foreign law.

II. Verification of the Working Hypotheses

Following the above review of important relevancies as the editor sees them, concluding remarks will be devoted to our most crucial problem: to verify the working hypotheses proposed in the Introduction against the facts and opinions presented by the six authors.

Generally speaking, both hypotheses, the three-level structure of law and the interaction between received law and indigenous law, are found verified in their basic formulations, together with the definitions of their component concepts. At the same time, it has also been found needful to elaborate the definitions of some of the concepts, and to improve the formulations of the hypotheses in further detail and appropriateness.

1. THE THREE-LEVEL STRUCTURE OF LAW

The definition of official law offered in the Introduction is to be maintained as "the legal system sanctioned by the legitimate authority of a country." So, too, is the definition of state law as the official law "directly sanctioned by the legitimate authority of the government of a state to have overall jurisdiction over the country." However, some undeniable suggestions are seen to crop up concerning classification of the subsystems of official law as well as arrangement of the relationships between them. For instance, religious law is demonstrated as a typical official law other than state law after modern reception of law. But its position, character and seriousness in the whole system of official law differ from country to country. Islamic law in Egypt and Iran can be classified into the same category, but each retains remarkable characteristics of its own; Hindu law in India is also religious law, but contains far fewer official provisions than Islamic law; Buddhist law in Thailand seems to be more obscure in the official system;[8] and religious law for the minorities in a country, such as the Copts in Egypt and the Moslems in India and Sri Lanka[9] may be rather regarded as incorporated into state law. Such variations of religious law at the official level should be further accurately identified to obtain a more systematic classification of official religious law. Little mention is found of official laws other than religious law. The facts and systematic arrangement of others should also be explored:

The given definition of unofficial law was "the legal system not officially sanctioned by any legal authority, but sanctioned in practice by the general consensus of a certain circle of people, whether within or beyond the bounds of a country" functioning with "a distinct influence upon the effectiveness of official law; in other words, those which distinctively supplement, oppose, modify, or undermine any of the official laws, including state law." The importance of unofficial law as defined in such a way is most emphatically argued in the report from India under the name of "people's law", in the report from Thailand by the "autonomous legal domains", and in the report from Japan by various examples. The reports from the other countries seem not to pay direct attention to unofficial law, but their descriptions are understood to suggest its influence, judging from the fact that their systems of official law have adopted so many unofficial legal practices. The existence and function of unofficial law as defined above are thus verified. On the other hand, it is clearly evident that further steps are necessary before the concept of unofficial law can be finalized. First, the number of collected facts is severely limited, considering those supposed to actually exist; related facts should be systematically collected from not only the six countries concerned, but from widely throughout the world. Second, classification and reclassification of the different types of unofficial law should be repeatedly attempted in collating the feedback of facts collected as suggested above. Third, as a result of such reclassifications, or, as we might have to say theoretically, as a methodological premise of such collection and classification, unofficial law should be redefined to be operationally used for empirical investigation of its referent. Such redefinition would necessitate differentiating unofficial law into various subtypes in accordance with the variations of the facts. Thus, finally, it is necessary to evolve a systematic arrangement of various unofficial laws functioning in a country, as well as a general theory of unofficial law in human society.

The definition of a legal postulate as "a value principle or value system specifically connected with a particular official or unofficial law which acts to found, justify, and orient the latter." is found basically verified, although the related descriptions may refer to it under different names and note different ways of its functionings. The official legal postulates are here of secondary importance, for there is nothing to mention beyond that established in model jurisprudence. Rather, the unofficial ones are our primary concern. Here again, it is found that further steps are needed similar to those for unofficial law cited above. First, systematic collection of the related facts; second, classification and reclassification of the collected facts; third, redefinition of the concept; and finally, systematic arrangement and general theorization. In addition to these, two problems are raised specifically concerning legal postulates. One is the mode of their mutual relationships in forming, more or less, the integration necessary to preserve national identity in a country, as suggested in the Introduction. The basic legal postulate identified in subject individual countries may be reasonably hypothesized to make an indispensable contribution to such integration, although in different ways and under different names, as seen by the everlasting *Shari'a* in Egypt and Iran, *Dharma* or *Dharmasastra* in India and Thailand, and the "amoeba-like way of thinking" in Japan. The possible integrating function of the basic legal postulate should be the first problem to be pursued. The other specific problem is the function of the indigenous legal postulates in relation to official law. Their function may appear at a glance to be confined to unofficial law, with the exception of those few adopted into official law. However, it is thought that some of them, including basic legal postulates, also exert some influence on official law, insofar as they function in the whole structure of law including official law.

Supposing that the whole structure of law of a country is composed of the three levels of official law, unofficial law, and legal postulates, the systematic relationship between them should be thoroughly examined. Such an examination has never been undertaken in model jurisprudence in the serious manner implied here. Indeed, model jurisprudence may have, in its own way, a perspective of the three levels, for it does admit some legal postulates supporting its positive provisions and obviously involves some provisions of unofficial origin; but the legal postulates and unofficial law considered by model jurisprudence are rigidly confined to those sanctioned by the legitimate authority of a state.

Others which may compete and conflict with official law are predestined to be rejected as irrelevant to law. Our perspective, on the contrary, is to recognize the whole body of unofficial laws, regardless of the apparent insignificance of some or many to official law, as an independent system equal to official law, at least in formal classification. In Western countries, official law may in reality be so dominant as to justify the rejection of unofficial law in our sense; however, generally in non-Western countries, and specifically in the six countries reported on herein, the situation is quite different. The influence of unofficial law upon the whole structure of law may vary from country to country, but seen overall it is surely so extensive and serious as to threaten the formal structure and effectiveness of official law. Truly, as seen by the proponents of model jurisprudence, official law may have the capacity to reject unofficial law at its command, but that rejection never results in the annihilation of the unofficial law in reality. The reality is nothing more nor less than a continuous struggle between the two, with coexistence as the best, and the undermining of the official law as the worst possible cases.

One of our first problems, then, is to clarify the relationship between official law and unofficial law, each supported by its own legal postulates – in other words, to probe deeply into the interrelationships and interactions between them. Although model jurisprudence has, unfortunately, rarely presented reliable achievements in this respect, there are some suggestions to be found. For instance, Henry Maine early pointed out three agencies to bring official law into harmony with society: fiction, equity, and legislation (1917: 15). As referred to in the Introduction, contemporary comparative lawyers take for granted differences in the conception of law by different cultures. Recent scholars, having sociological or anthropological perspectives, are expanding such suggestions in various ways: searching for means of conflict management developing out of the domain of official law (cf. Blankenburg *et al.*, 1980; Nader, 1980); disclosing the in reality flexible boundary between official law and popular practices (cf. Kadish and Kadish, 1973; Allott, 1980); emphasizing differences in symbolic acceptance of official law (cf. Podgorecki *et al.*, 1973; Gusfield, 1981); and presenting a variety of examples of unofficial laws adopted into official judicial procedure in non-Western countries.[10] There are found invaluable data concerning the mutual channelling and influencing between official law and unofficial law, among which not only overt but also covert examples should be carefully observed. Covert relations are specifically noted here because they have been hitherto neglected, and because unofficial law has been hidden or ignored despite its actual influences as a friend or rival of official law.

2. INTERACTION BETWEEN RECEIVED LAW AND INDIGENOUS LAW

The relationships pointed out above, harmonious or conflicting, between official law and unofficial law may appear to overlap those between received law and indigenous law, insofar as official law is identified as received law, and unofficial law as indigenous law. However, minimal reflection will make us realize that such identification is too cursory to visualize the real state of contemporary law in non-Western countries. From the methodological point of view, the criteria of the two dichotomous classifications are different from one another: "official or unofficial" is relegated by a formal criterion – whether sanctioned by the legitimate authority of a state or not, while "received or indigenous" is relegated by a substantial one – whether the origin of law is foreign or native. Different criteria must bring forth different results. Furthermore, concerning the reception of law, much more complicated facts, which I shall outline below, are presented in the reports from the subject six countries.

First, the originally received law often tends, as hypothesized in the Introduction, to be converted in a long course of assimilation into law which may reasonably be called indigenous. Islamic law in Egypt and Iran, Chinese law in Japan, and Indian law in Thailand evidence this tendency. Even Western law received in modern times may eventually come to be called indigenous law in the future; the leading lawyers of Sri Lanka are proud of their official law received from Holland and England, calling it, "Roman-Dutch law unique in the world." The conversion tendency may be particularly remarked in a country which once received one foreign law and later received another. Second, the destiny of modern received law is variable. To emphasize some comparative features: in Iran, it was embodied in wide areas of legislation, but by and large mutilated in reality; in Egypt, it was accommodated to more indigenous laws; in Sri Lanka, it was compounded by the two main origins of Dutch law and English law; in India, it was apparently rejected by a persistent "people's law," even under the formal supremacy of the English-law-based system; in Thailand, it was purposively codified, admitting some validity of indigenous law and legal postulates; and in Japan, its formal systematization has been distinguishably achieved. Third, the reception of law is, in reality, similar to the relationship between official law and unofficial law; that is, continuous interaction or struggle between received law and indigenous law, each with its supporting legal postulates. Fourth, the process and outcome of the reception of law must be observed and analysed with due consideration to the whole process of historical development of the particular country in which such interaction and struggle occurred, and not from the limited perspective of examining only the results of the acceptance of Western law, disregarding the whole process, as is practised in the orthodox methodology of comparative law in model jurisprudence.

The last point suggests a critical requirement for the accomplishment of our purpose; that is to observe and analyse reception of law within the whole course of historical development of a people's cultural heritage. Assessments of the results of the receptions of law may vary, ranging from most successful to least successful, with many degrees between the two extremes. But the whole process and outcome must be viewed with the total history of the people concerned – a history in which they have endeavoured to preserve their cultural identity in law against other peoples. Here, then, is hypothesized one or more basic legal postulates of a country functioning throughout its history to provide the people with the criteria with which they are enabled to determine, from among many possibilities, what kinds of law they should develop selectively and, especially related to our topic, what foreign law and to what extent it should be received or rejected, in order to preserve their cultural identity in terms of law. Such a postulate or postulates cannot be of a received nature insofar as each group of people concerned has preserved its national identity in history, but must be of an indigenous nature, however it or they may have involved or assimilated received law. The "identity postulate of indigenous law" may thus be an appropriate name for such a postulate or postulates.

The six countries here reported on have kept their legal independence, relying upon their respective legal identities, however their histories may appear to include various difficulties in that endeavour. In each of the countries, a basic legal postulate has been found functioning to maintain minimum integration within the whole structure of law. The question then arises of examining whether or not, or rather of demonstrating that, such a basic legal postulate forms the above suggested identity postulate of indigenous law of each country. Among the many related sub-questions, an especially important one is the nature of the relationships between the two types of basic legal postulates, indigenous and received. Theoretically, it should be possible to differentiate clearly one from the other. In reality, however, they may be inseparably related to each other to give consonant effects upon the whole structure of law of the receiving countries, even while they may be dissonant in various ways. It should then be questioned whether or how resonant effects are realized between the two types of postulates in order to form an identity postulate of indigenous law; this is, of course, a question which is deeply concerned with the relationship between official law and unofficial law.

The hypotheses of interaction between received law and indigenous law as stated in the Introduction are thus found to be basically verified, together with the definitions of received law and indigenous law, in both the broad and narrow senses. The next problem to be explored may be to identify accurately the entire picture of the reception of law in its interaction with the indigenous law of the countries concerned, together with elaborated reformulation of the major tool concepts, received law and indigenous law, and to theorize that picture into a consistent conceptual scheme applicable to other countries, Western as well as non-Western[11].

Notes

1 The summaries which follow are limited by my own ability to understand the reports from other cultures on the one hand, and by the specific intention here to verify the two working hypotheses stated in the Introduction. Readers are, of course, free to interpret and appreciate in their own way the whole descriptions of each of the authors. The authors may be free to do so, as well.

2 Cf. Jhering's noted statement that Roman law ruled over the known world at three different times in human history, that is, through the unification of the Roman Empire, the unity of the Catholic Church, and the reception of Roman Law (Jhering, 1965: 3–5; italics mine).

3 The author of the Iranian report is a political scientist who was educated in The United States and is presently teaching in Saudi Arabia after having worked at Teheran University. The author of the Egyptian report is a legal scientist who has worked at a national research institute.

4 The first foreign culture diffused into the Sri Lankan native culture was the Indian culture, which brought Buddhism. The two cultures amalgamated to such an extent as to form what may be characterized as an indigenous culture. The second foreign culture, Islam, formed a minority group abiding by Islamic law. The third, Christianity, eventually brought Western law into the country by three agents: Portugal, which left rare influences in law; Holland, which left unique influences in the present "Roman-Dutch law;" and England, which exerted decisive influences upon contemporary official law. After independence, the country chose a socialist system. Sri Lanka, then, is a rare example, and may be the most complicated example of reception of law in the world.

5 The information on these tribal laws, although a secondary one based on the field surveys of some anthropologists, is of high value, because the tribal law of mountain peoples living in the vast area ranging from India, through Burma and Thailand, to the Indo-Chinese Peninsula has been sparsely reported, in spite of a significance comparable to the tribal laws of well-noted areas in Africa, North America, and Oceania.

6 There is a good example in point. Thailand has had a well-formalized constitution, but it was wholly or partially revised almost every time a cabinet was replaced, usually by *coup d'état.* Such frequent revisions of constitutions never occur in Western countries. In fact, Thai people tend not to take such a revision as an alteration of the basic norm of

the nation, but rather as a natural course of revision of a kind of administrative law subject to the unwritten, unalterable fundamental norm of the nation.

7 This is not to say that Sri Lanka has no conspicuous unofficial law. On the contrary, various kinds of unofficial law exist, as suggested in Note 9. They are simply unobserved by the Sri Lankan author.

8 The positive provisions which are referred to in the Thai report as directly related to Buddhism are very few, even though the constitution, however frequently it has been revised, has continued to declare that the King, protector of all religions, must be a Buddhist.

9 The Moslems in Sri Lanka enjoy abiding by Islamic law, the important part of which is officially sanctioned along with some other indigenous laws, including ones for the Buddhist Sinhalese and the Hindu Tamils (for further details, see Tambiah, 1972: 143–225).

10 We have no apt references which systematically concentrate on this point, although recent reports on conflict management from non-Western societies include useful data on it. Some of them can be found in Allott and Woodman (1985).

11 POSTSCRIPT: After I completed the Conclusion, I personally devised another scheme, "three dichotomies of law" to improve on "the three-level structure of law."

First, law may be *official law* which is "the legal system and its components sanctioned by the legitimate authority of a country", or *unofficial law* which is "the legal system and its components which are not officially sanctioned by any legitimate authority but sanctioned in practice by the general consensus of a certain circle of people, whether within or beyond the bounds of a country, and which present distinct influences upon the effectivity of official law, supplementing, opposing, modifying or even undermining any of the official law, especially state law". Second, law may be in the form of *positive rules* which are "the formalised verbal expressions of particular regulations to designate specified patterns of behavior", or *postulative values* which are "particular values and ideas and their systems specifically connected with a particular law to ideationally found, justify, or else supplement, criticize the existing positive rules". Finally, law may be *indigenous law*, "law originated in the native culture of a people", or *transplanted law*, "law transplanted by people from other cultures, whether voluntarily received or involuntarily imposed". (Cf. Chiba, 1984: 17–20)

References

Allott, Antony N.
1980. *The Limits of Law*. London: Butterworths.
Allott, A. N., & Woodman, Gordon, R., eds.
1985. *People's Law and State Law: The Bellagio Papers*. Dodrecht: Foris Publications Holland/U.S.A.
Blankenburg, Erhard, *et al.*, eds.
1980. *Alternative Rechtsformen und Alternativen zum Reicht*. Opladen: Westdeutscher verlag.
Chiba, Masaji, ed.
1984. *Law and Culture in Sri Lanka: A Research Report on Asian Indigenous Law*. RGAIL Working Paper. Tokyo: Research Group on Asian Indigenous Law, Tokai University.
Gusfield, Joseph R.
1981. *The Culture of Public Problem: Drinking-Driving and the Symbolic Order*. Chicago: The University of Chicago Press.
Jhering, Rudolf von.
1965. *Der Geist des Rechts*. von Fritz Buchwald, Herg. Bremen: Carl Schünemann.
Kadish, Mortimer, & Kadish, Sanford.
1973. *Discretion to Disobey: A Study of Lawful Departures from Legal Rules*. Stanford: Stanford University Press.
Maine, Henry Sumner.
1917. *Ancient Law*. Everyman's Library. London: J. M. Dent.
Nader, Laura, ed.
1980. *No Access to Law: Alternatives to the American Judicial System*. New York: Academic Press.
Podgorecki, Adam, Kaupen, Wolfgang, Van Houtte, J., Vinke, P. & Kutchinsky, Berl.
1973. *Knowledge and Opinion about Law*. London: Martin Robertson.
Tambiah, H. W.
1972. *Principles of Ceylon Law*. Colombo: H. W. Cave.

About the Authors

Chiba, Masaji
Professor, Faculty of Law, Tokai University, JAPAN.
Baxi, Upendra
Director, The Indian Law Institute, New Delhi, INDIA.
Kasemsup, Preedee
Professor, Faculty of Law, Thammasat University, THAILAND.
Nezami, M. Asaad
Professor, College of Arts, Riyad University, SAUDI ARABIA.
Tiruchelvam, Neelan
Lawyer, Colombo, SRI LANKA.
Yassin, El Sayed
Director, Centre for Political & Strategic Studies, Cairo, EGYPT.

Index

Alphabetical order is word-by-word Page numbers followed by 'n' refer to chapter notes, those followed by 'r' are to references.

For Product Safety Concerns and Information please contact our EU representative GPSR@taylorandfrancis.com
Taylor & Francis Verlag GmbH, Kaufingerstraße 24, 80331 München, Germany

www.ingramcontent.com/pod-product-compliance
Ingram Content Group UK Ltd.
Pitfield, Milton Keynes, MK11 3LW, UK
UKHW022112190926
475702UK00013B/1391
* 9 7 8 0 4 1 5 8 6 1 6 9 4 *